MW00998048

ADVANCE PRAISE FOR *CIPHERS OF TRANSCENDENCE*

'Patrick Masterson is the very soul of what Aquinas called *sapientia*, a fetching blend of intelligence, wit and humanity, a master of both the speculative and the practical, which is reflected in the range and depth of this outstanding collection of studies. A well-deserved and ringing tribute to one of the luminaries of Irish philosophy and intellectual life.'

John D. Caputo, Syracuse University

'*Ciphers of Transcendence* is a superb collection of essays from a group of experts in the areas of philosophy of religion and ethics and of the history of philosophy in the classical, medieval and more modern eras. All the essays are concerned in some way with the notion of 'transcendence' which is something that ought to mean more to us as we so readily fight among ourselves and trash our earth-bound world. All the authors have had some connection with Professor Patrick Masterson either in Ireland or in other parts of Europe and so the volume stands as a fitting tribute to him who is one of Europe's more interesting and important modern thinkers.'

**William Lyons MRIA, Emeritus Professor,
Trinity College Dublin**

'This is an impressive collection of essays honouring Patrick Masterson – philosopher, university president and novelist – who has long played a central role in Irish intellectual life. Along with eminent colleagues from other countries, some of the best-known Irish philosophers have contributed to the volume, which paints a lively picture of important issues in contemporary philosophy of religion, metaphysics, and ethics. Highly recommended.'

Philipp W. Rosemann, National University of Ireland, Maynooth

'This is a splendid collection of essays, illuminating diverse philosophical themes by many of the significant voices in the Irish philosophical scene. The writers and essays pay due honour to Patrick Masterson, himself a significant contributor to philosophical and academic matters in Ireland for many decades.'

William Desmond, Villanova University

'A rich and wide-ranging volume, which explores the perennially fascinating notion of transcendence from a host of different, and often highly illuminating, perspectives.'

John Cottingham, University of Reading

CIPHERS OF TRANSCENDENCE

CIPHERS OF TRANSCENDENCE

ESSAYS IN PHILOSOPHY OF RELIGION
IN HONOUR OF
PATRICK MASTERSON

EDITED BY

FRAN O'ROURKE

IRISH ACADEMIC PRESS

First published in 2019 by
Irish Academic Press
10 George's Street
Newbridge
Co. Kildare
Ireland
www.iap.ie

© Fran O'Rourke & individual contributors, 2019
'Remembering Bóthar Buí' © Estate of Seamus Heaney.

9781788551175 (Cloth)
9781788551182 (Kindle)
9781788551199 (Epub)
9781788551205 (PDF)

British Library Cataloguing in Publication Data
An entry can be found on request

Library of Congress Cataloging in Publication Data
An entry can be found on request

All rights reserved. Without limiting the rights under copyright reserved
alone, no part of this publication may be reproduced, stored in or
introduced into a retrieval system, or transmitted, in any form or by any
means (electronic, mechanical, photocopying, recording or otherwise)
without the prior written permission of both the copyright owner and the
above publisher of this book.

Irish Academic Press gratefully acknowledges financial support from University
College Dublin; National University of Ireland; European University Institute;
Cardinal Connell Educational Fund; College of Arts and Humanities, University
College Dublin; College of Social Sciences and Law, University College Dublin;
School of Philosophy, University College Dublin.

Typeset in Adobe Garamond 11.5/14.5 pt

Jacket image: Untitled (from *Meditations*) by Patrick Scott, 2007.
© Stoney Road Press and Patrick Scott.
Frontispiece: Portrait of Patrick Masterson by Derek Hill

CONTENTS

TABULA GRATULATORIA

Luke Amentas
Fergus Armstrong
Maria Baghramian
Edith Blennerhassett
Angelo Bottone
Guy Boulanger
Jim & Mary Boylan
Conor Brady
Hugh Brady
Eileen Brennan
Niamh Brennan
Cathal Brugha
Helen Burke
Canon Foundation in Europe
John D. Caputo
Deirdre Carabine
Gerard Casey
Ken Casey
Eamonn Ceannt
Danny Cheriyan
Una Claffey
Patrick Clancy
Suzy Cohen
Anthony & Mary Collins
Donald Collins
John Connell
Art & Emer Cosgrove
Stephen Costello
Pat Coyle
Tim Crowley
Margot Cullen
Mary E. Daly
Rev. Patrick H. Daly
Patrick J. Daly
Fergus D'Arcy
Andrew J. Deeks

Rev. Gerard Deighan
Dermot Desmond
William Desmond
Judith Devlin
John Dillon
John Blake Dillon
Dominican Studium, Dublin
Eileen Donnelly & John
    Masterson
Michael Dore
Margaret Downes
Brendan Drumm
Brendan Duddy SJ
John Dudley
Ciara Dunne
Joseph Dunne
Michael W. Dunne
Ricca Edmondson
Barbara FitzGerald
Barre Fitzpatrick
Michael Foley
Vincent Foley
Órfhlaith Ford
David & Geraldine Frame
David & Naomi Frame
David Quintus Frame
Imogen Frame
Phoebe Frame
Thomas Frame
Paul Gallagher
Colin Garvey OFM
Rev. J. Anthony Gaughan
Augustine Gibney
Michael Gill
Julie & Don Godson
Rev. Patrick Gorevan

Michael & Marianne Gorman
Jeremiah Hackett
John Haldane
Attracta Halpin
Jack Hanna
Eoghan Harris
Mary Harvey-Ling
Philip Harvey
Triona Harvey
Joseph Hassett
Catherine Heaney
Marie Heaney
Mark Patrick Hederman
Lorraine C.J. Heffernan
Frank Hegarty
Gabriel Hogan
Iseult Honohan
David Horan
John Horgan & Mary Jones
Brian Howlett
Gemma Hussey
Teresa Iglesias
Tom Inglis
Richard Kearney
John & Nora Kelly
Sinead Kelly
Mary Kennedy
Brid Kerrigan
Helga Kerstin
Brigid Laffan
Felix M. Larkin
Mette Lebech
Dara Lynne Lenehan
David Lenehan
Emma-Jane Lenehan & Donal
    O'Riordan

James Lenehan
Jim & Dara Lenehan
Mark Lenehan
Patrick & Bernadette Lenehan
Rosemary Lenehan
Thomas Lenehan
Eleni Leontsini
Francis J. Litton
William Lyons
Keith & Liz MacDonald
Alasdair MacIntyre
Carol MacKeogh
Philip Maddock
Maurice Manning
Lara Marlowe
Martin Family
Archbishop Diarmuid Martin
Seamus & Anita Martin
Adrian & Marion Masterson
Eric & Deirdre Masterson
James & Mary Masterson
Laurence Masterson
Laurence & Catherine
  Masterson
Louis & Vanessa Masterson
Lucy Masterson
Naomi Masterson
Patrick K. Masterson
Robin Masterson
Rosemary Masterson
J.C.C. Mays
Therese McCall
Declan McCourt
John McCourt
Michael McDowell
Moore McDowell

Alan Moore
Max Moore
Dermot Moran
Michael Moriarty
Evelyn Murphy
Marie Murray
Siobhan Nash-Marshall
Martin & Carmel Naughton
Turner Nevitt
Jo Newman
Philip Nolan
Denis O'Brien (Dublin)
Denis O'Brien (Paris)
Eilis O'Brien
Brendan O'Byrne
John O'Callaghan
Msgr Ciarán O'Carroll
Noreen O'Carroll
Oliver O'Connor
Tom O'Connor
William J. O'Connor
Michael O'Doherty
Ann O'Dwyer
James O'Gara
Deirdre O'Grady
Paul O'Grady
Declan O'Keefe
Nicky O'Kennedy & Peter
  Kruseman
Patricia O'Loan
Andy O'Mahony
Felix O'Murchadha
Helen O'Neill
Cyril O'Regan
Fran O'Rourke
Seán David O'Rourke

Kevin & Geraldine O'Sullivan
Niamh O'Sullivan
Patrick O'Sullivan
Philip Owende
Joyce Padbury
Philip Pettit
Brendan Purcell
Lochlann & Brenda Quinn
Andrea Robiglio
Philipp W. Rosemann
Michael P. Ryan
Patrick Sammon
Colin Scott
Anngret Simms
Mark Simpson
Andrew Smith
Brendan Smith
Niamh Smythe
Robert Sokolowski
Maria Steen
Neil Steen
Hugh Stirling
Macken Stirling
Robert Stirling
Joan Tallon
Michael Tallon
Henning Tegtmeyer
Denys Turner
D. Vincent Twomey SVD
Thomas van Velsen
David Walsh
Patrick Walsh
Peter Wicks
Msgr John Wippel
Markus H. Wörner
Patrick Zoll SJ

FOREWORD

The doyen of university presidents emeriti, Patrick (Paddy) Masterson remains one of UCD's most admired scholars and leaders, twenty-five years after he was its President. A Festschrift is the crowning accolade for an academic and the present volume is testament to the high esteem with which Paddy Masterson is regarded by his peers. It is also a token of gratitude from his Alma Mater. I am delighted to be associated with its publication.

Paddy Masterson graduated from UCD in 1958 with a BA in Philosophy, First Class Honours, first place, and with a scholarship from the NUI to undertake doctoral studies at the Université Catholique de Louvain in Belgium where he was awarded a PhD *avec grande distinction* in 1962. He returned to UCD to join the Department of Metaphysics and pursued an illustrious career, first as a scholar, author and teacher of philosophy, and subsequently as an academic leader. He was appointed Dean of the Faculty of Philosophy and Sociology in 1980, became Registrar in 1983 and served as President from 1986 to 1994.

Paddy has always been a man of action and his foresight during his presidency set a firm footprint on the campus arena that inspired his successors. Back in the 1980s, Irish universities experienced 'serious reductions in State funding', which presented an enormous challenge for UCD as it continued to expand on the Belfield campus. Undeterred, Paddy established a President's Development Council and appointed a Director with responsibility for alumni relations, relations with donors and sponsors, and fundraising. Among his legacies, supported by philanthropy, are the magnificent *aula maxima*, O'Reilly Hall, and the UCD Michael Smurfit Graduate Business School at Carysfort, Blackrock. Also under his presidency, UCD's first custom-built research facility, the Biotechnology Centre, and the massive second phase of the James Joyce Library, were completed.

Perhaps his most transformative action for the University was the purchase of land and residential property and the construction of student residences on campus. Roebuck Castle, purchased in 1986, became a hall of residence; the first student village, Belgrove, was opened in 1990; and the second, Merville, in 1992. From then on UCD sought to create a vibrant campus environment where the student community lives and works.

More important than the expansion of the campus, Patrick Masterson was committed to the primacy of scholarship in the University. This year marks the thirtieth anniversary of the Newman Fellowship Programme, which he established to provide promising early-career researchers with donor-funded bursaries at a time of prolonged economic recession. Since 1989 the programme has flourished, and close to two hundred two-year post-doctoral fellowships have been awarded across the full spectrum of academic disciplines. The Newman Fellowship Programme, initiated by President Masterson, is his *monumentum aere perennius*.

Paddy left UCD to take up the position of Principal of the European University Institute of Florence in 1994 but has always kept in touch with *his* university and remains Professor Emeritus of Philosophy of Religion here. Outside of Ireland, he has been honoured in Portugal, Italy, the United States, and his beloved France. He shares his intellect and wit by continuing to publish in philosophy and his more recent passion, fiction. We wish him many more years of philosophical and creative endeavour. On behalf of the academic community I express my sincere gratitude to Patrick Masterson for an outstanding contribution which continues to enrich the lives of the staff and students of University College Dublin.

Andrew J. Deeks
President, University College Dublin

INTRODUCTION
CIPHERS OF TRANSCENDENCE

FRAN O'ROURKE

I. CIPHERS OF TRANSCENDENCE

The vocabulary of the philosophical community has been enriched by a variety of words borrowed from the German language. One thinks readily of *Weltanschauung, Lebenswelt, Zeitgeist* or, of more recent currency, the brooding term *Angst*. Of happier association is the joyous word describing the volume present to hand. *Festschrift* is literally a 'festive writing' – a celebratory anthology, *florilegium*, or garland of writings. The dictionary defines *Festschrift* as a 'miscellaneous volume of writings from several hands for a celebration', especially 'one of learned essays contributed by students, colleagues and admirers to honour a fellow scholar'. The present volume is a congratulatory gift of admiration and gratitude which befits a circle of philosophers who wish to celebrate in a special way a dear and honoured master. The authors render festive tribute to Dr Patrick Masterson, expressing their esteem and affection for a distinguished friend, teacher and colleague.

Those familiar with the academic career of Patrick Masterson will recognize the significance of the title *Ciphers of Transcendence*. Specializing in the philosophy of religion Masterson has devoted much reflection to those aspects of experience which signpost the existence of God who, although transcendent, must in some manner – albeit indirectly – be accessible to humans. Religion in its myriad manifestations throughout history is concerned with the Transcendent, i.e. a being enthroned beyond the realm of finite human experience, invariably called God. The origins of the word 'religion' shed light on its significance. Cicero (106–43 BC) classically stated: 'Religion is that which brings men to serve and worship a higher order of nature which they call divine.'[1] Thomas Aquinas (one of Patrick Masterson's master thinkers) cites that definition as well as the etymology offered by Cicero, according to which 'a man is said to be religious from *religio*, because he often ponders over and, as it were, reads again (*relegit*), the things which pertain to the worship of God'. According to that etymology, Aquinas remarks, 'religion would seem to take its name from reading over those things which belong to divine worship because we ought frequently to ponder over such things in our hearts'.[2] Aquinas also cites a second etymology, equally classic and perhaps as plausible, which would have the term derive from '*religare*', 'to bind'. That etymology was proposed by the fourth-century Christian apologist Lactantius, who wrote:

> We are created on this condition, that we pay just and due obedience to God who created us, that we should know and follow him alone. We are bound and tied (*religati*) to God by this chain of piety, from which religion itself received its name, not, as Cicero explained it, from careful gathering ... The name of religion is derived from the bond of piety, because God has tied man to himself, and bound him by piety; for we must serve him as a master, and be obedient to him as a father.[3]

St Augustine favoured this explanation,[4] and concluded his treatise *On True Religion* with the exhortation: 'Let our religion bind us to the one omnipotent God (*religet ergo nos religio uni omnipotenti deo*), because no creature comes between our minds and him whom we know to be the father and the truth, i.e. the inward light whereby we know him.'[5] While Lactantius' explanation may seem more obvious, the consensus of scholars seems to favour Cicero. Both explanations, however, convey important aspects of what is a ubiquitous, perennial, and distinctively human phenomenon.

Since it is axiomatic that God transcends human reality, the question of his existence and nature is problematic for human understanding. Attitudes range from self-convinced theism, through sceptical agnosticism, to dogmatic atheism. In each position will be found nuanced and graded affirmations of transcendence. The dictionary translates the Latin verb *transcendo* with a variety of related terms such as 'to climb', 'pass', 'cross', 'step over', 'overstep', 'surmount', 'excel', 'exceed', 'surpass'. Basic to its meaning are the notions of 'crossing over' or 'going beyond' – both finding expression in classic philosophy in the terms 'transcendental' and 'transcendent'. Thinkers in ancient and medieval philosophy referred to the 'transcendental' characters of reality, i.e. features not confined to any particular category or division of reality, but which extend beyond boundaries to everything that exists. Most important among these properties are goodness, truth, and unity (arguably also beauty), qualities which were in turn interpreted as ciphers or intimations of a supreme 'Transcendent' reality which surpasses the entire finite universal realm, occupying a dimension beyond the range of human experience. The term 'transcendental' suggests a *horizontal* infinity that universally embraces all beings without limit in its comprehension. The term 'Transcendent' indicates a *vertical* direction, pointing ultimately towards a perfect being which surpasses in infinite measure the limits of finitude, and which is the creative cause of the finite universe. Man is at the centre-point of the world, the axis and fulcrum of the horizontal and vertical, but is born to ascend.

The vertical orientation of human life was significant in Greek philosophy. According to Plato's etymology, 'anthrôpos' (ἄνθρωπος), the Greek for man, means 'upward gazer': 'The word ἄνθρωπος implies that other animals never examine, or consider, or look up at what they see, but that man not only sees but considers and looks up at that which he sees, and hence he alone of all animals is rightly called ἄνθρωπος, because he looks up at (ἀναθρεῖ) what he has seen (ὄπωπε).'[6] Aristotle understood human anatomy as a function of man's higher destiny. Instead of forelegs and forefeet, he has hands and arms, which allow him turn his upper body toward the higher regions of the universe.[7] There is transcendent purpose in the distribution of limbs: 'Man is the only animal that stands upright, and this is because his nature and essence are divine. Now the business of that which is most divine is to think and to be intelligent; and this would not be easy if there were a great deal of the body at the top weighing it down, for weight hampers the motion of the intellect.'[8] Aristotle declared that while 'man is the best of the animals ... he is not the highest thing in the world'.[9] The poet Pindar expresses the contrast between man's ephemeral life and his brighter destiny: 'We are things of a day. What are we? What are we not? The shadow of a dream is man, no more. But when the brightness comes, and God gives it, there is a shining of light on men, and their life is sweet.'[10]

Affirmation of a Transcendent – however understood – is recognition of a reality beyond the here-and-now; it is to state that the physical world is not all there is, denying that 'the place we occupy seems all the world'.[11] Denial of the transcendent may be the result of lengthy theoretical reflection; alternatively – and frequently in the contemporary world – it may emerge as a form of habitual practice, from an absence of reflection on the deeper questions of human life and destiny. As the French writer Paul Bourget remarked: 'One should live as one thinks, otherwise sooner or later one ends up thinking as one has lived.'[12] Failure to reflect on deeper questions may lead to the assumption that there is no such deeper meaning; that there is nothing beyond the immediate sense world. Practice usurps reflection.

The French philosopher Ferdinand Alquié asserted: 'It is in the metaphysical affirmation of transcendence that man finds his most authentic truth.'[13] A century ago Max Weber lamented the loss of transcendence: 'The fate of our times is characterized by rationalization and intellectualization and, above all, by the "disenchantment of the world" (*Entzauberung der Welt*).'[14] In an interview given in 2010 Seamus Heaney remarked: 'The biggest shift in my lifetime has been the evaporation of the transcendent from all our discourse and our sense of human destiny.' Having attributed this partially to the loss of authority suffered by the Catholic Church, he continued: 'But more bewildering still is exile into a universe with no up or down, no internalized system of moral longitude or latitude, no sense of a metaphysical roof over our heads.'[15] Paul Hewson (U2's Bono) insists on the importance of transcendence: 'It is becoming clear that the material world is not enough for anybody. We had a century of being told by the intelligentsia that we're two-dimensional creatures, that if something can't be proved, it can't exist. That's over now. Transcendence is what everybody, in the end, is on their knees for, running at speed toward, scratching at, kicking at.'[16]

Modernity has robbed mankind of its gods and leeched the world of mystery. Our sense of wonder has largely evaporated; there is little that astonishes or startles us. The world has become all too familiar. We assume science has solved the great questions, with little residue for reflection. It could be argued that the lack of a sense of transcendence springs from the loss of wonder. St Thomas defines wonder (*admiratio*) as 'a kind of desire (*desiderium*) for knowledge; a desire which comes to man when he sees an effect of which the cause either is unknown to him, or surpasses his knowledge or faculty of understanding'.[17] Wonder is 'a kind of fear resulting from the apprehension of a thing that surpasses our faculties: hence it results from the contemplation of the sublime truth'.[18]

The Greeks attributed the origin of philosophy to wonder. Wonder is the transcending motion together of mind and heart since, as Aquinas remarks, contemplation terminates in the affections.[19] Aristotle observed that men first wondered about immediate problems but gradually advanced to the greater realities of nature and finally to the origin of the universe itself.[20] Wonder is the reflective admiration of that which we know but do not fully comprehend; it contemplates the mysterious. To philosophize, as the German philosopher Josef Pieper points out, is to step beyond – to transcend – the workaday world of daily concerns and utility goals, to adopt a reflective attitude towards the totality of being.[21]

The term 'ciphers of transcendence' is most frequently associated with the thought of the twentieth-century German philosopher Karl Jaspers. Patrick Masterson has adapted the term to refer to those 'experimental clues that enable us to attain a rational or philosophical affirmation of God. But they are ciphers which, as such, cannot directly disclose his existence. They have to be "deciphered" by philosophical argument which argues that his existence can be affirmed as a theoretical truth condition of these features of experience.'[22] In the following paragraphs 'transcendence' is taken to refer in the broadest sense to any dimension which surpasses the immediate level of sense experience here and now. The word 'cipher' indicates that the aspect of transcendence is not immediately given but must be extrapolated through reason and reflection.

These remarks are set within the context of what Patrick Masterson refers to as 'metaphysical realism', more precisely the 'moderate rational realism developed effectively by Thomas Aquinas and which reaches back for its inspiration to Athens and Jerusalem, to Plato and Aristotle and Judaeo–Christianity'.[23] I propose to consider transcendence as it may be discerned in three successive steps. These are: the affirmation of an intelligible independent reality beyond the isolated self; the affirmation of the universal realm of being to which I belong; and the affirmation of a creative infinite Being, who is the source of the finite universe. While the last of these is the most significant and far-reaching, the divergence between theism, agnosticism and atheism is largely determined by the initial methodic option regarding cognition and its relation to reality. Here precisely lies the divergence between classical and modern philosophy. Whereas ancient philosophy sought to disclose the hidden meaning of the cosmos, confident in the faith that an objective meaning could be discovered, the concern for modern philosophy was whether we can know anything whatsoever with certainty. The modern question centres, not upon the world, but upon human cognition; this preoccupation eventually led to the scepticism which has characterized much of philosophy ever since, and a turn away from the Transcendent.

For René Descartes (1596–1650) consciousness is a closed world, limited to internal ideas or representations: we know only what is *in* the mind. This principle was unquestioningly followed by the British empiricists and Immanuel Kant, who maintained that what I directly know are not things themselves but appearances, impressions, or ideas of things. The direct realism of traditional philosophy gave way to an indirect realism, a position shared equally by Continental idealism and British empiricism. In the words of John Locke, 'the mind, in all its thoughts and reasonings, hath no other immediate object but its own ideas, which it alone does or can contemplate'.[24] If all we know are the contents of our mind, what grounds have we to affirm the reality of an independent world? The logical conclusion, drawn by the Irishman George Berkeley, was that reality itself consists of nothing but perceptions.

KNOWLEDGE AND TRANSCENDENCE

The first moment of human transcendence is the act of knowledge, in which the individual traverses from the subjectivity of the isolated self to an independent world beyond consciousness. In any simple sensation I am in direct contact with the physical world here and now. Such at least is the common-sense conviction of mankind in general and was for the most part the assumed natural attitude of pre-modern philosophy. The question of the 'outside world' became a stumbling block because of the method adopted by the father of modern philosophy. Descartes prioritized the so-called principle of immanence, according to which, in order to be known, an object must be 'in' the mind or consciousness, i.e. the mind can know directly only its own contents.[25] There is a quantum of truth in this: in order to be known the object must be somehow present to the mind. Descartes' error was his failure to understand that when transferred from the physical domain, the word 'in' assumes a different meaning. If the water is in the bottle it cannot simultaneously be in the bucket. The tradition of Aristotle, on the other hand, maintains that the water can be physically in the bottle but simultaneously, in a unique non-physical intentional mode, also 'in' my consciousness: such is the marvel of knowledge.

Descartes' assumption was uncritically adopted by most modern philosophers, not only by idealists and rationalists such as Immanuel Kant, but even by many of a sensist, empirical, outlook such as Locke and Hume. This position had defining consequences for the question of God. If the mind only knows its own contents, and is incapable of affirming the independent existence of an independent world beyond itself, it lacks the foundation for asserting an infinite reality beyond the realm of finite being. It cannot rely on the principle of causality to argue from the world as effect to the existence of a transcendent cause.

Descartes' inversion of the relation between reality and knowledge brought about what Immanuel Kant (1724–1804) appropriately termed a 'Copernican revolution' in philosophy. Kant overturned the meaning of the word 'transcendental', ascribing to it a meaning exactly the contrary of its traditional significance: 'I entitle *transcendental* all knowledge which is occupied not so much with objects as with the mode of our knowledge of objects in so far as this mode of knowledge is to be possible *a priori*.'[26] Instead of universal qualities pertaining objectively to all existent things whatsoever, the term came to denote the subjective capacities of all knowledge whatsoever. Kant reversed the assumption that cognition must conform to the object, requiring instead that the object must submit to our cognition. He argued that all we can know are phenomenal appearances and that we are incapable of knowing things as they are in themselves. Instead of the object making cognitive representation possible he asked how the representation makes the object possible. Judged from the point of view of traditional realism, Kant remained within the circle of Cartesian immanentism, a position that precluded him from affirming the independent existence of an objective world, and by implication of a divine transcendent cause.

Notwithstanding his immanentist interpretation of knowledge, Kant recognized the innate human inclination to posit transcendent realities. Man is possessed of a profound disposition towards metaphysics – a *metaphysica naturalis*: 'Human reason proceeds impetuously, driven on by an inward need, to questions such as cannot be answered by any empirical employment of reason, or by principles thence derived.'[27] Kant however is unable to pursue such questions realistically since there is no intuition of the supra-sensible; sense knowledge alone has positive content. The principle of causality cannot be invoked to go beyond the world of appearances. He posits as 'regulative' the ideas of self, world, and God, which guide and order human inquiry; these are aspirational but have no actuality in themselves. The metaphysical impulse, though ineradicable, is void and illusory. While Kant recognizes our zeal to know God, the world, and the self, their reality lies beyond the competence of knowledge.[28]

Kant's transcendental idealism is diametrically opposed to the 'transcendental idealism' of Plato, which was in fact an exaggerated realism. Plato was the great oracle of transcendence in ancient philosophy. 'Transcendent' here refers to the realm of ideal forms with the Good at its zenith, which Plato posited beyond the sense world. It denotes thus an indispensable dimension of reality: reality is more than what is experienced by the senses. Plato viewed things in their profound dimensions: each thing is insufficient in itself; finite and fluctuating it cannot stand alone but reaches to a reality beyond, which, though transcendent, is innerly present to it. In Rilke's phrase, 'Transitoriness rushes everywhere into a profound Being.'[29] To guarantee the reliability of scientific knowledge Plato posited a world of subsistent Ideas beyond the empirical world. In his zeal to affirm the object of true knowledge, free from change and imperfection, he rejected the role of sense experience. His methodic error is suitably conveyed by Kant:

> The light dove cleaving in free flight the thin air, whose resistance it feels, might imagine that her movements would be far more free and rapid in airless space. Just in the same way did Plato, abandoning the world of sense because of the narrow limits it sets to the understanding, venture upon the wings of ideas beyond it, into the void space of pure intellect. He did not reflect that he made no real progress by all his efforts; for he met with no resistance which might serve him for a support, as it were, whereon to rest, and on which he might apply his powers, in order to let the intellect acquire momentum for its progress.[30]

The key to any satisfactory solution of the problem must lie between the extremes of Plato and Kant. This was provided by Aristotle.

Man is an ecstatic being. Human nature is not a closed system, but is open to the world at every level. We are nourished physically by our immediate environment and intellectually by the wider universe. We find fulfilment by traversing the frontiers of the self in engagement with the non-self. Paul Ricoeur remarked: 'I express myself in expressing the world;

I explore my own sacrality in deciphering that of the world.'[31] Knowledge is a clear instance of ecstatic transcendence. Cognition occurs only when the human capacity is activated; of itself the cognitive apparatus is entirely passive. The intellect is a virginal slate on which characters must first be inscribed. Knowledge begins with the action of the physical objects on the senses. Descartes' pure *cogito* is an abstraction isolated from our first experience of the world. Aristotle's thinker is marked by its openness to the world.

It is easy to see why divergence regarding the ultimate question of the existence of a transcendent God begins with the initial choice of philosophic method, in response to the question: what do I know? A.N. Whitehead remarked: 'The ancient world takes its stand upon the drama of the Universe, the modern world upon the inward drama of the Soul.'[32] For Descartes the unshaken ground of truth (*fundamentum inconcussum veritatis*) is the self-experience of subjective thought, as conveyed in his famous '*Cogito ergo sum*': 'I think, therefore I am.' For Aristotle and Aquinas, the foundation of truth is the datum of immediate sense experience: *Aliquid est*, 'Something is.' Rather than Descartes' *Cogito*, their motto would read: '*Res sunt, ergo cognosco, deinde cogito*': 'Things are, therefore I know, thus I think.' Descartes not only placed knowledge of the independent world in doubt but closed the path of metaphysical reasoning towards the Transcendent.

Compounding the problems stemming from Descartes' closed consciousness was his obsession with clear and distinct ideas. Jacques Maritain has remarked that the tragedy of modern philosophy was the divorce of intelligibility from mystery.[33] Profound and sublime thoughts are rarely clear and distinct; philosophy reflects most significantly upon the mysterious – those truths (*clair-obscurs*) that embrace, sustain and transcend us, rather than problems that lie detached before us. Leonard Cohen sang: 'There is a crack in everything, that's how the light gets in.' Ralph Waldo Emerson, the transcendentalist poet of the mid-nineteenth century, wrote: 'There is a crack in every thing God has made',[34] but qualified this in his journal: 'God has made nothing without a crack, except Reason. What can be better than this?'[35] Finitude, the deep fracture in things, is a cipher whose transcendence reason illuminates. Our mind, however, since it is measured for finite existence, is overwhelmed by the luminosity of sheer existence. William Blake asserted: 'If the doors of perception were cleansed everything would appear to man as it is – infinite. For man has closed himself up, till he sees all things through narrow chinks of his cavern.'[36] There is a dissymmetry between the intellect's capacity to know and the intelligibility of being. Human cognition is dazed by the all-embracing and ever-present radiance of existence. Aristotle remarks: 'As the eyes of bats are to the light of day, so is the intellect of our soul towards the things which by nature are most manifest of all.'[37] The existence of things is what is most apparent of all, yet faced with the mystery of Being we approach the border between light and dark. Confronted by what is indefinite and undefined we are prone to metaphysical dizziness. Considered in respect of their origin creatures are shade and dark compared to the light of infinite Being. What is opaque in itself seems relatively clear, while the plenitude of luminosity overwhelms through excess. Our knowledge of God is eclipsed by the divine brightness, which blinds us into darkness. But light is best perceived out of the dark: whoever digs deep enough will view the stars even in daylight.

TRANSCENDENCE TO THE WORLD

Reflection on sensation provides valuable insight into the wider horizon of human transcendence, namely that of endless and unconditioned existence. Not only do I affirm the reality of the sensed object, but in pronouncing the word 'is', I affirm the most universal and profound value possible for human knowledge: that of existence itself. There is more to perception than meets the eye. Not only do I comprehend the object as sensed here and now, but in affirming it as real I gain insight into the fact that the first activity exercised by the sense datum is existence itself: the first thing that each thing does is 'to be'. I recognize as fundamental the primary perfection and value of being. Reflecting on this affirmation I grasp the intransgressible distance between being and non-being. I recognize moreover that the object before me shares the fundamental act of existing with every other existing individual. The notion of being is verified in the sense-object acting upon my tongue, eye, or ear, but its meaning is not limited either to it or to any other possible object of knowledge. This is to discover the transcendental character of being: the value and perfection of existence is not limited to the here and now, or to any particular mode of being, but has unrestricted significance and value; it traverses all limits and categories. It has an absolute or infinite value.

In the simple affirmation of the humblest object we implicitly assert the transcendent and transcendental character of existence. This was the great intuition of the Greek thinker Parmenides, who first grasped the absolute character of reality hidden in the simple words, 'something is': Being IS. Parmenides' consent to the absolute character of Being is momentous. It is a simple intuition of the starkness with which reality imposes itself. 'It is necessary both to say and to think that being is; for being is and non-being cannot be.'[38] It is an insight into the absolute and enduring value of Being, removed from non-being, transcending all change and diversity. Being is at the origin of everything: there is nothing more elementary and nothing beyond it. Being is absolute: it is bounded or restricted by nothing (*absolutum*). Once Being is given, non-being is impossible. The recognition of Being as primordial, first wrought in reflective language by Parmenides, is faithfully captured by S.T. Coleridge:

> Hast thou ever raised thy mind to the consideration of EXISTENCE, in and by itself, as the mere act of existing? Hast thou ever said to thyself thoughtfully, IT IS! heedless in that moment whether it were a man before thee, or a flower, or a grain of sand? Without reference, in short, to this or that particular mode or form of existence? If thou hast indeed attained to this, thou wilt have felt the presence of a mystery, which must have fixed thy spirit in awe and wonder. The very words, There is nothing! or, There was a time, when there was nothing! are self-contradictory. There is that within us which repels the proposition with as full and instantaneous light, as if it bore evidence against the fact in the right of its own eternity.
>
> Not TO BE, then, is impossible: To BE, incomprehensible. If thou hast mastered this intuition of absolute existence, thou wilt have learnt likewise that it was this, and no other, which in the earlier ages seized the nobler minds, the elect among men, with a sort of sacred horror. This it was which first caused them to feel within themselves a something ineffably greater than their own individual nature.[39]

'Not to be': impossible; 'to be': incomprehensible. Louis Pasteur similarly remarked, 'The notion of infinity has the dual character that it imposes itself upon us and yet it remains incomprehensible.'[40] Such is the affirmation of existence: it imposes itself upon our consciousness, yet lies beyond our comprehension.

If we consider what occurs when we affirm the reality of what is given in sensation, we gain valuable insight into the meaning implicit in the basic concept that is involved: we invoke and activate the universal concept of being. Spontaneously and simultaneously I also implicitly affirm the totality of existence. My thought moves swiftly, deepens and expands, from 'this is' to 'the totality of being is'. The absolute and necessary character of being is implicit in asserting the existence of the sense particular: 'This is.' 'This' refers to the sensible, particular, here and now; 'is' expresses a universal absolute. This was the value of Parmenides' discovery: Being has also an absolute character; nothing limits or opposes it. The fact that there is now something in existence means that there was never a time or state in which there was nothing. Julie Andrews has reliably assured us: 'Nothing comes from nothing, nothing ever could.' Nor will there ever be a state of non-being, since being cannot pass in its entirety into its opposite, which would be total annihilation. The writer Francis Stuart liked to remark that everything would have been much simpler if nothing had ever existed![41] To ponder such a possibility is apt to induce mental vertigo, the unbearable lightheadedness of non-being. Existence imposes itself with irrefutable vehemence; given even the most insignificant finite entity, we are obliged to affirm the totality of the universe as absolute and infinite. In pronouncing 'Reality is' I express a universal truth which holds without exception for everything in existence: I express a transcendent truth.

'Transcendence' in this context refers to the mind's unrestricted openness to reality as a whole; the intellect is *capax universi*, capable of universal knowledge. In cognition the human person transcends the here and now to embrace the totality. In adopting the universal attitude of cognition towards the universe of the real, by attending to such concepts as 'the totality of the real', 'the universe', 'being', 'everything that is', I transcend the limits of space and time and become, in Plato's phrase, a 'spectator of all time and existence'. This universal capacity of human mind was for Aristotle the defining characteristic of the human soul. Concluding his treatise on psychology, he wrote: 'The soul is somehow all things.' There is a correspondence between spirit and the totality. According to the Arabic philosopher Avicenna (980–1037), the ultimate perfection which the soul can attain is to have delineated in it the entire order and causes of the universe. Cognitively or intentionally (in the order of knowledge) the ultimate horizon of reflection is the totality of the real, of all-which-is. Hamlet remarks: 'I could be bounded in a nut-shell, and count myself a king of infinite space.'[42] The protagonist in the Second World War film 'Pimpernel Smith' uses the inspiring password 'The mind of man is bounded only by the universe', as a signal to alert those whom he is about to spring from captivity.

Being is a 'transcendental' perfection. The concept of being surpasses every category; it is not limited to any specific kind or particular manner of existing. When I affirm of anything, however insignificant, that it 'is', I recognize that the meaning or value expressed in the verb 'is', is not confined to the particular thing here and now: it can refer to anything whatsoever. Being cannot be reduced to any particular kind, determination or mode of being. All forms of a priori reductionism are unwarranted. There could be other worlds of which we are unaware, 'parallel universes' or modes of existence which surpass the measure of human thought. This is the ultimate marvel of existence: we cannot pin it down, or confine it to any category. Philip Larkin spoke of 'unfenced existence'.[43]

Being is the ultimate realm of human thought, the universal and ubiquitous element of the human spirit: the ebb and flow of all we do, the buoyancy and ballast of what we know, the keel on which rests each intellectual advance. It is the anchor of every affirmation, the north which guides our quest – equally each point which encompasses the boundless sphere both of what we know and what yet remains uncharted. Through his participation in universal being, man transcends time and space; he traverses all boundaries and categories. This is the enigma of human nature: man is finite in his being; he is not the whole of being, nevertheless, through cognition, he embraces the totality of the real. Blaise Pascal (1623–1662) remarked: 'By space the universe contains me as a speck; by thinking I contain it.'[44] Cognitively the ultimate horizon of reflection is the totality of the real, the entirety of all-which-is; human being has through spirit a unique relation to the totality. The mind has an unrestricted openness, both factually and imaginatively. This was understood by the poet Andrew Marvell (1621–1678):

> The Mind, that Ocean where each kind
> Does streight its own resemblance find,
> Yet it creates, transcending these,
> Far other Worlds, and other seas.[45]

The awareness that one personally participates in the grand totality is a source of abundant fascination. The realization that I share with everything the most fundamental perfection of existence – that I am part of a greater universe which evinces eternity, infinity and absoluteness – is an awesome thought. Arthur Koestler chose the term 'oceanic sense' (borrowed from Freud, who coined the term only to belittle the experience as infantile) to describe the overwhelming feeling that one belongs to something ineffable and immeasurably greater than oneself.[46] The comparison of finding oneself immersed within a fathomless realm without horizon provides an apt physical analogy. The sense of being part of 'something greater', cradled in the generous embrace of the Whole, is perhaps the sentiment of those who proclaim themselves to be 'spiritual rather than religious'. How does this differ from the transcendence that defines religion? Religion involves the third transcendence noted above, namely that of an infinite personal cause, creator of the finite universe, to whom one owes gratitude and obeisance. What distinguishes the 'religious' from the 'spiritual' person is that the former acknowledges existence as gift from a generous creator.

Man as transcendent

Before passing on to the kind of reasoning which leads to the affirmation of a vertical transcendent just noted, it is worth considering the nature of transcendence that distinguishes human beings. There are indeed multiple layers of transcendence, corresponding to diverse graded perfections observed in the empirical world. This is to be observed in the ways in which individual beings rise above the limiting conditions of space and time, 'here and now'. A hierarchy of transcendence is to be observed in the world around us. At the basic level plants rise above the inert surroundings of the material world through the powers of nutrition and propagation. The miracle of transcendence is present in the weed growing in the cracked pavement. By contrast with matter, whose existence is entirely dispersed and extended throughout its constituent parts, plants have their own individual intrinsic principle – 'nature' – which allows them to inwardly construct themselves and spontaneously establish relationships with their environment. They are endowed with a minimal interiority; in this measure vegetal reality transcends the material. Animals in turn rise above animate plant life with the added perfection of local self-motion; zoological life is more perfect than the botanical. There is moreover a hierarchy within the animal kingdom, some species exhibiting amazing powers of instinctive knowledge, activity which may analogically be described as clever. All animals, however, are captive within their environment; their behaviour is seasonal and instinctive. Man alone – to some degree – rises above the conditions of his environment. As Josef Pieper has formulated it, animals have an environment, man has his world.[47] That world is precisely the domain of being, the total universe of the real, as described in the previous paragraphs. Robert Bolt vibrantly portrayed the hierarchy of creation in the words of Sir Thomas More: 'God made the *angels* to show him splendour – as he made animals for innocence and plants for their simplicity. But Man he made to serve him wittily, in the tangle of his mind!'[48]

Man is a *microcosm* of the greater, universal, order of being. This may be understood in two ways: *intentionally* (explained above as cognitive transcendence) and *ontologically*: he unites in a single being the various levels of existence: material, biological, spiritual. A traditional motif in philosophy sees man as a 'frontier' being, occupying the horizon between two worlds, the material and spiritual. Various levels of transcendence are to be observed within human nature. Man uniquely embodies within the unity of the self the diverse levels of existence, material, animate and biological. In common with all living things he rises above the material conditions of the exclusively physical, and rising above the vegetable he shares with other animals the powers of self-movement and sensation. Can human nature be explained exhaustively in physical, material or biological terms? Human nature is manifestly corporeal and biological; is it exclusively so? It has been argued by many philosophers that a number of activities indicate that man is capable of processes which go beyond the limitation of material reality, thereby indicating the presence of a non-material principle. That is to say, human reality cannot be entirely explained either by the physical or biological sciences, but exhibits the distinctively human quality of spirit.

Aristotle gave a number of reasons why the soul must be non-material. Referring to Anaxagoras he argued that the soul knows all things only because it is 'unmixed' (ἀμιγῆ)[49] with the body.[50] If it were corporeal, it would have a determinate quality (such as hot or cold), which would make cognition of its contrary impossible. It would also require a physical organ, similar to those of the senses.[51] The difference is clearly illustrated by the fact that a sense organ can be damaged if overused (the ear by loud sound, the eye by bright light), whereas the intellect cannot be affected in this way; the intellect is not impaired by thinking too intensely about difficult problems.

Aristotle declared: 'There is no such thing as face (πρόσωπον) or flesh without soul (ψυχή).'[52] An occasionally held view throughout the history of philosophy, which has increased in popularity and is today widespread, maintains on the contrary that there is no place for the soul: psychic life is a product of the brain, humans are exclusively material. This position may rest upon the assumption that all reality is essentially material in nature, a supposition that needs to be questioned. Friedrich Albert Lange famously began his 1866 study *The History of Materialism* with the statement: 'Materialism is as old as philosophy, but not older.'[53] The point of Lange's remark is that philosophy may sometimes be the source of its own problems. The doctrine of materialism, that human nature may be explained exclusively in terms of matter, rests upon the more fundamental belief that all reality is material. This is a metaphysical claim of great magnitude, one which derives, I suggest, from a simple methodic error, namely that reality or existence may be identified with one of its particular modes or determinations, specifically its perceptible mode. It is true that material bodies are the first objects of human cognition and the proper realm of human knowledge. It is a gratuitous assertion, however, to conclude a priori that material bodies are all that exist. The notion of existence does not exclude in advance the possibility of reality of a different modality than that of matter.

If it were material, the intellect could not receive within itself the intelligible natures of all things; but since it is open to receive all reality intelligibly within itself, it is not restricted to any material mode. The immateriality of the intellect is established in the first place by its universality, the clearest proof being its unlimited openness to every possible object. Whereas each of the sense faculties depends upon a specific sense organ, and is directed towards a particular material object here and now, located narrowly in time and space, the intellect is open to the totality because it has no such organ. Its universality is a consequence of its immaterial capacity. Its target is universal reality – the unrestricted totality of beings in general.[54] According to Aristotle, while sensation grasps the particular, the intellect understands the universal.[55] Sensation is confined to the here and now, while 'nimble thought can jump both sea and land'.

The cognitive openness of the human intellect to the totality of being is one of the key aspects of human transcendence. It has traditionally been taken as an indication of man's spiritual nature. The other main characteristic of the human spirit is reflection, i.e. the ability of the mind to turn back upon itself and its contents. Along with the mind's universality of scope, the power of self-reflection has been regarded as proof of the spiritual character of human nature. The power of self-reflection follows indeed from the soul's universality. Because of its universal scope, the intellect may introspectively and concomitantly know every cognitive act of the individual, whether sensible or intellectual. The intellect knows itself, Aristotle suggests, as it does any other immaterial object.[56] Reflexivity as an indication of the soul's immaterial nature was emphasized by the fifth-century Neoplatonist writer Proclus (410–485), who in proposition 15 of his work *Elements of Theology* asserts: 'All that is capable of reverting upon itself is incorporeal (ἀσώματον).' Proposition 171 states: 'Intellect is indeed truly incorporeal, which its reversion upon itself makes clear, for bodies are incapable of such reversion.' Matter cannot bend back upon itself. In his commentary on the *Liber de Causis* Aquinas quotes with approval Proclus' reason for the immateriality of intellect:

> No body is naturally suited to turn toward itself. For if that which turns toward something is in contact with that toward which it turns, then it is clear that all the parts of the body that turns toward itself will be in contact with all [the rest of its parts]. This is not possible for anything that has parts, because of the separation of the parts, each of which lies in a different place.[57]

What these authors have in mind is the inability of material reality, defined by mutual exteriority of parts (*partes extra partes*), to return upon itself in reflection. Put simply, parts get in the way. The components of any material object are external to one another; they have no cohesive unifying interiority. Through his conscious experience man possesses reflective self-experience, indicating an interior life which cannot be explained on materialistic principles. As for the difference between man and other animals, Teilhard de Chardin states compellingly:

> If we wish to settle this question of the 'superiority' of man over the animals ... I can only see one way of doing so – to brush resolutely aside all those secondary and equivocal manifestations of inner activity in human behaviour, making straight for the central phenomenon, *reflection* ... Admittedly the animal knows. *But it cannot know that it knows*: that is quite certain. If it could, it would long ago have multiplied its inventions and developed a system of internal constructions that could not have escaped our observation. In consequence it is denied access to a whole domain of reality in which we can move freely. We

are separated by a chasm – or a threshold – which it cannot cross. Because we are reflective we are not only different but quite another. It is not merely a matter of change of degree, but of a change of nature, resulting from a change of state.[58]

Since human nature is a complex reality, displaying a diversity of capacities that exceed the bounds of the spatio-temporal existence, many philosophers have asserted that human destiny ultimately lies beyond the material world: that what is most distinctively human is not subject to the corruption that affects everything in the visible material world. At its ultimate, most fundamental and supreme level, the question whether or not man has a transcendent destiny (whether he participates in an absolute or infinite reality) is focused on the prospect of immortality. Is death the end, or is there persistence and personal survival? One author has put it well: 'The human participation in the infinite is captured by the belief in a non-physical soul. The existence of an immortal soul has been a fundamental axiom of philosophical thought since prehistory. The immortal soul is, in Wordsworth's term, "our life's star".'[59]

While the ultimate question of human transcendence is that of personal immortality, the fundamental and final question of transcendence, absolutely and *per se*, is whether there exists an infinite and eternal self-sufficient being who is the source of all existence and every created perfection. If there is such a cause it must of necessity be intelligent and personal, since a cause cannot impart what it does not itself possess. Supporters and opponents alike agree that the most serious 'arguments' for the existence of God are the so-called 'cosmological' arguments, i.e. those based on the existence and nature of the visible world, rather than on an analysis of ideas (the 'ontological argument'), or on the need for a final justification of morality. Common to cosmological 'demonstrations' is the conviction that finite reality is a sign – cipher – for the Transcendent. It is also agreed that the classic arguments for God's existence are Aquinas' Five Ways (*Quinque Viae*), each of which takes as its point of departure an empirical datum, which when *analyzed* in light of the principles of identity, sufficient reason, and causality appeals to the existence of a transcendent cause.

Aquinas' Fourth Way (*Quarta Via*) takes as its point of departure the hierarchy of graded transcendence observed in the natural world.[60] Existence exhibits many degrees of perfection. This is manifest within our own experience; even within the mineral world we recognize levels of beauty and value. That which is living exercises greater powers than inanimate existence; in the vegetable realm there are objective grounds on which we judge some individuals to be more beautiful or more perfect than others. A greater degree of individuation is observed in the animal world, where self-movement and self-preservation are characteristics of the individual. Most marvellous of all, however, is the quantum leap – a *saltus qualitatis* – from beast to man. Incorporating within himself the properties of the inorganic, vegetal, and the animate, man rises beyond these and assumes a relationship towards all of reality. With the emergence of spirit there blossoms forth through self-reflection the vast world of human culture which opens upon the infinite and the eternal, the absolute and the universal. Each individual is obliged concretely to assume personal responsibilty for his ultimate destiny within the universal spectrum of existence.

Goodness is realized in diverse degrees. The universe displays an ascending scale of existential perfection: the plant is superior to the mineral, the animal is more perfect than the plant, man more noble than the beast. We observe basic qualities or perfections such as life, beauty, goodness, truth and unity; considered in themselves these imply no limit or imperfection. Aquinas argues that if such a quality or perfection is shared by a multiplicity of individuals according to diverse degrees, none of these can itself be the source of that perfection.[61] To do so it would need to be the source not only of the perfection, but also of the limit restricting the measure according to which it enjoys the perfection. It would be both cause and effect – an impossible contradiction. Since diverse individuals possess the shared perfection, but none in virtue of itself, each must receive it from a source which as the essential fullness of that perfection itself contains its own explanation and self-sufficiency. Put another way, no individual which possesses imperfectly one of these pure perfections can itself be the adequate source of that perfection; its only source can be the very essence or unrestricted fullness of the perfection. Only a being which possesses a perfection without limit can cause the limitation of that perfection in those beings which receive it. As the plenitude of the perfection it is also the maximum according to which greater and lesser are affirmed. Aquinas remarks: 'More and less are predicated of different things, according as they resemble in different ways something which is the maximum.'[62]

It is not possible here to detail the various aspects of this argument, which would need much more elaboration for its full significance and implications to be justified.[63] Central to the reflection lies the principle of participation which Aquinas inherited from Plato: finite beings share, each according to its individual limited measure, in the plenitude of a self-subsistent reality which is their cause. Aquinas applied Plato's principle without falling into the error of exaggerated realism. Reginald Garrigou-Lagrange remarked that the Fourth Way, 'contains in condensed form all the dialectics of Plato', by which the soul convinces itself of the reality of the transcendental perfections.[64] It is a 'dialectic of the intellect' whereby reflection rises to the affirmation of a maximum perfection which is the cause of all limited instances. Garrigou-Lagrange also referred to the 'dialectic of love', which 'is within the reach of every soul eager for that Goodness which no particular good can satisfy'. It is the eros described in the renowned passage of Plato's *Symposium* which portrays the soul's gradual ascent from the initial sensual love of particular bodies and forms to a love of bodies in general, then to the soul and its virtues, before finally gazing upon the vast ocean of Beauty itself, which exists eternally and absolutely, infinite and immutable, by and of itself. A passage in Aquinas' *Summa Theologiae* echoes the élan of the *Symposium*:

> The first step consists in the mere consideration of sensible objects; the second step consists in going forward from sensible to intelligible objects; the third step is to judge of sensible objects according to intelligible things; the fourth is the absolute consideration of the intelligible objects to which one has attained by means of sensibles; the fifth is the contemplation of those intelligible objects that are unattainable by means of sensibles, but which the reason is able to grasp; the sixth step is the consideration of such intelligible things as the reason can neither discover nor grasp, which pertain to the sublime contemplation of divine truth, wherein contemplation is ultimately perfected.[65]

In the tradition of Plato, Aristotle, Aquinas and the tradition which they inspire, such is the culmination of the philosophic quest: the affirmation that there really exists a transcendent destiny. Any attempt to decipher that transcendence must accord with man's nature as body and soul, matter and spirit, sense and intellect. Plato's flight of transcendence was inadequately grounded; man is, he stated, a creature not of earth but of heaven (φυτὸν οὐκ ἔγγειον ἀλλὰ οὐράνιον).[66] Orphism, one of the main sources of his inspiration, more correctly saw man as the child both of earth and starry heaven. According to Aquinas, man walks the earth in the promise and hope of beatitude, a *viator* travelling towards the transcendent mystery. He states: 'The most wonderful thing of all is that earthly and corruptible man may be promoted to the possession of spiritual and heavenly things.'[67]

CONCRETE CIPHERS OF TRANSCENDENCE

It was suggested above that every being, by the simple fact of its existence, is a cipher of transcendence in so far as it reveals the transcendent character of universal being. All entities share in the absoluteness of the totality, to which nothing can be opposed. The transient and transitory betoken the transcendent, the infinitesimal reflects the infinite, the ephemeral heralds the eternal. As Aquinas remarks, there is nothing so contingent that it does not contain at least some necessity.[68] Such necessity derives from its participation in the infinite plenitude that is governed by the necessary laws of reality and thought.

Besides this universal token of transcendence discerned in every entity, we also observe objects or events which epiphanize the transcendent in particular ways — not only through their existence, but by virtue either of what they are or do. These may be understood initially in relation to the twin powers of the human soul, namely intellect and will; each of these faculties has an innate capacity for the infinite, under the mantle respectively of the true and the good.[69] Aquinas remarks that 'the spiritual soul is capable of the infinite because it can grasp the universal'.[70] The mind thirsts for truth, the heart hungers for happiness.

TRUTH

Truth is the intellect's transcendent good.[71] Marked by a universal capacity (*capax universi*) the mind has an unrestricted need for truth. That is why the physicist seeks a 'Theory of Everything', and the philosopher asks the ultimate question 'Why does anything (or everything) exist?' Neither is satisfied with partial truths. The intellect pursues exhaustive understanding; regardless of how detailed our discoveries of the world, the drive to know remains unsatisfied with finite answers. The intellect's desire stretches to the infinite. While this may appear unattainable or even illusory, as Kant assumed, we have a grounded guarantee that the totality is intelligible even if it exceeds our intelligence. The law of non-contradiction is a warrant that reality is not condemned to absurdity and will not deceive us. A concrete hallmark of the transcendent nature of truth is its independence from every condition and circumstance. If on 15 April 2019 there was a hailstorm on the Acropolis, the statement 'On 15 April 2019 there was a hailstorm on the Acropolis' will be forever true.

The Good

Aristotle defined the good as that which all things seek. His definition applies to all agents, including animals which instinctively pursue goals to satisfy their needs. Humans act consciously in view of ends. Even if what we desire is harmful we do not desire it *because* it is injurious, but in so far as it promises an apparent good. As the faculty of the good the will is incapable of choosing evil as such: the good is a priori its normative object. Plato placed the Good at the apex of the Forms since it is the source of every value and the goal of all desire. In her celebrated address in the *Symposium* to those in search of Love, Diotima explains that the desire for beauty is finally fulfilled only in the complete possession of infinite beauty.

The attainment of a partial end gratifies a fleeting desire and provides passing satisfaction. The intellect, however, with its capacity for the infinite recognizes that finite goods are limited and that none can provide complete contentment. The will yearns for total happiness; heartened by 'the holy flame of discontent' we are not satisfied by ephemeral delights. Diotima expresses the élan of desire as it ascends from particular, limited, instances to the unique and infinite fullness of Beauty itself. Finite goods point towards a fullness which they imperfectly reflect. A common motif in Western thought is God's total goodness and perfection as the goal of human desire. In his *Confessions* Augustine proclaims: 'You have made us for yourself, O Lord, and our heart is restless until it rests in you.'[72] Aquinas expounds in detail:

> It is impossible for any created good to constitute man's happiness. For happiness is the perfect good, which quiets the appetite altogether since it would not be the last end if something yet remained to be desired. Now the object of the will, that is, of man's appetite, is the universal good, just as the object of the intellect is the universal true. Hence it is evident that nothing can quiet man's will, except the universal good. This is to be found not in any creature, but in God alone, because every creature has goodness by participation. Therefore God alone can satisfy the will of man, according to the words of Psalm

102.5: 'Who satisfies your desire with good things.' Therefore God alone constitutes man's happiness.[73]

According to Aquinas, only in complete union of mind and will with the divine goodness and truth shall the mind of man be filled and his heart stilled.

BEAUTY[74]

Beauty is the fusion of truth and goodness. It is the epiphany of reality as it illuminates the mind and pleases the will. It is the pre-eminent adumbration and foretaste of the Transcendent. While every entity is theoretically an epiphany of Beauty – although sometimes difficult to recognize as such – some individuals are immediately appealing. In his novel *The Death of Virgil* Hermann Broch wrote: 'Certainly many instances of earthly beauty – a song, the twilit sea, the tone of the lyre, the voice of a boy, a verse, a statue, a column, a garden, a single flower – all possess the divine faculty of making man hearken unto the innermost and outermost boundaries of his existence.'[75] On seeing the exquisite beauty of the Parthenon marbles for the first time the artist Benjamin Robert Haydon stated: 'I felt as if a divine truth had blazed inwardly upon my mind.'[76]

NATURE

We live our lives in intimate communion and exchange with our surrounding environment. Although we transcend the natural world in various ways, we are rooted in universal nature which nourishes and sustains us. Beyond the utility of survival the world draws us upward and outward by its beauty and majesty, suggesting something greater than ourselves. In mythology the powers of nature – birth, water, fire, growth, etc. – were personified and given theomorphic personalities. At a simple level humans have a natural affinity with the beauty of their natural surroundings; we are entranced by the mystery of the night sky, the simplicity of a sunlit dewdrop, the vastness of deserts or fertile plains, the majesty of mountain peaks and the subtle beauty of a flower in bloom. We marvel at the harmony across diverse domains of the world. The ecology of nature encapsulates in miniature the integrity of the metaphysical universe. The underlying marvel of nature is its indomitable power of self-renewal, which rather than atrophy or entropy renews itself season after season. In recent times we have become aware of the dangers we can inflict upon its delicate harmony and are conscious of a duty to something greater than ourselves. In ancient times the Presocratics recognized the primordial value of basic elements such as earth, air and water. In our own time we have begun to appreciate that nature must not be taken as a given, but valued as a gift.

Nature in its endless variety offers countless occasions of marvel and delight. In a remarkable passage on Aristotle's *Parts of Animals* we read the following praise of nature's beauty:

> Every realm of nature is marvelous ... so we should venture on the study of every kind of animal without distaste; for each and all will reveal to us something natural and something beautiful. Absence of haphazard and conduciveness of everything to an end are to be found in Nature's works in the highest degree, and the resultant end of her generations and combinations is a form of the beautiful.[77]

MORAL OBLIGATION

We evaluate our actions in light of standards which measure their ultimate value. We are sometimes required to choose between expedient advantage and higher value.[78] Our freedom may oblige us to accept what is disadvantageous, even physically harmful, out of regard for something greater. There are throughout history inspiring examples of individuals who sacrificed life rather than abandon their ideals. One might think of a mother who choses to be killed rather than smother her child whose crying will betray their hiding place. Death with dignity is prized above survival at any cost: life at such a price is not worth living.

Any moral assessment or evaluation involves detachment from the conditions of a particular situation. This may be no more than a utilitarian evaluation of possible consequences in order to weigh one course of action against another. Such is the case even where there is no consideration of so-called higher values, but simply the maximization of practical benefit. Properly, however, one can only speak of a transcendent dimension where there is a consideration of higher values, such as the intrinsic dignity of the person. Immanuel Kant proposed the principle that rational beings can never be treated as means to ends, but always as ends themselves. It is sometimes assumed that the basic moral command is to respect the dignity of other persons, especially never to intend the direct killing of another. This is fine so far as it goes, but fails to recognize that one also has moral duties to oneself. Robinson Crusoe did not await the arrival of his man Friday in order to become moral.

One might regard as 'absolutist' the view that no innocent life should be unjustly sacrificed, even to secure the physical well-being of countless others. It was a fundamental principle of Roman law that justice must be done though the world might perish or the heavens fall.[79] Justice must be preserved regardless of consequences. The foundation of Socratic humanist ethics is that it is never right to do wrong.[80] While such a system may seem rigid and absolutist, a secure moral system requires such a bedrock which ultimately guarantees greater freedom.

CONSCIENCE

Conscience is often assumed to be a special faculty of moral evaluation and decision, an inner voice of private personal command; it is in fact simply the faculty of reason when applied to a particular action, the intellect as it judges a concrete situation.[81] It is the person's subjective norm of morality, relying on the habitual acceptance of an objective norm or standard. Such habitual knowledge is the summation of an individual's moral character, the self-knowledge of one's duty in the overall scheme of things. In assessing the moral value of an action the person judges herself against deeply-held values. Metaphorically one may speak of an inner voice: Socrates referred to his personal daimon. Conscience is one's own most deeply felt voice of self-evaluation in light of one's intimate and profound personal values. In this sense it is a cipher of transcendence. St John Henry Newman wrote: 'Conscience does not repose on itself, but vaguely reaches forward to something beyond self, and dimly discerns a sanction higher than self for its decisions, as is evidenced in that keen sense of obligation and responsibility which informs them. And hence it is that we are accustomed to speak of conscience as a voice ... or the echo of a voice, imperative and constraining, like no other dictate in the whole world of our experience.'[82]

Conscience denotes the deepest core of a person's self-evaluation, one's innermost sanctuary of self-worth and personal integrity. It is the compass and beacon of character. One's actions are meritorious because they are freely chosen and executed responsibly. Respect for freedom of conscience is thus a touchstone of the truly liberal society. The human commitment to truth and goodness transcends the social order. The dignity of the individual rises above one's role in society or history. That dignity comes from being an agent endowed with the freedom and obligation to determine one's conscious identity and autonomy, an identity which cannot be reduced to one's role within a socio-economic mechanism. It is the person's dignity to be an autonomous subject of moral decision and responsibility. Conscience has rights because it first has duties, namely the duty and obligation of each individual to shape her life for herself, in dependence upon and in cooperation with others. It is a duty that cannot be abdicated or delegated; no one else can do it on my behalf. The ultimate ground for moral obligation and universal duty is the status of each member of the human species as an individual consciously aware of his or her freedom within the totality of the real, and the inescapable demand to make one's life personally meaningful, with all the possibilities and limits of our common nature. The recognition of this demand in oneself and in others illumines the moral commands arising from our nature as free and rational beings, conscious of the need to make our way in the world, a task that confronts each and every human being.

There are many courageous examples in both literature and history of individuals who sacrificed life or physical well-being rather than abrogate the values they held supreme. To choose survival would be a negation of their deepest self; in choosing a higher value they transcended death. Holding divine law superior to that of the polis, Antigone – the all-time exemplary heroine of moral defiance – was willing to suffer death by disobeying the decree of King Creon in order to give her brother Polynices a decent burial. Socrates preferred to drink the hemlock rather than unjustly condemn his fellow citizens. Thomas More went joyously to death rather than renounce his religious beliefs. In the twentieth century there were inspiring examples of persons who died willingly rather than abdicate their deeply held values. The Lutheran theologian Dietrich Bonhoeffer and the Jesuit philosopher Alfred Delp are only two of countless witnesses to transcendent principles of dignity and freedom. Such deaths make sense only in light of a belief in life beyond the poisoned cup, executioner's axe or gas chamber. By their actions those individuals were affirming that continued physical existence was not worth living if basic values were disavowed, that there was a higher court. In our time it is not unknown for individuals to suffer personal or professional disadvantage by resisting coercive violence to conscience. In the political sphere to compel an individual to act against his or her conscientiously held beliefs is a dictatorship of democracy.

TIME

Our awareness of time comes with movement. We are conscious of 'before' and 'after', according as events emerge out of the future, unfold within experience, and exit into the past. Our ability to relate anticipation, attention and memory in a synthesis of the tenses indicates that we rise above the limits of time and movement. We are neither hostages of the past, captive to the present, nor debarred from the future. We transcend the moment in anticipation and reminiscence. Some animals have an estimative power analogous to memory but are unable to consciously recall the past: they live in the timeless instant. They are unaware of the continuum that binds remembrance and expectation, the *Nacheinander* of remote past and distant future.

Plato described time as 'a moving image of eternity'.[83] He was fascinated by the instant, that unique moment of occurrence, the unheralded and unpredictable moment of becoming, which he referred to as the 'all-of-a-sudden' (ἐξαίφνης). It is the surprise moment poised between new and old. The 'sudden' or 'instant' is the suspended intersection between rest and movement, movement and rest, the merging of presence with absence, the condition of time that is itself timeless: 'Rather, this queer creature, the instant, lurks between motion and rest – being in no time at all – and to it and from it the moving thing changes to resting and the resting thing changes to moving.'[84] It is 'that peculiar kind of unified presence which mediates between simple presence and simple absence'.[85] In such a moment occurs the sudden illumination of the Beautiful as revealed in Plato's *Symposium*.

Time ripens into eternity. The dynamic actuality of the 'now', intensified into a unity of the tenses, is a simulacrum of God's timeless and untimely perfection. Boethius defined eternity as the 'whole, simultaneous and perfect possession of endless life' (*interminabilis vitae tota simul et perfecta possessio*).[86] This concept allows us conceptually and imaginatively to adopt the stance '*sub specie aeternitatis*', which nowadays we might refer to as the 'view from nowhere', or better the 'view from everywhere'.

ART

James Joyce wrote in his student notebook: 'Art is the human disposition of sensible or intelligible matter for an esthetic end.'[87] All art seeks to reconfigure the given world through a physical medium, verbal or material. The artist transcends immediate experience by creating a new image or representation.

While he makes use of many stratagems and techniques, his most valuable vehicle is symbol. Symbolization is a mental activity which unites two objects, whereby one suggests or represents the other; it is unique to human intelligence. Such a unifying function is possible only for an agent with the capacity to relate to all of reality. Animals can react to signs, many engage in the use of simple tools, but they can never create symbols. Symbolic activity is distinctively human, involving the transcendence of what is immediately given in order to relate it to something distant or dissimilar.

LANGUAGE

Language encapsulates man's capacity and impulse for self-transcendence. Using sensible symbols he seeks to surpass the confines of the material world. As Frege well put it: 'Signs have the same importance for thought as for seafaring the discovery of using the wind to sail against the wind.'[88] Man's citizenship of two worlds, material and spiritual, is nowhere better epitomized than in the activity of language: a material medium invested with metaphysical meaning. There is an inner tension between the sensible quality of the symbol and the reality it seeks to convey. Meaning struggles with the physical sign; its tension derives from the dual character of symbol, and the impetus to convey a non-material meaning through a material sign. Words are somehow a summation of man's sensible and intellectual unity. Of its very nature language is oriented towards its own transcendence. This intentional character lies at the heart of all knowledge and symbol. The achievement of language is to denote a reality which it cannot exhaustively express; its supreme accomplishment is to recognize its inability to express the ultimate mystery.

Language never adequately expresses the reality of what is given in experience. Thus is inspired the continual dialectic at the heart of language whereby it seeks to overcome its own limits, to complement its own inadequacy in the face of the real which it cannot adequately comprehend. The transcendence of what is to be said beyond what remains unuttered reaches deeply into the nature both of language and thought in their relationship towards reality. This power of self-transcendence which we detect in language is but symptomatic of man's capacity to reach beyond himself, to affirm and explore the other as always something more.

There is much talk of both artificial language and artificial intelligence, most of it misconceived. To speak of 'artificial' intelligence is to describe analogously and by approximation a mechanistic calculation that feebly mimics human thought. Computers are equipped to translate lengthy passages of prose – more or less satisfactorily – but they could never create poetry. They cannot conceive new metaphors nor, any more than animals, initiate or recognize symbolic behaviour. It is imaginable that a computer, encoded with complicated algorithms, might produce a formulaic 'poetry', but the result would derive ultimately from the human programmer. A computer could never recognize the seventy odd tropes that add nuance to human language. It could never distinguish between irony and litotes, much less detect if the use of litotes is itself ironic.

MUSIC

Music could be described as the metaphysics of sound. Among the arts it has the most immediate power to raise the mind beyond the here and now. It is also the most emotive. Music enters the ear, affects the heart, and elevates the mind. Music is 'metaphysical sound' because of the manner in which it is organized, coordinating such essential elements as melody, rhythm, tone and harmony. Musical order is rooted in frequencies of physical vibration, resulting in ascending or descending pitch. Its meaning and appeal, however, rise above the physical to inspire profound insights; it has the power to convey emotions of grandeur and elation, or of tragedy and sadness. The order and harmony of music are experienced as a continuity in the stream of time, but they have a presence that rises above the flow. It has a universality beyond language, to be shared by persons of every background. Music is in all cultures the clearest celebration of life.

Of the arts music most of all eludes definition. Is there meaning in music? Paraphrasing Aristotle, that is a deaf man's question.[89] Musical meaning is not propositional: it does not adhere to logic. Only rarely is it representational, as in Beethoven's 'Pastoral', but even here the meaning exceeds the images provoked. Music may be associative, evincing an emotional resonance, but this is personal and circumstantial. It is not possible, for example, to interrogate the meaning of the third movement of Sibelius' Fifth Symphony; any attempt would fail to grasp its inherent power and presence. Great music has the seductive ability to lead mind and sentiment to a profound and sublime dimension, defying definition, of what is great and beautiful. That is its exhilaration.

The view that music has the power to signal transcendence was common among ancient and medieval thinkers. Influenced by the Orphic mysteries, Pythagoras taught that music made the soul attentive to the order and beauty of the cosmos. Plato believed that the gods endowed men with a sense of rhythm and harmony, which are an imitation of spiritual order and harmony.[90] According to Aristotle, music imitates the movement of human emotions.[91] For Plotinus musical harmony reflects the beauty of the ideal realm. Music, he believed, transports the listener beyond the natural world to the highest beauty. Contemplating universal proportion in the intelligible realm the soul is beautified and becomes God-like.[92] For Augustine music is an analogue of transcendent beauty. He defined music as 'the science of measuring well' (*scientia bene modulandi*),[93] the 'modulation' (*modus* = measure) of rhythm and time in the movement of pleasing sounds, especially sweet and graceful song (*suavissime canens, et pulchre saltans*).[94] The right motion of music, with its well-ordered ratios which delight the ear, is desired for its own sake and is pleasing through itself.[95] Augustine regarded music as an intermediary between the corporeal and incorporeal, the earthly and the divine. Responding to its symmetry and rhythm, the soul discerns the order of creation, and is attuned to the 'hymn of the universe' (*carmen universitatis*).[96] The soul moves from the beauty of music, perceived by the senses, to a contemplation of transcendent Beauty.

* * *

Watching via satellite after midnight on 17 April 2019 a performance of Berlioz's *Requiem* in Notre Dame, rebroadcast by the French–German station *Arte* in homage to the magnificent edifice at her saddest hour, I could also look across the city of Athens to the floodlit temple dedicated to the virgin goddess Athena. The architects and masons of both votive monuments knew they were building, in Thucydides' phrase, a 'possession for all ages' (κτῆμά τε ἐς αἰεί),[97] content in the knowledge they would not live to see their work completed. Such is the transcendence of art, conveyed in the adage: 'Life is short, art is long' (Ὁ βίος βραχὺς, ἡ δὲ τέχνη μακρὴ, *Ars longa, vita brevis*). Horace defiantly declared the immortality of his work: *Non omnis moriar*, 'I shall not all die.' In his celebrated prayer on the Acropolis, Ernest Renan minted the phrase 'Greek miracle' to describe the unprecedented achievements of the human will and intellect that blossomed in the ancient Hellenic world. That miracle is man's transcending power, the exploits of which have since flourished far and wide.

Some years ago I had a frightening experience while sailing around the promontory of Mount Athos, when a furious storm threatened to send our small vessel to the bottom of the Aegean. As I held tight to the gunwale, beside me an elderly Orthodox monk sat calmly while the boat rose and sank, battered by wind and wave. Was he not afraid? His serene reply was the best definition of transcendence I have heard: 'There is more than this, there is more than this!'

II. Portraits of Transcendence

Each of the essays in the present volume deals, either directly or indirectly, with some aspect of the wider theme of transcendence. Some authors consider the topic as it arose in the history of philosophy, others consider it from a specific thematic point of view. Together they present a comprehensive overview of the importance of transcendence as a fundamental aspect of human experience.

In the opening essay, 'The Cosmic Aspect of Truth in Plato', John Dillon examines Plato's doctrine of *alêtheia* as a divinely ordered structure of reality, the nature of which can be grasped by the human mind through a rigorous sequence of intellectual exercises, but on the basis of an innate capacity. It is in Plato's view an entirely rational state of affairs which can in theory be realized politically, by a select few 'philosopher-kings'.

In 'Plotinus and Transcendent Truth' Andrew Smith explains that from the very beginning Greek philosophers, including Heraclitus, Parmenides, Empedocles and, above all, Plato, had set as one of their goals the discovery of 'truth' about the nature of man and the universe. Plotinus claimed to have found Truth itself, a conclusion partly intended as response to the sceptics' critique of all claims to knowledge. This claim rests on the identification of the object of knowledge with the knowing subject: this identification is Truth itself. In Plotinus' ontological system Truth is closely linked with beauty and eternity as essential aspects of the intelligible universe. Truth, beauty and eternity are not merely components of the intelligible but rather aspects of it as a whole and identical with it.

My essay 'Beauty from Plato to Aquinas' considers the classic definition of beauty as that which simply in its apprehension pleases the eye or ear. While variations are found among ancient and medieval thinkers, the essential components of the traditional definition (integrity, harmony and splendour), are already found in the dialogues of Plato. Aristotle, uniquely in the tradition of Western aesthetics, makes no mention of splendour. While Aquinas' most comprehensive definition of beauty is presented in a theological context, his grasp of beauty is firmly based on sense experience. Aquinas extends the consideration of harmony beyond that of the individual to the synoptic harmony of the universe.

In 'The Manifestation of God as the Speaking of Creation in Scottus Eriugena' Deirdre Carabine explains the Irish thinker's understanding of creation as the speaking of the thought that exists eternally in the Word. Eriugena's view is that creation is the simultaneous revelation and concealment of God (at both the human and divine levels). His understanding of creation as theophany, i.e. of creation as the 'showing of God', implies that the universe is theocentric because all reality is a manifestation of the unmanifest. For Eriugena, when God creates, God reveals God's self, and therefore, God creates God's self. In other words, just as revelation is creation, creation is revelation. God's self-revelation is the deepest concealment because it is a displacement of God into otherness, into what is both God and not-God. Revelation is concealment and concealment revelation.

In 'A Teacher and Two Students: Albert the Great, Thomas Aquinas, Meister Eckhart' Denys Turner considers this triangle of thirteenth-century theologians as a model of philosophical and theological exchange between teachers and students. Albert taught Thomas and Eckhart, Dominican friars like himself, but greatly different in personal style and temperament. Thomas was terse, dispassionate, cool, his was the mind of a teacher; Eckhart was wordy, flamboyant, hot, his rhetoric the style of a preacher. They also differed in matters of theological substance, Thomas being inclined to a more materialist and Aristotelian emphasis than Eckhart's idealist and Platonist inclinations. However they shared a common selfless conviction, that what is common to teaching and preaching is the passing on to others of what they had first contemplated for themselves. From their teacher Albert they had learned of the need to keep in play the inner conjunction of the word and the deed, of utterance and act. Denys Turner suggests that the practice of all three raises a question about our own university teaching practices today, when the inner relation between word and action is increasingly threatened by utilitarian priorities on the one hand, and dilettantish reactions on the other. He recalls that years ago Paddy Masterson exemplified better priorities.

It is a particular delight to include in this volume the text of a lecture by Patrick Masterson's dear friend and colleague, the late Cardinal Desmond Connell. In 'St Thomas and the Medieval Synthesis' Connell illustrates how Aquinas drew on the twin sources of Plato and Aristotle, filtered through numerous followers and commentators, to shape a novel synthesis that combined Greek philosophical sources with intellectual elements from the Judaeo-Christian tradition. He emphasizes the cultural kinship between the biblical notion of creation out of nothing and the Neoplatonist recognition of the primacy of existence. Although it maintained that the universe emanated by necessity from the transcendent principle, as opposed to the Christian doctrine of creation as a free gift, Neoplatonism asserts that all things derive from the divine source. It has therefore much in common with Christian creation, which emphasizes the utterly radical role of existence and the absolute character of the creature's dependence upon God. St Thomas drew on Neoplatonist elements to correct Aristotle, who maintained that the world existed eternally, separately from God. Connell suggests that the metaphysics of Aquinas is fundamentally Aristotelian, but recast in light of his unique and original notion of existence as the gift beyond essence that grounds human freedom. In this context Aquinas raises Aristotle's naturalist view of human nature to a new autonomy and dignity.

In 'Hegel and the Infinite' Cyril O'Regan focuses on Hegel's subversion of the Western philosophical tradition's binary opposition between infinite and finite, and its correlative theological contrasts between the uncreated and created, creator and creature. In a revolutionary move Hegel insisted that the infinite is properly understood only when it encompasses the finite in a whole rather than being contrasted with it. For Hegel the relation between God and the world is both two-way and intrinsic rather than extrinsic: God is as much a function of the world as the world is a function of God. In essence, God only becomes God in and through his relation to the world.

In 'Epiphany and Hopkins' Richard Kearney explains and compares the concepts of epiphany and haecceity in the work of Gerard Manley Hopkins. The essay begins with a detailed analysis of Hopkins' final journal entry on the role of the Magi in the Christian feast of the Epiphany, twelve days after the Nativity. The second part of the essay examines the intimate liaison in Hopkins between his reading of epiphany and his poetic retrieval of Duns Scotus' notion of singularity or 'thisness' (*haecceitas*).

In 'Edith Stein's Philosophical Conversions: From Husserl to Aquinas and Newman' Dermot Moran presents the philosophical evolution of Edith Stein (1891–1942), who wrote her doctorate under Edmund Husserl. Born a Jew, she converted to Catholicism and became a Carmelite nun (Sr Teresia Benedicta a Cruce, OCD). She became a victim of the National Socialist policy of extermination of Jews and was subsequently declared a Catholic martyr and saint. She was known philosophically primarily for her doctoral thesis, *Zum Problem der Einfühlung/On the Problem of Empathy* (1917), and for her contribution as research assistant to Edmund Husserl, including editing his *Ideas* II (published posthumously in 1952). Stein was in discussion with leading philosophers of her day, including Husserl, Scheler, Heidegger, Hedwig Conrad Martius, Roman Ingarden, and, later, Jacques Maritain, among others. Before becoming a Carmelite nun she campaigned publicly on issues relating to women's rights in the workplace and especially on women's education (in a Catholic context). Her work contains original approaches to empathy, embodiment, the phenomenology of emotional life, the unique nature of the person, the structure of social and collective intentionality, and the nature of the state. In her later work, she developed an original philosophy of being and essence (including a defence of 'individual essences') that united the resources of phenomenology and Thomist metaphysics. As a convert to Catholicism, she took a particular interest in the writings of John Henry Cardinal Newman, a fellow convert, and translated several of his major works. In his chapter, Moran outlines her philosophical development and focuses in particular on her 'conversions', first to philosophy and phenomenology, then to Catholicism, and to life in a religious order, and, finally, to Thomistic metaphysics, which she interpreted in a new and original light.

In her essay 'Religious Symbols in the Philosophical Anthropology of Paul Ricoeur' Eileen Brennan sets out to establish what the French philosopher means by 'transcendence'. In order to do so, one must first explain what Ricoeur means by 'the fault', a term with many possible meanings. As examples he lists (1) the law, (2) passions such as ambition and hate, and (3) the experiences of defilement, sin and guilt. Understanding what Ricoeur means by sin allows us to retrieve a once-prominent instance of 'transcendence', namely deliverance or salvation. Thus, if sin is a matter of enslaving my own freedom, as Ricoeur claims it is, transcendence is 'what liberates freedom from the fault'. Ricoeur's reflections on transcendence serve his wider objective of developing a philosophical anthropology, the central category of which is the acting and suffering human being. Ricoeur is critical of the modern age for having lost sight of the essential connection between human beings and the sacred, believing that it is his philosophy of symbols alone that can make that connection visible again.

In his essay 'Icons of Infinity: Rothko, Levinas and Jean-Luc Marion' Mark Patrick Hederman notes that around the same time both Rothko and Levinas became aware of the 'possibility of transcendence beckoning from within immanence'. For Levinas, the one reality which immediately introduced us to a world beyond our time-space capsule was encounter with the face of another person. To meet the Other is to have the idea of Infinity. In painterly terms it suggests the impossibility of representing the face on a canvas. Such a façade cannot reveal the secret of interiority, or the mystery of infinity. Rothko eventually created a visual structure which unmasks the illusion of penetrating vision. Phenomenologists had described the contours of this illusion whereas Rothko created visual antidotes to our otherwise restricted perspective. Painting the void forced him to become aware of the perspectival framework of his own visionary apparatus which prevented him from seeing the bigger picture. Jean-Luc Marion introduced the notion of a 'saturated phenomenon', to describe certain objects which have such overwhelming 'givenness' that they overwhelm our structures of perception. Rothko's later paintings create such portals to infinity and may be seen as examples of such saturated phenomena.

In 'Wisdom after Metaphysics?' Markus Wörner begins with a common-sense approach to the notion of wisdom, drawing on the results of Positive Psychology. Wisdom is to be understood as a mode of being in the world based on a general attitude of openness rather than on the specialized capacities of an intellectual, moral or religious elite. It is within the competence of *Homo sapiens* as such. Its acquisition results in a trustworthy harmony of cognitive and emotional habits (intellectual and ethical virtues) which are suited to confront fundamental, existential questions regarding the meaning of life. Wisdom comes in degrees and increases with experience.

In 'Experience and Transcendence' John Haldane responds to Patrick Masterson's questioning of Jean-Luc Marion's displacement of traditional inferences from experience to a transcendent cause with appeals to pure phenomenology. Haldane places the idea of transcendence in the context of a series of contrasts with the 'factual' and in exploring these he argues against interpretations that would consign value and transcendence to the domain of non-cognitive subjectivity. Following a reflection on the aesthetics of architecture he returns to the issue of experience as evidence for God and suggests a way in which value and meaning may be signs of divine activity.

In his essay 'Ethics in the Forest: Otherwise Approaching God' Joseph Dunne introduces Charles Taylor's image of the 'forest' as symbolizing an opening in ethical life to the possibility of radical self-transformation through responsiveness to what can most fully inspire a person's love, when this is a supremely high good that is beyond the call of duty and of a rich or flourishing life. In exploring the ethical–spiritual terrain of the forest, Dunne elucidates a Christian variant in which human life is lived as God-related. Noting how this variant has been deeply interfused with Western philosophical reflection, he analyses correspondences between it and the Socratic tradition, especially as formulated in Aristotelian ethics and as practised through Stoic spiritual disciplines. But his main concern is to show how the Christian Gospel's deep divergences from the whole Socratic tradition transfigure ethical life and recast the meaning of – and what is to count as – 'virtue'. He concludes by suggesting that this forest perspective can help to bring into sharper relief weaknesses in the motivational sources of modern secular morality, especially in face of the unabashed vitalism of contemporary neo-Nietzscheanism.

In her essay 'The Concept of Person in Healthcare Ethics' Noreen O'Carroll focuses on the problem of moral status and how to resolve it. Having moral status means having rights. 'Person' is the commonly accepted designation for moral status, denoting a subject of rights, but disagreements arise about the application of the word. Is an embryo a person? Is someone who has suffered irreversible brain-damage still the person she/he formerly was? Does someone in the advanced stages of dementia still manifest the characteristics of personhood? O'Carroll argues that discussions about such questions appear to be based on a common understanding of 'person' but in fact, interlocutors frequently use the word with two very different meanings, derived from the definitions of Thomas Aquinas and John Locke, respectively. These underpin two radically different approaches to care. She argues that the challenge for those who want 'person' to function as a criterion for moral status in healthcare is to ensure that the meaning assigned to the term includes the phenomenon of identity through the changes that occur in organic existence. She concludes that only a definition of 'person' in the tradition of Aquinas successfully meets that criterion.

In his essay 'Ethics without Transcendence' Philip Pettit argues that the idea of the valuable, however conceptualized, gains traction only in light of a contrast with that which is attractive to our desires. We may not find the valuable attractive, or the attractive valuable. To follow the attractive rather than the valuable in the case of conflict is, in an important way, to fall short of what it is to perform properly as a human being. Where then do we as human beings, unlike other animals, get the idea of the valuable and grant it authority over desire? While Patrick Masterson has argued that it represents the irruption of a transcendent reality into our ordinary experience of the world, Pettit proposes a more mundane explanation. He suggests that as mutually reliant creatures we seek to assure others that we will continue to believe, desire and act as we now say we will; we give one another this assurance in so far as we avow our attitudes and pledge our actions, accepting that there is an especially high cost involved in not displaying an attitude avowed or not performing an action pledged. The idea of the valuable is nothing more or less than the idea of acting in accordance with our pledges, even when doing so frustrates conflicting desires.

In his essay 'Suffering as a Cipher of Transcendence' Brendan Purcell discusses human suffering in light of Patrick Masterson's reflections on God and transcendence. Can a loving God permit the sufferings caused by natural disasters, animal suffering, or the suffering of innocent children? The existence of moral evil poses the most serious objection to the existence of a good God. Purcell considers the refusal of Peter Singer and Stephen Fry to accept the laws of the natural world and the fact of human freedom. He cites the lives of Chiara Badano and Etty Hillesum as providing a wider horizon on suffering to that envisaged by those who see it as precluding a good God. He considers in conclusion the widest horizon of all, that of Jesus' experience of God-forsakenness on the cross as itself a cipher of something akin to the suffering of the Trinity sublating human suffering into the mystery of Divine love.

In 'Is Desire Desirable? The Question that Discloses the Person' David Walsh suggests that the question of desire obliges us to consider it within the context of the life of the person whose character is being formed or deformed in response to the pulls of desire. The classical identification of the soul as the locus of the struggle does not adequately account for the capacity to stand apart from the self that is thereby being enacted. Plato and Aristotle resort to more specific characters or personae, such as the philosopher or *spoudaios*, to suggest the self-distancing involved. Missing is a more articulate account of the person as such. Yet the discovery of nous, the apex of reason, is the beginning of that development. A deeper understanding of self-distancing becomes available only through revelation, where the split between the will and what it fails to do raises the division into consciousness. However, an adequate philosophical account of the self that is capable of transcending itself would require the language of presence and absence that is the distinctively modern contribution.

In 'About What do Contemporary Atheists and Theists Disagree?' Alasdair MacIntyre suggests that, apart from the obvious conclusion regarding the existence or non-existence of God, a more fundamental divergence concerns what needs to be explained and what it is to understand. He distinguishes between two kinds of questions, each eliciting appropriately different styles of explanation. Some questions interrogate particular states of affairs, others the underlying order of the universe and the cosmos itself. The latter surpass scientific explanation, referring to distinctive features of human life involving intention and purpose. The distinction has been denied by those who insist that ultimately all genuine explanation is scientific, with the implication that the theistic account of the nature of things must be false. Theists, on the other hand, appeal to the need for truth as a good beyond science that provides direction in a person's life. Physics has no place for intentionality-informed, intentionally effective agents and, paradoxically, cannot therefore explain how physicists are possible. What demands explanation, MacIntyre argues, is that the universe of quantum mechanical and relativistic theories should accommodate human agency. He suggests that in modern atheism disagreement about God involves disagreement about the nature of the universe.

We are honoured to be able to include an unpublished poem, 'Remembering *Bóthar Bui*', by Seamus Heaney, written by the poet for Paddy Masterson's beloved wife Frankie. I am most grateful to the Heaney family for permission to reproduce the autograph manuscript.

The volume concludes with the text of an autobiographical talk given by the honorand, entitled 'My Life in Philosophy', in which Paddy Masterson gives an intimate and fascinating account of his introduction to the philosophical life and subsequent academic career. From his talk we learn much of the person and philosophical commitment of Patrick Masterson. We are grateful for his permission to include it as a fitting conclusion to our celebration of the life and work of a distinguished person and eminent philosopher.

ENDNOTES

1   Cicero, *De Inventione* 2, 161, trans. H.M. Hubbell (Cambridge, MA: Harvard University Press, 2000), p. 329.

2   *ST* II-II, 81, 1.

3   *The Divine Institutes* IV.28, trans. William Fletcher (Grand Rapids, MI: Eerdmans, 1979, p. 131)

4   Augustine, *Retractationes* 1, 13.

5   *De Vera Religione* 55, 113, trans. John H.S. Burleigh, Augustine, *Earlier Writings* (London: SCM, 1953), p. 282.

6   *Cratylus* 399c, trans. B. Jowett, modified.

7   *Part. An.* 2, 10, 656a10–13; 4, 10, 686a25–7.

8   *Part. An.* 4, 10, 686a27–31, trans. Peck, p. 367.

9   *EN* 6, 7, 1141a33; 6, 6, 1141a21.

10 Pindar, *Pythian Odes* 8, 95–7.

11 John Clare (1793–1864), 'November'.

12 Paul Bourget, *Le démon de midi* (Paris: Plon, 1914), vol. 2, p. 375.

13 Ferdinand Alquié, *Philosophie du Surréalisme* (Paris: Flammarion, 1955), p. 211.

14 Max Weber, *From Max Weber: Essays in Sociology*, eds H.H. Gerth and C.Wright Mills (London: Routledge, 2009), p. 155.

15 Interview with Jody Allen Randolph in *Close to the Moment. Interviews from a Changing Ireland* (Manchester: Carcanet, 2010), p. 205.

16 Interview with David Frick, 'U2 Finds What It's Looking For', *Rolling Stone*, 1 October 1992. From a later interview: 'As dark as it gets, we are looking for shiny moments. Those shiny moments, for me, are the same as they've always been. There are big words for them, like transcendence... For a hundred years people have been told they don't have a spirit, and if you can't see it or can't prove it, it doesn't exist. Anyone who listens to Smokey Robinson knows that isn't true.' Bill Flanagan, *U2 At The End of The World* (New York, NY: Random, 1996), p. 81.

17 *ST* I-II 32, 8.

18 *ST* II-II 180, 3 ad 3.

19 Ibid.

20 Aristotle, *Metaphysics* 1, 2, 982b17–19. See Fran O'Rourke, *Aristotelian Interpretations* (Sallins: Irish Academic Press, 2016), pp. 29–43.

21 See Josef Pieper, *Leisure the Basis of Culture* (London: Faber, 1968), p. 108–20.

22 Patrick Masterson, *The Sense of Creation. Experience and the God Beyond* (Aldershot: Ashgate, 2008), p. 2.

23 Patrick Masterson, *Approaching God. Between Phenomenology and Theology* (London: Bloomsbury, 2013), p. 33.

24 John Locke, *An Essay Concerning Human Understanding* (Oxford: Clarendon Press, 1975), p. 525.

25 See Patrick Masterson, *Atheism and Alienation. A Study of the Philosophical Sources of Contemporary Atheism* (Notre Dame, IN: University of Notre Dame Press, 1971), pp. 9–10.

26   Immanuel Kant, *Critique of Pure Reason* B 25, trans. Norman Kemp Smith (London: Macmillan, 1976), p. 59.

27   Immanuel Kant, *Critique of Pure Reason, B 21, trans. Kemp Smith, p. 56.*

28   See Patrick Masterson, ibid., pp. 17–18.

29   *Selected Letters of Rainer Maria Rilke, 1902 – 1926*, trans. R.F.C. Hull (London: Macmillan, 1946), p. 393.

30   Immanuel Kant, *Critique of Pure Reason*, B 8, trans. J.M.D. Meiklejohn (London: Dent, 1969), p. 29.

31   Paul Ricoeur, *The Symbolism of Evil*, trans. Emerson Buchanan (Boston: Beacon, 1967), p. 13.

32   Alfred North Whitehead, *Science and the Modern World* (London: Free Association, 1985), p. 174.

33   Jacques Maritain, *Creative Intuition in Art and Poetry* (New York, NY: Pantheon, 1960), p. 162.

34   Ralph Waldo Emerson, *Essays and Lectures* (New York, NY: Library of America, 1983), p. 292. Repeated in *Journals and Miscellaneous Notebooks*, vol. 5, 1835–1838, ed. Merton M. Sealts, Jr (Cambridge, MA: Belknap, 1965), p. 362.

35   Ralph Waldo Emerson, *Journals and Miscellaneous Notebooks*, vol. 4, 1832–1834, ed. Alfred R. Ferguson (Cambridge, MA: Belknap, 1964), p. 362. The first sentence is repeated in vol. 6, p. 198.

36   William Blake, 'The Marriage of Heaven and Hell', *The Poems of William Blake*, ed. W.H. Stevenson (London: Longman, 1971), p. 114.

37   *Metaphysics* 2, 1, 993a10–12. Aquinas wrote: 'Something is invisible in two ways. The first way is on account of itself, as a dark object; the other way on account of its exceeding the one seeing, as the sun does the eye of the owl. Thus, to us certain things are not clearly seen on account of a defect of their being, and certain others on account of their being excessive; and in this way God is inaccessible to us to a certain degree.' Referring to Pseudo-Dionysius' remark, 'All darkness is inaccessible', Aquinas explains: 'It is therefore the very same thing which here is light, and there darkness; but He is darkness inasmuch as He is not seen, and light inasmuch as He is seen.' (*Super I Tim.* 6, 3), trans. Chrystom Baer, Thomas Aquinas, *Commentaries on St. Paul's Epistles to Timothy, Titus, and Philemon*, (South Bend, IN: St Augustine's Press, 2007), p. 88.

38   Parmenides, Frg. 6.

39   S.T. Coleridge, *The Friend* I, ed. Barbara E. Rooke in *Collected Works* 4 (London, Routledge & Kegan Paul, 1993), p. 514. Emphasis in original.

40   Louis Pasteur, Inaugural speech to the Académie Française, 27 April 1882. The speech continues: 'I see everywhere in the world the inevitable expression of the concept of infinity. It establishes in the depth of our hearts a belief in the supernatural. The idea of God is nothing more than one form of the idea of infinity. So long as the mystery of the infinite weighs on the human mind, so long will temples be raised to the cult of the infinite, whether it be called Bramah, Allah, Jehovah, or Jesus …The Greeks understood the mysterious power of the hidden side of things. They bequeathed to us one of the most beautiful words in our language – the word "enthusiasm" – ἔνθεος – an inner god. The grandeur of human actions is measured by the inspiration from

which they spring. Happy is he who bears within himself a god, an ideal of beauty, and who obeys it; an ideal of art, of science, of patriotism, of the virtues symbolized in the Gospel. These are the living sources of great thoughts and great acts. All are lighted by reflection from the infinite.' Quoted in Rene J. Dubos, *Louis Pasteur. Free Lance of Science* (London: Gollancz, 1951), pp. 391–2.

41   In conversation with the writer Anthony Cronin, confirmed by Anne Haverty in a personal communication.

42   *Hamlet* II, ii.

43   Philip Larkin, 'Here', *The Whitsun Weddings* (London: Faber and Faber, 1964).

44   Blaise Pascal, *Pensées*, Frg. 348.

45   See also the English poet Fulke Greville, who wrote in 1633:
The mind of man is this world's true dimension
And knowledge is the measure of the mind;
And as the mind in her vast comprehension
Contains more worlds than all the world can find,
So knowledge doth itself far more extend
Than all the minds of men can comprehend.

46   Arthur Koestler, *Darkness at Noon* (London: Penguin, 1946), pp. 225–6.

47   Pieper, ibid., pp. 112–13.

48   Robert Bolt, *A Man for All Seasons* (London: Heinemann, 1961), p. 74.

49   *De An.* 3, 4, 429a18: ἀνάγκη ἄρα, ἐπεὶ πάντα νοεῖ, ἀμιγῆ εἶναι.

50   *De An.* 3, 4, 429a24–5: διὸ οὐδὲ μεμῖχθαι εὔλογον αὐτὸν τῷ σώματι.

51   *De An.* 3, 4, 429a25–6.

52   *Gen. An.* 2, 1, 734b24–5. Πρόσωπον is also the word for 'person'.

53   Friedrich Albert Lange, *Geschichte des Materialismus und Kritik seiner Bedeutung in der Gegenwart* (Iserlohn: Baedeker, 1887), p. 3.

54   A further indication of the universality of the psyche is its grasp of the universal concepts of those essences which are instantiated in countless substances. There is nothing whose essence cannot be the object of intellect, grasped in its immaterial intelligibility. See Aquinas *ST* I 86, 1 ad 3: Nihil intelligitur nisi immaterialiter.

55   *De An.* 2, 5, 417b22–3: τῶν καθ' ἕκαστον ἡ κατ' ἐνέργειαν αἴσθησις, ἡ δ' ἐπιστήμη τῶν καθόλου.

56   *De An.* 3, 4, 430a2–5.

57   Proclus, *Elements of Theology*, Prop. 15, trans. Robert Pasnau, *On Human Nature* (Cambridge: Cambridge University Press, 2002), p. 194. Drawing extensively on Aristotle for his psychology, Aquinas identified three arguments for the spirituality of the soul: First, because this operation covers all corporeal forms as its objects; therefore, it is necessary that the principle of this operation be free from all material forms. Second, because understanding concerns universals, whereas in a corporeal organ only individuated intentions can be received. Third, because the intellect understands itself; but this does not occur in a power whose operation is performed by means of a corporeal organ. See *In II Sent.*, 19, 1, 1. See *De Spiritualibus Creaturis*, art. 2: Perfectissima autem formarum, id est anima humana ... habet operationem omnino excedentem materiam, quae non fit per organum corporale, scilicet intelligere.

58 Teilhard de Chardin, *The Phenomenon of Man* (London: Fontana, 1965), pp. 182–3. The passage continues: 'From our experimental point of view, reflection is, as the word indicates, the power acquired by a consciousness to turn in upon itself, to take possession of itself *as of an object* endowed with its own particular consistence and value: no longer merely to know oneself; no longer merely to know, but to know that one knows. (*Non plus seulement connaître, mais se connaître; non plus seulement savoir, mais savoir que l'on sait.*) ... Now the consequences of such a transformation are immense, visible as clearly in nature as any of the facts recorded by physics or astronomy. The being who is the object of his own reflection, in consequence of that very doubling back upon himself, becomes in a flash able to raise himself into a new sphere. In reality, another world is born. Abstraction, logic, reasoned choice and inventions, mathematics, art, calculation of space and time, anxieties and dreams of love – all these activities of *inner life* are nothing else than the effervescence of the newly-formed centre as it explodes onto itself.'

59 Vyvyan Evans, *The Crucible of Language: How Language and Mind Create Meaning* (Cambridge: Cambridge University Press, 2015), p. 98. Reference is to Wordsworth's poem 'Intimations of Immortality'.

60 Patrick Masterson wrote his doctoral dissertation on the Fourth Way at the University of Louvain.

61 Reginald Garrigou-Lagrange formulated the principle as follows: 'When a perfection, the concept of which does not imply any imperfection, is found in various degrees in different beings, none of those which possess it imperfectly contains a sufficient explanation for it, and hence its cause must be sought in a being of a higher order, which is this very perfection.' *God: His Existence and His Nature* (St Louis, MI: Herder, 1941), vol. 1, p. 308.

62 *ST* I 2, 3.

63 See Patrick Masterson's excellent treatment of the Fourth Way in ch. 7, 'Analogy and Transcendence' of *The Sense of Creation* (Aldershot: Ashgate, 2008), pp. 85–106.

64 Garrigou-Lagrange, ibid.

65 *ST* II-II 180, 5 ad 3.

66 *Timaeus* 90a.

67 *Expositio super Job ad litteram*, 37.

68 *ST* I 86, 3.

69 See Shakespeare, *Hamlet* II, ii: 'What a piece of work is a man! How noble in reason! how infinite in faculty! in form, in moving, how express and admirable! in action how like an angel! in apprehension how like a god! the beauty of the world! the paragon of animals!'

70 *ST* I 76, 5 ad 4: Anima intellectiva, quia est universalia comprehensiva, habet virtutem ad infinita.

71 Aquinas, *In Periherm.* 1, 3, 29. Also *Contra Gentiles* 1, 59, 498; *Q. Disp. De Ver* 1, 8; *Q. Disp. De An.* 3, 1.

72 *Confessiones* 1, 1.

73 *ST* I-II 2, 8, trans. Laurence Shapcote (Chicago: Encyclopaedia Britannica, 1991), p. 622.

74 For an extensive treatment see my essay 'Beauty from Plato to Aquinas' in this volume.

75 Hermann Broch, *The Death of Virgil* (New York, NY: Grosset & Dunlap, 1965) p. 135.

76 Benjamin Robert Haydon, *The Autobiography and Journals*, ed. Malcolm Elwin (London: Macdonald, 1950), p. 78.

77 *Parts of Animals* 1, 5, 645a16–26, trans. William Ogle, *The Complete Works of Aristotle*, ed. Jonathan Barnes (Princeton, NJ: Princeton University Press, 1991) vol. 1, p. 1004.

78 Patrick Masterson discusses the contrast in Chapter 6 of *The Sense of Creation*.

79 *Fiat iustitia, et pereat mundus / Fiat iustitia ruat caelum.*

80 *Crito* 49ab. See also Romans 3. 8: 'It is not licit to do evil that good may come of it.'

81 *ST* I-II 19, 5, *Sed Contra*.

82 John Henry Newman, *An Essay in Aid of a Grammar of Assent* (London: Burns and Oates, 1874), p. 107.

83 *Timaeus* 37d.

84 *Parmenides* 156de, trans. Mary Louise Gill & Paul Ryan, in Plato, *Complete Works*, ed. John M. Cooper (Indianapolis, IN: Hackett, 1997), p. 388.

85 Jussi Backmann, 'All of a Sudden: Heidegger and Plato's *Parmenides*', *Epoché* 11/2 (2007), p. 400.

86 Boethius, *Tractates, De Consolatione Philosophiae* (Cambridge, MA: Harvard University Press, 1973), p. 422.

87 James Joyce, *Occasional, Critical, and Political Writing*, ed. Kevin Barry (Oxford: Oxford University Press, 2000), p. 104.

88 Gottlob Frege, *Begriffsschrift und andere Aufsätze* (Hildesheim: Olms, 1964), p. 107.

89 Asked if absolutely everything could be expressed scientifically, Albert Einstein replied: 'Yes, it would be possible, but it would make no sense. It would be description without meaning – as if you described a Beethoven symphony as a variation of wave pressure.' See Ronald W. Clark, *Einstein: the Life and Times* (London: Hodder and Stoughton, 1973), p. 191.

90 See Plato, *Republic* 398–403, *Ion* 534.

91 Aristotle, *Politics* 8, 5, 1340a19–20.

92 See Plotinus, *Enneads* I 3 [20] 1. 19–34; V 9 [5] 11. 7–13.

93 Augustine, *De Musica* 1, 2, 2.

94 Ibid., 1, 3, 4.

95 Ibid., 1, 2, 3.

96 Ibid., 6, 11, 29.

97 Thucydides 1, 22, 4, trans. Charles Foster Smith (Cambridge, MA: Harvard University Press, 1956), p. 41.

THE COSMIC ASPECT OF
TRUTH IN PLATO

JOHN DILLON

I must confess to having a long-standing adversative relation with the concept of truth, particularly in philosophical and theological contexts, which I recognize as being unreasonable. It is partly due to problems with the etymology of the word in Greek, such as I discuss below. On the level of 'normal', non-philosophical, or non-theological, discourse, the enquiry after the truth of some verbal account, or physical manifestation (such as, perhaps, the cause of an explosion, or the break-down of a computer) is an attempt to ascertain whether the account given, or the sense-datum received – it might be a sight, a sound, or even a smell – accords with what *really* is the case, or what *really* was the cause of the phenomenon. This, I suppose, would constitute a simple form of the 'correspondence theory of truth', but it is not at all what metaphysical or theological seekers after Truth would generally have in mind.

What I want to enquire into on the present occasion, in honour of an old friend who is himself a serious and persistent seeker after Truth,[1] is the following: When the Greek philosopher Plato (or through him, Socrates) speaks of 'truth' (*alêtheia, to alêthes*), what are the connotations of that term, and what does he intimate to us concerning the preferred means of attaining it? My contention would be that the quest for Truth (at least in, so to speak, its *capitalized* form!) is always for Plato a quest for insight into the structure of reality – a systematic enquiry, which uncovers the way the world works, and the organizing principle or principles behind it. This indeed would not be unreasonable, if, as seems possible, the distinguished philosopher Martin Heidegger was right in his interpretation of the rather mysterious word *alêtheia* as a sort of negation of *lêthê*, thus signifying 'an undoing, or peeling away, of the forgetfulness of, or obliviousness to, the true nature of things' (in his case, of Being), with which we are afflicted by reason of the dominance of our normal, 'everyday' (*alltäglich*), consciousness – that is to say, *Unverborgenheit*.[2] Heidegger in fact sees Plato's Allegory of the Cave, in the *Republic* Book 7, as a particularly good representation of this 'forgetfulness', in virtue of which we – the prisoners, as Plato tells us – assume that the shadows being paraded for us on the cave wall are the whole of reality, a level of consciousness from which we have to be forcibly liberated, and dragged upwards out of the 'cave-like dwelling', to view the true state of affairs in the world above.[3] Now, Heidegger's etymology of *alêtheia* has never, I think, attained complete acceptance in classical philological circles,[4] but I must say that I can come up with nothing better, and I think that it certainly helps to elucidate the peculiar nature of *alêtheia*, in its broader, as opposed to its 'correspondence', sense. Heidegger certainly makes a very plausible case for this in his exegesis of the two levels of reality in Plato's Cave image. Plainly, there are a number of factual 'truths' of which the released prisoner becomes cognizant, e.g. that the figures on the screen, which he formerly took for reality, are in fact merely shadows cast, from a fire, by objects which are themselves mere images, in wood or stone, of 'real' things (with which he as yet, however, has no acquaintance); or that the ultimate source of light in the upper world, up into which he is unwillingly dragged, is the sun. But these individual propositions, true though they are, are only insignificant elements of the overall fabric of Truth.

This, as it emerges, is a coherent vision of the way things are, and of the generative principle of reality, the 'Sun', representing 'the Good', or the rational principle which drives the universe forward.[5] Heidegger's acute observation[6] that the true opposite of *alêtheia* in this sense is not *pseudos*, but rather *lêthê*, 'forgetfulness,' or 'obliviousness' (of the way things are, and of one's own true nature) leads me to make the connection (which I am not quite sure that Plato actually intends us to make) between the ascent of the prisoner from the cave into the upper, 'real' world, and the descent of the souls into reincarnation, in the Myth of Er in Book 10, where they journey through the plain of Lethe, and then drink from the waters of the river Ameles ('self-neglect'), the consequence of which is that they 'become oblivious to everything' (*pantôn epilanthanesthai*).[7] Now this obviously means that they forget all the details of what has transpired in the upper world, and specifically their 'choice of lives', but I think that it is also intended to mean that they become oblivious to the overall structure of reality, the 'way things are'. This is something that at least some few people – no doubt those who have drunk *moderately* of the waters of Ameles,[8] but even of those only a minority – can come to gain a recollection of, at least to some extent, as they go through this life, either by 'divine dispensation' (*theia moira*), or through having the good fortune to meet up with someone like Socrates, who has received such dispensation, and is inspired to help others to achieve similar insight.[9]

This, then, is one model of truth which I find interesting. What I would like to do here is to examine a number of other significant passages from the Platonic dialogues, which may serve to elucidate Heidegger's – and, I believe, Plato's – view of truth in the sense of *Unverborgenheit*. Let us start with one from the end of the *Gorgias*, where Socrates has come through his long dialectical contest with first, Gorgias, then his follower Polus, and then the bumptious aristocratic Athenian 'might is right' advocate Callicles, culminating in a myth of the afterlife, involving a last judgment of souls. He concludes as follows: 'Now I have been convinced by these stories, Callicles, and I am considering how I may present to my judge the healthiest possible soul, and so I renounce the honours sought by most men, and, *working at the truth* (*tên alêtheian askôn*), I shall readily endeavour both to live and, when death comes, to die, as good a man as I possibly can be.'[10]

What intrigues me particularly here is the rather distinctive verb that he employs to govern *alêtheia*: *askeô* means 'to practise, work at' (the noun *askêsis* came in later times to denote monkish asceticism, among other things!). Woodhead, wishing to produce better English, renders it 'pursue', which is not unreasonable, but would better translate *diôkô*.[11] What Socrates has to mean here, surely, is a kind of *practising* – a form of 'mindfulness', one might say – for which the Arabic term, much favoured by Sufi philosophers, is *dhikr*, which leads the mind upwards to the contemplation of the source of its being, and the revelation of its true nature.[12] On the occasions when Socrates is recorded as falling into a trance, of which we observe one at the beginning of the *Symposium*, when he gets becalmed in a doorway on the way to Agathon's victory feast, and are told of another at the end, by Alcibiades – his night-long session of meditation when on military service at Potidaea – we may assume, I think, that he was in effect practising *dhikr*, though perhaps in pursuit of the solution to a particular existential problem, rather than in contemplation of the whole realm of Truth (though the one, I think, involves the other).[13]

At any rate, this may serve to remind us that the 'historical' Socrates – in so far as we can recover knowledge of such an individual! – was primarily concerned with discovering the truth about *himself*, rather than about the universe as a whole; and indeed he may have been the first individual in Greek history to identify such an object of search. This, it seems to me, is the deep significance of his rather light-hearted dismissing of Phaedrus' attempt to draw him out on the subject of the myth of Boreas and Oreithyia. Just to make conversation, Phaedrus ventures to ask him whether he believes the story of Boreas' abduction of Oreithyia to be true.[14] Socrates, after alluding, with some irony, to the attempts of *hoi sophoi* to give a 'scientific', allegorical, explanation of the tale, replies:

> I myself have certainly no time for that sort of thing, and I'll tell you why, my friend. I can't as yet 'know myself', as the inscription at Delphi enjoins, and so long as that ignorance remains, it seems to me ridiculous to inquire into extraneous matters. Consequently I don't bother about such things, but accept the current beliefs about them, and direct my inquiries, as I have just said, rather to myself, to discover whether I really am a more complex creature and more puffed up with pride than Typhon, or a simpler, gentler being whom heaven has blessed with a quiet un-Typhonic nature.[15]

This 'search for oneself' might be seen as having been initiated by Heraclitus, with his famous remark, 'I went in search of myself' (*edizêsamên emêuton*),[16] but, if so, Socrates elaborated it further. Socrates is indeed in search of the *truth* about himself: granted that he is truly a soul rather than a body, what sort of an entity is this soul? Whatever about the *real* Socrates, the Platonic Socrates, having abandoned the simplistic model expounded in the *Phaedo*, where all irrational impulses are distractions imposed by the body, unveils in the ninth book of the *Republic*[17] an answer to the question that he poses himself here at the beginning of the *Phaedrus*,[18] by producing his remarkable image of the soul as a composite of a 'many-headed beast' (the passions), a lion (the *thymos*, or spirited element), and a human being (the reason), all encased in a human form. The true essence of justice, which has been the topic of the *Republic* as a whole, becomes the following:

He who says that justice is more profitable (sc. than injustice) affirms that all our actions and words should tend to give the man within us complete domination over the entire man and make him take charge of the many-headed beast – like a farmer who cherishes and trains the cultivated plants, but checks the growth of the wild – and he will make an ally of the lion's nature, and caring for all the beasts alike will first make them friendly to one another and to himself, and so foster their growth.[19]

So Plato, in the guise of Socrates, feels that he has attained to the truth about the nature of the (embodied) soul, and therewith the proper means of managing his life. The proper control of the 'beast' and the 'lion' frees up the rational soul to pursue its quest for knowledge of 'the Good', which will reveal to it the truth about the way the universe is structured, and our place in it.[20] We find what seems to be a further refinement of this position at the end of the *Timaeus*, where an entity, the personal *daimôn*, which is presented back in the *Phaedo*[21] as a being distinct from, and superior to, the individual soul, and then in Book 10 of the *Republic*[22] as a guiding spirit that the individual soul chooses for itself, now becomes identified with the highest element in the individual soul itself:

And we should consider that God gave the sovereign part of the human soul to be the *daimôn* of each one, being that part which, as we say, dwells at the top of the body, and inasmuch as we are a plant not of an earthly but of a heavenly growth, raises us from earth to our kindred who are in heaven. And in this way we speak most correctly, for the divine power suspends the head and root of us from that place where the generation of the soul first began, and thus makes the whole body upright. When a man is always occupied with the cravings of desire and ambition, and is eagerly striving to satisfy them, all his thoughts must be mortal, and, as far as it is possible altogether to become such, he must be mortal every whit, because he has cherished his mortal part. But he who has been earnest in the love of knowledge and of true wisdom, and has exercised his intellect more than any other part of him, must have thoughts immortal and divine, if he lays hold on truth (*eanper alêtheias ephaptetai*), and in so far as human nature is capable of sharing in immortality, he must altogether be immortal, and since he is ever cherishing the divine power and has the *daimôn* within him in good order (*eu kekosmêmenon*), he will be singularly happy (*eudaimôn*).[23]

This remarkable passage, envisaging as it does a higher, almost 'semi-detached', element even within the rational soul, constituting the proper conduit for knowledge of 'the truth', which is to say, the understanding of the true nature of the intelligible world (and the physical world in its dependence on it), shows Plato appropriating the popular concept of the 'guardian daemon' for the purpose of postulating an element in the human soul which is in a particular way 'divine', as being in potential direct contact with the realm of divine Truth – a concept which was to have a lively afterlife in later Platonism, particularly with such thinkers as Plutarch and Plotinus.[24] This, it seems to me, must be regarded as the culmination of a long process of reflection by a man much given to meditation on these subjects – both the nature of the human soul and the nature of things in general.

This brings me back, from what has been something of a digression into the search for the truth about one's own nature, to our proper theme, which is Plato's view of the nature of cosmic Truth. In renewed pursuit of this, I will turn back to the *Phaedrus*, but this time to the Myth of the 'Heavenly Ride', where once again, as in the Allegory of the Cave, we are presented, though from a rather different angle, with a vision of the intelligible world, the vision of which is enjoyed, in this context, not by an embodied soul which has had the good fortune to 'ascend', but rather by rational souls destined ultimately to be human, before they have descended. This level of reality is described as follows:

Of that place beyond the heavens none of our earthly poets has yet sung, and none shall sing worthily. But this is the manner of it, for assuredly we must be bold to speak what is true (*to alêthes*), above all when the subject of our discourse is truth (*alêtheia*). It is there that true being dwells, without colour or shape, and intangible; reason alone, the pilot of the soul, can behold it, and all true knowledge focuses on this realm. Now even as the mind of a god is nourished by reason and knowledge, so also is it with every soul that has a care to receive her proper food; wherefore when at least she has beheld being (*to on*) she is well content, and contemplating truth (*theôrousa t'alêthê*) she is nourished and prospers, until the heaven's revolution brings her back full circle.[25]

The connection made here between contemplating the truth and being nourished by it is notable. Intelligible reality is seen by Plato as providing sustenance for the mind. The souls of both gods and men proceed to feast upon the Forms of the various virtues that present themselves to their view. Just below, at 248b–c, we find the following: 'Now the reason why the souls are willing and eager to see the location of the plain of Truth (*to alêtheias pedion*) lies therein, that the pasturage that is proper to their noblest part comes from that meadow, and the plumage by which they are borne aloft is nourished thereby.' So browsing on the contents of the meadow of Truth is good for the growth of the soul's 'plumage', which is what keeps it 'aloft', and in touch with the intelligible world.

This is all, of course, expressed in a mythological mode, but we may suitably end, perhaps, with a non-mythological passage which illustrates well, I think, Plato's use of *alêtheia* in a 'cosmic' sense, the conclusion of Socrates' interrogation of the slave-boy in the *Meno*. Once Socrates has secured Meno's agreement that the boy did not acquire his ability to recognize the truths of mathematics in this life, he is enabled to draw the conclusion that his soul must always have known these truths:

> Socrates: If, then, there are going to exist in him, both while he is and while he is not a man, true opinions which can be aroused by questioning and turned into knowledge, may we say that his soul has been forever in a state of knowledge? Clearly he always either is or is not a man.
>
> Meno: Clearly.
>
> Socrates: And if the truth about reality (*hê alêtheia tôn ontôn*) is always in our soul, the soul must be immortal, and one must take courage and try to discover – that is, to recollect – what one doesn't happen to know, or, more correctly, remember, at the moment.[26]

So there we have it. A potentiality of access to the truth is something that we have always with us, acquired before birth by the soul when it is free to browse in the meadow of Truth, and when this is actualized on the plane of human existence, such access fosters and nurtures the rational faculty of the soul, until, in particularly favoured cases, it attains a comprehensive vision of reality, which is denominated 'the Good' – and which, in the ideal state of the *Republic*, qualifies the person so favoured to rule the state, as a benevolent dictator (or rather, as a member of a board of such). Not many individuals, it must be recognized, will attain to that level of insight, but most of us can expect to achieve at least some intimations of it. The first step, certainly, is to come to view the physical world as a realm of shadows, which reveal, at best, merely intimations of reality, if properly evaluated; and this is followed by a fairly steep learning curve, though culminating, at the end of the tunnel, in the light of an intelligible Sun.

A final thought.[27] All this talk of 'beholding' and of 'vision', however, should not lead us to assume that the objects of intellectual vision, including the Good itself, are ultimately 'out there', external to the mind of the person who has attained *noêsis*, full intellectual comprehension of the Truth. Plato does indeed make copious use of the language of vision, which, on the physical plane, implies an external object to be viewed, but there are sufficient indications, in a number of key passages, that he understands intellectual 'vision' as a process of 'internalization'.

First of all, in the extended passage from Book 9 of the *Republic* discussed earlier, and particularly in the passage 585d–587a, where the pleasures proper to each of the three levels of soul are being contrasted, the talk is not of 'viewing' or 'contemplating', but rather of 'being filled and satisfied' (*plêrousthai*), as in the following passage: 'If, then, to be filled with what befits nature is pleasure, then that which is more really filled with real things would more really and truly cause us to enjoy a true pleasure, while that which partakes of the less truly existent would be less truly and surely filled and would partake of a less trustworthy and less true pleasure.'[28]

Here the whole emphasis is on the internalizing of the 'pleasures' concerned, which in this case are intellectual pleasures, such as are in fact identical with the 'objective' Forms which the soul is elsewhere portrayed as contemplating. Again, in the *Timaeus* passage quoted above, we may note that the enlightened sage does not so much 'behold' Truth, as 'lay hold' (*ephaptetai*) of it, and this enables him to straighten out all the crookednesses and irregularities of the circuits of his soul arising from his original embodiment.[29] And even in the myth of the *Phaedrus*, quoted above, where the disembodied soul is portrayed as 'beholding' the Forms, it is also described as being 'nourished' (*trephetai*) by the vision, and 'being feasted' (*hestiastheisa*), which may reasonably be understood as a process of internalization of the Forms.[30] So, when all is said and done, Truth, though certainly having an objective existence of the intelligible realm, is also 'within' us – and such, I trust, has been the experience of our distinguished honorand!

Endnotes

1 Indeed, this essay may be viewed against the background of our honorand's fine study, Patrick Masterson, *Approaching God: Between Phenomenology and Theology* (London: Bloomsbury, 2013).

2 See Martin Heidegger, *Vom Wesen der Wahrheit*, translated as *The Essence of Truth* (London and New York: Continuum, 2002).

3 *Rep.* 515a.

4 Though I note that it is essentially accepted by the standard Greek dictionary of Liddell, Scott and Jones, s.v. *alêthês*.

5 We may note that each of the 'preliminary studies' which should occupy the aspirant Guardians, arithmetic, geometry, stereometry, astronomy and harmonics (532d–531d) have as their object to raise the soul to a vision of real being (*ousia*), 'truth', and the Good, regarded as equivalents; cf. e,g, 526b3 (arithmetic); 527b9 (geometry); 530b4 (astronomy).

6 See Heidegger, *The Essence of Truth*, pp. 94–104.

7 *Rep.* 621a–b.

8 *Rep.* 621a8–9.

9 It must also be said that, in the ideal state of the *Republic*, the Guardians would attain this insight, in the form of a vision of the Good, after their laborious fifteen-year preparatory training in dialectic.

10 Gorgias 526d6–e1, trans. Woodhead, modified.

11 Others, in their embarrassment, have sought to emend the verb, e.g. to *skopôn*, 'considering', but these are rather desperate remedies.

12 See on this, e.g. Henri Corbin, *Alone with the Alone: Creative Imagination in the Sufism of Ibn Arabi* (Princeton, NJ: Princeton University Press, 1969), pp. 246–71.

13 *Symp.* 174e–175b; 219e–220a.

14 *Phaedrus* 229c, trans. Hackforth.

15 *Phaedrus* 239e–230a, trans. Hackforth, slightly altered.

16 Fr. 101.

17 *Rep.* 588b–589b.

18 I sidestep the awkward question of the relative priority of *Phaedrus* and *Republic*! From the dramatic perspective, Socrates' puzzle, as expressed here, is prior.

19 *Rep.* 589a5–b6, trans. Shorey.

20 In fact, the connection between the accurate comprehension of justice and injustice and the essence of truth (*autê hê alêtheia*) is made already by Socrates in the *Crito,* 48a.

21 *Phaedo* 107d–108c.

22 *Rep.* 617e.

23 *Tim.* 90a–c, trans. Jowett, slightly emended.

24 See my papers, 'Plutarch and the Separable Intellect', in A.P. Jimenez & F.C. Casadesus Bordoy (eds), *Estudios sobre Plutarco* (Madrid: Ediciones Clásicas, 2001), pp. 35–44, (repr. in *The Platonic Heritage*, (Aldershot: Ashgate, 2012), Essay 11); 'Fravashi and Undescended Soul', forthcoming, in a Festschrift for John Rist.

25 *Phaedrus* 247c–d, trans. Hackforth, slightly emended.

26 *Meno* 86a5–b3, trans. W.K.C. Guthrie.

27 I am much indebted, in this final section, to a recent insightful article by Eric Perl, 'The Motion of Intellect: On the Neoplatonic Reading of *Sophist* 248e–249d', in *The International Journal of the Neoplatonic Tradition* 8 (2014), pp. 135–60.

28 *Rep.* 585d–e, trans. Shorey.

29 *Tim.* 90c2.

30 *Phaedrus* 247d4 and 247e3.

PLOTINUS AND
TRANSCENDENT TRUTH

ANDREW SMITH

In one of his most profound explorations of the nature of intellect
Plotinus makes 'truth' one of its essential components: 'If there is not
truth in Intellect, then an intellect of this sort will not be truth, or truly
Intellect, or intellect at all. But then truth will not be anywhere else either.'[1]
This is no mere grandiose rhetorical gesture, but a claim grounded in his
deepest insights into the metaphysics of Being and the conclusion of the
long search for 'truth' in the Greek philosophical tradition, a conclusion
that trumps all other theories with the claim to have found Truth itself.

For the search after 'truth' (ἀλήθεια) is a leading theme of Ancient
Greek philosophers. Although the word is not used by him in the existing
fragments, Heraclitus, for example, claims that the utterances of his
personal λόγος are a unique and authentic expression of the universal
λόγος.[2] Parmenides, too, frequently refers to his account of the oneness of
reality as a 'truth'[3] which is to be distinguished from mere opinion (δόξα),[4]
and Empedocles also claimed privileged access to the truth of things,[5] and
distinguishes 'Truth' (Νημέρτης) from Obscurity (Ἀσάφεια).[6] Access to
'Truth' was not, however, a view that went unchallenged. Xenophanes
declared that men have access only to what is 'like the truth'[7] and that:
'No man knows, or ever will know, what is clear about the gods and about
everything I speak of; for even if one chanced to say what is perfectly the
case, yet oneself knows it not; but seeming is wrought over all things.'[8]

The Sophist Protagoras later pursued a similar line when he declared:
'About the gods I am not able to know whether they exist or do not exist,
nor what they are like in form; for the factors preventing knowledge are

many: the obscurity of the subject, and the shortness of human life.'[9] His book entitled 'On Truth' contained the famous relativist claim that man is the measure of all things, a claim that was severely criticized by Plato in the *Theaetetus*.[10] As interpreter of Plato, Plotinus found important references to 'truth' in the description in the *Phaedrus* of the 'plain of truth', where true dialectic is illustrated by the winged ascent of the soul.[11] Plotinus' frequent designation of the transcendent intelligible universe as 'true' echoes Plato's description of the world of Forms.[12]

But, of course, Plato's confidence about the possibility of attaining certain knowledge (truth), as demonstrated in the dialogues of the middle period, was not shared by the followers of the New Academy and the later sceptical tradition. And it is partly in response to this latter challenge that Plotinus provocatively demonstrates how one can attain 'truth'. The immediate epistemological context for Plotinus is the sceptic's attack on a theory of knowledge based on the assumption that the intellect is a recipient of external data, which it processes as impressions.[13] On this theory the contents of the intellect are images of objects, which themselves lie outside it; the intellect therefore apprehends only a copy of the objects rather than the real or 'true' objects. It is a criticism that could be applied both to our knowledge of the sensible world as well as to our grasp of Platonic Forms. Plotinus' response, which involves a radical revision of the sort of Platonic view held, for example, by Longinus, the contemporary head of the Academy in Athens, was to modify the relationship of the mind to the objects of its intellection as independently existing entities by claiming that the intellect is identical with the objects of thought:[14] 'If one grants that the objects of thought are as completely as possible outside Intellect, and that Intellect contemplates them as absolutely outside it, then it cannot possess the truth of them and must be deceived in everything it contemplates. For they would be the true realities; and on this supposition it will contemplate them without possessing them, but will only get images of them in a knowledge of this sort.'[15]

So radical was this interpretation that Porphyry, one of the more important members of his school, initially opposed it vigorously within Plotinus' seminar, before finally accepting the idea and writing in its defence.[16] It is an interpretation which became a key element in the Neoplatonic theory of intellect,[17] and which provided ample justification for Plotinus' stress on the discovery of 'truth'. For, in claiming that true knowledge consisted not merely in seeing but in *being* its objects, Plotinus had moved from a correspondence theory, what is true, to a theory of ontological identity in which the intellect is truth.

What then was that investigation into the relationship of 'truth and the intelligible and Intellect' which Plotinus promised at the beginning of his treatise 'That the Intelligibles are not outside Intellect'?[18] The discussion of the relationship of Intellect to the intelligibles is a theme which is extensively represented in a number of intense treatises, mostly in the fifth *Ennead*. It is also a doctrine which has been richly analysed by modern interpreters of Plotinus.[19] My concern here is the notion of 'truth', which has received less attention. It is, perhaps, easy enough to see what he means by it: a designation of knowledge that is authentic. But, if 'truth' is not merely a label for 'authentic knowledge', can we identify for it a particular status, role or mode of operation in the constitution and operation of intellect?

To begin with we might note that truth is linked with beauty and eternity as occupying a special position in the intelligible world. For example in the treatise on *Time and Eternity* we read the following:

> And we should not suppose that eternity has come to intelligible reality accidentally from outside, but eternity is in that reality[20] and is from it and with it. For it is seen to be in it from its very nature because when we see all the other things too, which we say are there, existing in it, we say that they are all from its Being and with its Being. For what exists primarily must exist along with the primaries and in the primaries; *since beauty is in them as well as from them, and truth is in them.*[21]

These three are, then, essential aspects of his intelligible universe. Each of them is applicable to that world as a whole rather than to any particular component of it. Beauty, for example, is not one Form amongst the others, but rather, even if it is to be designated as a Form, it is one which provides order and structure to the totality of Forms, since beauty is shown to be an ordering principle within the universe. Eternity, too, is applicable to the nature of the intelligible world as a whole, as a mark of the exclusion of all temporal sequence in that world and the simultaneity (τὸ ἅμα) of its constituent elements. Truth, too, is applicable to the whole intelligible universe when it is conceived as a self-thinker in which, as we have seen in our discussion of V 5 [32] 1–2, there is a unity of thinker, thinking and object of thought. Truth, then, is the expression of that identity. Each of these three expresses a particular essential feature of the intelligible universe as a whole. But while it may be possible, as we shall see, to learn a little more about their function and status in the intelligible world, it is not so easy to pin down and assign to them a particular ontological identity. Unlike his successors, who were more inclined to devise a precise taxonomy for features of the intelligible world, Plotinus avoids such a frozen presentation and a proliferation of entities in preference to an unceasing enquiry into the dynamism of Intellect. And throughout his project to unravel the workings of transcendent reality he never loses sight of the inherent difficulty that is presented by the limitations of discursive reason, which always divides what is in itself indivisible. And yet it is those very divisions and distinctions which he exploits in order to construct a whole which is one and many at the same time.

We have already seen Plotinus' analysis of Intellect in terms of epistemological principles. Another of his key ideas is that the intelligible world may be analysed in terms of five fundamental or primary categories, which he extracts from Plato's *Sophist*. Is truth to be identified with any of these categories or *genera* or is it to be considered as an additional genus? The five are movement, rest, sameness, difference, and Being. They may be conceived as essential aspects of intelligible reality. In Intellect we have both 'movement', because intellect is an activity, the activity of thinking, and 'rest', for it is always in possession of the object of its thinking. Intellect, too, is both identical with the object of its thinking and may also be distinguished from it. Similarly the thought content of Intellect is both plural – the many different Forms – and one – expressing the unity and coherence of the whole in which each part is also in a sense both itself and the whole. These four genera thus form the foundation of the complex diversity in unity of the Intelligible World. We then must finally add 'being', for the intelligible world, as well as each of its elements, is what really exists – as opposed to the physical world, which is a world of becoming. In the second of his treatises devoted to the subject of the categories, where he discusses in detail his theory of the five primary genera, we find that Beauty and even Intellect are not identified with any one of them. In fact he can speak of the genera as being 'elements' (στοιχεῖα) of Intellect.[22] It seems, then, unlikely that truth is to be identified with any of them. In fact truth would seem to be more similar in status to Beauty and Intellect. It is instructive to follow the enquiry which Plotinus conducts in VI 2 [43] in the course of establishing the necessity for each of these genera and their role in the constitution of the intelligible. For in the course of this enquiry he looks at certain other factors to ascertain whether they can be added to the list of five genera. What he says to exclude them will help us to understand a little more their status and role, even though this is in fact incidental to his main intention which is to say why they are not categories.

Now whilst Plotinus does not explicitly discuss the status of truth and eternity in the context of the five genera, he does discuss the status of One, Good and Beauty; and we may learn something from these about the status of truth, which, as we have seen, is closely allied to beauty and eternity. After establishing the five genera he raises the question whether there are just these five or whether there are more. It is a question which is never fully answered except in so far as he eliminates a number of candidates: oneness, good, quality, quantity, relation and beauty. We need not here dwell further on his choice of candidates; quality, quantity and relation will have been suggested by the Aristotelian categories of the physical world, although 'quality' is for Plotinus an important and controversial topic in the context of the Forms; Beauty and the Good are obvious Platonic metaphysical concepts (and both also are mentioned together by Aristotle in a passage which Plotinus makes use of);[23] and Oneness is clearly of serious metaphysical importance for Plotinus.

Oneness is dealt with at length in VI 2 [43] 9–12. To begin with Plotinus is careful to note that 'One' in its primary sense applies only to the ultimate principle, the One, and cannot be predicated in this sense of anything else. Of course the intelligible world can be described as a one-being, a plurality in unity; but it does not have the same signification as when 'One' is applied to the One itself, but oneness in a different sense, namely, being one. A similar argument is applied to the Good, which can properly be applied only to the highest principle. Like 'One', 'Good', too, is not predicated of the ultimate principle; rather it is the cause of goodness in others. He commences by excluding the application of 'Good' to what is below the One in the sense in which it applies at that level (i.e. the level of the One itself) – 'not in that way in which the first is' (οὐκ ἐκείνως ὡς τὸ πρῶτον).[24] And he next excludes it from being applied to a potential genus in the sense of a quality (οὐχ ὡς ποιόν). The final qualification for Good to be accepted amongst the primary genera is that its essence is identical with its existence, i.e. any 'quality' is internal to itself and not brought in from outside: 'but is in itself' (ἀλλ' ἐν αὐτῷ). This, too, is rejected on the grounds that the 'goodness' of each of the genera would be different and in each case identical with one of the existing five. He gives only one example: the Good for Being would be its return towards the One; but this is movement (κίνησις), which is already one of his categories. Thus Good cannot be a separate category, but is predicated of each of the categories, although in a way which in each case is identical with the essence of that category.[25]

Eternity, although suggested, as we have seen, as one of the essential aspects of the intelligible world, is summarily dismissed as a category,[26] perhaps because Plotinus was already planning his detailed treatment of the theme in III 7 [45], which was composed immediately after VI 2–3 [43–45]. It is, however, later confirmed as being an essential feature of intelligible reality as a whole.[27]

When he comes to discuss Beauty at VI 2 [43] 18 he entertains three possibilities: (1) it bears the same relationship to the One as Good; (2) it is a kind of light from the One illuminating the intelligible world represented by the Forms; (3) it is one with Being ('But if the beautiful is nothing else but substance itself, it has been included in what was said about substance.')[28] Plotinus may be seen here to be repeating his hesitation elsewhere about the exact status of Beauty,[29] and it is not clear which, if any, of the above possibilities he rules out. But what is certain is that he does not want to include it as a primary genus in its own right. But what he goes on to say is interesting. If, he argues, we are talking about beauty as we experience it, then it is a kind of 'movement', a movement which leads us upwards (to ideal Beauty). He then identifies this movement with the movement involved in knowing, which also, at the highest level (of stable knowledge), involves rest. This then leads him to intellect which, he argues, is not one of the genera but rather a compound (σύνθετον). Being (and we may also assume the other genera too) is said to be an element of Intellect (στοιχεῖον). The immediate result of his discussion is the distinction of Intellect from the five genera: 'But Intellect, since it is Being as intelligent and a composite of all the genera is not one of the genera; and the true Intellect is Being with all its contents and already all beings, but Being in isolation, taken as a genus, is an element of it.'[30] He then goes on to distinguish Intellect from the Forms, which as universal Forms have the ranking of species of the primary genera and as (secondary genera) to their even more specific expressions: 'But righteousness and self-control[31] and virtues in general are all particular activities of Intellect; so that they are not among the primary genera, and genus and species [of virtue] are posterior.'[32]

Intellect is not, then, to be identified with the Forms in their particularity but it is, of course, identical with 'Being with all its contents and already all beings'.[33] The Forms are activities of Intellect, and here Plotinus is anticipating his complex analysis of the relationship of Intellect as a whole to particular intellects and intelligibles in Chapter 20.[34] We must, then, distinguish Intellect both from the five genera and from Forms. Beauty and eternity would seem to occupy a similar position, distinct from the Forms and yet somehow identical with Being and Intellect, when these are understood as constituting the intelligible world as a whole. We may also now include truth since in his conclusion to the treatise he briefly mentions truth (VI 2 [43] 21. 43, what is 'true and primary' in intellect), along with beauty (VI 2 [43] 21. 11–12, 'the greatness and beauty in intellect'), and eternity (VI 2 [43] 21. 53–4).

Let us return to the passage from the treatise on eternity which we cited earlier (III 7 [45] 4.1–8) and examine more closely the formula 'in … from … with'. 'In' here does not mean 'in' as 'in a substrate'[35], e.g. as a quality inheres in a substrate, but rather 'is included in'. 'From' indicates that eternity, beauty and truth are not external in origin but are generated from the Intelligible and this is then qualified by 'with', which indicates that they are coterminous in existence and not sequential. To be 'in' is a corollary of 'to be from and with', i.e. beauty is not an external but internal product, which is made clear by the clause '*because* when we see all the other things too, which are there, existing *in* it, we say that they are all *from* its being and *with* its being'; i.e., to be 'in' implies internal origin and simultaneity. Thus taking the three together we can say that truth, beauty and eternity are embraced within the intelligible world *as a whole* (being 'in') by an act of simultaneous self-generation ('with' and 'from'). This wholeness and identity is expressed elsewhere more graphically in the case of Being and Beauty when Plotinus says: 'But the power in the intelligible world has nothing but its being and its being beautiful. For where would its beauty be if it was deprived of its being? And where would its reality be if it was stripped of its being beautiful? For in deficiency of beauty it would be defective also in reality.[36] For this reason Being is longed for because it is the same as beauty, and beauty is lovable because it is Being.'[37]

Beauty and Being are identical and are one, but at the same time may be distinguished conceptually from each other, just as intellect and its object are one but may also be distinguished from each other. The passage from III 7 [45] 4. 1–8 continues:

And some things[38] are, as it were, in a part of Being in its entirety, others are in the whole, just as this which is truly a whole is not something gathered from the parts, but has itself generated the parts, in order that in this way, too, it may be truly a whole. And truth is also not a concordance with another thing there, but belongs to each thing of which it is the truth. In fact this whole which is the true whole, if it is really to be a whole, must not only be a whole in the sense that it is everything, but must also possess the whole in such a way as to be deficient in nothing. If this is the case, nothing 'will be' for it. For if there will be something, it was deficient in that respect. In that case it was not a whole. But what could happen to it contrary to its nature? For it is not affected in any way. And so if nothing happens to it, it is neither going to do anything, nor will it be, nor was it anything. (III 7 [45] 4. 9–19)

Truth, as we have learned from V 5 [32], is to be found only when the thinking subject and the object of thought are identical. If they are not identical, intellect (the thinking subject) will possess only images of the objects and not the objects themselves. Thus Truth, too, then is an aspect of Being in its entirety, what is 'truly' a whole. Moreover a correspondence or concordance theory of truth, 'This is like that', will not suffice; truth is self-contained. We note that the whole is not 'gathered from the parts, but has itself generated the parts', which corresponds to the notion of generation 'from', which we noted earlier. What we learn from this passage is that truth permeates the whole of Intelligible reality and is not a property of just one aspect, as particular Forms or even genera would be, and that this is intimately linked to eternity – the simultaneity and timelessness of the intelligible world.

The status, then, of each of these, beauty, eternity, truth, intellect is in some way analogous. All of them are 'prior' to Form, are constituted in some way from the genera and are not only essential aspects of the intelligible world (Being as a whole), but are identical with it. Beauty, Truth and Eternity are, like Intellect, not identical with any one genus but an essential feature of all five genera, working together in mutual implication. The specific contribution of truth[39] is not merely identity (for that is the contribution of the genus 'sameness'), but an identity that transcends sameness and difference, the identity which expresses itself as epistemological certainty in an encounter with true reality, i.e. where Being and thinking are authentic, because its 'object', the intelligible world as a whole, is not only one with the thinker, but is itself 'true Being', i.e. it is self-identical as being constituted in, from and with itself.

Truth, then, proves itself to be something as substantial as Being itself and it is fitting to conclude with Porphyry's exhortation to raise ourselves to the level of Intellect: 'We shall enjoy the contemplation of intellect and be established with the incorporeal, and through the intellect, live with truth.'[40]

ENDNOTES

1 *Enneads* V 5 [32] 1. 65–8, trans. A.H. Armstrong, trans. (Cambridge, MA: Harvard University Press, 1984), vol. V, p. 161.

2 Frag. 1.

3 Frag. 1, 29–30; frag. 2, lines 4, 8, 18, 27.

4 Frag. 8, 50–2.

5 Frag. 23, 9–11; frag. 112.

6 Frag. 122.

7 Frag. 35.

8 Frag. 34.

9 Frag. 4.

10 I am avoiding here entirely the debate as to whether Plato in the *Theaetetus* had in fact given up the theory of Forms as a basis for a positive epistemology.

11 *Phaedrus* 248b6; *Enn.* I 3 [20] 4. 11; The same phrase is referred to again in VI.7 [38] 13. 34 with an emphasis on the expanse of the plain which intellect traverses.

12 E.g. V 8 [31] 5. 15 and Plato, *Phaedrus* 247c8; d4; *Republic* 509a6; 517c4.

13 Sextus Empiricus *PH* 2.72–5; *Math.* 7. 191–8; 357–8. See R.T. Wallis, 'Skepticism and Neoplatonism' in W. Haase (ed.), *Aufstieg und Niedergang der römischen Welt* 2.36.2, (Berlin: de Gruyter, 1987), pp. 911–54.

14 An idea which was also based on Aristotle's description of the divine intellect as a self-thinker (*Metaphysics* 12, 9, 1074b15–34) and his statement (*De Anima* 3, 4, 430a3–4) that thinker and object of thought are identical in the case of incorporeals.

15 V 5 [32] 1. 50–5, trans. Armstrong, pp. 159, 161.

16 Porphyry, *Life of Plotinus*, ch. 18.

17 Certainly as far as Intellect (the divine mind) is concerned, even if later Platonists had some doubts about the ability of the individual 'intellect' to attain it.

18 V 5 [32] 1. 35–6: 'We shall proceed to investigate how truth and the intelligible and Intellect are related...' Trans. Armstrong, p. 159

19 E.g. A.H. Armstrong, *The Architecture of the Intelligible Universe in Plotinus* (Cambridge: Cambridge University Press, 1940).

20 Reading <ἐν> ἐκείνῃ with Perna, Kalligas.

21 III 7 [45] 4. 1–8. Plotinus elsewhere regards beauty as being somewhat similar in its status to eternity. In his treatise 'On Love' we find the following remark: 'Eternity is

certainly akin to beauty and the eternal nature is the first to be beautiful and all that proceeds from it is beautiful.' (III 5 [50] 1. 44–6). He then goes on to refer to the Intelligible world in the following terms: 'a reality of this kind is all beautiful and eternal' (III 7 [45] 6. 1).

22 VI 2 [43] 18. 15.

23 Aristotle, *Metaphysics* 7, 6, 1031b10–14 and Plotinus VI 2 [43] 5. 6. See Christoph Horn, *Plotin über Sein, Zahl und Einheit* (Stuttgart/Leipzig, 1995), p. 111.

24 VI 2 [43] 17. 10.

25 He allows that we can call things 'good' and thus predicate goodness of them as a quality. But for Plotinus the regular notion of 'quality' is excluded from the intelligible world. Even Forms do not possess qualities, but what they are is identical with their existence.

26 VI 2 [43] 16. 6.

27 VI 2 [43] 21. 52.

28 VI 2 [43] 18. 6, trans. A.H. Armstrong (Cambridge, MA: Harvard University Press, 1988), vol. VI, p. 163.

29 I 6 [1] 9. 39–43; VI 7 [38] 22 and VI 7 [38] 32–3.

30 VI 2 [43] 18. 12–15, trans. Armstrong, p. 163.

31 Righteousness and Self-control are taken from the description of the intelligible universe in Plato's *Phaedrus* and used by him as standard indicators of Forms in general (see V 8 [31] 10. 13–14).

32 VI 2 [43] 18. 15–17, trans. Armstrong, p. 163.

33 VI 2 [43] 18. 13–14, trans. Armstrong, p. 163.

34 And see also VI 2 [43] 22. 25–6: 'When it is active in itself, the products of its activity are the other intellects.' Trans. Armstrong, p. 175.

35 This distinction is clearly stated by Plotinus: 'Motion is neither to be subsumed under Being nor to be ordered above it; rather, it is on a level with Being, but not as something, for it is the activity of Being and neither of them is without the other except in our conception of them, and the two natures are one nature: for being is actual, not potential. Even if you were to grasp each of them separately, both motion would appear in Being and Being in motion, just as with the One-Being, although each of them separately contains the other, still discursive reasoning says they are two, and that each Form is a double one.' (VI 2 [43] 7. 16–24, trans. Lloyd Gerson (ed.) (Cambridge: Cambridge University Press, 2018), p. 688.

36 The same point is made in III 7 [45] 4. 16–19, that if reality/being has a future aspect (will be), i.e. is not eternal, it will be deficient in respect of what will be for it.

37 V 8 [31] 9. 36–41, trans. Armstrong, pp. 267, 269.

38 The 'some things' that are in 'a part of being' are the Forms which are not all instantiated everywhere. The 'others' which are in the whole are eternity, truth and beauty.

39 The specific contributions of the others might be designated as follows: beauty assures order, eternity simultaneity, and intellect activity.

40 Porphyry, *De abstinentia* I.109, 11–13.

Beauty from Plato to Aquinas

FRAN O'ROURKE

On a visit to the University of San Diego I was told about the founder of that splendid institution. As well as being a practical woman who created a magnificent university, Mother Rosalie Hill was a person of inspiring ideals. Her motivating vision was expressed: 'Three things are significant in education: beauty, truth and goodness. But the only one that attracts people on sight is beauty. If beauty attracts people, they will come and find the truth and have goodness communicated to them by the kind of people here.' Her words may be summarized: delight in Beauty, know the Truth, love the Good. They call to mind the motto on the façade of the neoclassical opera house in Frankfurt: '*Dem Wahren, Schönen, Guten*' ('To the True, the Beautiful, the Good'), words inspired by the city's most famous citizen, Johann Wolfgang von Goethe, who wrote of the spirit's progress to the eternity of the true, the good, the beautiful.[1] The American romantic R.W. Emerson wrote in similar vein: 'Truth, and goodness, and beauty, are but different faces of the same All.'[2] This is probably as good a definition as one will find of what are known as the 'transcendental' perfections of being. Such properties are convertible with one another, and are coextensive with the grand totality – the universe of the real.

There is, however, a danger in Emerson's statement – a pantheist peril. He seems to confuse the 'transcendent', as absolute, with the universal features of reality known as the 'transcendental' properties of being. Philosophers distinguish, on the one hand, between the unique and transcendent principle of the universe – the ultimate reality of Plato and Plotinus – named equally as the One, Beauty, and the Good, and, on the other, those characteristics of unity, goodness, beauty and truth that belong to all realities, both finite and infinite. Unity, goodness, and truth are recognized as the most important of the transcendentals; many readers of Aquinas add the property of beauty. The Presocratic thinker Heraclitus was the earliest recorded thinker to consider beauty a universal character of the real: 'People disagree on what is beautiful although to God everything is beautiful.'[3]

PLATO

Among ancient philosophers Plato (428/427–348/347 BC) was the foremost champion of the Transcendent. He also implied a doctrine of transcendentals by stating that every being is good and beautiful.[4] Beauty, he believed, is supreme and gives to life its transcendent value. Diotima, in her lofty discourse on beauty in the *Symposium* proclaimed that 'a man finds it truly worthwhile to live, as he contemplates essential beauty'.[5] While beauty is easily experienced, its essence is difficult to define. Socrates remarks in the *Lysis*: 'I am quite dizzy myself with the puzzle of our argument, and am inclined to agree with the ancient proverb that the beautiful is friendly. It certainly resembles something soft and smooth and sleek; that is why, I daresay, it so easily slides and dives right into us, by virtue of those qualities. For I declare that the good is beautiful.'[6]

In Joyce's *A Portrait of the Artist as a Young Man* Stephen Dedalus remarks: 'Plato, I believe, said that beauty is the splendour of truth. I don't think that it has a meaning, but the true and the beautiful are akin.'[7] While the definition of beauty as *splendor veri* is nowhere to be found in Plato, it captures well one of his most profound intuitions. And despite Stephen's hesitation, the notion had most certainly a definite meaning for Plato. The Greek philosopher was the first to formulate what would become an important triad in the perennial tradition: Truth, Goodness, Beauty. In the *Phaedrus* he states: 'The divine is beauty, wisdom, goodness, and all such qualities.'[8] In the *Timaeus* he declares that the world is beautiful and its maker good.[9] The triad is affirmed, with some variation, in the *Philebus*:

> The power of the good has taken refuge in the nature of the beautiful; for measure and proportion are everywhere identified with beauty and virtue (μετριότης γὰρ καὶ συμμετρία κάλλος δήπου καὶ ἀρετὴ πανταχοῦ ξυμβαίνει γίγνεσθαι) ... We said that truth also was mingled with them in the compound ... Then if we cannot hunt

the good with one idea only, let us run it down with three – beauty, proportion, and truth, and let us say that these, considered as one, may more properly than all other components of the mixture be regarded as the cause, and that through the goodness of these the mixture itself has been made good.[10]

Here, alongside goodness, beauty, and truth are introduced the requisites of proportion and its cognate 'measure', both of which are allied to beauty, truth and virtue. Beauty requires measure, harmony and symmetry. At *Philebus* 66b Plato groups 'proportion, beauty and perfection' (τὸ σύμμετρον καὶ καλὸν καὶ τὸ τέλεον).

Aquinas' celebrated description of beauty as *visum placens*, that which pleases when seen, has its remote roots in Plato's dialogue *Hippias Major*.

> That is beautiful which makes us feel joy; I do not mean all pleasures, but that which makes us feel joy through hearing and sight. For surely beautiful human beings, Hippias, and all decorations and paintings and works of sculpture which are beautiful, delight us when we see them; and beautiful sounds and music in general and speeches and stories do the same thing ... The beautiful is that which is pleasing through hearing and sight.[11]

Apart from the *Enneads* of Plotinus, the *Hippias Major* is the only work in ancient philosophy to deal explicitly with the theme of beauty. Its author asks not just 'what is beautiful, but what the beautiful is'.[12] The fact that there is doubt about its authenticity does not diminish the validity of the definition offered in the dialogue. Discussing the nature of definition in the *Topics*, Aristotle cites as an example the definition of 'the beautiful as what is pleasant to sight or to hearing' (οἷον τὸ καλὸν τὸ δι' ὄψεως ἢ τὸ δι' ἀκοῆς ἡδύ).[13] Although grasped as symmetry by the eye, and as harmony by the ear, beauty is grasped ultimately by the soul; Plato relates beauty (καλόν) to intellect (διάνοια): 'This name, the beautiful, is rightly given to mind, since it accomplishes the works which we call beautiful and in which we delight.'[14]

It is therefore legitimate to attribute to Plato the thought, if not the formula, of beauty as *splendor veri*. Beauty shines through the brightness of truth. For Plato, beauty is the 'most radiant of all, and the loveliest (ἐκφανέστατον εἶναι καὶ ἐρασμιώτατον)'. Ἐκφανέστατον is what shines forth most powerfully; it is the fundamental 'epiphany'. Beauty is the clearest manifestation of the good, as confirmed in the *Phaedrus*:

> Beauty shone in brilliance among those visions; and since we came to earth we have found it shining most clearly through the clearest of our senses; for sight is the sharpest of the physical senses, though wisdom is not seen by it, for wisdom would arouse terrible love, if such a clear image of it were granted as would come through sight, and the same is true of the other lovely realities; but beauty alone has this privilege, and therefore it is most manifest and most lovely of all.[15]

Proportion had traditionally been recognized by the Greeks as a fundamental constituent of reality and beauty. According to Plato, nothing which is beautiful is without proportion; deformity and disproportion result in ugliness.[16] In the passage from the *Philebus* already quoted, Plato declares measure and proportion to be requisite elements of beauty; in the *Timaeus* he states: 'All that is good is beautiful, and what is beautiful is not without proportion; for an animal to be beautiful it must be well-proportioned.'[17] If an animal's parts are excessively large, it lacks due proportion and is consequently ugly. 'A body, for example, which is too long in the legs, or otherwise disproportioned owing to some excess, is not only ugly, but, when joint effort is required, it is also the source of much fatigue and many sprains and falls by reason of its clumsy motion, whereby it causes itself countless evils.'[18]

Plato refers on many occasions to the beauty of physical things, of animals (horses and apes); humans (boys and girls), inanimate materials such as wood, stone, ivory and gold.[19] Most beautiful and desirable of all, according to Plato, is the harmonious proportion and symmetry between soul and body: 'For with respect to health and disease, virtue and vice, there is no symmetry or want of symmetry greater than that which exists between the soul itself and the body itself.' If body and soul are not appropriately fitted towards one another, 'then the creature as a whole is not beautiful (οὐ καλὸν ὅλον τὸ ζῷον), seeing that it is unsymmetrical in respect of the greatest of symmetries'.[20] When soul and body are in proper harmony it is, for the one who has eyes to see, 'the most beautiful and admirable (κάλλιστον καὶ ἐρασμιώτατον)'.[21] Echoing Pythagoras' view of the relation between individual and cosmic beauty, Plato asserts that the living creature is most harmonious and beautiful when its parts mirror the form of the universe.[22] Drawing a practical conclusion from such a world-view, Plato urges that students of mathematics should develop bodily excellence by practicing gymnastics, while those exhibiting physical excellence ought to cultivate music and philosophy – this 'if either is to deserve to be called truly both beautiful and good'.[23]

Plato sought not only to explain the reality of beautiful things and how they are experienced, but also to explain why they exist; this was the rationale for his theory of Forms. There must exist an absolute and transcendent ground for beauty, an esssence of beauty in which beautiful individuals participate; beautiful things exist only because they share in the beauty derived from the generous and generative plenitude of subsistent Beauty which exists in itself. Not only are there beautiful things: there exists Beauty Itself.[24]

ARISTOTLE

Asked why we spend so much time on beauty, Aristotle (384–322 BC) supposedly replied: 'That is a blind man's question.'[25] Beauty is a frequent theme throughout his work. Like Plato he believed that it was ultimately a divine characteristic, but for different reasons. With his biologist's mind he perceived beauty as the perfection proper to natural substances in themselves. In the *Metaphysics* he generalizes and 'personifies' it, stating: 'In many cases the Good and the Beautiful are the beginning both of knowledge and of motion.'[26] While he does not appear to share with Plato and Aquinas a 'transcendental' concept, i.e. beauty as universally interchangeable with goodness, Aristotle occasionally attributes to it a higher status than to goodness, as when he states that goodness pertains to actions, whereas beauty is also in immovable things (τὸ δὲ καλὸν καὶ ἐν τοῖς ἀκινήτοις).[27] According to Aristotle, beauty is desired in itself: 'The beautiful (καλὸν) is that which is both desirable for its own sake and also worthy of praise; or which, being good, is pleasant because it is good.'[28]

Καλὸν expresses for Aristotle not only what delights the eye and ear, but also what appeals to our higher ethical sensibility – a nuance sometimes conveyed in English translation by the word 'noble'. He recognizes a bond between the ethical and aesthetic. Discussing the virtue of magnificence in the *Nicomachean Ethics* he compares the magnificent individual (μεγαλοπρεπὴς) with the artist, 'for he can see what is fitting and spend large sums tastefully... the magnificent man will spend such sums for the sake of the beautiful (δαπανήσει δὲ τὰ τοιαῦτα ὁ μεγαλοπρεπὴς τοῦ καλοῦ ἕνεκα)... he will consider how the result can be made most beautiful and most becoming (πῶς κάλλιστον καὶ πρεπωδέστατον) rather than for how much it can be produced and how it can be produced most cheaply.'[29] He explains further: 'For a possession and a work of art have not the same excellence. The most valuable possession is that which is worth most, e.g. gold, but the most valuable work of art is that which is great and beautiful, for the contemplation of such a work inspires admiration, and so does magnificence; and a work has an excellence – a magnificence – which involves magnitude.'[30] Worthy of note here is that beauty elicits admiration, i.e. delight simply through knowledge. Such delight is characteristic of the self-sufficient person, who seeks to 'possess beautiful and profitless things (τὰ καλὰ καὶ ἄκαρπα) rather than profitable and useful ones'.[31] Joining adjacent phrases in the *Nicomachean Ethics* we may summarily define Aristotle's entire ethics: 'Virtue aims at the beautiful' (τοῦ καλοῦ ἕνεκα· τοῦτο γὰρ τέλος τῆς ἀρετῆς).[32] This empirical insight rejoins the exalted ideal of Plato's Diotima, who declared that the purpose of human life is to contemplate essential beauty.

Thus there is for Aristotle, as for Plato, a beauty that is proper to soul; he remarks: 'Beauty of the soul is not so easy to see as beauty of body.'[33] His most explicit statement regarding empirical beauty may be found in the *Metaphysics*, where we also find the suggestion of a cosmic role for essential Beauty:

> The main species of beauty are orderly arrangement, proportion, and definiteness (τοῦ δὲ καλοῦ μέγιστα εἴδη τάξις καὶ συμμετρία καὶ τὸ ὡρισμένον); and these are especially manifested by the mathematical sciences. And inasmuch as it is evident that these (I mean, e.g., orderly arrangement and definiteness) (συμμετρία καὶ τὸ ὡρισμένον) are causes of many things, obviously they must also to some extent treat of the cause in this sense, i.e. the cause in the sense of the Beautiful.[34]

The symmetry and proportion of empirical beauty result for Aristotle from the organic order of parts within the unified whole. The role of orderly proportion is illustrated by three examples in the *Politics*: 'A painter would not let his animal have its foot of disproportionately large size, even though it was an exceptionally beautiful foot, nor would a shipbuilder make the stern or some other part of a ship disproportionately big, nor yet will a trainer of choruses allow a man who sings louder and more beautifully than the whole band to be a member of it.'[35] The preeminent signs of beauty are for Aristotle integrity and order or proportion. Beauty pertains to the fitness of nature, in particular the inner teleology of natural substances which Aristotle ultimately regards as a manifestation of beauty.[36] Natural beauty however seems to reveal a deeper cause; in one of his biological works Aristotle attributes beauty to the productive power of the divine: 'Of the things which are, some are eternal and divine, others admit alike of being and not-being, and the beautiful and the divine acts always, in virtue of its own nature, as a cause which produces that which is *better* in the things which admit of it.'[37]

Aristotle associates beauty with completenesss or perfection (τὸ κάλλιστον καὶ ἄριστον ... τὸ δὲ καλὸν καὶ τέλειον).[38] His account of 'perfection' is relevant to our discussion since, while it is possible to locate the notion of integrity in Dionysius (the acknowedged primary source for Aquinas' notions of beauty), it is more likely that Aquinas derived from Aristotle the notion of *integritas* as an essential prerequisite for beauty. The text from the *Metaphysics* may be helpfully divided as follows:

We call complete (τέλειον):

(1) That outside which it is not possible to find even one of the parts proper to it; ...

(2) That which in respect of excellence and goodness cannot be excelled in its kind, e.g. a doctor is complete and a flute-player is complete, when they lack nothing in respect of their proper kind of excellence... Excellence is a completion; for each thing is complete and every substance is complete, when in respect of its proper kind of excellence it lacks no part of its natural magnitude.

(3) The things which have attained a good end are called complete; for things are complete in virtue of having attained their end, since the end is something ultimate ... the ultimate purpose is also an end.

Things, then, that are called complete in virtue of their own nature are so called in all these senses, some because they lack nothing in respect of goodness and cannot be excelled and no part proper to them can be found outside, others in general because they cannot be exceeded in their several classes and no part proper to them is outside.[39]

We have noted that Aristotle agrees with Plato in defining beauty by its effect as that which gives delight. He also agrees that beauty is formally constituted by measure and proportion (μετριότης καὶ συμμετρία). By contrast with Plato, however, Aristotle does not include splendour among the criteria of beauty; in this he is at variance not only with his teacher but with the entire tradition of the West. As well as the primary characteristics of order, symmetry and limit, he especially emphasizes perfection or integrity. For his part he adds the pre-requisite of magnitude; this is required for beauty both of natural substances and artistic works, as he explains in the *Poetics*:

> A beautiful object, whether an animal or anything else with a structure of parts, should have not only its parts ordered but also an appropriate magnitude: beauty consists in magnitude and order (τὸ γὰρ καλὸν ἐν μεγέθει καὶ τάξει ἐστίν), which is why there could not be a beautiful animal which was either minuscule (as contemplation of it, occurring in an almost imperceptible moment, has no distinctness) or gigantic (as contemplation of it has no cohesion, but those who contemplate it lose a sense of unity and wholeness), say an animal a thousand miles long. So just as with our bodies and with animals beauty requires magnitude, but magnitude that allows coherent perception, likewise plots require length, but length that can be coherently remembered.

> A limit of length referring to competitions and powers of attention is extrinsic to the art: for if it were necessary for a hundred tragedies to compete, they would perform them by water clocks, as they say happened once before. But the limit that conforms to the actual nature of the matter is that greater size, provided clear coherence remains, means finer beauty of magnitude.[40]

Aristotle's explanation in the *Nicomachean Ethics* for the need of a proper magnitude is literally an *argumentum ad hominem*: 'Beauty implies a good-sized body, and little people may be neat and well-proportioned but cannot be beautiful.'[41] Magnitude is not in itself a constituent of beauty, but a necessary prerequisite; only substances of an appropriate size may be deemed beautiful: neither too big nor too small, but in proportion to the capacity of human knowledge. The emphasis on order and magnitude is also conveyed in the *Politics* where the desirable size of the polis is illustrated by comparison with a ship:

> For law is order, and good law is good order; but a very great multitude cannot be orderly: to introduce order into the unlimited is the work of a divine power – of such a power as holds together the universe. Beauty is realized in number and magnitude, and the state which combines magnitude with good order must necessarily be the most beautiful. To the size of states there is a limit, as there is to other things, plants, animals, implements; for none of these retain their natural power when they are too large or too small, but they either wholly lose their nature, or are spoiled. For example, a ship which is only a span long will not be a ship at all, nor a ship a quarter of a mile long; yet there may be a ship of a certain size, either too large or too small, which will still be a ship, but bad for sailing.[42]

Since for Aristotle the intrinsic order of anything results from its form, it follows that form (εἶδος) is the ultimate source and ground of an individual's beauty. The importance of form as a principle of unity and integrity is brought out in the following passage from the *Metaphysics*:

> While in a sense we call anything one if it is a quantity and continuous, in a sense we do not unless it is a whole, i.e. unless it has unity of form; e.g. if we saw the parts of a shoe put together anyhow we should not call them one all the same (unless because of their continuity); we do this only if they are put together so as to be a shoe and to have already a certain single form.[43]

When Aristotle states that a beautiful object must have an orderly arrangement of parts, he is referring to form. An individual's magnitude is likewise determined by its form; however not all forms are suited to manifest beauty to the human eye: they must be in proportion. Minuscule or gigantic objects are not proportioned to the capacities of the senses. In *De Anima* he is at pains to note that the senses also constitute a λόγος, i.e. ratio or proportion: there is a fitness between the perceiver and what can be perceived. Beauty is adapted to the receptive range of the sensory apparatus.

As with so many aspects of Aristotle's philosophy, analogy plays a pervasive role. We have seen that beauty depends on a suitable proportion between the senses and their object. Analogy emerges also at another level. Aristotle states that there is a beauty proper to each stage of a person's growth and development. This is suitably depicted in the *Rhetoric*:

> Beauty varies with each age. In a young man, it consists in possessing a body capable of enduring all efforts, either of the racecourse or of bodily strength, while he himself is pleasant to look upon and a sheer delight. This is why the athletes in the pentathlon are most beautiful, because they are naturally adapted for bodily exertion and for swiftness of foot. In a man who has reached his prime, beauty consists in being naturally adapted for the toils of war, in being pleasant to look upon and at the same time awe-inspiring. In an old man, beauty consists in being naturally adapted to contend with unavoidable labours and in not causing annoyance to others, thanks to the absence of the disagreeable accompaniments of old age.[44]

PLOTINUS

One of the most profound discourses on beauty in classical philosophy is that of Plotinus (204–270), the founder of Neoplatonism. It is significant that Plotinus' treatise on beauty was chronologically the first of his *Enneads*, an indication that he regarded beauty as the primary reality and centre of the universe. Plotinus was the first to systematically discuss beauty and, via Augustine and Pseudo-Dionysius, his influence stretched into the Middle Ages and beyond. Plotinus agreed with Plato and Aristotle that beauty is perceived primarily through sight and hearing, but refers also to the beauty of intellect and virtue. His treatise begins:

> Beauty is found for the most part in sight, but it is found also in hearing, both in the composition of words, as well as being found in music; indeed in all aspects of music, for both melody and rhythm are beautiful. And for those proceeding upwards from sense perception there are beautiful ways of life, actions, dispositions and items of knowledge as well as the beauty of the virtues. And if there is any beauty beyond even these, it will itself make it manifest.[45]

Plotinus begins by inquiring after the beauty that manifests itself through matter: 'Then what is it that has made us imagine bodies to be beautiful and our hearing to assent to sounds as being beautiful? And how can all the things that are directly concerned with soul be beautiful? ... What is it that stirs the gaze of those who look and turns them towards itself, draws them and makes them delight in what they see?' Plotinus faithfully sums up the traditional definition of beauty: 'It is said by virtually all that symmetry of the parts to each other and to the whole with the addition of fine colour is the cause of visual beauty, and that for visible things and in general all other things being beautiful is being symmetrical and measured.'[46] However he rejects this definition as inadequate:

> For those who hold this view nothing simple but only a compound is of necessity beautiful. And for them the whole will be beautiful, while the parts will not have their beauty from themselves, but as contributing to make the whole beautiful. And yet if the whole is beautiful the parts too must be beautiful; for it certainly must not be made up of ugly parts, but beauty must have taken hold of all the parts. [47]

If symmetry alone were the criterion for beauty, simple things could not be beautiful. For Plotinus unity is a prior characteristic: the more unified an entity, the more beautiful it is. Whatever is utterly simple is most unified of all. Moreover, to define beauty as symmetry is to suggest that only what is composed of parts could be beautiful; this implies, paradoxically, that none of the parts can be beautiful, only the whole. This would lead to the absurd suggestion that a beautiful object could be entirely composed of ugly parts. According to Plotinus, the parts must also be beautiful; symmetry alone does not constitute beauty: 'One must say that being beautiful is something other than and beyond proportion, and that proportion is beautiful because of something else.' [48]

According to Plotinus, beautiful sense objects cause spiritual delight by virtue of the luminous presence of form which is the source of their inner unity. There is deep kinship between the soul's cognitive power and the intelligible form; both derive from the Soul, and ultimately from Intellect. Intelligible form is what is beautiful.[49] Plotinus illustrates the importance of the intelligible form by contrasting a lump of stone with a statue modelled after an idea in the mind of the master.[50] The beautiful things of nature are likewise imbued with form, which is itself a sensible manifestation of Intellect. Plotinus remarks: 'Surely in each case [beauty] is form, which is the cause, which comes from the maker to the thing which comes into being.'[51]

Beauty ultimately derives from the Good. As Plotinus points out in his mature treatise VI 7, beautiful material things are desired not for their material element, 'but for the beauty imaged upon them. For each is what it is by itself; but it becomes desirable when the Good colours it, giving a kind of grace to them and passionate love to the desirers.' Intellect itself is not beautiful 'till it catches a light from the Good'.[52] He states succinctly: 'Beauty is what illuminates good proportions rather than the good proportions themselves, and this is what is lovable.'[53] The luminous presence of beauty is mediated through form, the most perfect of which is the living soul, which explains why 'there is more light of beauty on a living face, but only a trace of it on a dead one, even if its flesh and its proportions are not wasted away'. Thus, he asserts, an ugly living man is more beautiful than the statue of a beautiful man. He explains: 'The living is more desirable because it has soul; and this is because it has more the form of good; and this means that it is somehow coloured by the light of the Good.'[54]

Following Plato, Plotinus explains sensible beauty by its participation in the higher Forms, with Beauty at the apex: 'We affirm that things here are beautiful by participation in form. For everything which is formless but capable of receiving shape and form, as long as it is without a share of reason principle and form, is ugly and outside divine reason principle.'[55] Form is the decisive and determining principle of beauty, which dominates and unifies matter:

> The form draws near and arranges together the thing that is going to become composed as one from many parts, guides it to become a single complete entity and makes it one by the agreement [of its parts], since the form itself was one and what is formed must also be one as far as this is possible for something that is composed of many parts. Beauty is, then, established upon it once it has been brought together in unity and it gives itself to both parts and wholes.[56]

Ultimately, 'Beauty is in that higher world and comes from there.'[57] 'The greatest beauty in the world of sense is a manifestation of the noblest among the intelligibles.'[58] The ordered beauty of the cosmos is caused by the soul's presence in the sensible world: 'Just as rays from the sun light up a dark cloud, make it shine, and give it a golden appearance, so soul entered into the body of heaven and gave it life, gave it immortality, and wakened it from sleep.'[59]

In Plotinus' systematized universe, the source of all reality is the One, also named Beauty or the Good, which transcends everything finite and multiple; the One may also be termed Non-Being, by excess, since it shares none of the limits characteristic of beings. From it the entire universe of being emanates in a descending scale of diminishing perfection, order and beauty. From it flow forth the worlds of spirit, life and nature, down to unshaped matter – which is non-being through default. This world of material non-being is for Plotinus the realm of evil and ugliness. Pseudo-Dionysius would inherit this Plotinian scheme of things. More important, however, was the metaphysics of light which was central to Neoplatonism. Plotinus adopted Plato's famous analogy between the sun and the Good: as the sun illuminates the visible natural world, so the Good is the source of light and intelligibility throughout the entire universe. Light is the best analogue for reality in a world where being first occurs as the object of intellect. So understood, being is light, and light is being. Beauty is the luminous splendour of being. Plotinus' *Lichtmetaphysik* remained influential throughout the history of aesthetics.

AUGUSTINE

The authorities most frequently cited by Aquinas in reference to beauty are St Augustine (354–430) and Pseudo-Dionysius, both in the tradition of Plato and Plotinus. While Pseudo-Dionysius stressed harmony and clarity, Augustine repeatedly emphasized the importance of number as the foundation of such key elements as harmony, symmetry and proportion. The profound insight animating Augustine's aesthetic theory is summed up in his affirmation: 'We can only love what is beautiful. (*Non possumus amare nisi pulchra.*)'[60] Beauty is not contemplated in the abstract, but experienced in loving delight at the realities admired in visible creation: 'Consider all creation, the earth and the sea, what is on the earth and on the sea... They move you? They clearly move you. Why? Because they are beautiful.'[61] Beauty elicits joy and love. Augustine asks: 'Do we love anything but the beautiful? What then is the beautiful? And what is beauty? What is it that allures and unites us to the things we love; for unless there were a grace and beauty (*decus et species*) in them, they could not possibly attract us to them?'[62]

Augustine even finds beauty in such things as cock fights, rats, mice and worms; all such creatures are beautiful in their own kind (*video tamen omnia in suo genere pulchra esse*).[63] He is profoundly moved by countless examples of beautiful things in the world:

> Question the beauty of the earth, question the beauty of the sea, question the beauty of the air, amply spread around everywhere, question the beauty of the sky, question the serried ranks of the stars, question the sun making the day glorious with its bright beams, question the moon tempering the darkness of the following night with its shining rays, question the animals that move in the waters, that amble about on dry land, that fly in the air; their souls hidden, their bodies evident; the visible bodies needing to be controlled, the invisible souls controlling them; question all these things. They all answer you, 'Here we are, look; we're beautiful.' Their beauty is their confession. Who made these beautiful changeable things, if not one who is beautiful and unchangeable?[64]

Having relinquished Manicheism, discovered Platonism and converted to Christianity, Augustine's love shifted from the attractions of the flesh to a desire for God. His aesthetics was influenced most profoundly by Plotinus, whose treatise *On Beauty* he discovered in his early thirties (AD 385). The Neoplatonist's theory of transcendent beauty chimed with his newly found theism and guided his mature search for divine beauty. In one of the most celebrated of passages in Western spirituality Augustine lamented how he came late to the love of God, having been seduced in his youth by the beauty of things which would not exist, had they not been created by God:

> Late have I loved you, beauty so old and so new: late have I loved you. And see, you were within me and I was in the external world and sought you there, and in my unlovely state I plunged into those beautiful (*formosa*) created things which you made. You were with me, and I was not with you. The lovely things kept me far from you, though if they did not have existence in you, they had no existence at all.[65]

Enslaved as a youth to the pleasures and beauty of the physical world, and devoted as an adult to the mystery of divine beauty, beauty was a frequent theme in Augustine's writings, from his earliest to the latest, with frequent variations in the definitions provided. As with our familiarity with time, he acknowledges that beauty is easy to experience but difficult to define.

The definition of beauty proposed by Augustine in his early work *De Pulchro et Apto* was similar to that of Aristotle, namely that beauty is caused by integrity and proportion: 'I marked and perceived that in bodies themselves there was a beauty from their forming a kind of whole, and another from mutual fitness, as one part of the body with its whole.'[66] Beauty is primarily the harmony that suffuses the many aspects relating unity to diversity and diversity to unity in any individual, or in the totality of individuals. These relations are described variously by such terms as order, symmetry, proportion, mutual agreement, measure. Each of these terms implies all the others.

The many formulations of the elements of aesthetic appreciation in Augustine may be reduced to three: unity, order, and brightness.[67] While he deals explicitly with unity and order – frequently under the guise of the related aspects of number, proportion and measure – he does not explicitly consider brightness. However, he employs terms related to splendour, fulgence and brilliance with such frequency that it may be counted as one of his prerequisites for beauty.

For Augustine beauty consists primarily in harmony, i.e. the fitting proportion between parts suited to one another and which are mutually well ordered. Viewed in isolation parts may be unattractive, but together they form an ordered unity: 'though the parts may be imperfect the whole is perfect'.[68] Beauty therefore belongs primarily to the whole: 'Every beauty that is composed of parts is much more praiseworthy in the whole than in any part' (*omnis enim pulchritudo quae partibus constat, multo est laudabilior in toto quam in parte*).[69] This corresponds to Aristotle's emphasis on τέλειον, adopted by Aquinas as *integritas*. For Augustine the constituent elements that coalesce in the beauty of the whole are the cognate elements of harmony, order and unity; the three are inseparable: harmony results from the pleasing order of parts within the unity of the whole. Augustine sometimes refers only to one or other of these coordinates, but the three belong together. His statements that 'there is no ordered thing that is not beautiful' (*nihil enim est ordinatum, quod non sit pulchrum*),[70] or that 'unity is the form of all beauty' (*omnis pulchritudinis forma unitas*),[71] express different aspects of the same reality.

The harmony of music is for Augustine the paradigm for artistic or created beauty. In *De Musica* Augustine states summarily: Beauty pleases because of number: *pulchra numero placent*.[72] We find a clear exposé of the importance of number in *De Libero Arbitrio*: 'Look at the sky, the earth, and the sea, and at whatever in them shines from above or crawls, flies, or swims below. These have form because they have number. Take away these forms and there will be nothing (*formas habent, quia numeros habent: adime illis haec, nihil erunt*). Whence are these except from number? Indeed they exist only insofar as they have numbers.'[73] Montague Brown explains: 'Number is not merely enumeration and measurement, but also (and more importantly) proportion, harmony, integrity, and order. These are the same characteristics that make things beautiful; they are to be found in all things, from the simplest fly to the order of the universe and even to history as ordered by divine providence. The one constant is that beauty is ordered unity; it is the harmonious integration of constituent parts.'[74] Augustine expresses this as follows: 'In all the arts it is symmetry that gives pleasure, preserving unity and making the whole beautiful. Symmetry demands unity and equality, the similarity of like parts, or the graded arrangements of parts which are dissimilar.'[75]

Besides Plotinus, one of Augustine's greatest influences was Cicero, who cited two criteria for the beauty of the human body: proper proportion of limbs and 'softness of colour' (*quaedam apta figura membrorum cum coloris quadam suavitate*).[76] St Augustine follows this verbatim: 'For all bodily beauty consists in the proportion of parts, together with a certain agreeableness of colour (*partium congruentia cum quadam coloris suavitate*). Where there is no proportion, the eye is offended, either because there is something lacking, or too small, or too large.'[77] The core idea of Augustine's theory is that beauty is the harmonious relationship of parts. He illustrates this in a manner that is readily understood: 'In the visible appearance of a man, if one eyebrow be shaved off, how nearly nothing is taken from the body, but how much from the beauty!—for that is not constituted by bulk, but by the proportion and arrangement of the members.'[78]

'Beauty is a good gift of God' (*bonum Dei donum*).[79] Augustine had a deep love and admiration for the beauty of creation, since it is what best reveals the creator; it is the clearest link between creatures and their creator. Radically all things are good, and therefore beautiful, because they are created. To the words of Genesis, 'God saw everything that he had made, and behold, it was very good', Augustine adds: 'We also see the same, and behold, all things are very good.'[80] Bringing matter into existence God simultaneously, in the same act, gives it form – a multiplicity of forms – and thereby beauty.[81] Through form each thing receives the integrity of its nature.

The principle of form is fundamental in Augustine's metaphysics and central to his understanding of beauty. Form gives the individual its unity, shape and identity; it thus lies at the heart of beauty. To have a form or species is to be beautiful: 'every corporeal creature is beautiful in its own way, for it is held together by form and species'.[82] Among the Latin words for beautiful are *speciosus* and *formosus*, derived from the words for 'shape' (*species*) and 'form' (*forma*). There is for Augustine a hierarchy of beauty, determined by the various grades of perfection constituted by form. God is the most perfect Form, possessing the perfections of all others and therefore perfectly beautiful. Created forms are more or less perfect according to varying degrees, and whatever is deprived of form is devoid of beauty.

Augustine's approach to beauty is all-embracing. There is a hierarchy of beauty rising from the most lowly inanimate physical object, through the scale of living things – plants, animals, humans –, surpassed by the beauties of the soul, its perfections and virtues, which point as a cipher to supreme Beauty itself. All levels have their appropriate place within the hierarchy regardless of individual defects or ugly particularities: 'All have their offices and limits laid down so as to ensure the beauty of the universe. That which we abhor in any part of it gives us the greatest pleasure when we consider the universe as a whole.'[83] At the zenith is the divine plenitude of supernatural beauty. The origin and essence of beauty, from which all beautiful things derive, is divine Beauty. 'All things are beautiful because you made them, but you who made everything are inexpressibly more beautiful (*et pulchra sunt omnia faciente te, et ecce tu inenarrabiliter pulchrior, qui fecisti omnia*).'[84] Augustine echoes Plato, moreover, when he addresses God: 'My father, supremely good, beauty of all things beautiful. O truth, truth!'[85] God is the beauty from whom is all beauty.[86]

PSEUDO-DIONYSIUS

One of the most significant treatises in the entire history of Western theology was composed by an unknown writer of the fifth century, who for authorial enhancement adopted the literary persona of first-century Dionysius the Areopagite (*c.*500), convert of Saint Paul. In his influential treatise *On Divine Names* the enigmatic writer contemplated the mystery of the unknown God and evaluated the language used to refer to the inscrutable divinity who transcends all thought and utterance. Another work, *Mystical Theology*, described the mystical union of the soul with the hidden divinity. These writings rapidly acquired universal esteem due to the presumed authority of the writer who as *primus inter patres* enjoyed quasi-apostolic authority. Not until the Renaissance was it discovered that the author of these rich treatises had drawn upon the writings of the Neoplatonist Proclus (+485), and hence could not have been the first bishop of Athens. The writings themselves, however, were genuinely profound and expertly penned, exhibiting an authority independent of their putative authorship. Aquinas, as all medieval authors, assumed Dionysius to be the disciple of St Paul and regarded his writings with great reverence. His most extensive comments on beauty occur in his commentary on the Pseudo-Areopagite's treatise *On Divine Names*. He adopted from Dionysius the identity of divine beauty and goodness, and inherited the author's emphasis on harmony and clarity as formal constituents of beauty.

Although Dionysius does not define beauty explicitly, it is clear from the important passage of *Divine Names* 4 that he regarded harmony and splendour as its most important characteristics. Other qualities of transcendent beauty are its plenitude and stability, both akin to the third characteristic listed by Aquinas, *integritas*. Caroline Canfield Putnam has suggested: 'From the hints given him by Denis, St Thomas has probably drawn his notion of *integritas, sive perfectio* which he presents as one of the three requisites of beauty.'[87] Our earlier accounts suggest that Aristotle and Augustine were more likely sources since they placed explicit emphasis on unity and perfection; Aquinas' genius was to combine diverse streams of influence into an original synthesis.

Dionysius' starting point and central intuition is that it is God's essence to be the infinite plenitude of goodness and beauty. There is no distinction in him between Beauty and the Good. God's beauty is identical with his goodness; both names are affirmed conjointly.[88] Following the positive path of divine names, God is called Good because through goodness he creates the world, and Beauty because everything he causes is beautiful. Goodness and Beauty are together the primary names attributed to God. In Chapter 4 of *On Divine Names* Dionysius elaborates upon the distinctive characteristics which these properties have in common, and notes their primary effects. God is through love the creative origin of all things, the source of universal harmony, and goal of all desire.[89] Dionysius' aim is to praise God as transcendentally good and beautiful, not to explain the human experience of beauty. Since, however, our knowledge of God can only be gained through perfections discerned in creation, and because our concept of beauty is given through experience, he refers to the beautiful effects of divine goodness; it is from these that we are led to affirm God's causal beauty. Dionysius also perceives beauty and goodness at the finite level as identical: 'There is nothing which lacks its own share of beauty, for as scripture rightly says, "Everything is good."'[90]

Beauty and Goodness are the ἀρχή and τέλος of all beings. Dionysius plays on the similarity of the word for beauty (κάλλος) with the word 'to call' (καλεῖν); the Good calls all things toward itself, wherefore it is called Beauty.[91] Beauty has the power of illumination, investing creatures with resplendence and lustre, constituting them as images of the absolute. Dionysius writes: 'The Good is praised by the sacred theologians as beautiful and as beauty, as love and as beloved, and with all other divine names as befit the source of loveliness and the flowering of grace.' (τῆς καλλοποιοῦ καὶ κεχαριτωμένης ὡραιότητος θεωνυμίαι).[92] The word 'beauty' used here by Dionysius, ὡραιότης, has a special connotation: originally denoting the bloom of youth or ripeness of fruit, it expresses here the fullness of divine beauty. Dionysius has taken a word from nature and given it a supernatural spiritual meaning.[93]

The infinitely Good, according to Dionysius, is not only 'beautiful' but is 'beauty' itself. There is no distinction in the all-embracing transcendent Cause between the quality 'beautiful' and the essence of 'beauty'. In the case of beings we may distinguish between the perfection as such considered in itself without restriction and the finite measure manifest in creatures which have a limited share; by contrast, infinite beauty is infinitely beautiful. Creatures are beautiful, but the transcendent source is Beauty itself; only as essential and absolute beauty can it cause beautiful things:

> The supraessential Beautiful is called 'Beauty' because of the beauty it bestows on all things, each according to its nature; and because it is cause of the harmony and splendour in all things (ὡς τῆς πάντων εὐαρμοστίας καὶ ἀγλαΐας αἴτιον, *universorum consonantiae et claritatis causa*), flashing forth as a light on them all the beautifying

transmissions of its fontal ray; it bids all things to itself (whence it is called 'beauty') and gathers all in all unto itself.[94]

The infinite Good–Beauty pre-contains 'supereminently within itself the fontal beauty of everything that is beautiful' (ὡς παντὸς καλοῦ τὴν πηγαίαν καλλονὴν ὑπεροχικῶς ἐν ἑαυτῷ προέχον).[95] In the simple and supernatural nature of all beautiful things, every beauty and everything beautiful causally pre-exist as one.[96] Dionysius repeats his reference to harmony: divine beauty and goodness are the source not only of harmonious proportion within a beautiful individual, but of the harmonious unity that pervades the entire universe. 'From this beauty comes the existence of all beings, each beautiful in its own manner; from beauty come the harmonies, sympathies and communities of all things (διὰ τὸ καλὸν αἱ πάντων ἐφαρμογαὶ καὶ φιλίαι καὶ κοινωνίαι); beauty unites all things.'[97]

Dionysius expresses the universal causality of Beauty in Aristotelian terms: 'Beauty is the principle (ἀρχὴ) of all things: as *efficient* cause (ποιητικὸν αἴτιον), moving and embracing the whole through love for its beauty; as the limit of all things and as desired; as *final* cause (τελικὸν αἴτιον), since all things come to be for sake of Beauty; as *exemplary* cause (παραδειγματικόν), since all things are determined (ἀφορίζεται) according to it.'[98] The Good, Dionysius states, 'gives form to the formless' (το ἀνείδεον εἰδοποιεῖ), thereby conferring beings with their perfection and intelligibility.[99] The lines immediately following, in which the identity of beauty and goodness are affirmed, and their exhaustive and comprehensive causation, are distinctively Platonic: 'Beauty is therefore the same as the Good, since all things in each mode of causality seek (ἐφίεται) the beautiful and the good; there is nothing among beings that does not share in the Beautiful and the Good.'[100] We may even say that 'nonbeing also shares in the Beautiful and the Good, because non-being, when applied transcendently to God in the sense of the denial of all things, is itself beautiful and good'.[101]

Of seminal significance for the subsequent tradition of Western aesthetics is Dionysius' identification of divine beauty with light, and his emphasis on its power of divine splendour. 'Thus the Good is also praised by the name "Light", just as an archetype is revealed in its image.'[102] Beauty is the illuminative presence and splendour of the Good, the clearest sensible paradigm for its all-infusive power and beneficence. Dionysius' use of the language and imagery of light is further evidence of profound Platonist influence.

When Dionysius states that transcendent Beauty is the cause of harmony, he has especially in mind the universal harmony among beings rather than the proportion between parts of a single individual – an aspect which, as we shall see later, was emphasized in his commentary by Aquinas. Dionysius affirms:

> From it derives the existence of everything as beings, what they have in common and what differentiates them, their identicalness and differences, their similarities and dissimilarities, their sharing of opposites, the way in which their ingredients maintain identity, the providence of the higher ranks of beings, the interrelationship of those of the same rank, the return upward by those of lower status, the protecting and unchanged remaining and foundations of all things amid themselves. Hence, the interrelationship of all things in accordance with capacity. Hence, the harmony and the love which are formed between them but which do not obliterate identity. Hence, the innate togetherness of everything. Hence, too, the intermingling of everything, the persistence of things, the unceasing emergence of things. Hence, all rest and hence, the stirrings of mind and spirit and body. There is rest for everything and movement for everything, and these come from that which, transcending rest and movement, establishes each being according to an appropriate principle and gives each the movement suitable to it (ἐφαρμογαὶ καὶ ἀσύγχυτοι φιλίαι καὶ ἁρμονίαι τοῦ παντός).[103]

It is important to note the empiricism of Dionysius. Despite his emphasis on the primacy of negative theology, and the superiority of the mystical knowledge of God, Dionysius recognizes that our knowledge of divine nature is necessarily grounded in experience, mediated through our grasp of created perfections as participations in a transcendent source. We only know of God what is revealed in the limited reflections of creaturely participations. All divine realities, even those revealed to us, are known through their participations; what they are in their origin and ground is beyond intellect, being and knowledge. When we give to the divine hiddenness such names as 'life', 'being', 'light' or 'word', our mind grasps only the powers (δυνάμεις) descending to us from the divinity which cause being, light and wisdom. We ourselves observe no life or being which resembles the absolutely transcendent Cause of all things.[104]

We have knowledge of participated perfections although we remain ignorant of the essential perfections themselves in their original plenitude. Although deficient such knowledge is necessary and valid: this is how God ordained things. There is a revealing passage in *The Celestial Hierarchy*, 1, 3:

> He modeled it on the hierarchies of heaven, and clothed these immaterial hierarchies in numerous material figures and forms so that, in a way appropriate to our nature, we might be uplifted from these most venerable images to interpretations and assimilations which are simple and inexpressible. For it is quite impossible that we humans should, in any immaterial way, rise up to imitate and to contemplate the heavenly hierarchies without the aid of those material means capable of guiding us as our nature requires. Hence any thinking person realizes that the appearances of beauty are signs of an invisible loveliness. The beautiful odours which strike the senses are representations of a conceptual diffusion. Material lights are images of the outporing of an immaterial gift of light... Order and rank here below are a sign of the harmonious ordering toward the divine realm.[105]

Beauty as a divine property is first disclosed, therefore, under the veil of material adornment. In this important passage Dionysius confirms that the initial experience of beauty is sensible and material. The renowned historian of aesthetics Władysław Tatarkiewicz is thus mistaken when he states that the aesthetics of the Pseudo-Dionysius was speculative, abstract, and removed from experience: 'Neither before nor since has there been an aesthetics more transcendental, more a priori, and more divorced from the real world and from normal aesthetic experience.'[106] That Dionysius, on the contrary, is well familiar with the devices of aesthetic experience is evident from the following corrective:

> We cannot, as mad people do, profanely visualize these heavenly and godlike intelligences as actually having numerous feet and faces. They are not shaped to resemble the brutishness of oxen or to display the wildness of lions. They do not have the curved beak of the eagle or the wings and feathers of birds. We must not have pictures of flaming wheels whirling in the skies, of material thrones made ready to provide a reception for the Deity, of multicolored horses, or of spear-carrying

lieutenants, or any of those shapes handed on to us amid all the variety of the revealing symbols of scripture. The Word of God makes use of poetic imagery when discussing these formless intelligences but, as I have already said, it does so not for the sake of art, but as a concession to the nature of our mind. It uses scriptural passages in an uplifting fashion as a way, provided for us from the first, to uplift our mind in a manner suitable to our nature. [107]

Because Dionysius is best known for his devotion to transcendent realities, there is a temptation to assume he had little interest in the material world: this would be incorrect. This strong empirical side is doubtless of Aristotelian origin. Thus we read in *The Celestial Hierarchy*:

> Forms, even those drawn from the lowliest matter, can be used, not unfittingly, with regard to heavenly beings. Matter, after all, owes its subsistence to absolute beauty and keeps, throughout its earthly ranks, some echo of intelligible beauty. Using matter, one may be lifted up to the immaterial archetypes. Of course one must be careful to use the similarities as dissimilarities, as discussed, to avoid one-to-one correspondences, to make the appropriate adjustments as one remembers the great divide between the intelligible and the perceptible.[108]

In accordance with the path of positive naming (which rises from visible effects to their invisible source) Dionysius states that the transcendent Beautiful is called 'Beauty' because it confers beauty on all things – on each according to its nature – and because it is the cause of harmony and splendour in all things. The transcendent Beauty, he states, flashes forth its rays of beauty to all things, and in return calls all things together in unity towards itself. The supraessential Beauty is thus both the source and end of all creatures, their efficient and final cause.

While he employs the language of Aristotelian causality, the influence of Plato is particularly evident in Dionysius' emphasis on the absolute character of divine beauty:

> And they name it beautiful since it is the all-beautiful and the beautiful beyond all. It is forever so, unvaryingly, unchangeably so, beautiful but not as something coming to birth and death, to growth

or decay, not lovely in one respect while ugly in some other way. It is not beautiful 'now' but otherwise 'then', beautiful in relation to one thing but not to another. It is not beautiful in one place and not so in another, as though it could be beautiful for some and not for others. Ah no! In itself and by itself it is the uniquely and the eternally beautiful (ἀλλ᾽ ὡς αὐτὸ καθ᾽ αὑτὸ μεθ᾽ αὑτοῦ μονοειδὲς ἀεὶ ὄν). It is the superabundant source in itself of the beauty of every beautiful thing.[109]

The passage borrows directly from Plato's *Symposium*:

First, it always *is* and neither comes to be nor passes away, neither waxes nor wanes. Second, it is not beautiful this way and ugly that way, nor beautiful at one time and ugly at another, nor beautiful in relation to one thing and ugly in relation to another; nor is it beautiful here but ugly there, as if it were beautiful for some people and ugly for others… It is not anywhere in another thing… but existing itself forever, by itself and with itself, it is eternally one in form (ἀλλ᾽ αὐτὸ καθ᾽ αὑτὸ μεθ᾽ αὑτοῦ μονοειδὲς ἀεὶ ὄν). All other beautiful things share in it, in such a way that while these come to be or pass away, it is neither diminished nor increased nor suffers any change.[110]

Dionysius exerted profound influence on Aquinas' theory of beauty. Dionysius' emphasis on the Platonist characteristics of harmony and splendour is an obvious source for two of Aquinas' constituents of beauty, *consonantia* and *claritas*. Aquinas' third requisite, *integritas*, although not specifically named, is also implicit in Dionysius' diagnosis of creatures. To state that the transcendent principle of Beauty confers beauty on each thing, in accordance with what it is in itself (οἰκείως ἑκάστῳ καλλονὴν),[111] indicates an interiority and selfhood within each creature which is aptly captured by the Latin *integritas*. The qualities of stability, plenitude, and constancy which mark the transcendent are likewise features of *integritas*.

THOMAS AQUINAS

As his pupil in Cologne, Thomas Aquinas (*c.*1225–1274) transcribed Albert's commentary on Dionysius' treatise *On Divine Names* and was doubtless influenced by his master, who defined beauty as the 'splendour of form shining on the proportioned parts of matter' – a definition that included the important elements of splendour, form and proportion.[112] Aquinas' most elaborate treatment of beauty is also to be found in his commentary on *The Divine Names*. Dispersed throughout many of his other works we find tangential remarks on beauty, *obiter dicta* in relation to diverse topics. Scholars have trawled his writings in an attempt to construct a Thomistic aesthetics. In so far as a comprehensive theory of beauty may be identified in Aquinas, it may be summarily expressed in the following assertions:

Pulchra enim dicuntur quae visa placent ('Those things are said to be beautiful which please when seen.')[113]

and

Ad pulchritudinem tria requiruntur: integritas, consonantia, et claritas ('Three things are required for beauty: integrity, harmony, and clarity'.)

The first statement is a nominal description of beautiful things, an empirical description or designation *per effectum* rather than an ontological explanation. The second is an analytic definition expounding the metaphysical properties or principles causing beauty. The first provides the subjective aspects of beauty as experienced, the second the objective elements which ground the experience.

According to Aquinas, God is the infinite essence of beauty, and every creature is in its own way beautiful. God is transcendent Beauty, beauty a universal quality of all creatures. Opinions are divided on the question whether or not Aquinas considered beauty a transcendental property of reality; at issue is the precise meaning of 'transcendental': does it suffice that beauty be coextensive with goodness and truth – and by implication with being –, or must it make explicit an added concept to the notion of 'being'?[114] Aquinas states unambiguously that both goodness and truth are transcendental qualities of being. 'Good' expresses a relation of reality to the will, 'truth' a relation to intellect. There is, however, no single faculty which has beauty as its unique and specific object; beauty is the joint object of the cognitive and appetitive faculties, and is therefore related to both goodness and truth. In *ST* I, 5, 4 ad 1 Aquinas states that beauty and goodness are in reality identical, since both are rooted in form: 'goodness properly relates to the appetite ... beauty relates to the cognitive faculty'. (*Bonum proprie respicit appetitum... Pulchrum autem respicit vim cognoscitivam.*)[115] This does not mean that beauty is simply goodness apprehended by intellect (that would abolish the distinction between *pulchrum* and *verum*), but is that which gives delight simply when known. When an individual is desired as good, its form functions as final end; when experienced as beautiful, form gives pleasure by the simple fact of being perceived. As Etienne Gilson notes, 'beauty relates to form as known, whereas goodness relates to form as desired'.[116]

It is important to clarify the significance for Aquinas of the metaphysical notion of form. *Forma* translates Aristotelian εἶδος and refers to the inner principle that determines the nature or essence of an individual; substantial form is the co-principle – along with prime matter – which constitutes the individual as a specific kind of substance. Together with the related term *species*, *forma* carries the connotation of beauty: *speciosa* and *formosa* both mean 'beautiful'. In order for something to be beautiful, it must first be complete in itself according to an appropriate nature: this is the function of *forma*. Form is not the outer shell or superficial shape of a thing, but its deepest and innermost defining element. It is the ontological root of a being's perfection, and the source of its intelligibility. Form is thus the ground of a being's existential and essential *integritas* as well as its intelligible *claritas*, since knowledge occurs through assimilation of form. Form is, moreover, the principle of organization whereby the parts of the individual are unified in harmonious *consonantia*. When something is determined within a particular species according to its appropriate form, it is by definition beautiful.[117]

Bonum and *pulchrum* are identical in reality but distinct in meaning. The good is that which is desired by the will and which, when possessed, satisfies the will; its nature is to calm the appetite when attained. By contrast it is the nature of beauty to appease the appetite simply by being known. The movement of the will towards the good is satisfied, its tendency arrested, when the object is possessed; the beautiful object, on the other hand, gives pleasure in the simple act of cognition, either sensory or intellectual. Desire and fulfilment are common to both: the good satisfies when possessed, beauty satisfies when apprehended. 'Beauty adds to the good a relation to the cognitive power (*vim cognoscitivam*), and hence that is said to be good which simply satisfies the appetite, while that is said to be beautiful, the mere apprehension of which pleases.'[118] To the attainment of goodness and the recognition of truth, beauty adds the experience of pleasure.[119]

Beauty is experienced in a cognitive act which begins in the senses but is fully achieved by intellect. When Aquinas defines *pulchrum* as '*id quod visum placet*', he understands *visio* to refer by extension not only to all sensual knowledge, but metaphorically to all knowledge whatsoever. He explains:

> Any word may be used in two ways – that is to say, either in its original application or in its more extended meaning. This is clearly shown in the word 'sight', originally applied to the act of the sense, and then, as sight is the noblest and most trustworthy of the senses, extended in common speech to all knowledge obtained through the other senses.[120]

All knowledge begins in the senses, but human knowledge is properly intellectual. There is increased intensity of pleasure as the experience of beauty deepens from the sensual to the intellectual. Beauty is indeed initially given to the senses but not fully grasped as such. While the senses enjoy a basic pleasure of physical beauty, they are incapable of grasping the deeper beauty-causing harmony that suffuses and governs a multiplicity of sense data distributed in space and time, such as a landscape or symphony. Beauty at its most complete and profound must be experienced intellectually. Aquinas asserts that only humans can grasp the beauty of sensible realities. Following Plato and Aristotle, he gives priority to sight and hearing as the 'most cognoscitive' (*maxime cognoscitivi*) of the senses, since they are closer to intellect.[121] Beauty pertains primarily to the audible and visible. Sight and hearing are better equipped than the other senses to minister to reason. We speak of beautiful sights and sounds but not of beautiful tastes and odours. Sight and hearing have a more profound and universal scope than taste, smell or touch, which require physical contact with the object of sensation. Sight is particularly praised for its greater universality: '[*Visus*] *est altior inter omnes sensus et universalior.*'[122] At the start of the *Metaphysics*, Aristotle states that we prize sight above the other senses because it is most revealing of the differences among the objects of experience.[123] Commenting on this passage, Aquinas states that it is the most knowing (*cognoscitivus*) of all our senses, hence the most spiritual, for the more immaterial a power is, the more perfectly it knows.[124] Sight has a special dignity; it is more spiritual and more subtle than any other sense.[125]

Beauty causes both sensual pleasure (*delectatio*) and intellectual delight (*gaudium*). Aquinas describes as natural love (*amor naturalis*) the movement of a faculty towards its connatural object; he distinguishes between sensitive and intellectual or rational love (*amor sensitivus vel intellectivus seu rationalis*).[126] Delight and pleasure are effected through the operation of sense and intellect: the more perfect the activity, the greater the delight.[127] Each faculty is perfected by objects proportionate to its capacity, and by the energy which actualizes it. There is an elemental pleasure in the simple experience of physical beauty. As Aquinas explains, 'the senses delight in things duly proportioned, as in what is after their own kind – because even sense is a sort of reason, just as is every cognitive faculty'.[128] There is thus a proportion and clarity proper to the sense faculties that perfects them in their activity The proper object of the intellect is the essential form of the known object: in grasping the form it is perfected in its operation; form is moreover the objective source of beauty.

Intellectual delight is superior to emotional pleasure;[129] while the senses can perceive harmony and *claritas*, they are unable to grasp relationships among diverse elements or proportions between one thing and another; this is unique to reason and intellect.[130] Aquinas thus asserts that only humans can enjoy sensible beauty: 'The senses are given to man, not only for the purpose of procuring the necessaries of life, for which they are bestowed on other animals, but also for the purpose of knowledge. Hence, whereas the other animals take delight in the objects of the senses only as ordered to food and sex, man alone takes pleasure in the beauty of sensible objects for its own sake.'[131] Aquinas explains elsewhere why beauty is properly the object of reason: 'Beauty consists in a certain clarity and due proportion. Now each of these has its roots in the reason, because the light that makes beauty seen, and the establishing of due proportion among things belongs to reason. Hence since the contemplative life consists in an act of the reason, there is beauty in it per se and essentially.'[132]

INTEGRITAS, CONSONANTIA, CLARITAS

Dionysius had explicitly noted *consonantia* and *claritas* as the properties of beauty; Aquinas adds *integritas*. In his commentary on the *Sentences* he cites Aristotelian magnitude as a third requirement to complement Dionysian harmony and lustre. In the *Summa* he prioritizes *integritas* instead. Although he includes it only once among the three required characteristics, it could be argued that integrity or perfection is the ground of the other two; I have suggested that the integrity of the individual is rooted in substantial form. Harmony or *consonantia* can only be fully present if the object is perfect in itself according to its nature. Likewise, at the deepest level, *claritas* requires perfection of the object or completeness of form. Intelligibility derives from the form of the individual as exemplar of the defining essence; the individual is understood by the abstractive assimilation of the form present in the material conditions.

Francis J. Kovach refers to integrity or perfection as the *formal principle* of beauty; and proportion, and clarity or splendour as its *material principles*.[133] Alternatively he refers to order as the 'synthetic principle' of beauty; and integrity, proportion, and clarity as its three 'analytical principles'.[134] He notes that Aquinas refers to order on its own in at least six texts on beauty; in eleven texts he refers to just one of the analytic principles; in six texts to two principles; and to all three in only three passages.[135] Despite the frequency with which the phrase '*tria requiruntur*' is cited as a resumé of his aesthetic theory, it is expounded in detail by Aquinas on only one occasion; this occurs, significantly, in a theological context, a fact often ignored by commentators. At *ST* I, 39 Aquinas asks if the Fathers of the Church have correctly assigned to the persons of the Blessed Trinity their essential properties or so-called 'appropriations': eternity, beauty, and joy. Aquinas refers to St Hilary, fourth-century bishop of Poitiers, who wrote: 'Nothing can be found lacking in that supreme union which embraces, in Father, Son and Holy Spirit, infinity in the eternal, his likeness in his image, our enjoyment in the gift.' (*Aeternitas in Patre, species in Imagine, usus in Munere*).[136] Having attributed eternity to the Father, Aquinas proceeds to explain why beauty is attributed to the Son, second member of the Trinity:

> Species or beauty has a likeness to the property of the Son. For beauty includes three conditions, 'integrity' or 'perfection', since things that lack something are by the very fact ugly; due 'proportion' or 'harmony'; and lastly, 'brightness' or 'clarity', whence things are called beautiful which have a bright colour.

> The first of these has a likeness to the property of the Son, inasmuch as he as Son has in himself truly and perfectly the nature of the Father (*habens in se vere et perfecte naturam patris*).

The second agrees with the Son's property, inasmuch as he is the express image of the Father (*imago expressa patris*). Hence we see that an image is said to be beautiful, if it perfectly represents even an ugly thing (*aliqua imago dicitur esse pulchra, si perfecte repraesentat rem, quamvis turpem*). This is indicated by Augustine when he says 'Where there exists wondrous proportion and primal equality' (*tanta convenientia, et prima aequalitas*), etc.

The third agrees with the property of the Son, as the Word, which is the light and splendour of the intellect (*quidem lux est, et splendor intellectus*), as Damascene says. Augustine alludes to the same when he says: 'As the perfect Word, not wanting in anything, and, so to speak, the art of the omnipotent God', etc.[137]

It is noteworthy that Aquinas at the outset introduces *pulchritudo* as the equivalent of *species*. With creative insight, Aquinas justifies Hilary's attribution of beauty to the second person of the Holy Trinity: Christ enjoys integrity or perfection because he 'has in himself truly and perfectly the nature of the Father' (*habens in se vere et perfecte naturam patris*). He has due 'proportion' or 'harmony' because 'he is the express image of the Father' (*imago expressa patris*), and has splendour or *claritas* since he is *Logos* or Word, signifying 'light and splendour of the intellect' (*quidem lux est, et splendor intellectus*).

Aquinas' statement '*Ad pulchritudinem tria requiruntur: integritas, consonantia, et claritas*' is correctly cited as his most comprehensive and satisfactory analytic definition of beauty. Most frequently he specifies only harmony and splendour, characteristics emphasized by Pseudo-Dionysius. In his early commentary on the *Sentences* of Peter Lombard, he omits integrity, but includes magnitude as stipulated by Aristotle. He states:

According to Dionysius, two things come together in the account of beauty, namely, consonance and lustre. For he says that God is the cause of all beauty insofar as he is the cause of consonance and lustre, just as we say that men are beautiful who have proportionate members and a resplendent colour. To these two the Philosopher adds a third when he says that beauty does not exist except in a sizable body; so that small men can be called well-proportioned and pretty, but not beautiful.[138]

It has been suggested that magnitude is the equivalent of *integritas*, but this is unconvincing; the concepts of *magnitudo* and *integritas* are distinct, Aquinas understands *integritas* as synomymous with *perfectio*.

AQUINAS' EMPIRICAL APPROACH TO BEAUTY

One of the few personal facts we know about Aquinas is that he was excessively corpulent. There is the dubious legend that he needed a circle cut into the table to allow him dine with comfort. Was he concerned with bodily appearance? It would be good to think that he was health-conscious, and appreciated that a healthy mind inhabits a healthy body. Was he vain? Given his legendary humility and piety, we may scorn the thought. In his prayer *Qua ad Caelum Adspirat* Aquinas, however, beseeches the Almighty to endow his body with 'beauty of splendour' (*da etiam corpori meo, largissime remunator, claritatis pulchritudinem*)![139] He is of course referring to the splendour of the glorified body (*claritas corporis gloriosi*). Aquinas' prayerful motivation is evidence against what in the past was a common charge – indeed a prejudice –, namely, that his philosophical theory of beauty lacked empirical foundation. It was supposed that he considered beauty in the abstract, applying an a priori definition, or merely transferred the notion of divine beauty to creatures. The charge does not fit well with his philosophic method since, as for his teacher Aristotle, it was axiomatic for Aquinas that knowledge necessarily begins in the senses. The sensible is a preamble to the intelligible;[140] only from sensible realities do we progress to a knowledge of the suprasensible.[141]

Aquinas states that the beauty of the body differs from that of the spirit, and differs for this and that body.[142] Throughout his writings we find multiple references to physical or sensible beauty. As an example of *claritas* he refers to the luminosity of the Milky Way.[143] He remarks in his early *Commentary on the Sentences* that beauty enhances the marriage union.[144] In his mature treatise *De Veritate* he gives the example of a woman who by reason of her beauty merits marriage to a king.[145] He notes that 'the home of a lord looks better in the city than in the country'.[146] In his Commentary on the *Nicomachean Ethics* Aquinas endorses Aristotle's statement that the pleasure of the eye is the beginning of love, suggesting that 'pleasure at the sight of a woman is the beginning of love for her, for no one begins to love a woman unless he has been first delighted by her beauty'.[147]

THE METAPHYSICS OF BEAUTY

Aquinas' most explicit and extended remarks on beauty are to be found in his commentary on *The Divine Names* of Pseudo-Dionysius, in which God is praised as identically the Good and Beauty. It is also his most profound treatment of the question, since he is dealing with the foundation of beauty, i.e. its origin in God and the relation between the divine plenitude of essential beauty and its limited participations in creatures. Beauty is affirmed as the original and ultimate reason and purpose for creation.

While Aquinas' commentary is an elaboration upon Dionysius' brief remarks, it is clear that he endorses the author's approach to beauty. The central element in their common teaching is the Platonically inspired theory of participation, according to which beauty is affirmed differently of God and creatures. God is essentially beautiful and is Beauty itself; creatures are beautiful through their participation in beauty. Aquinas explains that in God, who is first cause, 'the beautiful and beauty are not to be divided as if the beautiful is other than beauty, since the first cause alone through its simplicity and perfection comprehends the whole, i.e. all things, in one'. Thus while that which is beautiful, and the essence of beauty, are in creatures distinct, 'God comprehends both in himself as one and the same.'[148] The reason is that a beautiful creature has only a limited share in beauty: it is beautiful, but is not the essence of beauty, whereas God is not only beautiful, but is himself the essential plenitude of beauty. In creatures that which is beautiful and beauty itself are distinguished as participant and participated: the beautiful participates beauty, but beauty itself is a participation in the first cause that makes all things beautiful.[149] Participation is the metaphysical ground of similitude: the participant resembles the participated, since the effect resembles its cause; in causing the being of creatures, God imparts a share of his beauty.

Aquinas refers to the two primary characteristics of beauty which Dionysius[150] states are caused by God, harmony and clarity: 'And he shows in what the meaning of beauty consists, when he adds that God so transmits beauty in so far as God is "the cause of harmony and clarity (*causa consonantiae et claritatis*)" in all. Thus we call a man beautiful because of a fitting proportion in size and position, and because he has a bright and shining colour.'[151] Aquinas emphasizes the proportional character of beauty: 'It should be taken proportionately in other things that each thing is called beautiful according as it has clarity of its own genus whether spiritual or corporeal, and in so far as it is constituted in due proportion.'[152] Aquinas explains that, according to Dionysius, God causes *claritas* because he imparts, as with a flash, to all creatures a share of his luminous ray which is the fountain of all light. The flashing emissions of the divine ray are participations in his likeness; it is these radiations that produce beauty in things.[153]

To Dionysius' briefest mention of *consonantia*, Aquinas elucidates that God causes a twofold harmony in things: firstly by ordering ('calling') all creatures towards himself[154] and, secondly, by establishing mutual harmony among creatures towards each other.[155] God gathers together all in all (*congregat omnia in omnibus*) towards himself as their common and final end. This is to be understood in terms of Platonist participation: 'Higher things are in the lower by participation, and lower things in the higher through a certain excellence; thus all things are in all. Because all things are found in all according to a certain order, it follows that everything is ordered to the same final reality.'[156] A little later in his commentary Aquinas elaborates:

> It has been said that harmony (*consonantia*) belongs to the nature (*ratio*) of beauty, hence everything pertaining to harmony proceeds from divine beauty. And so he adds that through divine beauty there is concord among rational creatures in matters of intellect, for those who agree on the same opinion are in harmony. There is also friendship with regard to affection, and communion with regard to action and external matters. Universally all creatures, whatever union they have, they have by virtue of the beautiful.[157]

All harmony and concord among beings, their friendship, communion and unity, derive from the power of the beautiful. Divine beauty causes the existence of 'all the substantial essences' (πᾶσαι τῶν ὄντων αἱ οὐσιώδεις ὑπάρξεις),[158] not only in their unities or identities, but also in their differences and distinctions. Dionysius speaks of 'communions of contraries' and 'non-mixtures of unified things',[159] a *reconciliatio oppositorum* or unity of the similar and different. Even things that are dissimilar, Aquinas remarks, agree in some respect,[160] and ultimately all things lead back to the causality of the beautiful, exhibiting consonance, which is of the essence of beauty.[161] Most fundamentally all parts of the universe, Aquinas notes, agree by virtue of their existence, which is the profound source of their affinity and unity (*Omnes partes universi conveniunt in ratione existendi*).[162]

The beauty of the universe requires that there be diversity and gradation; a single being alone could not make manifest the infinite splendour of the Creator.[163] The universe constitutes an ordered and harmonious hierarchy, with due proportion and agreement among the various levels. Aquinas spoke of the 'wondrous connection of things' (*mirabilis rerum connexio*),[164] whereby the highest members of an inferior level touch the lower members of the next degree.[165] As harmony of sound results from a due proportion of number, the component parts of the universe are fitted together to result in a harmonious whole: 'From all the parts of the universe one totality of things (*una rerum universitas*) is constituted.'[166] Aquinas asserts that the 'highest beauty' (*summus decor*) of things is the order among distinct grades among creatures, even suggesting that the perfection of the universe (*perfectio universi*) arises from the ordered unification of evil and good things.[167]

The beauty of the universe consists in the harmony, proportion, order and mutual solidarity of beings infused with a shared desire for their unique and universal end. All creatures 'conspire' to produce universal concord and harmony, through due order and proportion.[168] The order of the universe (*ordo universi*) is for Aquinas 'the ultimate and noblest perfection in things' (*ultima et nobilissima perfectio in rebus*).[169] Thus while beauty is first experienced in the sensible appreciation of a physical body which presents itself to our senses with clarity and proportion, exhibiting its proper integrity or wholeness, the highest appreciation of beauty is contemplated in the universal harmony of all creatures as a unified universe. The beauty of the universe is more than that of individuals: it is their community. To form such a community they must be adapted towards one another. As the harmony of music is caused by due numerical proportion, so also the order of things in the universe. There is profound solidarity and affinity among all beings because of their common participation in the first perfection of existence. Creatures produce together a diapason of universal harmony.

Aquinas brings his unique metaphysical insight to bear on Dionysius' statement that the existence (*esse*) of all things comes from divine beauty (πᾶσι τοῖς οὖσι τὸ εἶναι), by explaining *claritas* as the effect of *esse*, measured through the form of the individual being which partakes of divine splendour:

Clarity is a feature of beauty, as has been said before. Every form, however, through which a thing has existence (*esse*) is a participation in divine brightness (*omnis autem forma, per quam res habet esse, est participatio quaedam divinae claritatis*). And he adds that individual things are beautiful according to their own nature, that is, according to their own form (*singula sunt pulchra secundum propriam rationem, idest secundum propriam formam*). Thus, it is obvious that the *esse* of all things comes from divine beauty.[170]

We may conclude from his commentary on *The Divine Names* that for Aquinas the beauty of a being is identical with its act of existing; beauty is not merely an ornament shimmering on the surface of things but is their very existence. In Chapter 4 of his commentary Aquinas states: 'The beauty of the creature is nothing other than the likeness of divine beauty participated in things.'[171] And in the following chapter he states: 'Created being itself (*ipsum esse creatum*) is a certain participation and likeness of God.'[172] Divine beauty is the source of existence in all things (*ex divina pulchritudine esse omnium derivatur*).[173] A being's existence is its beauty; its beauty is its existence. Each being is an irradiation of the divine brilliance, participating in divine being and beauty.[174]

Emphasizing the intimate connection between goodness and beauty, Aquinas refers to the importance of form: 'Nothing exists which does not participate in beauty and goodness, since each thing is beautiful and good according to its proper form.'[175] And again: 'A form is a certain irradiation coming forth from the first brightness; but brightness pertains to the essence of beauty.'[176] Etienne Gilson remarks, 'Everything is beautiful as having a form (through which it has *esse*), and this form is a sort of a participation of the divine clarity.'[177] The most important aspect or effect of beauty is brilliance or clarity. *Claritas*, or radiance, is the ontological splendour of form, which is the intelligible medium in which the actuality of existence is revealed. The ontological splendour of finite creatures shines through the brilliance of form. The bond between beauty and form may be understood in light of Aquinas' assertion in *Contra Gentiles* that 'form is nothing else than a divine likeness that is participated in things', citing Aristotle that form is 'something divine and desirable'.[178]

Aquinas emphasized the role of form as the ground of intelligibility, i.e. the intelligible clarity of the individual. Intellectual cognition is achieved through the assimilation of the intelligible form. So much Aquinas had in common with Aristotle, but he disagreed with Aristotle's doctrine that form or essence (*eidos, essentia*) is the deepest principle of actuality within the individual. Aquinas maintained that it is form which determines essence, but that of itself essence is powerless to be; it requires a deeper actualizing principle in order to exist. Form is the inner principle that determines what a thing is in its essence, but is itself in need of its own act of existing (*esse*) which causes it to be. Form is the instrumental medium through which the individual receives existence (hence beauty) according to a particular mode, but has of itself only potency towards existence. Aquinas deepened Aristotle's notion of actuality beyond that of form to affirm the actuality of existence, the act of being, *actus essendi*, which is denoted by the verbal infinitive, 'to be', Latin *esse*. Whereas for Aristotle the deepest level of actuality is a thing's form, determining its essence (*what* it is), for Aquinas the most profound and intimate actualizing principle is its act of being (*actus essendi*), which makes something be: not *what* it is, but in the first place to *exist*. It is this primordial, originative act, which is for Aquinas the real origin of a thing's *claritas*. He notes that 'the very actuality of a thing is as it were its light (*ipsa actualitas rei est quoddam lumen ipsius*)'.[179] Form, according to Aquinas, is the actualizing principle of essence, determining the material potency to be a certain *kind of thing*; it is the mediating principle, the measure through which a being receives its existence.[180] It is itself in turn, however, in need of actualization by the more primordial actuality of existence, the *actus essendi* or *esse*, which is the act of all acts and the perfection of all perfections.[181]

Esse, or *actus essendi*, is the radical source of beauty in all respects, since it is the cause of integrity, clarity, and harmony in each entity, and in the universal totality of beings. In his *Commentary on the Sentences* Aquinas stated: 'The integrity of a thing follows upon its primary perfection which is its very existence.'[182] It endows each individual with its interior unity and organic wholeness. It is the original *claritas* conferring the radiance of actuality, i.e. beauty as the luminous splendour of being. Diversified throughout a multiplicity of forms, it is the root of universal harmony among creatures, since existence is what all things have in common.

Commenting on Dionysius, Aquinas provides the radical reason for the very existence of the universe, namely God's love of his own beauty. A finite cause, he explains, acts in order to acquire something that it lacks, whereas a perfect cause acts out of love for what it possesses. The passage reads:

> An agent cause acts by virtue of a desire of the end, because it is an
> imperfect agent and does not yet possess what it desires. However, it

pertains to a perfect agent to act out of love for what it possesses, and for this reason Dionysius adds that Beauty itself which is God, is the efficient, moving and supportive cause, 'by love of its own beauty'. Since God possesses his own beauty, he wishes to multiply it as far as possible, namely through communication of his own likeness.[183]

Elaborating further on the causality of divine beauty, Aquinas explains that God is not only the efficient, but also the final and exemplary cause of all things. He is efficient cause because he gives to all things their *esse*, moving and preserving them in existence. God is final cause of the universe since 'all things are made so that they may imitate divine beauty in some way'. (*Omnia enim facta sunt ut divinam pulchritudinem qualitercumque imitentur.*)[184] He is also exemplary cause, 'for all things are distinguished in accord with the divinely beautiful, and a sign of this is that no one cares to make an image or representation, except for the sake of the beautiful'.[185] Aquinas touches here on the deepest reason for artistic creation, which he applies analogically to the creation of the world by the infinite artist. God creates the universe in order to share his beauty, and to draw us into the mystery of that gift. For Dionysius and Aquinas, divine beauty is the origin and purpose of creation: out of love for his beauty God multiplies it through the communication of his likeness. He makes all things, that they may imitate divine beauty. As Jacques Maritain remarks, 'There cannot in fact be any purely "gratuitous" work of art—the universe excepted.'[186]

* * *

All humans by nature delight in the beautiful. From time out of mind, in all cultures and in every tradition, beauty has enchanted hearts and fascinated minds. The Greek proverbs, τὸ καλὸν φίλον ('beauty is a friend'),[187] and χαλεπὰ τὰ καλά ('beautiful things are difficult'), seem at variance, yet convey together a profound truth. Easy to love, beauty cannot be properly defined; beyond explanation, it is the primitive gift. Beauty is that which simply pleases when known; our perception does not err. Kant rightly defined the beautiful as that which gives universally pleasure without a concept.[188] Beauty is spontaneously experienced, without theory or practise. It is that character of being which attracts through loving admiration, and simultaneously appeases the desire it awakens. According to Aquinas beauty evokes joyous love and intellectual delight; it ennobles and exhilarates. He commends Aristotle's assertion that one cannot live without pleasure: those who find no joy in spiritual delight look to pleasures of the body: 'Every human being loves beauty: carnal people love carnal beauty, spiritual people love spiritual beauty.'[189] He remarks that a person who without good reason abstains from all pleasures is as insensible as a rustic lout.[190]

Beauty is the highest aspect under which reality is experienced. We respond more immediately to the beautiful than to truth or goodness. Beauty embraces and exceeds the transcendental character of goodness and truth, which find in beauty their higher manifestation. Beauty adorns truth and goodness with a garland of glory. It is the luminous revelation of reality at its most sublime and profound. Beauty brings us into immediate community with the transcendent; the simplest material beauty is a cipher of the infinite and absolute. Etienne Gilson has remarked: 'The beautiful is a transcendental of being, and to approach being as such is always to reach the threshold of the sacred.'[191] Beauty is the joyful glory of being, whether in the most humble sense reality or the deepest spiritual experience. Charles Baudelaire commented: 'It is the admirable, immortal, instinctive sense of beauty that leads us to look upon the spectacle of this world as a glimpse, a correspondence with heaven. Our unquenchable thirst for all that lies beyond, and that life reveals, is the liveliest proof of our immortality.'[192]

Dostoevsky's character Prince Myshkin reportedly proclaimed that beauty alone would save the world.[193] Interrogating the phrase in his Nobel lecture, Alexander Solzhenitsyn asked, 'What sort of a statement is that? For a long time I considered it mere words. How could that be possible? When in bloodthirsty history did beauty ever save anyone from anything? Ennobled, uplifted, yes – but whom has it saved?' Solzhenitsyn pointed to a peculiarity in the essence of beauty, namely its 'convincingness': it 'bears within itself its own verification ... and forces even an opposing heart to surrender'. He concludes:

> So perhaps that ancient trinity of Truth, Goodness and Beauty is not simply an empty, faded formula as we thought in the days of our self-confident, materialistic youth? If the tops of these three trees converge, as the scholars maintained, but the too blatant, too direct stems of Truth and Goodness are crushed, cut down, not allowed through – then perhaps the fantastic, unpredictable, unexpected stems of Beauty will push through and soar to that very same place, and in

so doing will fulfil the work of all three? In that case Dostoevsky's remark, 'Beauty will save the world', was not a careless phrase but a prophecy?[194]

Another of Dostoevsky's characters declares: 'Mankind can live without science, can live without bread; only without beauty can it not live, for then there would be nothing at all to do in the world! The whole secret is here, the whole of history is here! Science itself would not exist for a moment without beauty.'[195] Beauty leads us indeed to the mystery of the universe. We love because we experience beings, especially persons, as beautiful, admired and loved for their own sake; our noblest ideals, deepest desires and loftiest aspirations find selfless pleasure in their intrinsic beauty. For the classical thinkers whom we have considered, the profound human impulse towards beauty was a cipher of a greater dimension of the cosmos. This assumed deeper meaning for Christian authors, for whom all existence derives from the infinite self-love of absolute Beauty who in a sharing of that love freely gifts to mankind a vestige of his being, a foregleam of infinite and eternal beauty.

ENDNOTES

1 Johann Wolfgang von Goethe, 'Epilog zu Schillers Glocke', *Werke* I (Hamburg: Wegner, 1952), p. 257.

2 R.W. Emerson, *Nature* (Boston, MA: Houghton Mifflin, 1903), p. 24.

3 Heraclitus, Frg. 102.

4 *Timaeus* 53b, *Lysis* 216d. See also the implied suggestion in *Theaetetus* 186a.

5 *Symposium* 211d, trans. W.R.M. Lamb (Cambridge, MA: Harvard University Press, 1939), p. 207.

6 *Lysis* 216cd, trans. W.R.M. Lamb (Cambridge, MA: Harvard University Press, 1939), p. 49.

7 James Joyce, *A Portrait of the Artist as a Young Man* (New York, NY: Norton, 2007), p. 183.

8 *Phaedrus* 146e: τὸ δὲ θεῖον καλόν, σοφόν, ἀγαθόν, καὶ πᾶν ὅ τι τοιοῦτον.

9 *Timaeus* 29a: εἰ μὲν δὴ καλός ἐστιν ὅδε ὁ κόσμος ὅ τε δημιουργὸς ἀγαθός.

10 *Philebus* 64e–65a, trans. H.N. Fowler (Cambridge, MA: Harvard University Press), pp. 389–91.

11 *Hippias Major* 297e–298a, trans. H.N. Fowler (Cambridge, MA: Harvard University Press, 1939), p. 399.

12 *Hippias Major* 287de: ἐρωτᾷ γάρ σε οὐ τί ἐστι καλόν, ἀλλ' ὅ τί ἐστι τὸ καλόν.

13 *Topics* 6, 7, 146a22.

14 *Cratylus* 416d, trans. H.N. Fowler (Cambridge, MA: Harvard University Press, 1939), p. 113.

15 *Phaedo* 250d, trans. H.N. Fowler (Cambridge, MA: Harvard University Press, 2001), p. 485, slightly modified.

16 See *Sophist* 228a.

17 *Timaeus* 87c, my trans., after Donald J. Zeyl, *Plato. Complete Works*, ed. John M. Cooper (Indianapolis, IN: Hackett, 1997), p. 1286.

18 *Timaeus* 87e, trans. R.G. Bury, (Cambridge, MA: Harvard University Press, 1929), p. 239.

19 See Francis J. Kovach, *Philosophy of Beauty* (Norman, OK: University of Oklahoma Press, 1974) p. 217.

20 *Timaeus* 87cd, trans. Bury, pp. 237–9.

21 *Timaeus* 87de.

22 *Timaeus* 88cd.

23 *Timaeus* 88c: εἰ μέλλει δικαίως τις ἅμα μὲν καλός, ἅμα δὲ ἀγαθὸς ὀρθῶς κεκλῆσθαι. Trans. Bury, p. 241, modified.

24 See *Phaedo* 100cd.

25 Diogenes Laertius 5, 1, 20: πρὸς τὸν πυθόμενον διὰ τί τοῖς καλοῖς πολὺν χρόνον ὁμιλοῦμεν, τυφλοῦ, ἔφη, τὸ ἐρώτημα.

26 *Metaphysics* (= *Met.*) 5, 1, 1013a22, trans. Hugh Tredennick (Cambridge, MA: Harvard University Press, 1933), p. 211.

27 *Met.* 13, 3, 1078a32.

28 *Rhetoric* 1, 9, 1366a33–5, trans. Rhys Roberts in *The Complete Works of Aristotle* (*CW*), ed. Jonathan Barnes (Princeton: Princeton University Press, 1991), vol. 2, p. 2174, and John Henry Freese, (Cambridge, MA: Harvard University Press, 1926), p. 91.

29 *Nicomachean Ethics* (= *NE*) 4, 2, 1122a34–1122b10, trans. David Ross, *CW*2, p. 1771.

30 *NE* 4, 2, 1122b15–18. I follow the original Ross translation rather than *CW*2.

31 *NE* 4, 3, 1125a11–12, trans. W.D. Ross, *CW*2, p. 1775.

32 *NE* 3, 7, 1115b12–13.

33 *Pol.* 1, 5, 1254b38–9, trans. Jowett, *CW* 2, p. 1991.

34 *Met.* 13, 3, 1078a36–78b5, trans. Hugh Tredennick, (Cambridge, MA: Harvard University Press, 1962), p. 193.

35 *Politics* 3, 8, 1284b8–13, trans. H. Rackham, (Cambridge, MA: Harvard University Press, 2005) p. 245.

36 For Aristotle on the beauty of nature see *Parts of Animals* 1, 5, 645a16–26.

37 *Generation of Animals* 2, 731b24–7.

38 *Met.* 12, 7, 1072b32–4.

39 *Met.* 5, 16, 1021b12–1022a1, trans. Ross, *CW* 2, p. 1613, slightly amended.

40 *Poetics* 7, 1450b34–1451a12, trans. Stephen Halliwell, (Cambridge, MA: Harvard University Press, 2005), pp. 55–7.

41 *NE* 4, 3, 1123b7–8, trans. Ross, *CW* 2, p. 1773. See Aquinas, *In I Sent.*, dist. 31, q. 2, a. 1.

42 *Pol.* 7, 4, 1326a29–b2, trans. Jowett, *CW* 2, p. 2105.

43 *Met.* 5, 6, 1016b11–16. I follow the original translation by Ross.

44 *Rhetoric* 1, 5, 1361b7–14, trans. Freese, p. 55.

45 *Ennead* I 6 [1] 1. 1–6, trans. Andrew Smith (Las Vegas, NV: Parmenides, 2016), p. 45.

46 I 6 [1] 1. 20–5, trans. Smith, p. 46.

47 I 6 [1] 1. 25–30, trans. Smith, p. 46.

48 I 6 [1] 1. 38–40, trans. Smith, p. 47.

49 I 6 [1] 6. 11–32.

50 V 8 [31] 1. 7–19.

51 V 8 [31] 2. 14–15, trans. Andrew Smith, (Las Vegas, NV: Parmenides, 2016), p. 46, modified.

52 VI 7 [38] 22. 5–12, trans. A.H. Armstrong (Cambridge, MA: Harvard University Press, 1988), vol. 7, pp. 155–7.

53 VI 7 [38] 22. 25–27, trans. Armstrong, p. 157.

54 VI 7 [38] 22. 27–34, trans. Armstrong, pp. 157–9.

55 I 6 [1] 2. 13–15, trans. Smith, p. 48.

56 I 6 [1] 2. 18–23, trans. Smith, pp. 48–9.

57 V 8 [31] 13. 22, trans. Smith, p. 68, modified.

58 IV 8 [31] 6. 23–4, trans. A.H. Armstrong (Cambridge, MA: Harvard University Press, 1984), vol. 4, p. 417.

59 V 1 [10] 2. 20–2, trans. Lloyd Gerson (ed.) (Cambridge: Cambridge University Press, 2018), p. 535.

60 *De Musica* 6, 13, 38.

61 *Sermo* 19, 5.

62 *Confessiones* 4, 13, 20, trans. J.G. Pilkington in *Basic Writings of Saint Augustine* I, ed. Whitney J. Oates (New York, NY: Random House, 1948), p. 52.

63 *De Genesi Contra Manichaeos* 1, 16, 26.

64 *Sermo* 241, 2. St Augustine, *Sermons on the Liturgical Seasons*, III/7 (230–272B), trans. Edmund Hill, O.P. (New Rochelle, NY: New City Press, 1993), p. 71.

65 *Conf.* 10, 27, 38, *trans.* Henry Chadwick (Oxford: Oxford University Press, 1991), p. 201, slightly modified.

66 *Conf.* 4, 13, 20, trans. Pilkington, p. 52.

67 See Montague Brown, 'Augustine on Beauty, Number, and Form', *Studia Patristica* 43 (Leuven: Peeters, 2006), pp. 33–8.

68 *De Vera Religione* 40, 76, trans. John H.S. Burleigh, Augustine, *Earlier Writings*, (London: SCM, 1953), p. 264.

69 *De Genesi contra Manichaeos* 1, 21, 32, trans. Ronald J. Teske, SJ, *Saint Augustine. On Genesis* (Washington, DC: Catholic University of America Press, 1991), p. 80.

70 *De Vera Religione* 41, 77.

71 *Epistula* 7.

72 *De Musica* 6, 13, 38.

73 *De Libero Arbitrio* 2, 16, 164, trans. Anna S. Benjamin & L.H. Hackstaff, Saint Augustine, *On Free Choice of the Free Will* (Englewood Cliffs, NJ: Prentice Hall, 1964), p. 73.

74 Brown, p. 34.

75 *De Vera Religione* 30, 55, trans. Burleigh, p. 252.

76 Cicero, *Tusculanae Disputationes* IV, 31. See *Tusculan Disputations*, trans. J.E. King (Cambridge, MA: Harvard University Press, 1989), pp. 358–60.

77 *De Civitate Dei* 22, 19, trans. Marcus Dods, in *Basic Writings of Saint Augustine* II, ed. Whitney J. Oates (New York, NY: Random House, 1948), p. 640, slightly modified.

See *Epistulae* 3, 4: Quid est corporis pulchritudo? Congruentia partium cum quadam coloris suavitate.

78 *De Civitate Dei* 11, 22, trans. Dods, p. 163.

79 *De Civitate Dei* 15, 22.

80 *Conf.* 13, 28, 340. See *Genesis* 1.31.

81 *Conf.* 13, 33, 344. See also *De Vera Religione* 18, 36, and *Genesi ad Litteram* I, 1, 15: 29.

82 *De Vera Religione* 20, 40, trans. Burleigh, p. 244.

83 *De Vera Religione* 40, 76, trans. Burleigh, p. 264.

84 *Conf.* 13, 20, 28, trans. Chadwick, p. 289.

85 *Conf.* 3. 6, 10: Mi pater summe bone, pulchritudo pulchrorum omnium. O veritas, veritas. Trans. Pilkington, p. 33.

86 *Liber de Diversis Quaestionibus* 83, q. 44: Quia omne pulchrum a summa pulchritudine est, quod Deus est.

87 Caroline Canfield Putnam, *Beauty in the Pseudo-Denis* (Washington, DC: Catholic University of America, 1960), p. 88n89.

88 See *On Divine Names* (= *DN*) 4, 7, 704B, 141–2; 4, 8, 704D, 147; 4, 9, 705A, 148; 4, 10, 705B–708A, 151–5); 4, 18, 713D, 185. References are to chapter, paragraph, *Patrologia Graeca* III, and Greek text in Thomas Aquinas, *In Librum Beati Dionysii De Divinis Nominibus* (= *In DN*), ed. Ceslas Pera (Turin: Marietti, 1950).

89 Dionysius treats of beauty in chapter 4 of *On Divine Names*. See *DN* 4, 7–8, 701C–704D, 132–48; *DN* 4, 10, 705B–708B, 151–9.

90 *Celestial Hierarchy* (= *CH*) 141C, trans. Colm Luibheid, *Pseudo-Dionysius. The Complete Works* (New York, NY: Paulist Press, 1987).

91 *DN* 4, 7, 701C, 135. Dionysius here relies on Plato's *Cratylus* 416c.

92 *DN* 4, 7, 701C, 134.

93 Putnam, pp. 17–18.

94 *DN* 4, 7, 701C, 135, trans. C.E. Rolt (London: SPCK, 1972), p. 95, modified.

95 *DN* 4, 7, 704A, 138, trans. Rolt, p. 96, modified.

96 Ibid.

97 *DN* 4, 7, 704A, 139, my trans. after Luibheid.

98 *DN* 4, 7, 704AB, my trans.

99 *DN* 4, 3, 697A, 111.

100 *DN* 4, 7, 704AB, 141, my trans.

101 *DN* 4, 7, 704B, 141, trans. Luibheid.

102 *DN* 4, 4, 697BC, 113, trans. Luibheid.

103 *DN* 4, 7, 704BC, 143–5, trans. Luibheid.

104 *DN* 2, 7, 645AB, 56.

105 *CH* 1. 3, 121C–124A, trans. Luibheid.

106 Władysław Tatarkiewicz, *History of Aesthetics*, vol. 2. *Medieval Aesthetics* (The Hague: Mouton, 1970), pp. 27–8.

107 *CH* 2, 1, 137AB, trans. Luibheid. See also the continuation of this important passage, 137B–D.

108 *CH* 2, 4, 144BC, trans. Luibheid.

109 *DN* 4, 7, 701C–704A, 136–8, trans. Luibheid.

110 *Symposium* 210e–211b, trans. Alexander Nehamas and Paul Woodruff, *Plato. Complete Works*, ed. Cooper, p. 493, modified.

111 *DN* 4, 7, 701C, 135.

112 Albertus Magnus, *Super Dionysium De Divinis Nominibus*, ed. Paul Simon (Münster: Aschendorff, 1972), Cap. 4, § 72, p. 182.

113 *ST* I, 5, 4 ad 1. For an alternative formulation see *ST* I-II, 27, 1 ad 3: *Pulchrum autem dicatur id cuius ipsa apprehensio placet.* ('Beauty is said to be that, the very apprehension of which pleases').

114 See Francis J. Kovach, *Scholastic Challenges to Some Mediaeval and Modern Ideas* (Stillwater, OK: Western, 1987) p. 89: 'There are two reasons for calling beauty a unique transcendental. For beauty is the only relative transcendental of two termini (the intellect and the will) and the only transcendental that includes all the other transcendentals.'

115 *ST* I, 5, 4 ad 1: Aquinas repeats verbatim his distinction between *pulchrum* and *bonum* in his commentary on *The Divine Names*. See *In DN* IV, v, 356: Quamvis autem pulchrum et bonum sint idem subiecto, quia tam claritas quam consonantia sub ratione boni continentur, tamen ratione differunt: nam pulchrum addit supra bonum, ordinem ad vim cognoscitivam illud esse huiusmodi.

116 Etienne Gilson, *The Elements of Christian Philosophy* (New York, NY: Mentor-Omega, 1963), p. 175.

117 *Formosa* ('finely formed', 'shapely'), is synonymous with *pulcher;* Cicero coined the word *formositas* for beauty. Formosa is the former name of the island of Taiwan, so called by Portuguese sailors who, when they sighted the island in 1542, referred to it as *Ilha Formosa*, 'beautiful island'. The Modern Greek word for 'ugly' is άσχημος, literally 'unformed'.

118 *ST* I-II, 27, 1 ad 3.

119 See *ST* II-II, 145, 2 ad 1.

120 *ST* I, 67, 1.

121 Iᵃ-IIae q. 27 a. 1 ad 3. See Jacques Maritain, *Art and Scholasticism and The Frontiers of Poetry* (New York, NY: Scribner, 1962), p. 23. See Plato, *Hippias Major* 297e–98a.

122 *Quaestio Disputata De Anima*, art. 13: Unde visus est altior inter omnes sensus et universalior. See also *In Psalmos* 44, 2; *In 2 de Anima*, lect. 14, 417–8; *In 3 de Anima* lect. 6, 668: Dicit ergo quod visus est praecipuus inter alios sensus, eo quod est spiritualior; *Summa Contra Gentiles* (=*CG*) 3, 53, 2302; *ST* I, 91, 3 ad 3. (Unless otherwise stated, references are to the Marietti editions of Aquinas.) Augustine conveys the thoughts of both Plato and Aristotle by noting that vision and hearing are most noble, resembling reason to some extent in grasping their objects as wholes. See *De ord.* 2, 11, 32–3; *De lib. arb.* 2, 7, 16–19; 14, 38.

123 *Met.* 1, 1, 980a1–4.

124 *In 1 Metaph.*, lect. 1, 5–9.

125 *In 2 De Anima*, lect. 14, 415–18.

126 *ST* I-II, 26, 1.

127 *ST* I-II, 32, 1; also I, 4, 1; I-II, 3, 2.

128 *ST* I, 5, 4 ad 1.
129 See *ST* I-II, 31, 4 ad 3.
130 *ST* II-II 58, 4c.
131 *ST* I 91, 3 ad 3.
132 *ST* II-II 180, 2 ad 3, trans. Fathers of the English Dominican Province, *The Summa Theologica* II (Chicago, IL: Encyclopaedia Britannica, 1984), p. 609.
133 Kovach, *Philosophy of Beauty*, p. 162.
134 Ibid., p. 163. See *In DN* IV, xxi, 554: Requiritur enim ad pulchritudinem et claritatem forma et commensuratio quae ad ordinem pertinet.
135 Francis J. Kovach, *Die Ästhetik des Thomas von Aquin* (Berlin: De Gruyter, 1961), p. 105n8.
136 *ST* I, 39, 8, obj. 1: 'Dicit enim Hilarius, Aeternitas est in Patre, species in imagine, usus in munere.'
137 *ST* I, 39, 8.
138 *In I Sent.* 31, 2, 1, sol. and ad 4.
139 *Opuscula Theologica* II, p. 288: Da etiam corpori meo, largissime remunator, claritatis pulchritudinem, agilitatis promptitudinem, subtilitatis aptitudinem, impassibilitatis fortitudinem. See *The Aquinas Prayer Book. The Prayers and Hymns of St. Thomas Aquinas*, translated and edited by Robert Anderson and Johann Moser (Manchester, NH: Sophia Institute Press, 2000), pp. 52–3. On the glorified body see *ST* III, 45, 2; *ST* Suppl. 85, 2.
140 *In DN* IV, ix, 414.
141 For references see Francis J. Kovach, *Scholastic Challenges*, p. 203n11: Aristotle: *Post. An.* 2, 19, 100a3–14; *Met.* 1, 1, 980a28–981a12; Thomas: *In 2 Post. An.*, lect. 20, n592; *In 1 Met.*, lect. 1, nn 10–17; *In 1 Post. An.*, lect. 42, n 378, and lect. 30, n 251.
142 *In DN* 4, 5, 339: Alia enim est pulchritudo spiritus et alia corporis, atque alia huius et illius corporis.
143 *Super Meteora*, lib. 1 cap. 12 n. 3.
144 *In III Sent.* 2, 2, 1, 92.
145 *De Ver.* 26, 6.
146 *In Psalm.* 18, 3.
147 *In 9 Eth*, l. 5, n 1824.
148 *In DN* IV, v, 336.
149 *In DN* IV, v, 337.
150 *DN* 4, 7, 701C, 135.
151 *In DN* IV, v, 339.
152 *In DN* IV, v, 339.
153 *In DN* IV, v, 340.
154 Aquinas cites Dionysius' etymological explanation of the word for beauty (κάλλος) deriving from the word καλεῖν, 'to call'.
155 *In DN* IV, v, 340.
156 *In DN* IV, v, 340.
157 *In DN* IV, v, 349.
158 *DN* 4, 6, 704B, 143.

159 *DN* 4, 6, 704B, 144.

160 *In DN* IV, vi, 361: Dissimilia in aliquo conveniunt.

161 *In DN* IV, vi, 361.

162 *In DN* IV, vi, 364.

163 *CG* 3, 97, 2724. See Fran O'Rourke, *Pseudo-Dionysius and the Metaphysics of Aquinas* (Notre Dame, IN: University of Notre Dame Press, 2005), pp. 261–8.

164 *CG* 2, 68, 1453.

165 *De Spiritualibus Creaturis*, art. 2; *CG* 2, 91, 1775. See O'Rourke, p. 264.

166 *In DN* IV, vi, 364, trans. James F. Anderson, *An Introduction to the Metaphysics of St Thomas Aquinas* (Chicago, IL: Regnery, 1953), p. 97.

167 *CG* 3, 71.

168 *In DN* VII, iv, 733.

169 *CG* 2, 45.

170 *In DN* IV, v, 349.

171 *In DN* IV, iv, 337.

172 *In DN* V, ii, 660.

173 *In DN* IV, v, 349.

174 *In DN* IV, v, 340.

175 *In DN* IV, v, 355.

176 *In DN* IV, vi, 360.

177 Gilson, *Elements*, p. 177.

178 *CG* 3, 97.

179 *In Librum De Causis*, lect. 6, 168. According to Aristotle the certainty of knowledge is grounded in actuality. See *Met.* 9, 10, 1051b25–32.

180 *ST* I, 77, 6.

181 See the celebrated passage of *De Potentia* 7, 2 ad 9: Hoc quod dico esse est actualitas omnium actuum, et propter hoc est perfectio omnium perfectionum.

182 *In IV Sent.* 26, 2, 4: Integritas attenditur secundum perfectionem primam, quae consistit in ipso esse rei.

183 *In DN* IV, v, 352.

184 *In DN* IV, v, 353: Omnia enim facta sunt ut divinam pulchritudinem qualitercumque imitentur.

185 *In DN* IV, v, 354.

186 Jacques Maritain, *Art and Scholasticism and The Frontiers of Poetry* (New York: Scribner, 1962), p. 73. See *Art et Scolastique* (Paris: Rouart, 1927), p. 125: 'Il ne peut pas y avoir d'oeuvre d'art purement "gratuite", – l'univers excepté.'

187 *Lysis* 216c.

188 Immanuel Kant, *Critique of the Power of Judgment*, trans. Paul Guyer (Cambridge: Cambridge University Press, 2006), p. 104: 'That is beautiful which pleases universally without a concept.' See *Kritik der Urteilskraft* in *Kants Werke V* (Berlin: de Gruyter, 1968), p. 219: 'Schön ist das, was ohne Begriff allgemein gefällt.'

189 Aquinas, *In Psalmos Davidis Expositio*, 25, 5: Bonum et pulchrum est omnibus diligibile. Unde omnis homo amat pulchrum carnales amant pulchrum carnale, spirituales amant pulchrum spirituale.

190 *ST* II-II 152, 2 ad 2: Ad secundum dicendum quod ille qui abstinet ab omnibus delectationibus praeter rationem rectam, quasi delectationes secundum se abhorrens, est insensibilis, sicut agricola.

191 Etienne Gilson, *The Arts of the Beautiful* (New York, NY: Scribner, 1965), p. 182.

192 Charles Baudelaire, *Selected Writings on Art and Artists* (Cambridge: Cambridge University Press, 1981), p. 204.

193 Fyodor Dostoevsky, *The Idiot*, trans. Alan Myers (Oxford: Oxford University Press, 2008), p. 402.

194 https://www.nobelprize.org/prizes/literature/1970/solzhenitsyn/lecture/ (Accessed 5 October 2018).

195 Fyodor Dostoevsky, *Demons*, trans. Richard Pevear and Larissa Volokhonsky (London: Vintage, 1994), p. 486 (adapted).

THE MANIFESTATION OF GOD AS THE SPEAKING OF CREATION IN SCOTTUS ERIUGENA

DEIRDRE CARABINE

INTRODUCTION

In this essay, I wish to examine a number of closely interlinked concepts, all focused on the notion of God's creation explicated in the *Periphyseon* of the ninth-century Irish philosopher-theologian John Scottus Eriugena. Despite serious scholarly detective work, little is known of his life except that he was born in Ireland and was a scholar, poet and translator (from Greek to Latin), working at the Court of Charles the Bald in France. While a 'likeness' did feature on an Irish five-pound note prior to the introduction of the euro, he is still not widely known or appreciated in the land of his birth, despite the influence he was to exert on later theological thought in the Latin West, not only in his own right but through his translations of the works of the Pseudo-Dionysius.

Before examining the concept of creation in Eriugena, I begin with a word of caution: the pre-suppositions with which we approach any thinker of the medieval period – some of them new and some undoubtedly centuries old – need to be kept in mind. While it is impossible to strip away the layers of the intervening centuries, neither can we interpret the ideas of the ancients in the mindset of the present – especially with regard to negative theology, a task begun some decades ago by Jacques Derrida and continued by many others since. While the new take on Dionysius and negative theology has excited and inspired many, and reading Dionysius, Eriugena, and others through a different lens can be invigorating, to remove their ideas from their original contexts can constitute an injustice.[1]

One of the earliest scholars of Eriugena writing in English famously noted that he was the loneliest figure in the history of medieval thought; to those preoccupied with the genesis of his ideas, he was a striking Greek 'moment' in the history of western scholasticism.[2] While these views are finally being laid to rest through a new understanding of the Irishman as an original thinker (albeit standing on the shoulders of those who went before him into uncharted waters), nevertheless, there remains a lingering cloud of suspicion over those who, in the past, have dared to be original, to step outside the hegemony of the day. This, most certainly, is what Eriugena did when bringing together ideas from the Greek East and the Latin West, broadly classified as Dionysius the Areopagite, Maximus the Confessor, and Gregory of Nyssa on the one hand, and Ambrose, Boethius, Augustine and the canon of the day on the other.[3] And we should not forget that both sets of sources relied on different forms of Platonism: the Latin West on Plotinus and the Greek East on Proclus. This is what makes Eriugena's voice different from many of those who have sung in the choir of theology. As Hilary Mooney notes: 'It is indeed one of his greatest gifts to posterity to have transferred these themes (unknowableness of God, Christocentric anthropology, and *theosis*) with their Eastern nuances to the Carolingian world.'[4] His originality, sadly, meant that Eriugena's majestic work on nature suffered various condemnations and, for a time, was marginalized in later medieval thought. Although, like all things prohibited, it survived under the radar, so to speak, and we find his writings, ideas and translations re-surfacing in the twelfth and thirteenth centuries, finding a modified voice in the writings of the Victorines and Bonaventure among others.[5]

The central thematic I wish to develop in this essay is the idea that creation is the speaking of the thought that exists eternally in the Word. Eriugena's rigorously pursued negative theology, derived from his reading primarily of the Pseudo-Dionysius, results in the logical conclusion that creation is the simultaneous revelation and concealment of God (at both the human and divine levels). In this sense, a negative theology and negative anthropology are central to Eriugena's understanding of creation as theophany, i.e. of creation as the 'showing of God'.[6]

NATURA IN THE *PERIPHYSEON*

Although much of Books III and IV of the *Periphyseon* constitute a fascinating hexaemeron, i.e. commentary on the biblical account of the six days of creation, the whole work is as wonderful and stimulating an account of reality as are the mighty *Enneads* of Plotinus. Like Origen before and Aquinas after him, Eriugena set out to map and explicate the entire process of reality and, in so doing, came to some startling conclusions. Our current understanding of the world (and the way we see it at all levels) is, of course, coloured by recent innovations, technological and other. As humanity journeys further into the twenty-first century, we appear to have reached a new high in the human conquering of the world, a high that continues to perpetuate the idea of Francis Bacon, who declared that through science, nature's secrets would be laid bare for all humanity to probe and exploit. But, dare I say that in gaining all this knowledge, we appear to have lost the sense of marvel that lies at the heart of reality? Eriugena, living in a very different world, presents us with another understanding of reality – one that continually points up the mystery of all things – which appears to be contradictory: on one level nature is wholly unknowable, and yet it is, at the same time, at least partially knowable. Creation cloaks God with a veil of obscurity while at the same time it is revelatory of God. The aporias resulting from our *duplex theoria* ('double contemplation', our different way of looking at reality) accurately pinpoint the contradictory and complex nature of realities. I return to this point below.

For Eriugena, *natura* is simply everything: God, angels, humans, and all else – the oneness of the myriad aspects of reality is central in Eriugena's thought. The long shadows of Plotinus, Proclus, and Dionysius are most certainly cast over him as we find our Irishman grappling with the fundamental categories of being and non-being, both of which he discusses under the genus *natura*, which becomes a study of how the unknowable God is revealed through creation while at the same time remaining hidden and obscure. *Natura*, then, is 'all things that are and are not',[7] an initial comprehensive packaging of everything into a 'system', for want of a better word, that forms a fundamental way of interpreting and describing reality, all reality. It is thus that Eriugena begins his exploration of how the uncreated creator, through the primordial causes in the Word, begins a journey of self-manifestation.

In an attempt to unpack *natura* and tell the story of creation, Eriugena explains the four comprehensive divisions as the lens through which he will explicate reality: that which creates and is not created (God), that which creates and is created (the Primordial Causes, the ideas of all things that exist eternally in divine Wisdom), that which is created and does not create (human nature), and that which is uncreated and does not create – that to which all things will eventually return (III 621A–622A).[8] The fourth division (that which is not created and does not create) has been the focus of some debate: if it neither creates nor is created, then logically it cannot be (I 442A). However, Eriugena's way of thinking about and expressing the mystery at the heart of all reality is not bound by the logic of language and thought (although it is constrained by the limits of rationality). Our *duplex theoria* tends to conceive of God in relation to created reality that has a beginning and an end, thus making a distinction in relation to God's nature. In contemplating *natura* in its comprehensiveness, the human mind, through *divisoria* and *resolutiva*, echoes the rhythm of creation itself that is in eternal movement from God and back to God. In the *Periphyseon*, we understand God as both creator and not creator in the sense of the first and fourth divisions of nature. But there is a fundamental sense in which this is not the only way of thinking about God and not-God.

The subtle dialectic operative in Eriugena's thought is not easily explained, because the bottom line is that created reality *is* the manifestation of God. It is in this way that Eriugena's conception of the universe is theocentric because all that is really is the manifestation of the unmanifest, and the tremendous diversity of the universe remains a fundamental unity. All differences, however, are not in some way resolved into sameness: it is precisely because they are different that they form a unity in their source. The procession of God into created effects means that all things have the one primordial cause, all things have the same beginning, and ultimately, all will have the same end. All things are, therefore, bound together in the unity of their cause: 'The beauty of the whole established universe consists of a marvellous harmony of like and unlike ... an ineffable unity.' (III 638A) This unity is not a synthesis resulting from strict logical thought processes whereby Eriugena can 'resolve' the four divisions of nature into one, but as a unity that already pervades all diversity and difference because creation is the showing of God (and, of course, as I hope to show, God's simultaneous concealment).

SPEAKING CREATION IN THE WORD AND *NIHILUM*

Etienne Gilson, back in 1954, made the following pertinent summary of this idea:

The God of Eriugena is like unto a principle which, incomprehensible in its simplicity, reveals itself at a stroke in the multiplicity of its consequences. This self-manifestation of God is the true meaning of creation in Eriugena's doctrine. This is why he often calls it a 'theophany', that is to say an apparition of God'. For God to create is to reveal himself, and since to create is to reveal, to say that God reveals himself, is tantamount to saying that he creates himself. In other words, just as revelation is creation, creation is revelation.[9]

And while this is true, we can also counter that God's self-revelation is the deepest concealment because it is a displacement of God into otherness, into what is both God and not-God.

How then does Eriugena come to the conclusion that creation is God's self-making, the process of the going forth from God into God? First, the goodness of the uncreated creator 'creates' the primordial causes, the externalization of the ideas of all things in the Word, in Wisdom eternally. This is what Eriugena says: 'Therefore descending first from the superessentiality of His Nature, in which He is said not to be, He is created by Himself in the primordial causes and becomes the beginning of all essence, of all life, of all intelligence ... and thus going forth into all things in order He makes all things and is made all in all things, and returns into Himself, calling all things back into Himself.' (III 683A–B) The laws of causality are in effect turned upside down. If we do not read this as the logical conclusion of a rigorously applied negative theology, we can easily read this concept in Eriugena as pantheistic, as was, of course, bound to happen.

Eriugena's thoughts on *nihilum* in Book III of the *Periphyseon* constitute a fascinating treatise on the subject, first admirably explicated by Gustavo Piemonte in a 1968 essay.[10] The nothingness from which all things are created has to be God's self because there can be nothing co-eternal or co-existing with God. Creation *ex nihilo* simply has to be understood as creation *ex Deo*. This important development of Dionysian thought in theological discourse occurs as Eriugena attempts to protect the simplicity of the divine nature, a thematic to which he returns time and again in the *Periphyseon* (e.g. III 677C). The *nihilum* from which all things come cannot be the privation of being, as he demonstrates to his always-astute *alumnus*: numbers exist eternally in the Monad (from the number one come all numbers; from unity comes multiplicity). In this way the *nihilum* of Genesis is nothing other than the divine Wisdom (III 681A: *nihil per excellentiam*) in which all things are created (Psalm 104:24).[11] It is here that we find the precursor of Nicholas of Cusa's treatise on God becoming not-other (*De li non aliud*).

Therefore, in a fundamental apophatic sense, God and creation cannot be regarded as two separate natures, but are ineffably one and the same (III 678B). This means that creation does not exist *per se* but participates in God. Creation can be understood then as illusion in that it is not (in) itself but is the showing of God. In the view of Michael Sells, this is 'the confusion of cause and effect' mentioned above.[12] However, I am not convinced that this confusion exists if we read Eriugena through the lens of Werner Beierwaltes' explication of dialectic.[13] As Donald Duclow put it, 'The divine *nihil* constitutes the ground for theophanic self-creation, which in turn cannot be thought apart from the transcendence which it manifests in the otherness of created essence and being.'[14] Everything, both sensible and intelligible, is an appearance of that which is non-apparent (III 633A); as Eriugena succinctly notes: God is *principium, medium, et finis* (III 689A). Once more relying on Dionysius, Eriugena makes the bold assertion that God makes all things and is made in all things (III 633A). Everything is 'God stuff'; everything is made from God, including 'God'. *Natura* then, is from God, in God, and is God: *facit omnia et fit in omnibus et omnia est* (III 634A). This logically (and theologically) impossible is beyond speech and rational, earth-bound thought, as the reaction of the alumnus shows (he declares himself to be surrounded on all sides by the dark clouds of his thoughts). Thus, in taking a Dionysian idea slowly and painstakingly to its ultimate, and somewhat audacious, conclusion (without the One there can be no multiplicity),[15] Eriugena states that all things not only are eternal in the Word but *are* the Word (III 641A): 'All things are at once both eternal and made in the Word.' (III 641C) The Word makes all things and is made in all things. Another reaction of the *alumnus* here provides a touch of humanity and at the same time points up the boldness of the ideas which the *nutritor* has been developing when he insists that he is bewildered and struck dumb as a dead man (III 646C).[16] He then outlines his apparent objections by summing up all that has been said (III 646C–649D) as going against everything he has been taught. Then, in a rather clever literary (and most likely theological) move, the master figuratively falls to his knees in prayer (III 650B) – after all, how can a faithful seeker of truth be capable of heresy?

In the subsequent paced teasing out of the matter to the satisfaction of the *alumnus*, Eriugena explains that just in the same way that numbers are both eternal in the Monad and yet are made in the ways in which they appear (III 660C), so too all things are both eternal and made, are both God and not-God. And there was never a time when the things that are were not because they reside eternally in God's Word, God's Wisdom (III 665B). As both eternal and made, an apparent antinomy between the atemporal and the temporal is set up, as noted by Michael Sells[17], but this is a typical Eriugenian formulation: it simply affirms the simultaneous truth of both statements, and stretches the mind beyond the traditional understanding of creation as a temporal event. And lest we raise our theological eyebrows disapprovingly, Eriugena can extract himself from any taint of pantheism that might well be levelled at him not only by relying on a negative theology, but most importantly by appealing to the authority of 'Saint' Dionysius. As I have noted elsewhere, his assertion that God is all things, the one great underlying metaphysical theme of the *Periphyseon*, is finally shown to be inadequate in the light of the truth that God is none of the things:

> The constant checks and balances in Eriugena's portrayal of the complexity of *natura*, the affirmations and denials, the reminders that the immanent is also the transcendent and the transcendent immanent, are strong indications that there can never be a 'reconciliation' of the perceived tension between the two because that is precisely the way reality is structured. Any fixed points in the human understanding of God are constantly movable as the rational power of the mind is continuously pushed up to and at times over the limits of its comprehension. And yet, the presence of God in all things is one reassurance that speech [about God] is, after all, possible.[18]

But despite the protests of the *alumnus*, the *nutritor* does not back-pedal: the process of creation is the *nihilum* of Genesis, the no-thing becoming some-thing (becoming other than God) through divine wisdom. The unknowable reveals itself through creation and in so doing becomes something that both itself and created effects can know. Logically, the divine nature cannot know itself, but when descending into the principles, it begins to know itself in something (III 689A–C). The paradox of creation is that the original darkness of God, which is 'no-thing', becomes something, becomes other. When God becomes other than God through causality, God can know God's self and can also be 'known' by creation. And at the same time creation obscures God because it is other than God. 'Invisible it is seen, and while it is being seen it is invisible' (III 633C). This complex understanding of creation as the creation of 'God' eventually finds full voice in Meister Eckhart when the creature exclaims: 'When I flowed forth from God, all creatures declared: "There is a God".'[19] And again: 'Therefore I am my own cause according to my essence, which is eternal, and not according to my becoming, which is temporal.'[20] In this sense, another paradox is set up in the relation between God as creator and God as not-creator (all things are eternally in God). As Ernesto Mainoldi notes:

> He is conceived as creator in consideration of the things that are created by Him; He is conceived as non-creator when considering that the creation is eternally in Him as uncreated and this uncreated status cannot admit its negation, that is to say creation. Creation is then impossible because God is *natura quae non creatur et non creat*, but creation is at the same time possible because God is creator as well.[21]

God's fullness above being is the 'no thing' which is the negation of some thing, but through its becoming it becomes the negation of the negation: the divine nature becomes 'other' than itself. God becomes not-God through the process of *ek-stasis*, literally God's going out from God into the appearances of God. The transition from nothingness into something, indeed into all things, is 'self-negation' but there is, paradoxically, no 'self' to negate until the movement into the causes begins, 'for as yet there is no essence'. (III 683A) 'For if the understanding of all things is all things and It alone understands all things, then It alone is all things … For It encircles all things and there is nothing within It but what, in so far as it is, is not Itself, for It alone truly is.' (III 632D–633A) Creation, therefore, does not refer to the making of things that exist outside of God, but the exteriorization of God's thought as spoken in the Word. And indeed, if God is revealed through the process of manifestation, then God was not God before God created. It is in this sense that we can understand Meister Eckhart's so-called audacious statement: 'If I were not, God would not be either.'[22] In creation, then, God makes God's self: 'God, by manifesting Himself, in a marvellous and ineffable manner creates Himself in the creature, the invisible making Himself visible and the incomprehensible comprehensible and the hidden revealed and the unknown known.' (III 678C) And lest we think that Eriugena is speaking about the reality of the Incarnation, he insists that he is speaking of the act of creation as the ineffable descent of the Good so that all things can be (III 678D), another important Dionysian motif.

It is thus that revelation is concealment and concealment revelation. The ineffable *processio* into creation means that the very process of creation is theophany: the appearance of God as other than God, the 'becoming' of God, while at the same time God remains other than not-God. God goes out to become not-God, to become creature while remaining God, that is, God-in-otherness. The otherness that divine creation causes is, therefore, both itself and something else, and the otherness of creation to the creator and the otherness of the creator to creation are the 'stuff' of reality.

Here is the fundamental crux of the matter: 'It follows that we ought not to understand God and the creature as two things distinct from one another, but as one and the same. For both the creature, by subsisting, is in God; and God, by manifesting Himself, in a marvellous and ineffable manner creates Himself in the creature.' (III.678C) Again, lest the *alumnus* disagrees, Eriugena has this to say about God and Nothing:

> So that [Nothing] is the name by which it is necessary to call God, Who alone is what is properly meant by the negation of all things that are, because He is exalted above everything that is said or understood, Who is none of the things that are and are not, Who by not knowing is the better known. And so agreement will be reached between us, who seemed to disagree. (III 686D–687A)

Thus, Eriugena affirms the simultaneous truth that God is both above all and in all things. In the *Mystical Theology* Dionysius had highlighted the distance between the soul and God, using the image of Moses ascending the mountain to be in the same place as God. In the *Divine Names* he changed tack and used Paul as the example of intimate divine indwelling. Eriugena does it differently and resists the idea of Moses as exemplar: he takes the ontological route and shows instead how God's inherent presence in creation is God's self-nearness.[23] For this reason he consistently points up the fact that God and creature are one – a logical idea since there is nothing but God.[24] And just as God is unknowable in God's self, so too is the human unknowable: I am and remain, in reality, no matter how puffed up in the body I inhabit, an idea in the mind of the unknowable God. As Carlson notes: 'The superessential God who remains beyond all that can be spoken or understood is a God beyond the definition or circumscription of any place (or time); indeed, he is the placeless place of all places, "present to all things by his immeasurable circumambience of them" (I 523B) – and thus in that very presence to all things beyond those things.'[25] Bernard McGinn sums this up neatly: 'God knows all things under him, but he cannot know what he is because he is not a "what", that is, a particular reality capable of being defined ... We are most truly image of God in our inability to grasp or define our true nature, which precisely as *imago Dei* remains forever mysterious.'[26]

The unveiling of God (the *aperikaluptos* spoken of so passionately by the Pseudo-Dionysius, although with a different focus) is the act of creation, the Good calling all into being. For something to be understood it has to be, and when created reality is, it can in some measure be understood, but not fully so. In so far as it is, it can be understood (because it is something); in so far as it is God's manifestation of God's self, it is incomprehensible. Creation then, *ousia*, is fundamentally unknowable because it is God. This is why it can be understood as a process of alterity: God becoming not-God is simultaneous revelation and concealment. Willemien Otten explains:

> Central to Dionysius's use of negative theology throughout all this is the introduction not just of a dialectic between the human and the divine – that much was to be expected from the outset – but the setting in motion of a kind of reverse divine striptease: an unveiling of the divine which results not in its undressing but in its redressing, as the divine bareness becomes more and more hidden.[27]

The *ekstasis* that is God's going out of God's self that paradoxically results in God becoming other than God's self, does not reveal God *per se*, but rather shows *that* God is, because God is not a what! Eriugena's most eloquent expression of the simultaneous truth of God revealed yet obscured is as follows: 'Everything that is understood and sensed is nothing else but the apparition of what is not apparent, the manifestation of the hidden, the affirmation of the negated, the comprehension of the incomprehensible

... the understanding of the unintelligible, the body of the bodiless, the essence of the superessential, the form of the formless.' (III 633A–B)

CALLING CREATION BACK INTO GOD

According to Eriugena's circular conception of the drama of creation, in the return, the complementary movement occurs: the creature goes out to become not creature, but God (deification) while still remaining creature. Paradoxically, in the descent of God as other, God remains not other and God is known both by God's self through *what* God has become and also *by* what God has become (III 689B). This is stated in a passage which we have had occasion to previously consider:

> Therefore descending first from the super-essentiality of His Nature, in which He is said not to be, He is created by Himself in the primordial causes and becomes the beginning of all essence, of all life, of all intelligence... and thus going forth into all things in order He makes all things and is made all in all things, and returns into Himself. (III 683A–B)[28]

However, if we take Eriugena's fundamental assertions to their ultimate conclusions, we could perhaps say that when God becomes not-God, the eschatological implication would be that deification occurs, not only as Ambrose and the others would have it at the end of the drama of creation, but also in the moment of God's theophanies. Is this a simple stretch of the imagination too far? While one aspect of Eriugena's thought can be understood as an elucidation of the process of *resolutio* when God shall be 'all in all', the fact that things exist means that God is, in an ineffable way, already 'all in all', although this is more difficult to appreciate from an earthbound perspective. [29] God cannot be understood as either 'this' or 'that', yet God is precisely 'this and that' (I 468B), a very definite confusion of the laws of causality. 'But if the creature (is) from God, God will be the Cause, but the creature the effect. But if an effect is nothing else but a made cause, it follows that God the Cause is made in His effects.' (III 687C)[30] That means we can say that creation is already God, already deified, because its very identity is God. The truth of this statement rests on the idea that while God, as cause, is 'made' in God's effects, God remains above created effects in the darkness and unknowability of God's hidden essence, as the mighty Plotinian One remains above all duality in majestic rest.[31] In this way, the basic concept described in the *Periphyseon* (God is all things) is constantly thwarted by the affirmation of the dialectical truth of God's concealment of God's self not only in creation but also in the darkness of inaccessible light.

In Eriugena's thought the return does not imply the destruction of otherness, but a resolution of this otherness back into unity without negating the otherness that has been called into being. This is a very important point and one that is frequently misunderstood, leading to dark mutterings of pantheism and heresy. The eschatological unity that signifies the final act in the great drama of creation is a unity that, paradoxically, admits of distinction. It is not the annihilation of the otherness of God, but its perpetual celebration. In other words, the original thought that is spoken in the Word remains always: it cannot be un-thought. Elsewhere I have noted that the 'going out' of God into otherness is perhaps more significant than the 'going back' into God described by Eriugena as the return of all things to their source – not so exciting! In creation, being can say: 'I am not God! I am God's otherness.'[32] Creation is in itself the affirmation that it is not God because it is something else. In a similar fashion, the deification that occurs when Eriugena conceives of God being all in all remains a thought that exists eternally in the divine darkness.

The whole of *natura* is a unity characterized by diversity and difference, even in the final *resolutio*. In the act of creation, which Eriugena sometimes describes as a flowing out from or diffusion from God, things still remain in their cause and will ultimately return to it. 'For the whole river first flows forth from its source, and through its channel the water which first wells up in the source continues to flow always without any break to whatever distance it extends. So the Divine Goodness and Essence ... first flow down into the primordial causes ... flowing forth continuously through the higher to the lower; and return back again to their source.' (III 632B–C) This understanding of the ineffable descent of the supreme Goodness as simultaneously the cause of all things and indeed as all things, can constitute a real problem for many, and Eriugena's conception of God's creation was ultimately misunderstood despite his strong assertions that creation is not something apart from God, but is the ontological participation of the creature in God as demonstrated by 'Saint' Dionysius.

CONCLUSION

Used as we are to understanding the divine nature from either the perspective of transcendence or the perspective of immanence, Eriugenian formulations such as unmanifest/manifest, invisible/visible (by no means original to him), stretch the mind in both directions simultaneously, for the one cannot be understood without the other: God both is all things and is not all things. The idea that God is manifest in creation is true, but the fact that God remains transcendently unmanifest is also true. And yet, neither is true when understood singly; the 'problem' is resolved by coupling both truths in a dialectical formulation that reveals the tension between, and the simultaneous truth of both. The truth of the statement, 'God is all things', is constantly undermined by the basic distinction between the divine essence and theophany, which is a forceful reminder that, as an apophatic understanding demonstrates, a comprehensive account of reality can never be attained. All that is said about the creative process in the *Periphyseon* is constantly under threat from the continuous moments of denial that something can be said about the divine nature. The noetic tension between the simultaneous knowability and unknowability of God is a constant feature of Eriugena's thought that cannot be explained away, indeed cannot be explained further as it is grounded in an ontological conception of how 'nothing' becomes otherness and difference.

It is this wonderful account of creation that I find particularly relevant many centuries after Eriugena disappeared from the pages of recorded history. In an age where technological advances continually push back the frontiers of human knowledge to the point where humans are beginning to embark on the process of creation themselves (the human genome project, animal and human cloning), Eriugena consistently points up the shadowy and yet exciting mystery that lies at the heart of all reality: that creation is the manifestation of God, and in the deepest, most secret folds of nature, lies the divine. And he does so in a way that is likely to appeal to those who are not particularly interested in the Christian account of creation – in a way which post-moderns and perhaps even new-agers could find stimulating and thought-provoking. The universe may well be better understood by human beings this side of the twentieth century, but the universe does not give up its secrets easily. I have noted elsewhere that the detailed and intricate harmony of the universe cannot be examined in the way we would examine the various parts of a symphonic score,[33] but I believe the whole can be grasped partly, even if not fully understood, just as we can grasp the reality of a vast mountain range hidden behind the cover of cloud.

ENDNOTES

1   For the historical origins of of negative theology and the *via negativa* see Deirdre Carabine, *The Unknown God. Negative Theology in the Platonic Tradition. Plato to Eriugena* (Eugene, OR: Wipf & Stock, 2015), and Fran O'Rourke, 'The *Triplex Via* of Naming God', *The Review of Metaphysics* 69 (2001), pp. 519–54.

2   Henry Bett, *Johannes Scotus Eriugena: A Study on Mediaeval Philosophy* (Cambridge: Cambridge University Press, 1925), p. 1.

3   On Eriugena's sources see Hilary Anne-Marie Mooney, *Theophany: The Appearing of God According to the Writings of Johannes Scottus Eriugena* (Tübingen: Mohr Siebeck Verlag, 2009), ch. 6; Werner Beierwaltes (ed.), *Eriugena: Studien zu seinen Quellen* (Heidelberg: Carl Winter, 1980); Bernard McGinn and Willemien Otten (eds), *Eriugena: East and West* (Notre Dame, IN: University of Notre Dame Press, 1994).

4   Mooney, *Theophany*, p. 38.

5   Paul Rorem, 'The Early Latin Dionysius: Eriugena and Hugh of St. Victor', *Modern Theology*, 24/ 4 (2008), pp. 601–14.

6   On the relationship between negative theology and negative anthropology in Eriugena see Willemien Otten, 'In the Shadow of the Divine: Negative Theology and Negative Anthropology in Augustine, Pseudo-Dionysius and Eriugena', *Heythrop Journal* 40 (1999), pp. 438–55.

7   On this initial division, *quae sunt et quae non sunt*, see Dermot Moran, *The Philosophy of John Scottus Eriugena. A Study of Idealism in the Middle Ages* (Cambridge: Cambridge University Press, 1989), pp. 214–18, and Gustavo A. Piemonte, 'L'expression 'quae sunt et quae non sunt': Jean Scot Érigène et Marius Victorinus', in G.H. Allard ed., *Jean Scot, écrivain* (Montreal/Paris: Bellarmin/Vrin, 1986), pp. 81–113.

8   References are to Eriugena's *De Divisione Naturae* (Greek *Periphyseon*) in volume 122 of Migne's *Patrologia Latina* as given in Iohannes Scotti Eriugenae, *Periphyseon*, eds. I.P. Sheldon-Williams, Ludwig Bieler, Édouard Jeauneau, Mark Allen Zier, published by the Dublin Institute for Advanced Studies, 1968–1995, vols. VII, IX, XI, XIII in the *Scriptores Latini Hiberniae* series. Translations are from Sheldon-Williams, *Periphyseon* III.

9   Etienne Gilson, *History of Christian Philosophy in the Middle Ages* (New York, NY: Random House, 1955), p. 119.

10 Gustavo A. Piemonte, 'Notas sobre la Creatio de nihilo *en Juan Escoto Eriugena*', *Sapientia* 23 (1968), pp. 37–58; see also Moran, *The Philosophy of John Scottus Eriugena*, pp. 212–40.

11 See Ernesto Sergio Mainoldi, 'Creation in Wisdom: Eriugena's Sophiology beyond Ontology and Meontology', in Willemien Otten and Michael I. Allen (eds), *Eriugena and Creation* (Turnhout: Brepols, 2014), pp. 183–222.

12 Michael A. Sells, *Mystical Languages of Unsaying* (Chicago, IL: University of Chicago Press, 1994), p. 42.

13   This is a theme Werner Beierwaltes has engaged with in many of his works, most
     notably his interpretation of Nicholas of Cusa's *De li non aliud*; see *Der Verborgene
     Gott: Cusanus und Dionysius* (Trier: Cusanus Institut, 1997); see Peter Casarella's
     pertinent comments on this concept in 'Cusanus on Dionysius', *Modern Theology*
     24/4 (2008), p. 674.

14   Donald F. Duclow, 'Divine Nothingness and Self-Creation in John Scottus Eriugena',
     The Journal of Religion 57/ 2 (1977), p. 119.

15   Pseudo-Dionysius, *Divine Names* 13, 2.

16   See the comments of Michael A. Sells, *Mystical Languages of Unsaying*, p. 53.

17   Ibid., pp. 54–5.

18   Deirdre Carabine, *John Scottus Eriugena* (Oxford: Oxford University Press, 2000), pp.
     65–6.

19   See the German sermon '*Beati pauperes spiritu*' in the translation of M.O'C. Walshe,
     Meister Eckhart Sermons and Treatises, vol. 2 (London and Dulverton: Watkins, 1981),
     p. 275.

20   Ibid.

21   Ernesto Mainoldi, 'Creation in Wisdom: Eriugena's Sophiology beyond Ontology
     and Meontology', p. 212.

22   Meister Eckhart, *Beati pauperes spiritu*, p. 275.

23   On this theme see Emmanuel Falque, 'Jean Scot Érigène: la théophanie comme mode
     de la phénoménalité', *Revue des sciences philosophiques et théologiques* 86 (2002), pp.
     387–421.

24   *P* II 528B; Willemien Otten comments on this complicated theme in Willemien
     Otten, 'Eriugena on Natures (Created, Human and Divine). From Christian-Platonic
     Metaphysics to Early Medieval Protreptic', in Isabelle Moulin (ed), *Philosophie et
     Théologie chez Jean Scot Érigène* (Paris: Vrin, 2016), pp. 131–2.

25   Thomas A. Carlson, *The Indiscrete Image: Infinitude and Creation of the Human*
     (Chicago, IL: University of Chicago Press, 2008), p. 92.

26   Bernard McGinn, 'Western Christianity', in Bernard McGinn, John Meyendorff, and
     Jean Leclercq (eds), *Christian Spirituality. Origins to the Twelfth Century* (New York,
     NY: Crossroad, 1988), p. 323.

27   Willemien Otten, 'In the Shadow of the Divine', p. 443.

28   See also *Hom.* XI 289B.

29   Eriugena himself says this in Book III 683C, but explains the difference in terms of
     the Fall and subsequent redemptive activity of the incarnate Word.

30   According to Willemien Otten's seminal work, this passage represents an inversion of
     the hierarchical order of cause and effect. 'Instead of God creating the world in his
     capacity of being its eternal cause, it is God who becomes created through his effects.
     Eriugena thus appears completely to overturn the logical order of events as he comes
     to make creation almost responsible for God's unfolding as its cause.' Willemien
     Otten, *The Anthropology of Johannes Scottus Eriugena* (Leiden: Brill, 1991), p. 71.

31   *Ennead* VI 7 [38] 39. 28–9.

32   Carabine, *The Unknown God*, pp. v–vi.

33   Deirdre Carabine, *John Scottus Eriugena*, p. 110.

A TEACHER AND TWO STUDENTS: ALBERT THE GREAT, THOMAS AQUINAS, MEISTER ECKHART

DENYS TURNER

The acknowledgement of debts to one's teachers is pretty much the default practice of academics; the acknowledgement of debts to one's colleagues – though often at least as great – is less common; colleagues seem the more easily taken for granted. If, as in my case, you were first taught by Paddy Masterson (in my final year as a philosophy undergraduate in University College Dublin) and then for a few years taught with him as a colleague in the same department, you twice over have reasons for gratitude. And you can add a third reason: within this volume there is among several others a small-scale reunion of Paddy, Philip Pettit and myself: the three of us for a period of a few years taught philosophy together until in due course Philip and I went our separate ways. With such colleagues as these it was a testing but also a bracing time, and for sure it was great fun.

It occurred to me that it would be for this reason appropriate on the occasion of celebrating Paddy's remarkable career as philosopher, teacher, author and senior administrator, to reflect more generally on the subject of university teaching and its attendant forms of comradeship, not exactly in the shared experience of the three of us, but in that of three academics of another age entirely, who were teaching and learning at the very dawn of the university as we know it in the West. One was a teacher, the other two his students. The students were Thomas Aquinas and Meister Eckhart; the teacher of them both, Albert the Great. And the lesson they teach us today is less in the content of what they as teachers and students learned and taught, more in what they understood teaching and learning to be.

For it tells us something that cannot fail to remind us of Paddy's academic career and of reasons for continuing gratitude for what it represents. For I suppose that one thing among others the three of us have had in common, but first learned of from Paddy, has been an aspiration above all to be an Albert the Great. For whatever there is to be said about any achievements of our own as philosophers, wasn't it something more that we have been teachers with a view to our students in due course outstripping us?

I

The story is told, though it's likely to be apocryphal, about a supposed thirteenth-century Muslim teacher, Mullah Nasrudin, who had a reputation for great wisdom. 'Mullah,' asked a student one day, 'how come you are so wise?' 'It's like this,' he replied: 'Every morning when I get up I start talking, and all day long I continue talking uninterrupted. But as I talk I look into people's eyes. And when I see a glint I write down what I have just said.' Student feedback collected anonymously after the event notoriously tells you little of value about your teaching performance. The glint and the glaze in the classroom on the other hand tell you the alarming truth on the spot. The glaze means you haven't pulled it off. The glint means they have and that they don't need you anymore; and it means that you have liberated them, above all from yourself. It means that you have successfully taught.

There was once in a house of studies in Cologne a famously dumb and rather overweight student who was so shy that I am sure he would have hidden behind his laptop had he been in possession of one, hoping that no one would notice him and that the professor would neglect to address any questions to him. Evidently he was so unreactive in the classroom that fellow students nicknamed him 'the dumb ox'. Their professor got to hear of this name-calling and remonstrated with the students: 'The day will come,' he told them, 'when this dumb ox will bellow so that the whole world will hear him', and promptly appointed him his personal research assistant and asked him to take over some of the classes himself. The student, of course, was Thomas Aquinas. The teacher was Albert the Great. My guess is that because the teacher, Albert, was in front of the class, looking the students in the eye, he could see where there was a glint, where the glaze. And we know that when in due course it was Thomas' turn to teach, he knew all about the glaze. For in that famous preface that opens his *Summa Theologiae* he was scathing about university teaching practices in his own time. Most theological teaching, he says, is so badly organized and repetitive and even pointless as to be relentlessly glaze-inducing. He knew from Albert how to do better.

The student died some six years before the teacher, Thomas in 1274, Albert in 1280. Sometime between those two dates Albert taught another Dominican student, a teenager, possessed of a very different intellectual temperament from taciturn Thomas. I have always imagined Albert to have found him, a certain Johannes Eckhardus (later to be known as 'Meister Eckhart') to have been that irritatingly opinionated sort of student who cannot be got to stop talking, in the classroom or out of it, always taking it for granted that he has something more interesting to communicate to the seminar than anyone else – and, which is more irritating still, usually being right, though we had rather preferred he hadn't told us so. We don't know what Albert thought of him, for nothing is recorded, though we do know what the student thought of Albert, since he quotes his teacher approvingly in a number of his sermons. Apart from their both having been students of Albert, Thomas and Eckhart share few things in common that I know of: both were Dominicans, they share the distinction of being the only Masters of Theology at the University of Paris who held their professorial chairs twice, and both were charged by high-ranking ecclesiastics with having held heretical theological opinions, Thomas being accused by the Bishop of Paris in league with the Archbishop of Canterbury in 1277, Meister Eckhart by Pope John XXII in 1329. Neither Thomas nor Eckhart was alive at the time of these condemnations so they were in no position to respond, though three years earlier in 1326 Eckhart had retorted sharply to a list of accusations of heterodoxy issued by a peculiarly unpleasant archbishop of Cologne, Henry of Virneberg. Happily, the reputations of Thomas and Eckhart survive today untroubled by late medieval scruples about their orthodoxy. Otherwise I cannot think of two more different intellectual and spiritual temperaments than those of Thomas Aquinas and Meister Eckhart.

So you the teacher never know, and it's important never to assume that you do know, what or who is lurking behind those laptop lids arrayed in front of you in the classroom. You may be the prestigious professor up at the front and doing the talking. But if you are, you ought always be prepared for it if, as things turn out, your role is to be an Albert the Great, shortly to be outshone by some of your students. But his students being better than him *is* his achievement as a teacher: to get the feel of what it must have been like for Albert, just imagine yourself being the physics teacher of both Albert Einstein and Nils Bohr.

II

Not that Albert was any sort of intellectual slouch himself, and though I shan't in any detail go into his research profile, as we call it today, it was considerable and, in several ways, especially in range, more impressive even than Thomas', never mind Eckhart's. For Albert was a botanist who knew how to classify species systematically, a student of animal behaviour, a mineralogist, and an alchemist of an experimental sort – he had his laboratories –, a scholar who commented on every one of the texts of Aristotle, albeit in defective translations; he was a theologian who compiled a fine commentary on the *Mystical Theology* of the Pseudo-Denys, and to cap it all he was for three years a bishop. Albert was a polymath, truly a university man: he wrote, of course, but my guess is that he preferred what we nowadays call 'research', above all in the laboratory, and it is little wonder given the range of his thought that in his own lifetime he was accorded the title of '*Doctor Universalis*'. So even if his influence, scientific and philosophical, is too limited by the methods of a pre-modern period to be felt as such within today's university curricula, his intellectual persona is iconic. If you were a university academic, you would want to be like Albert in generosity of mind and spirit. He loved learning. And he desired God. What more could you want?

You could rephrase that question. Since one thing more you could want is a teacher, you could ask: what more could you want in a teacher? The answer to that question, if you are a teacher, is that you could want your students to become better at it than you are. But note: if that is exactly what Albert wanted and got, a Thomas and an Eckhart who were better than he, it was in good measure because of Albert that they outshone him. *They* are his success. He taught them how to be better, and one can readily imagine that one of the best-known sayings of Thomas himself reflects his sense of indebtedness to his master: 'For even as it is better to enlighten than merely to shine, so it is better to give to others the fruits of one's contemplation than merely to contemplate.'[1]

Contemplata aliis tradere. It became a Dominican motto. It is easily said and with greater difficulty achieved. Here are some devices for avoiding the demands of your own professed teaching mission, the main one being to ensure that by hook or by crook we stay one step ahead of our own students. We out-jargonize them, we wrap up what we know in the private language of the elite, this vice being rampant among the philosophers, and more particularly those of the Hegelian or post-modern persuasions; but also it is not uncommon among sociologists, anthropologists and psychologists en masse, with literary theorists lagging not far behind. Then there are those emperors of the social sciences, the economists, whose forfeiture of intellectual and moral clothes was cruelly but deservedly exposed for all to see in 2008, though that was no laughing matter for the rest of us. And why did not the accountants protest long before the market's collapse, since they, if anyone did, must have known what was going on? Next in order of shamelessness, we theologians, who, as long ago as 1649 were declared by that great radical communist, Gerrard Winstanley, to be foremost among the merely 'verbal professors of freedom', as he called them, who steal the Bible from the people and hide the light of the world under the bushel of our jargon-ridden hermeneutics. And so we could go on, but won't, for the *trahisons des clercs* are easily and cheaply exposed, especially since we university people take particular pleasure, as I do now, in a form of ironic self-criticism that, being so readily and cheerfully admitted, is as easily thereby defused.

Thomas seems so different. We can observe in him all the contrasts with academic mentalities of this kind. He is so clear that he himself disappears. I am not sure what the psychological connection is between them, but do not teachers and taught alike observe some connection between terminological obscurantism and magisterial self-importance? J.L. Austin was a philosopher famous for his lucidity of style, whether in writing or teaching. He once asked at the end of a paper why anyone should find his arguments to be of any importance. To which he replied that importance is of no importance, only truth is. That is pure Thomas: for him you could say that clarity is to the life of the mind, especially to the mind of the teacher, what humility is to the moral life. For if tortuously obscure declamation is closely allied to self-importance, clarity in writing or in speech, by contrast, expresses the teacher's willingness to be exposed to counter-argument and contestation. Clarity in a teacher is vulnerability to the critique of the taught, who by way of the teacher's opening of the way for them into the life of the mind, can learn to travel on their own routes and not necessarily yours. For you are not important, your teaching is, and self-importance gets you in the way of effective teaching, and placing yourself as teacher in the light places your students in the shadows, mainly in yours. Casting light for others, as Thomas knew, makes you disappear. *Contemplata aliis tradere.*

Such is our self-effacingly plodding Thomas, the dumb ox. What about the scintillating Eckhart? He seems to be the opposite. Here in his sermons is a master rhetorician, self-consciously brilliant, he knows when to turn on the fine speech, and when to turn it off. He calibrates speech to an effect; his aim is to be spectacular. There are times when you are tempted to ask if he is not just a very smart show-off, smart like the very smart, usually male, student who is always the one to take the floor in the seminar, filling up the air-space with weighty jargon-words strung along in endlessly extruded sentences, like nothing so much as an out-of-control vehicle careering at high speed down the hill with failed brake pads, mixing his metaphors on the way down to an ugly verbal smash-up, as is this sentence I have composed by way of illustration and, to your relief, have hereby finished. Is Eckhart just a verbally self-indulgent show-off, a verbose mixer of metaphors?

Before answering, let us address another question. Who was it warned of the infelicitous nature of the mixed metaphor? And what was said to be wrong with them? Though I admit that the advice, let us say, that you should not cross your bridges before they hatch will work only because you recognize the two metaphors that get thus mixed, the fact is that in the doing of theology the joy of mixing your metaphors is not just the fun of annoying the pedants: it is essential theologically. For if all you can say of God metaphorically is that he is my rock, and being a rock he cannot also be a gentle breeze or, if either of these, then not my light or anything else lacking a lapidary nature, then you have probably thereby excised 148 out of the 150 Psalms from the canon of scripture on some literary dogmatist's scruple. The rhetorical pedants need to be warned off the poet's territory. Poet-theologians of Eckhart's kind dissent and will of theological necessity enthusiastically ignore them. To speak with any degree of accuracy of the divine you have to deploy every resource of language available because no one bit of it, or even all of it, will be adequate. That is Eckhart: his verbal virtuosity is a theological necessity and not a merely rhetorical ploy.

One can say that when it comes to styles of theological expression there are misers and there are spendthrifts. Thomas is a verbal miser: if there is a short-hand way of saying things, Thomas will find it, he cuts precisely – and by the way, though I know there are those who will be scandalized to hear it said, he is a poor poet and, as teachers go, his illustrative examples are unimaginatively feeble: for some reason or other he is obsessed with stones, which are appropriately heavy and inert.[2] Eckhart is a verbal spendthrift: his language is a proliferating riot of imagery, over-the-top is his default style, he scatters metaphors so profusely about it would seem almost to be at random: I suppose all this means is that he is a great poet. Thomas is verbally restrained, terse, economical, he aims at a pure lucidity so that his words, like his persona, move out of sight in themselves, they serve but to let the light through to the reality on the other side. Eckhart's language is dense, thick, his words draw attention to themselves, they are striking verbal events in themselves, actions done, performances. Listen to how differently they say the same thing, the laconic Thomas first, writing in a textbook of theology:

> In this life we do not know what God is. And so it is that by grace we are made one with [God] as to somewhat unknown (to us).[3]

That's it then, that is all you need to say. Supererogatory is the wordy Eckhart in a sermon:

> You should love God not because he is lovable, for God is not lovable, he is superior to love and loveableness. 'How, then, should I love him?' You should love God unspiritually, your soul must be without spirit, stripped of all spirituality. For so long as your soul is spiritual it has form; and as long as it has form it has neither unity nor union; and as long as it lacks union it does not love God, for real love is found in union. Therefore, let your soul be unspiritual; for if you love God as he is spirit, as he is person, as he is image, all that must go. 'Then how should I love him?' You should love him as he is, as non-God, as non-spirit, as non-person, as non-image, as pure undefiled unity, removed from all duality. And in that oneness may we ever sink down, out of something into nothing. May God help us. Amen.[4]

What, then, is the difference between the teaching miser and the preaching spendthrift, apart from terseness in the one, prolixity in the other? We could try out the distinction this way: teachers use words to clear the way for their students, so that they might understand something for themselves. Teachers move themselves out of the picture so the students can paint their own thoughts on a clean canvas. Teachers create independent minds, and notably in a lifetime of teaching Thomas created no school of his own, no followers, though Giles of Rome mistakenly thought of himself as one. It was the Dominicans who made Thomas their official theologian some decades after his death, though it is my guess that he himself would have been aghast had he known what some of the 'Thomists' would make of him. Preachers, by contrast, use words to effect a change in their congregations' lives, drawing them into the community of the Word preached. They create solidarities, and their words are the coinage of a community's exchanges. Then you might want to add a more general proposition: teachers use words to say something, preachers use words to do something, the one to signify a meaning, the other to effect an action.

Will that do it? Not quite, the distinction is a bit too tidy. Here's a truism that, even in so far as it is true, could hardly be more misleading: 'Actions speak louder than words.' Why misleading? Because while the truism is true in what it affirms, it is false in what it denies, for utterances too are actions, and put in such unqualified terms the disjunction between words and actions is unhelpful. After all, when I *say* 'I love you' do I not thereby *make* love to you; and the converse: when I *kiss* my lover, do I not thereby *say* 'I love you'? If in saying I do, so in doing I say. Utterances are actions that effect. And actions that effect do so by way of how they utter. It is only because of both these truths that Judas' kiss can be the bearer of so terrible an irony; for his action of kissing spoke with a forked tongue. If his kiss spoke love and friendship what his action of kissing did is betray his Lord and Master, so that his saying of love is undone by what the betrayal says, each subverts the other within a single act. Before Jesus is betrayed, therefore, treason is committed against language itself, against the very nature of speech as truth-bearing. And that, presumably, is why Jesus protests. For Jesus it would have been not so much Judas' betrayal of himself that offended, for he had known already at the earlier supper what was to happen and he had told Judas to get on with it. Harder to take must have been the mendacity of the manner, the kiss. For in that act was the betrayal of the foundations of speech itself, a betrayal that is so shamelessly mendacious that it seems to take even Jesus' breath away in astonishment. For it is reported that Jesus protested: 'Do you betray the Son of Man with a *kiss*?' Judas is not just a traitor. He is a poisoner of wells. He mocks even kissing.

So the conventional prioritizing of actions over words is a misleading over-simplification, words uttered themselves being actions. In consequence no less simplistic is the manner of making out the distinction between the teacher and the preacher in terms of that prioritization. And even when the clarification is granted, when, that is, it is conceded that words do things every bit as much as actions say things, it is plainly false, when it comes to relative volumes, that all actions are utterances *fortissimo* and every word's efficacy *piano*. After all, are we not told that it was in the Word that all began? For in that Word uttered was 'all that is made'.

III

Perhaps then we ought not to try too hard to distinguish between the teacher and the preacher, between our Thomases and our Eckharts. For my typecasting of these two may be true as to the emphases of each but not as to the whole of either. In any case Thomas preached occasionally and Eckhart was a university professor at the University of Paris for brief spells, though he completed no more than shortish fragments of his ambitious academic plans for what he called his *Opus Tripartitum*. So we do need to complicate matters a little, in particular we could do with a more nuanced account of how word and deed get together and interact in truthful speaking – for truth in speaking is what is in question in either case – and it helps to look at a few more complicated, if somewhat randomly chosen, ways in which word done and deed said have come apart.

Consider first that baffling fellow, the truth-telling and self-accusing hypocrite. My favourite is the Pardoner who appears as one of the pilgrims in Chaucer's *Canterbury Tales*. He is what once was known as a 'bounder', a shameless conman. He sells 'pardons', that is to say, by way of the supposed efficacy of the relics that he claims to possess (they are in fact entirely bogus) he professes to be able to sell remission of sins to such gullible penitents as will pay him the appropriate fees. Of course he is a splendid hypocrite – he is happy to admit it – he robs the poor, he tells us, by shamelessly preaching up the efficacy of his pardons in sermons on the evils of the desire for money. For, he says, 'My burden is and ever was: *Radix malorum est cupiditas.*' Now it is pretty clear that Chaucer's Pardoner, being no fool, is well aware that his fellow pilgrims know his claims for his relics are bogus and that they in turn know that he knows this. In short, he knows he is a hypocrite, and he knows his fellow pilgrims know he is a hypocrite. In view of which it is clearly pointless for the Pardoner to deny his all-too-blatant deceits: the only way out is, by way of shameless bragging, to get the self-criticism in first: 'See', he declares, 'the thoroughgoing hypocrite that I am: I preach that money is the root of all evil as a way of cheating people out of theirs with false pardons, many of whom can ill afford it. That's how I make a living, by conning the gullible, and you and I both know it. What a laugh!'

Now the significance of Chaucer's Pardoner for our purposes is to be found in the manner in which he disables the critical power of the truth precisely by way of the cynical blatancy of his telling it, precisely, that is, by shamelessly *not* lying. He is a hypocrite, but self-deceived is the last thing he is. Moreover, he is not so lacking in self-awareness as to suppose that anyone would believe him were he to deny that he is a cynical cheat. So he takes the words out of the mouths of his accusers and evacuates them of all moral force by appropriating them to himself. What he shows, alas, is that the truth does not always set you free: not at least when you have turned it full circle upon itself, like the snake that endlessly feeds itself on its own tail, re-growing its length as it is nourished by what it devours.

Now you may be familiar with a definition of a sacrament as 'a sacred sign that effects what it signifies', human words and bodily signs whose utterance instrumentally enacts divine things. Thomas was fond of the formula. But looked at from the point of view of our theme, the definition, at least when generalized for signs of any kind and not confined to the sacramental, is just as apt for good speech, whether of teaching or of preaching sorts. For the examples I have given so far have been negative, cases where the signification and the effectiveness have fallen apart from one another, or worse, mutually subvert – as when Judas' kiss says one thing and does another that says the opposite, speaks love and thereby does what says betrayal; or, as in the case of the Pardoner, who so tells the truth as to disengage it altogether from action. In each case, one way or another, the connection between sign and effect, or between both and truth, is sundered. All are bastard sacraments: each is a sort of Satanic Mass of speech, a parodic inversion of a truthful relation between word and action.

Nor is that all. For it is true that Judas' betrayal of Jesus is a special and one-off case, and that the Pardoner's is a fictional one, and we need a structural instance of the Judas case, instances where not just individuals but social and political and economic systems too are organized dislocations of truth and practice, constructions of lived falsehoods. And though the Pardoner's case is fictional, nonetheless, blatant cynicism, a rupturing of the inner and intimate relations which sustain the possibilities of truthful speech, can be an institutionalized practice, as we all know, or would know, if only we, in our universities and colleges, were to examine the truth of ourselves, of what we do, and of how we have in times and under pressures financial, or political, or both, too often institutionalized the doing of it. Please do not misunderstand: here I speak simply of a dangerous temptation, one that is peculiarly ours as academics. I am not pronouncing some pretentiously general condemnation.

IV

For now we have a couple of parables in different ways, if in equal truth, applying to the teacher and the preacher. They are parables that tell of antitypes in turn of Thomas and Meister Eckhart. As for teachers, for a start there is our notoriously wordy insider academic talk, our patois: its very technicality helps sustain the belief that we are doing something worthwhile, which we could be sure of if only that jargon did not serve so effectively to disguise from us the distinction between the sublime and the ridiculous. 'Too many notes!' exclaimed absurdly the Emperor of Austria, Franz Joseph II, upon hearing a performance of Mozart's *Marriage of Figaro*. 'Too many words!' is said with more justification of our universities and colleges where our theological curricula seem to be generated much as is the news on the media, on which there has to be something newsworthy to report every day, willy-nilly. Wonderful would be the day when CNN and the BBC close down for twenty-four hours on the grounds that nothing worth reporting has happened since yesterday. Wonderful thought, but impossible: there has to be something worth reporting today because they have a daily output to broadcast. As to theology, one might with justification propose a moratorium on all of it that cannot be shown to answer to real need, when so much of it, like Mount Everest, seems to be worth climbing only because it is there, and it's only there because there are schools of Divinity that need a curriculum. Snakes consuming their own tails once more come to mind.

And to see why, just look at how in the academic world we commonly construct the relationships between word and action. Look especially, since it is my field, at how we university theologians do it. The besetting temptation of the academic theologian is to succumb to the Pardoner's sin, to that enjoyment of an excess of blatancy whose other name is cynicism. Here's how at our worst we pull off the Pardoner's trick. In the University of Bristol where, in a former academic incarnation, I taught a class in political theology (as I think we used to call it) I would address the class as follows:

Liberation theologians of the Third World tell us of some meta-theological principles of their work, among which figures perhaps most prominently a neo-Marxist principle of the priority of practice over theory. By this they seem to mean that you cannot do theology, read and study the Bible, understand the doctrines of Trinity or grace and all the rest as if the community of faith which is sustained by those doctrines existed in some politically, economically, socially neutral space; and, having done that, hope to derive therefrom some Christian principles of political, economic and social action and commitment. On the contrary, they say that before all such doctrinal commitment comes a practical engagement, a 'preferential option for the poor' and that option must first be the starting point of all theological reflection and then mediate it throughout, including how one reads its own principal source, the Bible.

For whether in hermeneutics or in worldly action you have to take sides and not because, if you are right-minded, so you should, but because like it or not you do anyway. I think it was the Peruvian theologian Gustavo Gutierrez who once commented that no one ever built a bridge starting in the middle of the river, you have to choose from which side to start. And, he would go on to say, the very neutrality (as you believe it to be) of the space in the middle of the river in which you have situated your theological reflections, a neutrality which is, in a university, the only guarantee of their theoretical adequacy, is already an answer to the question of which is prior to which, theory to practice or practice to theory. For that stranded neutrality of the middle itself settles the question in favour of the priority of theory over practice. So here is where the fun begins. Here I am, standing before you in the university lecture hall, expounding and even advocating, by means and methods entirely theoretical and detached from practice, the methodological principle of the priority of practice over theory. A bit shameless, I admit, but there you are, that is the magic of university study. We are free to study anything, anyhow we like, with total freedom of thought, entertaining the priority of practice over theory on condition that it is as theory that we entertain it, thus divorced from practice.

Then we would all laugh at the irony of it all, and get shamelessly on with the properly detached business of university enquiry. Exemplary Pardoners all, did we not practise a kind of sophisticated transparency as a mode of deception?

V

The lesson: there is the liberating word, and then there is the word that entraps thought and action, containing it within the bounds of a self-referring rhetorical practice. And here we have our two Dominicans, the one, Thomas, terse, lucid, his words transparent enough that you can see through them immediately to the thought that lies beyond. His are words that do not confine and entrap thought, will not enclose thought within the limits of a self-referring pedagogical practice: thus you can make his thought all your own or not, agree with it or not. Neither is Thomas, their utterer, ever present within his teaching, for he disappears, and nothing within that enormous output draws any attention to himself. But neither is his disappearing-act a mere absence, his disappearing does its work, his silence as an ego speaks more volumes than his words. Thomas is all teacher, and those students unconsciously got him exactly right, little as they knew it, when they called him a 'dumb ox'. For Thomas has nothing to say for himself.

And as to Meister Eckhart: it is true that temperamentally he is of a very different nature from Thomas, he is spectacular where Thomas is plain, brilliantly exciting where Thomas is calmly downbeat, teasingly hyperbolic where Thomas will understate. Eckhart is poet to Thomas' plain prose. And yet Eckhart too, the preacher, rhetorician, word-master, used his poetic skills to draw attention not to his own word-mastery, still less to himself personally, but to the mystery of God that lies beyond all speech. Eckhart's language bends to a purpose, but it is God who bends it, and the purpose is his.

And for both of them, teaching and preaching overlap in ways that cut across our neatly academic divisions of labour. For they meet in a common perception of where it is that all that word-craft is leading, whether of this kind or that: to a silence on the other side of all words in which alone the Word of God can be heard. But, and here is the paradox that Thomas and Eckhart share: it takes all that multitude of words to get you to the silence, for it lies only on the *other* side of them.

And Albert? Of course we do not read his science any more, though we can truly admire his commitment in principle to the evidence of the laboratory. Otherwise, what do we need to say of him other than that he taught Thomas Aquinas and Meister Eckhart? Is that not enough? Isn't teaching done out of the same hopes as theirs, as all three of us did in UCD, Philip and I indeed, but above all Paddy?

ENDNOTES

1 *Summa Theologiae* II-II, 188, 6: Sicut enim maius est illuminare quam lucere solum, ita maius est contemplata aliis tradere quam solum contemplari.

2 Though I am inclined to think that his saying that the accusative singular of 'stone' (in Latin *lapidem*) is derived from the fact that if you drop one on your foot it will hurt it, *laedens pedem*, is the one and only joke I have been able to identify in his work.

3 *Summa Theologiae* I, 12, 13 ad 3.

4 Sermon 83, *Renovamini Spiritu* in *Meister Eckhart, The Essential Sermons, Commentaries, Treatises and Defense*, trans. and intro. Edmund Colledge and Bernard McGinn, (London: SPCK, 1981), p. 208.

St Thomas and the Medieval Synthesis

DESMOND CONNELL

Medieval Christendom inherited a culture already old, which derived its deepest inspiration and unifying force not from philosophy but from the Gospel preached by the Church on the authority of divine revelation. The Gospel is not a philosophy, a speculative creation of human reason reflecting on the world, its origin, its order and destiny, but a message of salvation addressed to man by God, inviting him to a new way of life on earth with a view to an everlasting destiny in the world to come. No doubt, the Christian message contains a teaching rich in its implications for philosophy, and the early centuries of Christianity saw the elaboration of this teaching, its development and defence, in the theological schools of Antioch and Alexandria, in the creeds and conciliar decisions, in the writings of the Fathers – and most particularly, so far as the West is concerned, in the works of St Augustine. If the Gospel provided the fundamental inspiration and unifying force, the manner in which it shaped the culture of Western Christendom is due in large measure to St Augustine. For the medievals St Augustine was the great exponent of Christian wisdom in the light of which the world and man's place in it made sense.

In the elaboration of his thought St Augustine borrowed freely, as the other Fathers had done, from the patrimony of Greek and Roman philosophico–religious speculation, criticizing it in the light of his Christian convictions and adapting it to his requirements. Convinced that Neoplatonism in particular – through which he passed on the road to his conversion – had glimpsed imperfectly and from afar something of the

Christian cosmic vision, he made use of congenial Neoplatonic themes such as the primacy of the spiritual, the hierarchy of perfection ordering all things according to their proximity to or remoteness from their divine source, the role of the ideas contained in that first of the Neoplatonic emanations from God: the Intelligence – according to which all things are formed and man's intellect illuminated.

Certain other themes he cast aside, themes more essential to Neoplatonism than St Augustine perhaps suspected. Neoplatonism vigorously asserts the transcendence of God; God is the incomprehensible one, beyond all our capacity to conceive, and utterly remote in his perfection from all that proceeds from him. But this procession has the character of an eternal and necessary emanation. The Neoplatonic God cannot properly be said to create things because their being is not an absolute gift of the free exercise of his generosity. They come forth eternally after the manner of an overflow of his perfection, as the waters emerge from a superabundant source, as the conclusions proceed from and manifest the richness of a principle, as rays come from a point which concentrates in its simplicity the fullness of light. In a sense one could say that everything is divine until the light is finally dispersed in the darkness, which is the symbol of matter.

Never did the Greeks come closer to the doctrine of creation than here in the Neoplatonic assertion that all things derive from the divine source. Plato had risen from the material world to the contemplation of a higher spiritual order in his world of ideas – which material things reflect only deficiently; he had advanced a lofty conception of the human soul and declared its affinity with the Ideas, and its immortal destiny. But his notion of God remained, at least in so far as he expressed it, nebulous and ambiguous. What is Plato's God? It is hard to say. Perhaps the demiurge of the *Timaeus*, who forms the world after the model of the Ideas, thereby imparting order, goodness and divine harmony, but he is in no sense a creator. For Aristotle the world is without origin. Eternally there with God, it is moved by him in the sense that it is drawn towards its perfection by an aspiration to imitate him, by its love; but God neither knows of its presence nor cares for its progress. Neoplatonism, by deriving all things from God, approaches – perhaps under Judaeo–Christian influence – the doctrine of creation; but nowhere is the originality of this doctrine better revealed than in the opposition between a Neoplatonic world proceeding necessarily and eternally like conclusions from their principle, and the Judaeo–Christian world gratuitously chosen and established in its being by the absolute freedom of the one who alone has the right to say 'I am'. 'Amen, amen, I say to you, before Abraham was made, I am.' St Augustine betrays no signs of confusion between the two doctrines or their implications. Perhaps this is not so clear in the case of other Christian Neoplatonists, despite the orthodoxy of their intentions. The question at least has been raised about John Scottus Eriugena.

From a philosophical point of view, the doctrine of creation is the most fundamental of the influences shaping the Christian mind. It brings to explicit awareness the utterly radical role of existence and the absolute character of the creature's dependence upon God as the one who gives and sustains existence. Between being young and being old, being whole and being maimed, being intelligent and being stupid, being virtuous and being depraved, the oppositions are indeed real but nonetheless relative, and none of them has any significance except for that which exists. But between existing and not existing the opposition is absolute. Without God's freely implemented choice the creature would not exist, and it is on the foundation of its existence that all its endowments rest. For that reason it is said to be made from nothing.

Creation, however, must not be seen merely as an assertion of the creature's total dependence on God. One must indeed say that apart from the creative act the creature is literally nothing; but that is not to say that it is nothing, because through creation it is. Creation is the gift of being, and although the creature's being is wholly from God, it possesses the being it receives as its very own. The gift is real. By creation it is established in the integrity of its own proper finite nature. This has far-reaching implications for theology and philosophy: for theology in that it establishes the foundation of the distinction between the order of nature and the order of grace; for philosophy in that it anticipates the contemporary objection that to acknowledge God must involve the depreciation or even the destruction of properly human and natural values. It must, however, be conceded that St Augustine is here less perceptive than St Thomas. The reason lies in Augustine's Neoplatonism with its denigration of matter and its manner of explaining the dependence of the human mind upon an illumination from above. The great crisis of the thirteenth century was caused by the appearance in the West of a new form of Neoplatonism, and to this we now turn.

In the thirteenth century the Christian West was presented with a challenge to the very foundations of its culture in the form of an alternative wisdom – the pagan wisdom of Aristotle, whose philosophy offered a technically developed and coherent rational account of the world, of God, of man, his nature and destiny, which not merely did not support the Christian vision but on fundamental issues was clearly incompatible with it. The weakness of the Christian position was that it was based on faith, whereas Aristotle could claim the authority of reason.

The story behind the development of this crisis is fascinating, but exceedingly complex. It involves, in the first place, the curious centuries-long migration of the writings of Aristotle – up to the twelfth century the West possessed only his Logic – from Greece through Asia Minor into Syria, the Arab world, across North Africa and eventually into Spain and on to Naples. On the way his works were translated and they accumulated commentaries and accretions so that by the time they reached the West his teaching appeared in a form that owed much to his Neoplatonist Arab and Jewish interpreters. The reasons for this seem clear. For centuries Aristotle had been known and studied in the Muslim world. But in the eyes of religious men Aristotle's teaching on God must have seemed disappointing. If then Aristotle's theology was inadequate the obvious thing was to provide him with something better, and this was done from Neoplatonic sources in the form of two works in particular: the *Theology of Aristotle* and the *Liber de Causis*. St Thomas was the first to discover that the *Liber de Causis* was not in fact by Aristotle. One of the beneficial effects of the Christian opposition as it developed was to make the Christians critical of the sources, of the interpretations of the commentators, and of the reliability of the translations.

In the second place, the arrival of the Greek and Arabic literature coincided with the growth of the schools under the impetus of the twelfth-century renaissance, and the emergence at the beginning of the thirteenth century of the universities: Paris, Oxford, Bologna, Naples, etc. The West was creating the appropriate environment in which to profit from the new learning.

In the third place, the beginning of the thirteenth century saw the foundation of the new mendicant orders, in particular the Dominican and Franciscan orders, and their entry into the universities. These provided the greatest of the masters: St Albert the Great, St Bonaventure, St Thomas Aquinas, John Duns Scotus – not to speak of a host of lesser figures.

From the earliest years of the century the ecclesiastical authorities gave evidence of some anxiety about the challenge that was to come. Provoked

by the excesses of Amalric of Bene and David of Dinant, the Council
of Paris under Robert of Courçon, the papal legate in 1215 forbade the
reading of the *libri naturales* of Aristotle at Paris, and although this retarded
the advance of Aristotle in Paris it did not exclude him (nor is it fair to say
that such was the intention of the decision). Aristotle could still be studied
privately. Moreover he was freely used elsewhere, especially in Oxford
(Roger Bacon) and in Toulouse. By the middle of the century it became
clear what was to be done and the man who saw this need and how it was
to be met was St Albert the Great. Fernand Van Steenberghen sums up his
achievement as follows:

> It is characteristic of superior minds that they can see through details
> and accidental circumstances to the clear vision of the needs of their
> times. Faced with the new situation created by the full-scale invasion
> of Greek and Arab learning, Albert realized that the hour had come
> for Christianity to complete its intellectual emancipation and to take
> an active part in the scientific movement. Aristotle must be welcomed
> and his teaching assimilated according to the special genius of Latin
> and Christian thought; the errors, deviations and lacunae of pagan
> learning would be more effectively overcome by a constructive effort
> of reflection and criticism than by prohibition and mutilation of texts.
> Following out this fundamental intuition, Albert conceived the idea of
> 'remaking Aristotle for the use of the Latin world'; and for this purpose
> he undertook the composition of an encylopaedic work destined to
> enrich Christian learning with all the scientific discoveries which the
> Greeks and Arabs had accumulated throughout their history.[1]

Pierre Mandonnet writes:

> His intention was to take all the scientific work, of which Aristotle
> was the principal component, and incorporate into it every useful
> element that antiquity, the Arabian masters, and his own experience
> could offer. So gradually he formed the idea of a work which would
> put within reach of students the sum total of scientific results acquired
> by the human mind up to his day.[2]

What he achieved personally was indeed impressive and far-reaching in its
influence: he stands at the origin of subsequent developments in theology,

mysticism, philosophy and science. But the greatest of his achievements was to inspire with his ideals the pupil who surpassed him: Thomas Aquinas.

Let us return to the Christian vision of the universe in divine revelation. Revelation is intrinsically historical. This is a fundamental characteristic that was bound to place it in opposition to the vision of the universe emerging in the first half of the thirteenth century with increasing clarity and definition from the pagan sources. God revealed himself and his purposes to a chosen people in the history of that people's relations with him. Not merely was revelation itself a gradual historical process, but its content was a historical drama. History is constitutive of revelation in a way in which, for example, the history of science is not constitutive of, but merely incidental to, science. Moreover, its properly historical character separates it *toto coelo* from the historically represented process of myth, which is no more than the presentation of abstract ideas in an imaginative concrete form (viz. Hegel and Averroes). Now history – unlike evolution – is rooted in freedom. The theme of revelation is the history of salvation, of the existential predicament of human freedom in the presence of the transcendent freedom of God. There is the history of salvation writ large, which is the explicit theme of revelation: the drama setting out from Creation, through the Fall, the vicissitudes of the chosen people, the Incarnation and Redemption, the rise of the new people, and destined to culminate in the final coming and judgment. It is a story with a beginning, a middle and an end. There is the history of salvation writ small: the drama of each one's response throughout the brief span of his life to God's initiative in so far as it is addressed to him personally. (Incidentally, it is only where humanity has a history that the individual can have one: where humanity is but a predetermined eternal succession of individuals, the individual will be the victim of fatalistic necessity.) In each case the drama involves a struggle against evil, the perversion of heart called sin because it is the rejection of the Creator and offensive to him. God is at the same time beyond the drama – it is not an issue for him personally because he is the sovereignly free Creator whose providence directs creation towards the consummation he has ordained (*suaviter disponens omnia*) – and a participant – because the Word was made flesh and placed himself in the power of evil in order to overcome it (*Mors mortua tunc est in ligno quando mortua vita fuit*).[3] The history of salvation with its paradox and drama provides the deepest inspiration of medieval art. The Christian mentality can survive only for as long as it retains its conviction about divine and human freedom. The pagan sources presented a direct challenge to both.

Consider for a moment, by way of a not altogether irrelevant digression, a certain vision of our own time as inspired by an interpretation of science. Science envisages matter eternally in motion, and into this fits the chance occurrence of evolving life. Life emerges necessarily at the moment when chance has presented the appropriate conditions. Evolution is not history, but the product of blind impersonal forces. History, however extended, is but an episode within evolution when man appears and with him the rise and disintegration of cultures within a span of time that opens out the inevitable prospect of their ultimate disappearance. In this case there is some provision for history, but within a framework of necessity and chance that deprives it finally of its point. Freedom is ultimately crushed by necessity, the person by the fatalistic prospect. Here we have materialistic evolution. Medieval Neoplatonism presented rather an idealistic evolution where the course of events resembled the necessary sequence of ideas in a logically determined system. In the long run the outcome for human freedom is the same (or, in contemporary terms, when Marx turned Hegel on his head he was still left with Hegel).

The thirteenth-century challenge to divine freedom was crystallized in the claim that the world is eternal. This might mean either – as in Aristotle himself – that the world is uncreated, without origin, always there, independent of God in its being. Such a world is neither willed by God nor even known to him. He has no part in its direction, no care for its destiny. On the other hand, it might mean – as in the Neoplatonic Aristotelianism of Avicenna (980–1037) – that the world proceeds eternally from God by a necessity of his being. Avicenna explained how the world proceeds from God by a gradated series of emanations. God immediately produces only the first Intelligence. From the first Intelligence proceeds the second Intelligence together with the first animated celestial sphere, over which it presides. From the second Intelligence proceeds the third Intelligence and the second animated celestial sphere – and so on until we come to the tenth and last Intelligence which presides over the sphere of the moon. The tenth Intelligence, called the *Dator Formarum* (Giver of Forms) is the principle from which proceeds the whole sub-lunary world, the world where we live, including the souls of men. It is also the active source of the formation of bodies in the course of the changes that occur in the world as well as the active source of man's intellectual life. Each man has but a passive capacity to understand the truth infused from above – in that sense he is equipped with his own intellect – but the active source of his understanding is a separate intelligence common to the whole of humanity. Avicenna's philosophy excludes the freedom of creation, its immediacy, divine knowledge of and care for the world. Providence is the affair of the *Dator Formarum* and we are remote from God. Men arrive in an eternal sequence that eliminates history and subjects them to fatalistic necessity. In making the *Dator Formarum* the active principle in the formation of bodies and in the process of human intellectual knowledge he undermined the integrity of creatures, of the natural order. It remained for Averroes, however, to deal an even more serious blow to human integrity – but we shall return to this presently.

What answer could Christians make to the claims of Avicenna? Obviously they had the word of God to which they adhered in faith. But revelation makes its assertions without elaborating rational justifications. What, then, is to be thought of the eternity of the world? A purely theological reply will take the form of direct contradiction. And many, including St Bonaventure, adopted the attitude that the hypothesis of an eternal world is a contradiction in terms. St Thomas, however, considered the question on its own merits metaphysically and he presented the curious conclusion that there is no contradiction in the hypothesis of an eternal world provided only that it be created. Aristotle claimed that the world is of its nature eternal, but it can be shown that his arguments do not prove his point. On the other hand, revelation says that the world had a beginning in time, and we accept this as a matter of faith; but there is no way of proving from reason that the world had to have a beginning – this is a matter for God's free decision and can be known only from revelation. The conclusion of St Thomas, evidently, stresses God's freedom, and it may at first sight look like a nice compromise that goes a bit of the road with everyone. This would be a mistake. It is in fact a conclusion arising out of a radical rethinking of the whole of metaphysics. The metaphysics of St Thomas is something quite new, the first genuinely original philosophy of the Christian era. It draws upon the wide variety of sources at his disposal – Aristotelian, Neoplatonist, Patristic, Jewish, Muslim – but it masters these sources and emerges as a genuine unity of thought, a synthesis expressing a new and deeper penetration of the question of being. That is its glory and the source of its enduring value. The metaphysics of St Thomas is fundamentally Aristotelian; it differs, however, in its new perception of the existential character of being. Now existence is the sphere of freedom as essence is the sphere of necessity. The metaphysics of Avicenna is dominated ultimately by essential necessities. He provided, it is true, a valuable hint concerning the originality of existence, a hint taken up eagerly by St Thomas, when he made the point that the creature does not exist in virtue of a necessity of its essence, but he lost sight of the implications of this point when he declared that it existed in virtue of a necessity of the essence of God. As Gilson remarks, this is the God of the Neoplatonist Plotinus, for whom God is 'He who is what he had to be', so completely determined by his perfection that he could not have done other than what he did. The God of St Thomas is simply 'He who is', possessing in its fullness the existential character of being, able, therefore, to give being absolutely as he freely chooses, and not in virtue of a necessity of his essence.

The name 'He who is', of course, is a revealed name. Can it be discovered also philosophically? It can, provided we develop our metaphysical insight into the mystery of being to the point where we see that finite being, precisely as finite, is caused in its very being. The cause in this sense of finite being is the infinite being, He whose very essence is constituted by the fullness of being. Can we know that such a one is free? Yes, because He who is being in its infinite plenitude can have no need of creatures. If he creates, then his act is the expression of sheer generosity: *et ideo ipse solus est maxime liberalis.*[4]

There is thus no way of deciding what God must have done by appeal to necessary reasons. But perhaps, as St Bonaventure claimed, an eternal world is a contradiction in terms. Here we must be careful about what we mean by eternal. To speak of an eternal world is not to speak of a world identical in its duration with God. The world's duration is temporal, the continuous successive duration of a reality subject to incessant change. It does not possess its being all at once, but in a continuous flux. It gains its future only by losing its present in the past. God, however, is changeless: his duration is the duration of an immutable now proportionate to the supremacy of his possession of being, beyond all distinctions of past, present and future. And so Boethius expressed the eternity of God in the constantly quoted definition as 'the complete, simultaneous and perfect possession of everlasting life' (*interminabilis vitae tota simul et perfecta possessio*). The two eternities, the eternity of God and the eternity of the world are not only distinct, but in the most absolute sense incommensurable. They cannot be put side by side and compared, any more than one could compare the content of a problem by taking a measuring rod. We might perhaps think that if the world is eternal God could not have created it, because if he is to create it he must somehow manage to get in before it. But this is to place God in time, to measure his act by time. We think of creation as if it involved a transition, a coming into being. But how could there be a transition from nothing to being? Nothing is not a real starting-point from which to set out, nor are there any stages to pass before being is attained. We think that there was a time when there was nothing created, followed by a time when it all began. But where there is nothing created, *ex hypothesi* there is not time. What then is creation? Viewed from God's side it is simply God's free act of will by which he gives the world existence. Viewed from the creature's side it is simply the relation of total dependence in virtue of which it holds its being in time from God. Let it be, and it is. The temporal duration of the world is simply an aspect of its created being. But whether that duration is infinite or finite is irrelevant to the metaphysical question of its creation. A world stretching back without beginning into a temporal past is just as dependent and just as much created as a world stretching back only in a finite duration.

Having clarified in this way the metaphysical understanding of creation, St Thomas was in a position to vindicate God's freedom and to deal with the objections arising out of Aristotelian and Neoplatonist doctrines of necessity. He also saw that the act of creation is exclusively divine. Against Peter Lombard he argued that no creature could mediate creation because no creature could give being in the absolute manner of the creator: it could not even be employed as an instrument by the creator, because an instrument presupposes something to which its instrumental causality is applied. But creation does not presuppose anything, it simply gives absolutely. Each created thing, therefore, is created immediately by God. And since the divine act of creation is the expression of a free intelligent choice, God knows intimately all that he creates. We come from God as known and chosen, and his providence keeps us in his care.

Would an eternal world have a history? In a sense this question is irrelevant because revelation assures us that the world, and the human species, had a beginning. But even in an eternal world St Thomas would have been obliged by his own principles to maintain that the human race had a beginning. Otherwise there would now be an actually infinite number of human immortal souls and he considered that an actual infinite number in being is a contradiction. It is interesting that in the eternal world of modern materialism the human race has a temporal origin. The difference is that it has no ultimate destiny but extinction.

But if God's creative causality is so total and pervasive, is there anything left for the creature to do? If God literally does everything, is the creature anything more than a puppet? Has it even the reality of a puppet, or is it reduced to a mere appearance? At stake here is the crucial question as to how seriously we are to take man's personal activity, and in particular the moral responsibility for his decisions that derives from the fact that his actions are inalienably his own. Deprive him of his responsibility and not only have you made nonsense of the history of salvation but you have destroyed the foundations of that personal dignity at the origin of all properly human values. Profoundly aware of the issues involved, St Thomas never wavered in his conviction that if the creature's being is God's gift, the gift is nonetheless, or rather for that very reason, thoroughly real. Against the Mahometan theologians who sought to glorify God by depriving the creature of its power to act, St Thomas replied that this is to deprive the universe of what is best in it. The greatness of God is not enhanced by the poverty of his creatures but by their perfection, and the perfection of anything is manifested and measured by its activity, the activity in which it exploits the riches of its being. It is one thing to assert this; to justify it is more difficult.

The issue here to some extent divided Platonism from Aristotelianism. Plato maintained that the world of experience is not fully real: it depends on a higher order of spiritual realities – the Ideas or Forms – which our world merely reflects imperfectly, by imitation or participation. The effect of his teaching was to drain the world of our experience of its full reality. Neoplatonism continued this line of thought with its emanationism: the further a thing is from the first source the less is its reality. Matter, which is the final stage in the process of emanation, is non-being. Aristotle rejected the Platonic conception of a separate world of Ideas or Forms: the realities of our experience are fully real and equipped with all that is required for their natural activity. He brought the Platonic Forms down to earth, giving each thing the intrinsic form which determines its nature as the source of its natural activity. The difficulty here, however, is that he made the world practically self-sufficient, leaving it dependent on God not for its being but only for the ultimate principle of its motion. This is Aristotle's naturalism.

St Thomas synthesized these apparently irreconcilable positions. With Plato he made the world dependent upon a higher order of reality, which he identified with God; with Aristotle he defended its genuine reality. This he was able to do through his doctrine of creation. God is not simply an infinite perfection in which creatures participate or which they imitate. Above all he is the self-existent perfection of being, and the proper effect of his causality is to give being. Because creation is the communication of being the creature is fully real and endowed with all the natural principles of a real activity. In this way Aristotelianism is fully incorporated into his theory and at the same time surpassed.

Aquinas' genius appears particularly in his analysis of the difference between the manner of God's causation and that of the creature. The creature cannot give being absolutely; it can give being only by effecting a transformation in something already existent. If I want to make a statue, I cannot say: let it be and it is. I must find some material on which I can work to produce it. In order to produce its effect, then, the creature presupposes something distinct from, and present to it, on which it can act. Fire can burn only if there is something combustible in its path. The creature acts on the other as it were from outside it. Nor can it produce something distinct from itself. If the effect it produces is distinct from it this is because the effect is produced in something already distinct. The effect of its action in fact is somehow to impart a likeness of itself to the other. If, for example, I were to cause you to make some choice I should really be imposing my will upon you. But God does not act in this way from outside; he does not simply change what is already there distinct from him, because his creative causality does not presuppose something already there to receive the effect of his activity; he produces it absolutely. That is why he alone can cause what is absolutely distinct from himself. Because he alone is infinite in being, with absolute power over being, he alone can produce what is other than himself *in its very otherness*. God acts, then, not from outside, as if the creature were already there confronting him; he acts from within, as the very foundation of its being and activity. When he acts he enables the creature to be and to act. The effect of his causality, then, is not, for example, to impose his will on me but to give me my being and activity as other than himself, as my very own; he places my freedom in my hands. The creature thus possesses its *esse proprium* and its *agere proprium*,[5] which it holds and exercises in complete dependence on God, and this is the metaphysical foundation of the integrity of created reality. The objection that creation undermines the integrity of the creature is based on a confusion between divine and created causality.

St Augustine had remained rather more dependent on Platonism. In particular he followed the Platonists in maintaining that man depends immediately on God for the special illumination he requires in order to grasp truth. Many of the medieval masters followed him in this conviction, notably St Bonaventure, and on this basis they considered that man had only to enter sincerely into himself in order to discover the presence of God. It was an attractive theme in the eyes of Christians. St Thomas rejected this. God has given man the natural principles which enable him to embark on the task of acquiring the truth proportionate to his own proper nature. The human intellect has no immediate access to God or other spiritual realities but must make its way laboriously from its experience through the senses of the material world to an indirect and purely analogical knowledge of God. Such is man's natural condition, and here St Thomas follows Aristotle faithfully. One could put the difference between St Thomas and St Augustine by saying that whereas St Augustine sees God as supplying for the deficiencies of his creatures in the natural order, St Thomas sees him as the creative cause of the sufficiency of the natural order. St Thomas expresses these convictions from the beginning of his career. At the end of his career he was obliged to defend them against the challenge of Averroes. Paradoxically the Averroist challenge derived not from Platonic but from Aristotelian sources.

The question of man's nature is one of the thorniest in philosophy, for although each one of us experiences himself as profoundly one, possessing the unity of a distinct and unique person, the various components in our make-up seem irreconcilable. We possess an animal nature subject to physical and biological laws and equipped with the senses which enable us to experience the world about us. At the same time we escape from the fascination of the immediately experienced through our intellectual capacity to think, to stand back from the world and question it, to apprehend ideals of unity, truth, beauty, goodness as principles of civilized living, to penetrate to some knowledge of the supersensible. Nor are we controlled and determined by emotion; we restrain and overcome instinctive reaction by the exercise of free, reflective self-control. Confronted with this duality of aspects, Plato divided man in two, a body and a soul, attributing the higher life to his soul, and tracing the soul's origin, with some suggestion of myth, to a preexistence in the higher world of spiritual reality. Aristotle insisted that man is one and plunged his soul firmly in matter. Man is a single composite reality composed of a soul, which is his form, and matter. The soul is immaterial, spiritual. What, then, is its origin? Can purely material biological processes account for the origin of a being with an immaterial form? To this question Aristotle has no real answer. What is worse, there is enough of reticence and ambiguity in his works, including the *De Anima*, to create some doubt as to whether the individual's soul is properly intellectual at all. Perhaps the active intellect is a separate substance. Alexander of Aphrodisias, one of his greatest Greek commentators, identified the active intellect with the divinity in *Metaphysics* Bk 12. Perhaps the intellectual principle is unique and separate from individual men. In this case the individual is not immortal.

This is precisely the position adopted by Averroes in the name of an authentic interpretation of Aristotle. Averroes asserts the separate existence of two intellects, one active and one passive. The active intellect is the tenth Intelligence, which presides over the sphere of the moon, and to this extent Averroes repeats the teaching of Avicenna. This active intellect, does not, as in Avicenna, infuse intelligible forms into the individual man's passive intellect, for the very good reason that the individual man has no passive intellect either. Rather, the active intellect abstracts intelligible forms from the individual man's sensory experience and communicates them to the separate passive intellect, which does the thinking for the whole of humanity. In other words, man is no more than a highly developed animal and completely corruptible. The individual man does not really think, but in him a separate intelligence, which alone is immortal, does all the thinking on the basis of his experience. The union of the intelligence with the individual man is extrinsic and terminates at his death.

It would be difficult to exaggerate the consequences of this position for Christian civilization. Gone is that centre of freedom and choice, the Hebrew *heart*, which lies at the origin of man's personal dignity. St Thomas saw that there was question not just of the separation of the principle of thought but of the principle of freedom as well, because, as Aristotle himself was aware, will follows intellect. Gone too is the prospect of man's immortal destiny. And the challenge was based on an appeal to the authentic Aristotle.

In his *De Unitate Intellectus Contra Averroistas* St Thomas undertakes the task of answering Averroes. With new translations of Aristotle and Themistius by his colleague William of Moerbeke at his disposal he was in a position to refute textually the Averroist interpretation of Aristotle and of his Greek commentators, Theophrastus and Themistius. Philosophically he analysed the arguments of Averroes, confronting them with the evidence of experience: 'each one experiences that it is he himself who understands understanding' (*experitur enim unusquisque seipsum esse qui intelligit.*)[6] He showed the weakness of the contention that the intellect is one because truth is one, and criticized severely the dualistic conception of the opposition between matter and spirit which Averroes believed made impossible the union of spirit and matter in the human individual. He asserted firmly the unity of man on the basis of the unity of his form: it is one and the same form, the spiritual, intellectual soul, united with matter, that is at the origin of man's being and of all his activities. And he was able to account for the origin of each soul through God's creative presence to the world.

Gérard Verbeke reflects on the nature of this intervention:

> St Thomas adopts a position opposed to the anthropology of Averroes: is it as a Christian or as a philosopher he does so? The question would be futile if the Angelic Doctor did not himself insist on the philosophical character of his arguments. In opposing the doctrine of the Arabian philosopher he is bent on defeating him on his own ground through recourse to the texts of Aristotle, Theophrastus and Themistius: he is convinced that the interpretation of these authors as given by Averroes is mistaken. But there is more; in his refutation St Thomas tells us explicitly that he does not wish to rely on the teachings of the faith, but on philosophical arguments: to those who claim to be philosophers he opposes a philosophical reply. That this is not at variance with his Christian conviction creates no problem. He means to justify his position at the bar of reason and enters into a purely philosophical dialogue with his philosophical adversaries.[7]

If European civilization owes a debt to medieval thought, and in particular to St Thomas, it is surely this defence of the integrity of man which is the precondition of genuine human values. It is not perhaps inappropriate to remark that a challenge similar to the Averroist lies at the origin of contemporary thought in Hegel.

I began by posing the question of the relation between faith and reason. Whatever answer one accepts, one cannot but be impressed by the gigantic monuments of speculation built laboriously through the exercise of reason in the teeth of destructive forces that would have razed to its foundations all Christian dwelling in the world. It is sometimes said that the medieval universe is tiny by comparison with the material universe we know today: but the medieval universe is more than the material universe – it is the universe of being, and placed alongside the world of today's materialists it is a vastness beyond compare. Very particularly it affirms the vastness of the being of man, of each individual human being, however enclosed he may be within the confines of a fragile biological existence. As the Psalm put it: 'For the inward mind and heart of a man are deep.' (63.6: *Profunditas est homo et cor eius abyssus*.) The questions that raises remain with us today.

ENDNOTES

1   Fernand Van Steenberghen, *La philosophie au XIIIe siècle* (Louvain: Publications universitaires, 1966), pp. 289–90. Author's translation.

2   Pierre Mandonnet, *Siger de Brabant et l'averroïsme latin au XIIIe siècle*, vol. 1 (Louvain: Institut Supérieur de Philosophie, 1911), p. 37. Author's translation.

3   From the antiphon for the Office of the feast of the Exaltation of the Holy Cross, 14 September: O magnum pietatis opus mors: mortua tunc est, in ligno quando mortua vita fuit. (O great work of piety: death then died when life was dead upon the cross.)

4   *ST* I 44, 4 ad 1: 'He alone is supremely generous.'

5   Its own existence and its own action.

6   *ST* I 76, 1.

7   Gérard Verbeke, 'L'unité de l'homme: saint Thomas contre Averroès', *Revue philosophique de Louvain* 58 (1960), pp. 248–9. Author's translation.

HEGEL AND THE INFINITE

CYRIL O'REGAN

This essay concerns Hegel's appeal to and use of the concept of the infinite to indicate the singular achievement of German Idealism and of his own philosophy as it moves decisively beyond Kant's transcendental Idealism and his critique of metaphysics. By no means, however, do Hegel's appeal to and use of the concept of the infinite and cognate concepts such as Being, Idea, and finally Spirit, leave behind Idealism as such. Rather Hegel's concept of the infinite is indicative of an attempt at radicalizing Kant's Idealism and thereby demonstrating that there is nothing that thought cannot think: not nature, not the self, and not the ground of the world, whether explicitly referred to by the name of God or not. Nor does Hegel's critique of Kant's critique of metaphysics lead to the installation of either classical metaphysics or its Leibnizian restatement, both of which Kant rejected in the *Critique of Pure Reason*.[1] Hegel's metaphysics is dependent on the epistemological turn and is thus entirely post-Kantian even as it generates and supports a metaphysics different in kind from the premodern and modern forms of metaphysics that preceded it. Hegel's metaphysics is expressed within the frame of absolute Idealism that leaves nothing unthought, and especially those realities that much of the classical Christian philosophical tradition judged to fall outside conceptual scrutiny either in whole or in part. Hegel's absolute Idealism then genuinely represents a 'revolution' in philosophical thought.

Although the concept of the infinite is not the truly foundational concept in Hegel's technical discussions – this is Spirit (*Geist*) – nonetheless it recurs throughout Hegel's career both as a placeholder for conceiving the comprehensive whole, which alone for Hegel is the truth,[2] and as an index of a shift in vision and assumption regarding the order of reality.

Whether one is talking about the classical metaphysical tradition or the metaphysics of Leibniz, to the degree to which the concept of the infinite or any cognate thereof is supplied, the infinite is one term of the complex binary infinite–finite, in which the infinite is everything that the finite is not and the finite is everything (negative) that the infinite is not. Put another way: before Hegel, and before German Idealism, of which Hegel can be counted as its most illustrious and perhaps also most illustrative member, the infinite–finite pair does not indicate simply a contrast, but contraries that are incapable of reconciliation. Hegel's absolute Idealism represents the subversion of this view; while he does not reduce the binary of infinite–finite to that of contrast, and might rightly be said to exaggerate the difference, he does suggest that their difference is sustained within unity in which each of the terms defines the other. For Hegel, this means that the infinite–finite pair is a dialectical rather than simple unity. That is, the infinite–finite pair is not a unity given in the beginning and which sustains mere contrasts rather than contradictions that need to be reconciled. Rather the unity is a synthetic unity of contraries given only at the end in and through the process of working through difference to unity and bringing this complex unity to consciousness. There is a second aspect to the Idealist revolution enacted and completed by Hegel. This has to do with the God-world, which Hegel believes essentially mirrors the metaphysical relation of ground to what is grounded and the logical relation of that which explains to what is explained. Hegel fundamentally questions the classical understanding of God as creator and the world as created. In the classical model God is thought of as self-caused and completely self-sufficient, and the created as caused, ontologically insufficient, and dependent on God for its existence and continuation. As Hegel aims, then, to correct classical and modern metaphysics, he also aims to correct traditional Christian and modern Christian views of God and the God-world relation.

With these two foci in mind, the present essay is divided into two main sections. The first section concentrates on Hegel's metaphysical revolution in which reality is conceived as a complex, self-constituting whole rather than as a static binary between an order of reality that serves as the ground or cause of another reality, which is metaphysically deficient vis-à-vis its ground. Crucially, unlike the classical tradition and unlike what we find in the post-Cartesian metaphysics of Leibniz, where the infinite determines the finite unilaterally, in Hegel's absolute Idealism the infinite and finite determine each other reciprocally. Just as the finite cannot be philosophically accounted for outside of its relation to the infinite, neither can the infinite be explained in the strict sense outside its relation to the finite. I want to underscore that the subversion of the axiom of metaphysical asymmetry between the infinite and the finite, which plays a central role in classical metaphysics and in the metaphysics of Leibniz, is crucial to identifying Hegel's thought, but also German Idealism more broadly. Although I want to insist that Hegel and German Idealism are unique in this respect – thus 'revolutionary' – I will identify Spinoza as an important antecedent, without, however, suggesting that his thought truly accounts for Hegel's position on the mutual dependence of the infinite and the finite. I also underscore that the dialectical relation between the infinite and the finite is central to the elaboration of a developmental ontology that is new in the history of philosophy. The main texts I call on to make my argument in the first section of the essay include *Faith and Knowledge* (1802), the *Phenomenology of Spirit* (1807), and the *Encyclopaedia of the Philosophical Sciences* (1821–31).[3]

The second of our two sections has as its focus Hegel's concept of God and his articulation of the God-world relation. With regard to the former I show how Hegel, unlike Kant and in reaction to Kant, thought that an elaboration of God was possible without repeating the problems of classical metaphysics and the metaphysics of Leibniz. In addition, again in contradistinction to Kant, Hegel demonstrates that he is open to Christian doctrine, and especially the Christian doctrine of the Trinity, without this meaning in the slightest that his Trinitarian thought is in line with that of the classical theological tradition. With regard to the second of the main tasks in this section of the essay, I refer to Hegel's subversion of the God-world relation as classically conceived and carried forward under new management in Leibniz. Hegel argues against divine self-sufficiency or aseity and the unilateral dependence of the world and human being on a divine that bears no intrinsic relation to its own expressions. Two of the texts prominent in the first section will again be called on, that is, the *Phenomenology* and the *Encyclopaedia*. Hegel's *Lectures on the Philosophy of Religion* (1821),[4] however, will also play a central role. In order to give a measure of determinacy and traction to the discussion, I will use Aquinas' view of the creator-created distinction in the *Summa Theologiae* as both representative of the traditional Christian view and as a foil to Hegel's view which self-consciously departs from the classical view by insisting that though the world would not be the world without God, it is also true that God would not be God without the world. I will attend briefly to Hegel's demand that one of the systemic handicaps of Christianity has been its mode of representation (*Vorstellung*) which cannot imagine the God-world relation as other than made up of two different objects, one infinite, one finite, which are externally related to each other. Unlike most modern rationalists Hegel thinks highly of Christianity. He is also convinced that its mode of representation has to be overcome if we are to see the truth that God and world are intrinsically related to and mutually dependent on each other. To round out my account of Hegel's articulation of God and the God-world relation I will briefly comment on Hegel's critique of Kant's critique of the proofs of God's existence, while again underscoring that Hegel does not repeat the classical forms of these proofs.

Before I get to my two main tasks, however, it is necessary to present a brief historical review of the use of the term infinity in the Western philosophical tradition and the Christian theological tradition with which in due course the philosophical tradition got bonded. First it should be said that the notion of infinity (*apeiron*) is as old as philosophy itself. It is the pivotal term in what we know of the thought of Anaximander. The history of the term infinity thereafter in the philosophical tradition is in part dialectical and in part a history of forgetting that the term originally applied to reality at its most intensive and comprehensive. The use of the term is in part dialectical in that in the dialogues of Plato, and particularly in the *Parmenides*, infinity or the unlimited is less associated with the unity that is the ground of reality than with appearance and plurality that are precisely its opposite. This redirection or relocation of infinity is continued in Plotinus, who again thinks of infinity or the unlimited in a negative fashion as applying to that material reality that is at the furthest distance from the One which is Being at its most real, both extensively and intensively.[5] This negative or privative view of infinity is the legacy inherited by the Christian tradition as it drew upon the categories of Platonism and other forms of philosophy in order to make itself comprehensible to itself and to Western high culture. Although Gregory of Nyssa might be an exception in entertaining infinity as Being as its most perfect,[6] representative Christian thinkers such as Augustine and Aquinas had little use for the term, stained as it was by its association with plurality and formlessness.[7] Arguably, it takes until the Renaissance period and the rise of mathematics for infinity to begin to recover the kind of authority it enjoyed at the very inception of philosophy. Nicholas of Cusa and Giordano Bruno were two of the more prominent Renaissance thinkers who brought infinity back into philosophical circulation. One can hypothesize that their interest in mathematics in general and the mathematical notion of infinity in particular proved influential. In both cases, however, it was found necessary to distinguish between mathematical or quantitative infinity and a much richer, more qualitative view of infinity as naming the very foundation of reality. Although it would be going too far to make a case for the genetic dependence of German Idealism on Renaissance Neoplatonism both with regard to the language and substance of the infinite, nonetheless, it is a proven fact that Schelling had read Giordano Bruno early in his career, certainly Bruno's great text on divine unity, but perhaps also his most famous text on the infinity and immensity of the world.[8] If in all likelihood Hegel did not read the works of Giordano Bruno by the time of the publication of the *Phenomenology* (1807), he had almost certainly read Schelling's *Bruno*. As evidenced by his *Lectures on the History of Philosophy*, Hegel familiarized himself with the work of Bruno later in his career. It is also worth pointing out that in his logic Hegel recalls Nicholas of Cusa's famous idiom about the coincidence of opposites to buttress his own view of contradiction as the basic dynamic of his developmental view of reality and self-consciousness.[9]

DIALECTIC: RECIPROCAL DETERMINATION, DEVELOPMENTAL ONTOLOGY

Although Hegel's speculative idealism can neither be identified with the subjectivism of Descartes nor the transcendental idealism of Kant, which outlines the conditions of the possibility of knowledge of the external world, nonetheless, it presupposes both. In his *Lectures on the History of Philosophy* Hegel underscores not only the monumental nature of Descartes' discovery of the *cogito*, but also Descartes' procedural scepticism which, in his view, sets the terms for the dialectical movement of knowledge towards absolute knowledge.[10] In the same text he also lauds what Kant had referred to as his Copernican revolution.[11] If Hegel essentially changes from being a religious thinker to a philosopher in the strict sense, in texts such as the *Difference Essay* and *Faith and Knowledge*,[12] he does so only in and through a reading of Kant. Although Hegel's reading of Kant is critical, this is not to gainsay that Kant's thought is indispensable for him. The main criticism of Kant is that transcendental thought remains within the horizon of 'reflection' (*Reflexion*), that is, within the subject–object horizon characteristic both of realism and idealism. What is required is a shift to a 'speculative' viewpoint. In advancing the claims of 'speculation' (*Spekulation*), as more than one commentator has pointed out,[13] Hegel has in mind its etymology. 'Speculation' derives from the Latin *speculare*, which means to see, and *speculum*, which means a mirror. What Hegel is suggesting is that in knowledge in its most perfect realization there is a perfect coincidence between knowing and the object of knowing. This is precisely what is denied by Kant who insists that all we can know are the phenomenal appearances and that we are incapable of knowing things as they are in themselves. For example, while Kant understands our zeal to know God, the world, and the self, strictly speaking the reality of each lies beyond the competence of knowledge. Hegel thinks that Kant not only has been cowardly in making a confession about the impotence of knowledge, but has been entirely wrongheaded. For Hegel, even in 1802, has a grasp of what achieves a clearer expression five years later in the *Phenomenology* (1807): to claim to be able to find the line between how reality appears and how it is really constituted, or translated into the idiom of the finite and infinite, to be able to make the contrast between the infinite and the finite, implies that one has already transcended the boundary that supposedly separates them. Hegel famously makes this point in an aphoristic way in the Preface of the *Phenomenology*. It is the task of the famous final chapter concerning 'absolute knowledge' to provide the outline of what this looks like. Hegel is perfectly clear about what he aims to achieve: (a) to provide a description of the 'way' to absolute knowledge rather than a demonstration; (b) once the 'way' has been shown, it is the task of science as such (*Wissenschaft*) to articulate a newly minted dialectical logic to make sense of the possibility of absolute knowledge – hence the *Science of Logic* (*Wissenschaft der Logik*) (1812).[14]

By the time of the *Phenomenology* (1807), then, Hegel is clear regarding the actuality of absolute knowledge which can account for everything that is known as well as all preliminary forms of knowing. Hegel's preferred language is now that of Spirit (*Geist*), although Love (*Liebe*) is an approximate in this text, as Being (*Sein*), Essence (*Wesen*), and above all Concept (*Begriff*) will later be in the *Science of Logic* as well as the *Logic* of the *Encylopaedia*. As is well known, Hegel does not refuse the language of Being and, positively understood, Spirit can rightly be regarded as a specification of the category of Being with which both logics begin.[15] At the same time, however, it is distinct from it in that with Spirit we are talking about Being that is actual rather than merely virtual,[16] and Being as it is coextensive with self-consciousness rather than being prior to consciousness. It is obvious that in both logics Hegel essentially pigeonholes the entire metaphysical tradition as based on an empty formality, which in effect cannot be distinguished from nothing.[17] It would be easy to accuse Hegel of sheer opportunism here, since the kind of view of Being that he is overcoming more nearly recalls that of Scotus than the view articulated by Aquinas in *De Ente et Essentia* and by Aristotle in his *Metaphysics*. The most salient trait of Being from the point of view of my topic is that it is unrelational. One of the tasks of moving from Being to Essence and from there to Concept is to clarify that Being is not separate from its instances that it covers (the logic of Essence) nor from the reflexive grasp of this intrinsic relation (the logic of Concept).

Throughout his highly disciplined work, then, Hegel remains tolerant of approximates. I have dealt briefly with a crucial set of approximates above. Another approximate for Being as the would-be origin is the infinite (*Unendlichkeit*). In fact, Hegel's reflection on the infinite, arguably, provides the best angle from which to get a clear view of the metaphysical revolution that is afoot in his earliest attempts at philosophy. The first major act of Hegel's philosophical revolution consists of his opposition to the entire metaphysical tradition, especially as that tradition was adopted by Christian thinkers, which insisted on the absolute independence of the infinite, the incommensurability of the infinite and finite, and their fundamental irreconcilability given the contradiction between them. Instead, Hegel suggests that the infinite cannot be truly independent if it is not fully complete, and it is not fully complete unless it encapsulates the finite that would otherwise stand over against it, thereby limiting it and essentially constituting it as finite. Far from downplaying the incommensurability between the infinite and the finite, which was a staple of the philosophical tradition, Hegel underscores it only to exaggerate it further. Hegel's point is that it is precisely as contradictories that the infinite and finite are internally related and thus reconciled, and thereby constitute the comprehensive unity that in a real sense is alone worthy of being identified as the infinite.

Although the details will take some time to work out, from the very beginning of his philosophical career Hegel argues for a displacement of what one might call the principle of the unilateral determination of the finite by the infinite and its replacement by the principle of reciprocal determination:

as the finite is determined by the infinite, equally the infinite is determined by the finite. Now the principle of unilateral determination is central to classical metaphysics. Nor is this principle fundamentally questioned in and by the metaphysics of Leibniz,[18] who though he sees that the finite can mirror the infinite, nonetheless claims that it depends on the infinite for its existence, essence, and preservation in being. For Hegel, in the *Difference Essay* and *Faith and Knowledge*, the principle of reciprocal determination is foundational to the new philosophy which is being articulated by Fichte and Schelling. As a burgeoning philosopher, although he fully embraces this newly fashioned principle, it is crucial for him to grasp how this new principle is articulated. In these texts written some five years before the *Phenomenology* Hegel definitely prefers Schelling's positive articulation of the principle to that of Fichte, largely on the grounds that of the two Schelling seems to be more able to demonstrate the unity between the infinite and the finite and between knowing and being than Fichte, who in the many iterations of his *Science of Knowledge* (*Wissenschaftslehre*) remains more or less stipulative when he is not suggesting that unity is less an achievement than a task.[19] Hegel's opposition to this progressive view of the infinite remains constant throughout his career and for him it is set aside as the 'bad infinite' (*die schlechte Unendlichkeit*).[20] By the time of the *Phenomenology* (1807), however, Hegel has become convinced that Schelling's particular view of the relationship between the infinite and finite is itself flawed in a number of different ways. First, the unity between the infinite and finite envisaged by Schelling is insufficiently dynamic. For Hegel, the basic problem is that the unity is a unity posited in the beginning that takes insufficient account of the difference – even contradiction – between the infinite and finite. Instead, Hegel thinks that the unity is best thought of as if it were 'immediate' (*unmittelbar*) in the pejorative sense of the word, that is, a unity given in the beginning as a brute fact. He opposes to this a unity that is gained in a dialectical process through which it becomes apparent that the finite is not simply finite any more than the infinite is simply infinite. The infinite–finite unity, therefore, is dialectically mediated. If we dispose – as we ought to – of the idea that there is some external agent behind the process, then we can speak of the process of unification or reconciliation as self-mediated.[21] Second, an early work of Schelling such as the *System of Transcendental Idealism* (1799) and other texts from Schelling's so-called Identity–Philosophy phase (*Identitätsphilosophie*) fail to think through the relationship between absolute knowledge, that is, knowledge which does not involve the subject–object distinction, and relative knowledge, that is, knowledge which does involve such a distinction. Relative knowledge or consciousness is thus thought of as having an external relation to absolute consciousness. The problem here is that there is no way to account for the movement of one form of consciousness to the other. Moreover, from the mature Hegel's point of view, Schelling makes the gravest of philosophical mistakes by thinking of the form of absolute knowledge posited in and as the beginning after the manner of unconsciousness rather than self-consciousness. Absolute knowledge or 'intellectual intuition' in Schelling is knowledge 'before' it has become differentiated into subject and object. In contrast, for Hegel, absolute knowledge is that knowledge which is subsequent and consequent to consciousness and is identified as self-consciousness. This self-consciousness, however, not only surpasses any and all forms of consciousness, it also recollects them. In doing so, the absolute form of knowing is not only different from consciousness, but is fully comprehensive because it includes all its individual and social forms.[22]

Nothing should detract from the revolutionary character of German Idealism in the history of philosophy and the uniqueness of Hegel's contribution that brings out the dynamic and dialectical implications of the principle of reciprocal determination brought to light by both Fichte and Schelling. Nevertheless, it is not inconsistent to suggest with regard to both German Idealism in general and Hegel in particular that the principle of reciprocal determination is anticipated in the modern period. Pride of place necessarily has to be given to Spinoza's *Ethics* which challenges the received wisdom that there is always more reality in the cause than in the effect. This is a constant in the metaphysical tradition, whether one is talking about Plato or Aristotle, Aquinas or Duns Scotus, Descartes or Leibniz. In the various propositions that make up the justly famous Book I of the *Ethics* Spinoza makes it perfectly clear that the universe of finite particulars fully articulates infinite substance. Without this articulation infinite substance would not truly be infinite substance. This is made especially clear in Spinoza's treatment in Book I of the relation between *natura naturans* and *natura naturata*.[23] The effect, which fully renders the cause, is thus fully coincident with that cause. It is the presence of ideas such as this in Spinoza that justifies interpretations of Hegel which suggest that Spinoza is the metaphysical influence par excellence in Hegel,[24] albeit an influence that presupposes Kant's transcendental turn. Of course, this does not mean that when Hegel distinguishes his thought from that of

Spinoza in his *Lectures on the History of Philosophy* he is being disingenuous or that he fundamentally misunderstands the degree of discontinuity between his metaphysics and that of the Jewish philosopher.[25] Spinoza does indeed provide a basic sketch of a metaphysics in which the whole, whether substance and its expression in attributes and modes, or *natura naturans* and *natura naturata*, provides a significant prompt for Fichte and Schelling in their elaboration of the principle of reciprocal determination. Even here, however, Fichte and Schelling bring to clarity an idea that was merely inchoate in the great rationalist. Even more importantly, there is no notice in *Ethics* I of the kind of dialectical developmental ontology that is the unique mark of Hegelian metaphysics. Much the same can be said regarding the relation between consciousness and self-consciousness. Throughout the *Ethics* Spinoza is able to distinguish between three different forms of knowledge – perceptual knowledge, conceptual knowledge, and trans-conceptual knowledge. Moreover, he insists that the trans-conceptual form of knowledge involves rising to the eternal point of view.[26] It is obvious that Hegel not only appreciates but makes use of these distinctions, and that his version of absolute knowledge has a good deal in common with Spinoza's species of trans-conceptual knowledge. Still, it is not only that there are a number of departures in critical details, but rather that Hegel attempts to show the relations between these forms of knowledge and how one gives way to the other.

GOD-TALK AND THE GOD–WORLD RELATION

We saw in the first section that Hegel differs from Kant in being willing to reinscribe metaphysics as well as insisting that when it comes to knowledge there are no fundamental limits to human beings' powers of knowing. For Hegel, the powers of knowing exceed what Strawson in his interpretation of Kant has felicitously referred to as the 'bounds of sense'.[27] What I would like to focus on now is another hugely important way in which Hegel exceeds Kant. On the most general and formal level, this has to do with how Hegel's very different understanding of the prospects of God-talk in philosophy and more specifically with how he affirmed, on the one hand, philosophy's capacity to speak to the relationship between God and the world and, on the other, philosophy's ability to demonstrate the existence and nature of God. I will deal in turn with each of these three aspects of Hegel's movement beyond Kant.

As is well known, the results of Kant's exploration in *The Critique of Pure Reason* of the conditions of possibility for maintaining standard Christian talk about who or what God is and specifying God's relation to the world are depressing. The price to be borne for recognizing what is in reach of knowledge and what is not in talk about God and God's relations is that essentially we have to put in brackets almost everything that natural philosophy or philosophical theology has yielded. It is important to remember, however, that despite the acknowledged influence of Hume, Kant is not behaving as a sceptic. He is not implying for instance that God does not exist, nor is he denying directly that God is the ground of the world. Nor again is he getting involved in learned disputes as to how to think of God's nature and his reality as creator. Kant wants to make a distinction between our natural tendencies to speak of God and God's relation to the world, and whether and how such tendencies can be philosophically justified.[28] While in Kant's view there is much that is artificial in philosophical theology, especially in the form given to it by Leibniz, nonetheless, he is prepared to concede that significant elements of this discourse track the natural movement of the mind. Kant, therefore, is not the 'all-destroyer' (*Alleszermalmer*) whom the Jewish philosopher Mendelssohn thought him to be.[29] There is good reason, then, to take Kant at his word in the Preface to the First Critique when he states that his intention in destroying knowledge – so-called knowledge – is to make room for faith.[30] Given what follows in *The Critique of Practical Reason* (1788) there are even more grounds. While remaining consistent with the results of his inquiry into the limits of theoretical knowledge in the First Critique, Kant also remains true to the hint he made regarding making room for faith. Faith now is practical or moral faith. That is, God is a postulate of practical reason. Kant contends that human beings discover an obligation to obey the pure moral law. This moral law is coextensive with autonomy since it is the supreme illustration of self-rule. Importantly, for Kant, the force of the obligation is internal and does not derive from a 'supreme lawgiver'. God, however, does come back into the equation. On pain of meaninglessness, happiness should correspond to morality. Precisely the observable lack of such parity leads Kant to suggest that we 'postulate' God as the power to effect such a correspondence by guaranteeing postmortem human existence in which virtue and reward may coincide.

From just about the beginning of his philosophical career Hegel disagrees with Kant regarding the general possibility of God-talk and the modes in which it is to be carried out. This is evident in Hegel's essay on Kant in *Faith and Knowledge*.[31] As indicated already, in that text Hegel moved beyond what he called 'reflection' – what later he calls 'understanding' (*Verstand*) – and insisted that knowledge reaches to the divine and is itself divine. For Hegel, Kant is a rationalist of the worst kind, that is, a rationalist who has lost his nerve and degenerated into a fideist, a thinker who makes a leap beyond reason.[32] This view remains steady thereafter, and receives a final and definitive expression in Hegel's extraordinary reflection on Kant as a kind of intuitionist in the Introduction to the *Encyclopaedia*.[33] Hegel is unimpressed by Kant's proposal that while God and God's relation to the world cannot be an object of reflection within the band of theoretical knowledge, God and God's relations can be reframed in terms of practical reason. Hegel is convinced that Kant has confused a conceptual need with a conceptual justification. That is, while one can understand the pathos behind the appeal to God to avoid a conundrum that has the capacity of making all life seem meaningless, the 'postulate' of God represents at one and the same time the easy way out and no way out at all, since God can either be rationally justified or not. And Kant's separation of practical reason from theoretical reason is simply a strategy to avoid dealing honestly with the looming problem of nihilism.

Of course, in Hegel's view, it is not as if Kant is the only religious thinker in modernity who, in the wake of Hume's scepticism, has been unable to mount a satisfactory defence of God-talk. There are other culprits. In *Faith and Knowledge* Hegel lists Friedrich Heinrich Jacobi and Johann Gottlieb Fichte as two other examples. Hegel also hints at deficits in the philosophy of religion of Friedrich Schleiermacher, to which he returns later in both *Lectures in the Philosophy of Religion* and elsewhere.[34] But as it goes with Being, so it also goes with God. The fact that Hegel disagrees with Kant and other modern philosophical thinkers does not mean that he reinstates the classical Christian metaphysical view of God as the transcendent extra-mental reality. This hedge is in play whether we are talking about Augustine who in *De Doctrina Christiana*[35] insists that God, who is signified in our discourse, nonetheless eludes our signifiers, or Pseudo-Dionysius who in *Mystical Theology* declares that God exceeds conceptual knowledge; or even Aquinas who, in the opening articles of the *Summa*, makes it plain that our knowing of God is the knowing of a finite subject who by definition cannot rise to the divine form of knowing. Hegel is contesting the assumption that God is an extra-conceptual signified and also challenging the supplement of epistemic limitation that goes hand in hand with this realist commitment. Similarly, his dispute with Kant does not mean that he repeats Leibniz who, in his *Monadology*, dramatizes the finitude of knowledge by thinking of every entity, constituted by will and knowledge, as defining itself as an unrepeatable perspective on the world, others, and God. Hegel, then, is inclined to see that the traditional scoping of God, Leibniz's reformulation, and Kant's alternative essentially mirror each other. In any event, the ground of their mistake is similar. As already indicated, the thinker who early on encourages Hegel to move beyond both the traditional and Kantian account of God is Spinoza, who spoke of a form of knowledge that rises to the divine point of view or that of eternity (*sub specie aeternitatis*). Somewhat later in his career, in passages that continue to support his emendation of Kant's view of the possibility of God-talk, Hegelian appeals to Spinoza and to Schelling are replaced by appeals to Christian mysticism and especially to the German mysticism of Meister Eckhart and Jacob Boehme.[36] The appeal to Meister Eckhart is especially salient in that Hegel essentially superimposes Eckhart on Spinoza. A clear case of this is to be found in the *Encyclopaedia*, in which Hegel speaks of the mind's understanding of God as God's understanding of himself: 'God is God only so far as he knows himself: his self-knowledge is, further, self-consciousness in man and man's knowledge of God, which proceeds to man's self-knowledge in God.'[37]

Here Hegel complexly recalls Spinoza's famous remark that the intellectual love of God in the human mind is God's love for himself, and Eckhart's equally famous saying that the eye with which human beings see God is the same eye with which God sees himself.[38] In any event Spinoza and Meister Eckhart, and more generally Spinoza and German mysticism – even if exceptional in the philosophical and theological traditions – provide warrant for Hegel's bold move in insisting that the mind can fully comprehend and not simply have intuitive access to God.

Again, if we consider how Hegel is moving beyond Kant, it is good to underscore just how easily God comes into philosophy. Hegel was convinced that metaphysics and philosophical theology mapped each other, and thus that God was equivalent to the ultimate ground of reality whether this went under the rubric of Being, the Infinite, or Spirit.[39] Hegel made this absolutely clear in early works, such as the *Difference Essay* and *Faith and Knowledge*, and he confirmed it in his discussion of 'revealed religion' and 'absolute knowledge' in the *Phenomenology*. In addition, he posited the connection in the *Science of Logic*,[40] and provided a fully elaborated demonstration of their equivalence in the *Encyclopaedia*.[41] This much, however, follows from what we have said already about Hegel's step beyond Kant. There is, however, another ingredient. As already indicated, Kant had little time for philosophical theology. Equally, however, Kant, the philosopher of the Enlightenment, who had as his motto 'dare to think' (*sapere aude*), objected in principle to dogmatic theology, an obscurantist and authoritarian discourse that betrayed reason. Also problematic for him was dogmatic theology's theoretical rather than practical reading of scripture.[42] In his elucidation of Christianity in the *Phenomenology* Hegel has none of the disdain affected by Kant when it comes to Christian doctrines. This is especially true of the doctrine of the Trinity. In his *Religion within the Boundaries of Reason Alone* Kant is particularly dismissive regarding the doctrine of the Trinity, insisting that of all the Christian doctrines it bears the least relation to action in the world.[43] For Hegel, however, the doctrine of the Trinity is key to the relationship between theology and philosophy, especially if the real and ultimate subject of philosophy is God, which is precisely what Hegel believes.[44] This sketch is fully filled out in *Lectures on the Philosophy of Religion* in which he thinks that the Christian doctrine of the Trinity offers a fundamental clue to speculative philosophy, whose main task is to articulate the relation and consequence of the dynamic movement of the infinite through the finite and back to the infinite. The details of Hegel's argument need not detain us here. Nor do we need to examine whether Hegel is true to the classical Trinitarian tradition of Augustine and Aquinas in his articulation. Suffice it to say that although he takes Christian doctrines seriously, he does not pledge allegiance to the dogmatic tradition.[45] The theological tradition is not authoritative *in se*. Hegel attends to Christian doctrines in general and the doctrine of the Trinity in particular because he sees that they can serve as material in a philosophical account of God. The Christian doctrine of the Trinity has to be reworked in order to yield a philosophical view of God which, while it will insist upon relations, will get rid of persons,[46] and think of divine actions as necessary rather than contingent. Put technically, what is given in representation (*Vorstellung*), which is the form of symbolization of objectifying finite consciousness, has to be elevated to concept (*Begriff*),[47] which involves both the overcoming of the subject and object distinction and the removal of any sense of contingency in divine action. Speculative philosophy demonstrates therefore not only that its content is God, but that it is the master discourse about God.

Central to Hegel's God-talk is his insistence on reciprocal determination when it comes to God's relation to the world. We have already seen this in the formal metaphysical register of Hegel's thought as he borrows and extends an insight he discovered in the thought of Fichte and Schelling. But more than Fichte and the early Schelling Hegel displays no embarrassment in mapping the God–world relation onto the more formal ground-consequent relation. Hegel was not satisfied with Kant's dismissal of talk about creation on the grounds that we do not have the conceptual means at our disposal to talk about causation when it comes to the entire universe. Divine causality had to be rethought and with it the God–world relation in its entirety. In a first move Hegel questions the prominence of efficient causality in philosophical and theological accounts of the creation of the world. He believes that the emphasis on efficient causality in modern forms of theism (Descartes, Leibniz) has been detrimental both philosophically and theologically in that it has led to a kind of extrinsicism between God and the world. The criticism is not made on behalf of an older philosophy or philosophical theology of the sort that one might find in Aquinas or even Bonaventure, in which formal and final causality are just as important as efficient causality. Hegel either does not know the medieval philosophical and theological tradition or has no interest in recalling it. He thinks that as with German Idealism in general he is forging an entirely new path in a post-Kantian environment. And to the degree to which the classical rendition of creation is recalled by reference to *creatio ex nihilo*,[48] it is evident that Hegel has no truck with it since its basic purpose, on his view, is to sustain divine transcendence and governorship over the world. Fair or not, Hegel thinks that both modern and traditional reflection on creation are regulated by a grammar of divine self-sufficiency and the complete dependence of the world on God. It is this basic grammar that he sees himself as contesting.

The classical instance of this grammar is, arguably, provided by Aquinas in the *Summa Theologiae* in which he posits that, while creatures have a 'real relation' to God, God does not have a 'real relation' to creatures.[49] This apparently enigmatic formulation translates easily into the following: creatures depend on God to exist and to be the kind of entities they are; God does not depend on the world for his existence or his nature. Hegel thinks that this is the theistic mistake par excellence, and that it is flawed from both an existential and conceptual point of view. From an existential point of view,[50] it is easy to see why theism would continue to lose currency in the modern world, for it effectively denigrates both the world and human being by making both absolutely alien from the divine. This existential intuition, expressed in Hegel's very earliest work, is carried forward in the discussion of 'unhappy consciousness' (*unglückliches Bewusstsein*) in the *Phenomenology* and later in his *Lectures on the Philosophy of Religion*. Equally important, however, is the conceptual flaw of the one-way dependence model. A major problem from Hegel's point of view is the invidious deployment of a logic of possibility. God's self-sufficiency is secured by granting that it was logically possible for God not to create the world. Since the world is and the world presumptively expresses God, why should possibility, implicitly in the classical tradition, explicitly in Leibniz, have any philosophical purchase? Should not actuality regulate possibility rather than possibility regulate actuality? Hegel is convinced that this simple reversal would prove a tonic to both philosophy and theology. In the opening section I mentioned that without it being determinative, Spinoza's *Ethics* exercises considerable influence on Hegel's overall metaphysical account. Of course, Spinoza's *Ethics* not only does not shy away from speaking about God; arguably, in advance of Hegel it constitutes the most sustained attack against classical theism in the history of philosophy.[51] God or Substance is expressed without remainder in the world. This means essentially that God or Substance is expressed without remainder *as* the world. One can add Meister Eckhart to this distinguished minority list. One of the many ways in which he departed from Aquinas is in his subversion of the meaning of the creator–creation relation. Contrary to Aquinas, Eckhart insists that just as creation cannot be without the creator, the creator makes no sense without creation. Thus there is reciprocal determination. Hegel, who knew little of medieval philosophical and theological thought, is quite familiar with the thought of the German mystic,[52] and uses him as leverage against the classical theistic tradition.

To deny that Hegel is a theist does not make him an atheist, even if this is how left-wing Hegelians such as Bruno Bauer and Ludwig Feuerbach constructed him. But if not a theist and not an atheist, how are we to describe his position? As regards labels, a number of scholars are of the view that the two available titles are those of pantheism and panentheism.[53] Of course, much depends on definition. Hegel does exhibit a preferential option for the complex whole when it comes to God. God is the all, the full dynamic of the infinite expressing itself in the finite, and not simply an independent infinite which, from Hegel's point of view, is a chimera. In this sense, pantheism is a possible title, and was in fact applied to Hegel's system during his lifetime. If, however, one identifies pantheism with the sum of material objects, then Hegel is clearly not a pantheist. Not only are ideas real for him, but he indicates time and again that a spiritual energy moves through all things and provides them with direction. It is in recognition of these differentials that commentators have applied the term panentheism, which literally means 'all in God'. This is probably the better of the two terms, since it rightly takes account of indelible non-reductive features of Hegel's non-theistic view. However it too can mislead, in that it might suggest a greater level of transcendence to world and human being than is illustrated in and by Hegel's thought. As a placeholder, panentheism has its uses, but it is hardly a fully adequate interpretive concept. In addition, titles tend to subsume unique intellectual frameworks under genera, thereby failing to do justice to the uniqueness of particular conceptual formations. Hegel's view of the God–world relation is one such unique formation. We do not understand Hegel's achievement by using either of the above labels. What needs to be underscored is not only how but why he revolutionizes philosophical discourse concerning the God–world relation. I remarked above that Hegel alters the grammar of the God–world relation. This is true. But it is also true that it is anticipated in a number of figures, with Spinoza and Eckhart being first among equals. What none anticipates, however, is the dynamic dialectical register of Hegel's thought. The divine infinite, given in the beginning and as the beginning, is not the true infinite, because it is not the true whole of the infinite and finite. The divine infinite becomes in and through the world, which is expressive of the divine infinite but in the mode of contradiction and opposition. It is in and through this opposition between the initial divine infinite and contrary world that the fully comprehensive divine infinite comes to be. The fully actual divine infinite is a result worked out in and through the cosmos and human beings. This is Hegel's unique vision.

There is one further aspect of Hegel's God-talk I want to mention. This is the way that Hegel critically engages Kant's rebuttal of the proofs of God's existence, and how he repositions them in a post-Kantian philosophical environment. For Kant there are two lines of argument against these proofs: first, the weakness of each of the three main arguments (argument from design, cosmological argument, and ontological argument); and second, their shared reliance on the ontological argument.[54] For Kant, the argument from design fails because there is no way to disprove that the observable order in the world is not immanent; the cosmological argument fails since it essentially rests on an equivocation concerning causality, that is, that one can speak of the causation of the world in the same way that one can speak of causation within the world; and finally the ontological argument fails in that there is an ontological chasm between the idea of something and the reality of something. In addition, both the argument from design and the cosmological argument depend ultimately on the ontological argument, for when the idea of God is introduced as an explanation for order and for the existence of the world, it is important that this God not be simply an idea in the pejorative sense. But as Kant points out there is simply no way to get from the idea of God to the actual existence of God, since in his argumentative *coup de grâce* 'existence is not a predicate'.[55]

In his free-standing examination of the proofs of God's existence,[56] as well as his continual recurrence to them in *Lectures on the Philosophy of Religion*,[57] Hegel once again thinks of himself as rebutting Kant while withholding support for the proofs either in their traditional or Leibnizian form. Sticking to the individual proofs, Hegel thinks of each as being admissible in a post-Kantian frame of thought, given a fairly simple set of conceptual adjustments. Instead of thinking of the argument from design as involving a process of inference from the observation of order in the universe to an artificer, he is convinced that to the degree to which the human intellect rises beyond understanding (*Verstand*) which is tied to time and analysis, it directly grasps this order and recognizes that its thinking also is an expression of this order. Similarly, the cosmological argument admits of revision that makes it immune from Kant's criticism in the First Critique. Again, God is not an inference, specifically an inference from the contingency of the world. Rather the intellect in the form of true reason (*Vernunft*) grasps the world as being an intrinsic expression (*Erscheinung*) of God. Finally, the ontological argument admits of revision, provided we rethink the nature of the concept. If the concept is understood subjectively as an idea in a finite mind, then Hegel thinks that Kant's objection to the ontological argument holds. However, if the concept is considered objectively as an intellectual reality oriented towards concrete illustration,[58] then God's existence follows. Indeed it follows necessarily. Once again Hegel can rely on a precedent established by Spinoza in *Ethics* Book I, where actuality is implied in the concept of infinite perfection.

Hegel's critical engagement with Kant regarding the proofs for God's existence cuts even deeper when we take into account his essential agreement with Kant concerning the integrative role the ontological argument plays in all three proofs. For Hegel, the scope of the ontological argument is comprehensive; it includes the ontological fields of the cosmological and teleological arguments by including the cosmos and history. Moreover, it includes these fields necessarily. The motor of this necessity is the dynamic and dialectic movement in and through which a 'conceptual' or 'notional' divine becomes a fully real or 'actual' (*wirklich*) divine. Speaking of the concept in *Lectures on the Philosophy of Religion* Hegel expresses it thus: 'It is immediately this universal that determines and particularizes itself... of positing a finitude, negating this its own finitude, and being identical with itself through its negation of this finitude. This is the concept as such, the concept of God, the absolute concept.'[59]

This is a real process to which reason (*Vernunft*) has access. In articulating his view Hegel suggests that he is both saving and justifying the view of the classical Christian tradition. Of course the departure from that tradition could not be more obvious. No thinker within the classical Christian tradition is remotely prepared to license a God who develops in both being and consciousness and who has the world and history as the arenas for such development. In addition, while Hegel also ascribes 'personality' to God, he does not do so in a way that would satisfy a theist. In the strict sense 'personality' (*Persönlichkeit*) is ascribable only to the term of the process of divine self-development and self-constitution.[60] He does not have in mind the tri-personal subject of either Augustine or Aquinas, at once perfect and self-sufficient and the source of creative, saving and sanctifying action.

CONCLUSION

This essay has focused on Hegel's account of the infinite and its relation to the finite in its metaphysical and theological registers. It has been central to my argument that Hegel's Idealism presupposes Kant's transcendental turn, while also being highly critical of both his attack against metaphysics and his prohibition of truly substantive God-talk. I have also emphasized, however, that Hegel leaves intact much – if not all – of Kant's criticisms of traditional and Leibnizian metaphysics and God-talk. Put more strongly, Hegel's critique of Kant does not reinstall either object of critique. Hegel essentially reframes both the 'infinite' and 'God' and their relations to the 'finite' and 'world' respectively. In what has to be regarded as nothing less than a revolution in philosophy, he makes both the infinite and

God a function of their expression in the finite world, and elaborates a developmental ontology which is at the same time a kind of speculative 'theogony',[61] an account of nothing less than the birth of God.

ENDNOTES

1 Immanuel Kant, *Critique of Pure Reason* (New York, NY: Macmillan, 1968). With regard to the first, see especially Kant's discussion of the Antinomies, pp. 397–484. With regard to the second, see pp. 485–93. The so-called Copernican revolution that Kant effects within philosophy is somewhat ironic since Kant argues that the world can be nothing more than the objective correlative of our finite apparatus of knowing, made up equally of sensory apprehension and conceptual apparatus.

2 The clearest expression of this is to be found in §20 (Preface) of the *Phenomenology* in which Hegel makes the famous assertion that 'the truth is the whole' (*Das Wahre ist das Ganze*). See *Phenomenology of Spirit* (Oxford: Oxford University Press, 1977), p. 11. The most rigorous argument for holism as defining of Hegelian thought is provided by Paul Franks. See Chapter 2 'Post-Kantian Monism' in Paul Franks, *All or Nothing: Systematicity, Transcendental Arguments, and Skepticism in German Idealism* (Cambridge, MA: Harvard University Press, 2005), pp. 84–145.

3 For convenient English translations of *Glauben und Wissen* (1802) and the *Differenzschrift* (1802), see G.W.F. Hegel, *Faith and Knowledge* (Albany, NY: SUNY Press, 1977); G.W.F. Hegel, *The Difference between Fichte and Schelling's System of Philosophy* (Albany, NY: SUNY Press, 1976).

4 G.W.F. Hegel, *Lectures on the Philosophy of Religion*, vol. 1 (Berkeley, CA: University of California Press, 1984), also G.W.F. Hegel, *Lectures on the Philosophy of Religion*, vol. 3 (Berkeley, CA: University of California Press, 1985). There are four versions of the Lectures, the 1821 manuscript of the Lectures, and three further renditions (1824, 1827, 1831) put together from student notes.

5 Plotinus – in line with Plato – tends to associate the unlimited or the infinite with evil (*Enneads* I 8; II 9) or with matter (II 4). In contrast, the ultimate principle of all of reality, which is named the One but also the Good, is never associated with the unlimited (III 7; V 2).

6 For two contemporary authors who underscore the uniqueness of Gregory of Nyssa in providing a positive account of infinity, see Michel Barnes, *The Power of God: Dynamis in Gregory of Nyssa's Trinitarian Theology* (Washington, DC: Catholic University of America Press, 2016) and David Bentley Hart, *The Beauty of the Infinite: The Aesthetics of Christian Truth* (Grand Rapids, MI: Eerdmans, 2004).

7 In the case of both Augustine and Aquinas – in line with Neoplatonism – evil and the unlimited tend to get associated. This is coded in the definition of evil as *privatio boni*, thus precisely the contrary to God who is the fullness and perfection of being. The genius of Augustine lies less in his use of this formula than in his sense of what is at stake for Christianity if it were to accept the view that evil were substantial, that is, a rival absolute to the biblical God.

8   Schelling's *Bruno* (1802), was written in his 'Identity–Philosophy' phase in which he was insisting on the absolute correspondence of knowledge and being. For an English translation see Michael G. Vater (ed.), *Bruno or On the Natural and the Divine Principle of Things* (Albany, NY: SUNY Press, 1984). For references to Bruno's *De Causa*, see pp. 63, 65.

9   Although there is no reason to suppose that Hegel's dialectic is based on Nicholas of Cusa's famous notion of *coincidentia oppositorum*, there are moments when Cusa's famous formula seems to be recalled. This is true in particular in Hegel's discussion of dialectic in the so-called 'Lesser Logic'. See *Encyclopaedia of Philosophical Sciences*, Part 1 (Oxford: Clarendon Press, 1975), §81–2, pp. 115–19.

10   G.W.F. Hegel, *Lectures on the History of Philosophy*, vol. 3, *Medieval and Modern Philosophy* (Lincoln, NE: University of Nebraska Press, 1995), pp. 220–51.

11   Hegel, *Lectures on the History of Philosophy*, vol. 3, pp. 252–89.

12   This is a view shared by Steven Crites and H.S. Harris, arguably the two great charters in English of Hegel's development from being a religious thinker to being a philosopher. See Steven Crites, *Dialectic and Gospel in the Development of Hegel's Logic* (Philadelphia, PA: University of Pennsylvania Press, 1998); H.S. Harris, *Hegel's Development: Towards the Sunlight (1770–1801)* (Oxford: Clarendon Press, 1972); H.S. Harris, *Hegel's Development: Night Thoughts (Jena 1801–1806)* (Oxford: Clarendon Press, 1983).

13   The commentator who does this best is Rodolphe Gasche. See his *The Tain of the Mirror: Derrida and the Philosophy of Reflection* (Cambridge, MA: Harvard University Press, 1988), pp. 41–5.

14   Hegel's *Wissenschaft der Logik* (1812) presents dialectical logic that avails both of Kant's and Aristotle's logic while differing from both in demonstrating the internal and hierarchical relations between the various logical categories. For Hegel, the logical categories are metaphysical. Nonetheless, the domain of their operation is the mind in so far as it has transcended finitude and temporality. The same is also true in the case of the so-called 'Lesser Logic', that is, the logic of the *Encyclopaedia*. In the *Encyclopaedia* as a whole, however, Hegel is anxious to show the relation between logical and real-world categories. Thus, there is a philosophy of nature and a philosophy of mind to supplement an articulation of logic.

15   Hegel underscores in both the 'Greater Logic' and the 'Lesser Logic' that the articulation of logical categories is connected with God, and that in his view dialectical logic is not only a post-Kantian form of metaphysics, but also a kind of theology. Hegel speaks in both cases, in a manner quite similar to that of Christian Platonism or Neoplatonism, of the logical categories being ideas in the mind of God before the creation of the world.

16   This is a point made with some force by Gerhard Schmidt, *The Concept of Being in Hegel and Heidegger* (Bonn: Bouvier, 1979), p. 129.

17   This is the opening move in both of Hegel's logics. There is a huge literature on Hegel's logic and on this move in particular. See especially Jean Hyppolite, *Logique et existence: Essai sur la logique de Hegel* (Paris: Presses Universitaires de France, 1953).

18   The crucial text here is, of course, the *Monadology* (1714) in which Leibniz argues that God is the supreme monad integrating the perception and consciousness of all other monads, defined as centres of desire, perception and consciousness.

19   Fichte's *Wissenschaftslehre* was first published in 1794 and went through a number of
      revisions before Hegel commented on it in 1802. A crucial point of aggravation was
      Fichte's insistence on the deferring of the unity between consciousness and being,
      enshrined in the Third Ground-Proposition that A ought to (*soll*) equal Non-A. For
      this point, see *Difference Essay*, pp. 71–2, also pp. 1–3, 39, 43; Hegel, *Faith and
      Knowledge*, pp. 159–62, 172. Hegel's opposition to Fichte continues in the texts of
      his mature period. See *Phenomenology*, (Preface), §17–23, §32; *Science of Logic*, pp.
      150–1; *Encyclopaedia*, part 1, §93–95, pp. 136–41; also §104, pp. 152–5; *Lectures on
      the Philosophy of Religion*, vol. 1, pp. 308, 422–3. The scholar who best captures the
      systemic importance of Hegel's resistance to Fichte on this point is George Seidel. See
      his *Activity and Ground: Fichte, Schelling, and Hegel* (New York, NY: George Olms,
      1976). See p. 96 for a summary statement concerning Hegel's critique of Fichte's
      'unrealizable eschatology'.
20   Hegel, *Encyclopaedia* 1, §81.
21   William Desmond is particularly eloquent on this point. See his *Hegel's God: A
      Counterfeit Double?* (Aldershot: Ashgate, 2003) pp. 41–2, 62–7.
22   The *Phenomenology* is structured by its two basic tasks, that is, an account of the vertical
      shifts in knowing from sense knowledge to self-consciousness in the individual knower,
      supplemented by an account of historical social-becoming. There are many commentaries
      on the *Phenomenology*. The two best are by Jean Hyppolite and H.S. Harris, respectively.
      See Jean Hyppolite, *Genesis and Structure of Hegel's Phenomenology of Spirit* (Evanston,
      IN: Northwestern University Press, 1974); H. S. Harris, *Hegel's Ladder I: The Pilgrimage
      of Reason* (Indianapolis, IN: Hackett Publishing, 1997); *Hegel's Ladder II: The Odyssey
      of Spirit* (Indianapolis, IN: Hackett Publishing, 1997). See also my long review essay
      of Harris's absolutely comprehensive two-volume commentary, 'The Impossibility of a
      Christian Reading of the *Phenomenology of Spirit*: H.S. Harris on Hegel's Liquidation of
      Christianity', in *The Owl of Minerva*, 33/1 (2001–2), pp. 45–95.
23   Spinoza speaks of *natura naturans* and its passive correlative *natura naturata* in
      Ethics Bk. 1, Prop. 29. This language is in ready circulation since late Renaissance
      Neoplatonism. It is especially prominent in the work of Giordano Bruno who was
      burned at the stake for heresy in 1600.
24   For a good account of the relation between Spinoza and Hegel, see Pierre Machéry,
      Hegel ou Spinoza (Paris: François Maspero, 1979).
25   In his *Lectures on the History of Philosophy*, vol. 3, Hegel criticizes the monist tendencies
      of Spinoza, as well as Spinoza's inability to link modes and attributes to Substance or
      God. For a synoptic account of Hegel's criticisms of Spinoza, see Cyril O'Regan, *The
      Heterodox Hegel* (Albany, NY: State University of New York Press, 1994), pp. 171–4,
      147–50.
26   Spinoza posits a 'third kind' of knowledge beyond the adequate knowledge of
      concepts early in the *Ethics* Bk. 2, Prop. 40. He gives it a full discussion in Bk. 5. The
      qualification of *sub specie aeternitatis* is to be found in Bk. 2, Prop. 44 and is again
      fully articulated in Bk. 5.
27   Peter F. Strawson, *The Bounds of Sense: An Essay on Kant's Critique of Pure Reason*
      (London: Routledge, 1975).

28 In the *Critique of Pure Reason*, while Kant insisted that knowledge of God, human freedom and the like could not be validated, this by no means entailed their non-existence. They perdured as regulative ideas. For a still useful account of the 'ideas of reason', see James Collins, *The Emergence of the Philosophy of Reason* (New Haven, CT: Yale University Press, 1967), 111–17.

29 Moses Mendelssohn: 'Ich kenne daher die Schriften der großen Männer, die sich unterdessen in der Methaphysik hervorgethan, die Werke Lamberts, Tetens, Platnners und selbst des alles zermalmenden Kants.' *Morgenstunden oder Vorlesungen über das Daseyn Gottes* (1785) in *Gesammelte Schriften, Schriften zur Philosophie und Ästhetik* III, 2, ed. Leo Strauss (Frommann-Holzboog: Stuttgart-Bad Cannstatt, 1973), p. 3. See *Morning Hours. Lectures on God's Existence*, trans. Daniel O. Dahlstrom and Corey Dyck (Dordrecht: Springer, 2001), p. xix.

30 Kant, *Critique of Pure Reason*, p. 29.

31 For Hegel on Kant, see Hegel, *Faith and Knowledge*, pp. 66–96.

32 The construction of Kant in *Faith and Knowledge* as a fideist is entirely forensic. Hegel knows full well that Kant regards Friedrich Heinrich Jacobi as irresponsible philosophically in speaking of *salto mortale* with respect both to the existence of the external world and God. For Hegel's somewhat abusive treatment of Jacobi in *Faith and Knowledge*, see pp. 97–153. The denigration persists throughout Hegel's entire career. See also *Lectures on the History of Philosophy*, vol. 3, pp. 410–22.

33 *Encyclopaedia*, vol. 1, §62–78, pp. 95–112.

34 Hegel attacked Schleiermacher's preference for intuition and feeling over thought very early in his career. See *Faith and Knowledge*, pp. 150–2. This set the pattern for the mature Hegel. Schleiermacher's notion of 'feeling' (*Gefühl*) is a preferred object of attack in *Lectures on the Philosophy of Religion*, vol. 1, pp. 268–9, 273. The most sustained critique of what might be called Schleiermacher's experiential foundationalism is Hegel's Preface to H.W.F. Hinrichs' *Die Religion in inner Verhältnisse zur Wissenschaft* (Heidelberg, 1822). For an English translation of this Preface by A.V. Miller, see appendix to Frederick G. Weiss (ed.), *Beyond Epistemology: New Studies in the Philosophy of Hegel* (The Hague: Martinus Nijhoff, 1974), pp. 227–44.

35 Augustine, *De Doctrina Christiana* 1, 6. For a convenient English translation, see *Teaching Christianity*, trans. Edmund Hill, OP (New York, NY: New City Press, 1996), p. 108.

36 In *The Heterodox Hegel* I spend considerable time excavating the mystical sources of Hegel's thought, which include Boehme as well as Eckhart. For the more specific influence of Eckhart, see O'Regan, *The Heterodox Hegel*, pp. 250–63. See also my articles, 'Hegelian Philosophy of Religion and Eckhartian Mysticism', in David Kolb (ed.), *New Perspectives on Hegel's Philosophy of Religion* (Albany, NY: SUNY Press, 1992), pp. 109–29; 'Eckhart Reception in the 19th Century', in Jeremiah M. Hackett (ed.), *A Companion to Meister Eckhart* (Leiden: Brill, 2013), pp. 629–68, esp. pp. 639–46.

37 *Encyclopaedia*, part 3, §564, p. 298.

38 For Spinoza, see *Ethics* Bk. 5 for Spinoza's use of the notion of *amor Dei intellectualis* (Props. 33, 36, 37). The crucial proposition is 36: *Mentis Amor intellectualis erga Deum*

est ispe Dei Amor quo Deus se ipsum amat ('The intellectual love of the mind towards God is that very love whereby God loves himself'). In *Lectures on the Philosophy of Religion* Hegel cites the famous identity passage condemned by Papal Bull in 1329: 'The eye with which I see God is the same eye in which God sees me. My eye and God's eye are one eye.' (*Lectures on the Philosophy of Religion*, pp. 347–8).

39 By explicitly identifying both Being (*Sein*) and Spirit (*Geist*) with God, Hegel makes himself extremely vulnerable to Heidegger's charge of 'ontotheology', that is, the mistake of confounding Being with the 'highest Being'. Heidegger charges Hegel with this error throughout his oeuvre. See Martin Heidegger, 'The Onto-Theological Nature of Metaphysics', in *Essays in Metaphysics: Identity and Difference* (New York, NY: Philosophical Library, 1960), pp. 35–67; also Martin Heidegger, *Hegel's Phenomenology of Spirit* (Bloomington, IN: Indiana University Press, 1988), pp. 98–100; 124–6.

40 At the beginning of the *Science of Logic* Hegel famously declares that the logical categories are God's ideas 'before' the creation of the world. He is here recalling Christian Neoplatonic ways of talking about divine ideas as prototypes in relation to concrete instances in the world. Still it should be remembered that the language of 'before' is not temporal and is intended to suggest ontological rather than temporal priority.

41 The very first paragraph of the 'Lesser Logic' opens with the declaration that the object of philosophy and religion is the same, that is, Truth, and that God and Truth are the same. See *Encyclopaedia*, Part 1, p. 3. Being and God are also identified in §85 and §86 (pp. 123–7). The demonstration of the unity of content of religion and philosophy occurs at the very end of the *Encyclopaedia*, where Hegel discusses the relation between the religious and philosophical syllogisms, that is, the summary statements of the dynamics of revelation and reason respectively. See *Encyclopaedia*, Part 3: *The Philosophy of Mind* (Oxford: Clarendon Press, 1971), §564–77, pp. 297–315. Importantly, the relation between the religious and philosophical syllogisms pertains to Spirit as such. For the best account of this relation, see Dale M. Schlitt, *Hegel's Trinitarian Claim* (Leiden: Brill, 1984), pp. 99–120, 227–48.

42 For a good translation of Kant's 1793 text *Die Religion innerhalb der Grenzen der blossen Vernunft*, see Immanuel Kant, 'Religion within the Boundaries of Reason Alone' in *Religion and Rational Theology*, vol. 6 of *The Cambridge Edition of the Works of Immanuel Kant* (New York: Cambridge University Press, 1996), pp. 41–215.

43 In *Religion* Kant casts aside the doctrine of the Trinity as an *adiaphoron*, that is, what falls outside religion, since there is no way to reduce it to Christian experience and/or to think of it as motivating ethical action.

44 There is a large measure of agreement on this point. In addition to my own *The Heterodox Hegel*, see among others Piero Coda, *Il negativo e la trinità. Ipotesi su Hegel* (Rome: Città Nouva, 1987); William Desmond, *Hegel's God: A Counterfeit Double?* pp. 103–20; Emil Fackenheim, *The Religious Dimension of Hegel's Thought* (Bloomington, IN: University of Indiana Press, 1967); Dale M. Schlitt, *Hegel's Trinitarian Claim*, ch. 6.

45 Hegel attempts to balance his affirmation of religious formulas as valuable, because they resist reducing religion to feeling, against his distaste for what he regards as the authoritarian nature of dogmas.

46 Hegel attacks the Nicene view of the Trinity as constituted by one essence and three persons in both the *Phenomenology* and *Lectures on the Philosophy of Religion*. See *Phenomenology*, §771; *Lectures on the Philosophy of Religion* 3, pp. 82, 193. In these passages Hegel is taking a position that is antithetical to the one adopted by Aquinas in *Summa Theologiae* I, 30, 1. For my discussion of this point see *The Heterodox Hegel*, pp. 126–40.

47 There are numerous discussions of the modes of religious and philosophical discourse throughout Hegel's work. The two most important discussions of relations are in the final two sections (7 and 8) of the *Phenomenology* and in section 3 of the *Encyclopaedia*, Part 3 especially §564–577. For my discussion of the relation, see *The Heterodox Hegel*, pp. 327–70; pp. 454–64.

48 Although it is obvious that Hegel does not support the standard 'creation from nothing' model, there are moments throughout his work where he does not seem to separate himself from the tradition. See *Difference Essay*, pp. 93–4, and *Science of Logic*, pp. 88–90. A real opening towards the standard model seems to be implied when he critiques Spinoza's famous dictum '*ex nihilo nihil fit*'. The support of the standard model, however, is more apparent than real. The world does not emanate from a divine ground, but arises dialectically from a divine ground which truly becomes itself in and through its production of a finite other.

49 Thomas Aquinas, *Summa Theologiae* I, 13, 7.

50 Hegel's writings in the 1790s were focused on trying to find alternatives for traditional forms of Christianity which he perceived to be moribund.

51 Although in Book I of the *Ethics*, as he argues for his naturalistic view of reality as Substance, Spinoza argues against emanationist accounts of the world, his prime target is the theistic account of creation exemplified in Jewish as well as Christian philosophical traditions.

52 For a brief account of the role played by Franz von Baader (1765–1841) as a conduit of the knowledge of Meister Eckhart in German Idealism in general and Hegel in particular, see Cyril O'Regan, 'Eckhart Reception in the 19th Century', in Hackett (ed.), *A Companion to Meister Eckhart*, pp. 633–8.

53 The commentator on Hegel whose analysis depends almost entirely on distinctions between theism, pantheism and panentheism is Raymond K. Williamson. See his *Introduction to Hegel's Philosophy of Religion* (Albany, NY: SUNY Press, 1984).

54 *Critique of Pure Reason*, pp. 495–530

55 *Critique of Pure Reason*, pp. 500–7, esp. p. 504.

56 See Peter C. Hodgson (ed.), *Hegel: Lectures on the Proofs of the Existence of God* (Oxford: Oxford University Press, 2011).

57 See Hegel, *Lectures on the Philosophy of Religion*, vol. 1, pp. 414–44. For a fuller discussion see O'Regan, *The Heterodox Hegel*, pp. 323–6.

58 Hegel provides a rich account of Neoplatonism in *Lectures on the History of Philosophy*, vol. 2, pp. 374–453. Werner Beierwaltes is especially strong on bringing out the close relationship between Neoplatonism and German Idealism. See his *Denken des Einen: Studien zur Neuplatonischen Philosophie und ihrer Wirkungsgeschichte* (Frankfurt: Klostermann, 1985); also *Identität und Differenz* (Frankfurt: Klostermann, 1980).

59   See Hegel, *Lectures on the Philosophy of Religion* 1, p. 436.

60   In his account of 'revealed religion' or Christianity in the *Phenomenology* (§771) Hegel makes it clear that he does not support the classical Christian view of the tripersonal Trinity. He continues his attack in *Lectures on the Philosophy of Religion*. See *LPR3*, pp. 82, 194, 283. The conclusive dismissal of the tripersonality of the divine, however, occurs in Hegel's treatment of the relation between religion and philosophy at the end of the *Encyclopaedia* (§564–77). It turns out that there are only two candidates for the ascription of 'personality', first, the level of the concept which completes the logic, and second, the level of Spirit, which supposes that the concept has externalized and gathered itself back to itself through nature and finite spirit. Ultimately, it is only the latter to which 'personality' is ascribable in the strict sense. This is very different from the way Aquinas talks about 'personality' in the Trinity in the *Summa Theologiae*. See *ST* I, 30, art. 1.

61   The scholar who has best brought out Hegel's repetition of theogony is Iwan Iljin, *Die Philosophie Hegels als kontemplative Gotteslehre* (Bern: Francke, 1946), especially p. 203 where he uses the term 'theogenetic process' (*theogenetische Prozess*).

Epiphany and Hopkins

RICHARD KEARNEY

Hopkins on Epiphany

On 6 January 1889, feast of the Epiphany, Gerard Manley Hopkins made his last known entry in his spiritual diary. It was written just five months before his death of typhoid fever, and its subject was, appropriately, the event of epiphany. In very poor health and in the midst of his annual Ignatian retreat, Hopkins consoled himself with the fact that if his own journey to University College on Stephen's Green was 'inconvenient and painful', so too was the Magi's journey to Bethlehem.[1] 'To seem the stranger lies my lot ... among strangers', is how one of his poems begins, identifying his plight with his migrant biblical predecessors. And yet, like those voyagers in the night, Hopkins himself was to experience an illumination in the midst of darkness – 'so much light ... more than I can easily put down'.[2] From that January moment on, though his health grew worse, his 'spirits got better';[3] and on his deathbed in June 8, he pronounced his last words to his family, 'I am so happy, I am so happy.'[4]

In his January entry on the Epiphany, we find Hopkins reconstructing the wise men's journey with a 'detective ingenuity' worthy of Kierkegaard's reconstruction of Abraham's journey in *Fear and Trembling*.[5] But, in this instance, we are dealing with a very different kind of event – not the sacrifice of a son (Isaac) on a mountain but the birth of a son (Jesus) in a cave. During the course of his extensive reflections on the Epiphany, Hopkins makes what I take to be six key observations. I will say a word about each in turn.

First, Hopkins makes much of the fact that the three Magi were strangers from afar – gentiles or 'Persian Magians', as he put it, 'who may have come from the ... borders of India'.[6] They came, he notes, in secret, unrecognized and unannounced; and it is telling that right after their visitation, the Holy Family themselves take flight into another foreign land, Egypt. There is a certain mixing of wonder and estrangement.

Second, the strangers came *after* the event of the birth itself – twelve days later to be precise. The Feast of the Epiphany on January 6 is known in Ireland as 'Little Christmas', marking the culmination of the Christmas cycle; and in the Eastern Orthodox tradition it is actually considered to be the real revelation of Christ's incarnate birth. The first event of Christianity is, in short, a revelation *après coup* by and for strangers. Epi-phany as aftermath. Or what Hopkins will call a poetics of 'aftering'.[7]

Third, Hopkins notes that the divinity of the child is recognized by the Magi thanks to a certain hermeneutic reading of signs. The visitors read the stars that guide their path in a way which Herod and the great multitude did not. So, for Hopkins, the three foreigners are the first Christian hermeneuts, so to speak, practicing an astronomical mix of 'ordinary science' and 'extraordinary science' – the latter serving as a certain 'white magic' or 'secret art' which 'bridges over the gulf between human and superhuman knowledge'.[8] By contrast, notes Hopkins, the 'star was nothing to ordinary observers, perhaps not visible at all to them'.[9] It is the three wise interpretants who can say – like certain poets and sages after them – '*we have seen*'.[10] Hopkins explains: '[The Magi] speak of their art, their observation, magisterially'; and the stellar illumination in the dark may well have been 'only visible after the practice of their art, some sort of evocation, had been gone through'.[11] In short, epiphanies come and go and may require a certain poetic–hermeneutic art in order to decipher the wondrous in the ordinary. Epiphanies are not *faits accomplis* but invitations to discernment. Calls for responses. Or, as Hopkins says in one of his poems, the engendering moment of incarnation 'breathes once, and, quenched faster than it came, / Leaves yet the mind a mother of immortal song'. Paul Mariani, Hopkins' biographer, offers this helpful gloss: 'The moment of conception, of poetic inspiration ... was all that was necessary to generate a poem, even if it took months, even years ... for the poem to come to fruition. The seed had been planted, and the poem would come in its own good time – "The widow of an insight lost she lives ...".'[12]

Fourth, the Magi bring sweet-smelling gifts of frankincense and myrrh to mark the *sensible* nature of the Incarnation – word made flesh. And this emphasis on the carnal character of the Epiphany is further confirmed by the presence of animals and the 'scandalous' fact that the divine child manifests as the very least of beings (*elachistos*), naked and homeless in a lowly feeding trough (manger). Here we have the epiphanic paradox, par excellence, of wonder in the wounded, the highest in the lowest, the first in the last.

Fifth, the Epiphany is, Hopkins observes, surrounded by darkness. The nativity occurs in a cave in the depth of winter since there is no room at the inns of Bethlehem. And it is rapidly followed by a further more ominous kind of darkness – the perilous flight into Egypt and Herod's slaughter of innocents. In other words, from the very outset, Epiphany is a momentary irruption of light in opacity. Or as Hopkins reflects, the star of Bethlehem shines 'at night'. A basic point he carries home in citing Marie Lataste's mystic vision of Mary presenting her son on the 'twelfth day' of the Epiphany: 'ce désert ne sera plus un désert, mais une douce oasis, où vous vous reposerez … après la course, après de rudes épreuves'.[13] Epiphany, Hopkins intimates, is always mediated – in this instance by the Madonna, as well as by the Magi. (Not to mention nocturnal shepherds and animals.) Divinity descends into time and space, persons and places. It marks a plural, dialogical transition between dark night and natal light, water and drought, torment and rest.

Lastly, Hopkins proposes that the epiphany be read in light of what he considers to be two other epiphanic events in Jesus' life: his baptism by John in the Jordan and the conversion of water into wine at the marriage feast of Cana. Two related wonders involving the miraculous power of water: one of the four primary material elements. In the immersion in the Jordan, Jesus performs a second kenotic birth, a further conversion of human to divine (after his first nativity in Bethlehem). He comes to baptism, Hopkins observes boldly, 'disguised as a sinner' and leaves cleansed and reborn. Once again, we witness the epiphanic paradigm of descent into darkness (*kenôsis*) and ascent into light (*anabasis*), a double move repeated over and over throughout Jesus' life – right up to the final rising from the empty tomb.

At Cana, concludes Hopkins, we meet yet a different disguise and a different conversion: this time with Jesus the 'guest' serving secretly as 'host' by providing wine which everyone present assumes comes from the householders. Jesus 'conceals the miracle at the moment', observes Hopkins, 'and increases it afterwards'.[14] And this temporality of before-and-after is central, as we will see, to the deep rhythm of epiphany; for just as Jesus tells his mother '*nondum venit hora mea*' ('my hour has not yet come') –

thereby marking a lapse in the revelation of his transforming power – so too the conversion of water into wine is not witnessed right away but only afterwards, *nachträglich*, in the 'effects' of the wine on the unsuspecting guests. This notion of temporal lapse or delay is, we shall note, pivotal to the logic of epiphany in Hopkins. Indeed the very prefix *epi-* in Greek carries this sense of something extra, additional, surplus. A beyond-the-bounds which signals a new temporality of before and after, too early and too late, already and not yet (as in the terms 'epilogue' or 'epigraph'). This is what Levinas, talking of revelation, calls the 'paradox of posterior anteriority': the opening of ordinary chronological time to eschatological time.[15]

One might recall again here the context of Hopkins' attention to these serial epiphanies in the life of Christ: namely, his own personal struggle to emerge from bouts of crippling depression. Such 'dark nights of the soul' were graphically captured in Hopkins' so-called 'terrible sonnets' – 'I wake and feel the fell of dark not day', 'Carrion Comfort', 'No worse there is none' – *viae negativae* which found their poetic counterparts in the *viae affirmativae* of poems such as 'When Kingfishers Catch Fire' or 'Glory be to God for Dappled Things'. We will return to these below noting how, for Hopkins, wonder is often born from woundedness.

HOPKINS ON HAECCEITY

Hopkins' reading of epiphany has telling implications, I suggest, for understanding his deep fascination with Duns Scotus' notion of *haecceitas*. Though Hopkins himself does not make a direct connection, I think what he has to say about these two key notions makes the hypothesis not only telling but compelling. The strange and difficult concept of haecceity, which has puzzled commentators for centuries, names the precious 'thisness' of each creature as it bears witness to the infinite in the infinitesimal. In his sonnet, 'Duns Scotus' Oxford', Hopkins describes the town he revisits – six hundred years after his Franciscan predecessor – in terms of the same concrete particulars that Scotus himself would have witnessed in his day:

> Towery city and branchy between towers;
> Cuckoo-echoing, bell-swarmèd, lark-charmèd, rook-racked, river-rounded.

And he pays his learned magister this highest accolade:

He [...] who of all men most sways my spirits to peace;
Of realty the rarest-veinèd unraveller; a not
Rivalled insight ...

Hopkins offers his most consistent account of Scotist *haecceitas* in Chapter 3 of his *Spiritual Writings*. Entitled 'On Personality, Grace and Free will', it addresses the question: how can God move a human will to attain a destiny beyond the powers of its nature, while leaving it free to act? His answer is that our freedom operates at the level of personality prior to actual existence. Several different personalities can be uniquely different as free persons while sharing the same universal human nature – an actualized nature which each human needs in order to ultimately display itself in a common public world (to become manifest one to another). This freedom of personality is described by Hopkins as pitch (*gradus*) – a notion which plays a pivotal role in his poetics and which he defines as follows: 'Pitch is a pre-existing determination of man towards his eternal destiny by his creator, but in such a sort that the man is left free to determine himself.'[16] This priority of pitch to natural existence seems to imply that there is a 'world of possible being', prior to actual existence, in which God sees and loves each unique person as fulfilling his divine calling before one actually does so. In other words, personality is first conceived as singular pitch in the mind of God but requires our free consent, with the aid of 'elevating grace', to be brought to full realization, afterwards. For pitch to be fully 'selved' as a unique act of existence, it needs to add (*epi*) reality to possibility, a second birth to the first birth, so to speak, in order to become visibly manifest (*-phany*) in natural reality. Or to put it in terms of Hopkins' reading of the Epiphany, the manifestation of the divine child to the Magi occurs after the initial birth of the child – on the twelfth day. Hopkins pointedly asks if this intriguing notion of pitch 'is not the same as Scotus' *ecceitas*'.[17]

The editor of Hopkins' *Spiritual Writings*, Christopher Devlin, puts all this in more metaphysical terms: 'Pitch can only exist in an existing substance, yet its distinctiveness is so much more than merely conceptual that it must be considered as a reality apart from the nature in which it exists... A possible pitch is certainly identical with the Divine Essence in so much as it is an idea in God's Mind. But in so much as it is an intention ad extra in God's Will, it exercises an influence outside the Divine Essence.'[18] Thus, in regard to time, Scotus made allowance for the extra perfection that can come to a finite substance which is already perfect in spirit, though not yet in fact.[19] After possibility comes actuality, after essence comes existence, after nativity comes epiphany, after Creation comes Redemption. Hence the significance of Hopkins' cryptic but telling note on the temporal deferral of epiphany: 'Twelve days = 6+6 – Creation and Redemption.'[20] The nativity is revealed in its after-effects. I repeat his explanation: 'The star may have been an altogether preternatural appearance, only visible after the practice of [the Magi's] art, some sort of evocation, had been gone through, not necessarily always there.'[21] In short, there is no Christianity without witness, no revelation without a certain art of interpretation and action.

Hopkins himself would consider poetry as one such art, in his own life, performing epiphanies of instress and inscape and disclosing the process of divine incarnation in nature, in a process which he called, revealingly, 'aftering' or 'over and overing'. (We will return to this.) Epiphany – whether it be through the witness of art or action – involves the 'lifting of one self to another', the natural to the divine and vice versa: 'as if a man said: That is Christ playing at me and me playing at Christ ... that is Christ being me and me being Christ.'[22] Epiphany thus reveals itself, for Hopkins, as that moment of poetic theopoiesis where 'Christ plays in ten thousand places / Lovely in limbs, and lovely in eyes not His / To the father through the features of men's faces' ('As Kingfishers Catch Fire').

But how exactly does 'pitch' relate to 'being in Christ'? Here Hopkins emphatically returns to the notion of 'thisness'. He is aware that for Scotus *haecceitas* was the 'final determinant in the scale of natures that descend the tree of Porphyry by way of communicable genus and species: it is that which stops the common nature in one member of the species from being communicable to other members' – that is, from being translated into common universal properties.[23] *Haecceitas* is what makes someone or something this and no other. Gilles Deleuze and Félix Guattari explain: 'Duns Scotus created the word and concept from *haec*, "this thing" ... you will yield nothing to haecceities unless you realize that that is what you are, and that you are nothing but that.'[24] Deleuze remarks that 'not content to merely analyse the elements of an individual [Scotus] went as far as the conception of individuation as the "ultimate actuality of form"'.[25] Haecceity, in sum, is where the buck stops once and for all, where the person is manifest in his or her irreducible uniqueness and individuality, where one says, '*Ecce*': behold who comes, this one very particular person! And everyone is one such person. Which is why James Joyce names his unique universal hero of *Finnegans Wake*, HCE – Here Comes Everybody![26]

Hopkins exploits the felicitous homonymy here between the Latin-Romance spelling of *ecceitas* (without a 'h') and the exclamation, '*Ecce*' – as in '*Ecce Homo*' when Pilate announces Jesus to the crowd in Jerusalem, or '*Ecce Agnus Dei*' when John the Baptist announces Jesus at the Jordan (Hopkins explicitly cites this Latin greeting in his entry on the Epiphany). Individuality as *haecceitas* is intrinsic to being but prior to existence, since no natural existence is *de se haec*. More precisely, for Hopkins as for Scotus, 'being' (in the divine) is not only 'existence' (in nature) but also and quintessentially a 'process of coming into existence from a state of possibility in the creator's mind' – that is, qua 'essence or *esse* conceived by God'.[27] Scotus conceived individuality, accordingly, as the culmination of a process of becoming the *ultima realitas entis*. Its cause, like its pitch, remains ultimately a secret, a mystery to humans: '*Ratio intima haecceitatis non est quaerenda nisi in Divina voluntate.*'[28] Pitch, as Hopkins admits, 'is really "a thread or chain of pitches" *between* the actual self and the ideal self'.[29]

The Scotist double idea of finite being as i) already there, and ii) always-still-coming-more-fully-into-existence (*semper in fieri*), is intimately linked to the concept of '*personalitas*'.[30] And it leads Hopkins to some fascinating, if highly complex, reflections on the relation of proportionality between (a) Divine Personality vis-à-vis human personality, and (b) the infinite vis-à-vis the infinitesimal. These reflections not only pertain to the naked incarnate child, witnessed in the Epiphany, but echo the words of the Psalmist, *abyssus abyssum invocat*: 'For a self is an absolute which stands to the absolute of God as the infinitesimal to the infinite.'[31] Hopkins boldly affirms that the 'blissful stress of selving in God' is, when translated *ad extra*, the stress of creation, and can only fully be understood in terms of the Trinity.[32] But Hopkins breaks off at this point, apparently unable to say more in prose. No metaphysical account of the analogy or univocity of divine–human being can, it seems, adequately articulate this mystery. Perhaps only poetic language – and in Hopkins' case a singularly innovative and idiosyncratic poetry – can hope to fathom this unfathomable secret. Philosophy and theology can make no ultimate sense of these incommunicable and untranslatable imponderables. (Indeed Duns Scotus' own repeated attempts to do so merely earned him the epithet of 'dunce' from his contemporaries.) And, finally, where even poetry fails, the best we can do, Hopkins suggests, is to embrace loving actions which accompany and outstrip faltering words, beyond all logical propositions.[33]

Here, ultimately, Hopkins reckons with the mystery of continuous creation (*ensarkôsis*): namely, the perpetual coming of word into flesh – an audacious notion which both Scotus and Hopkins endorsed.[34] At the limit of thought and language, the most Hopkins can stammer is this: 'So that this pitch might be expressed, if it were good English, the doing be, the doing choose.'[35] In the heel of the hunt, Hopkins, the Classics scholar and professor, opts for Scotist praxology over ontology, suggesting that Aristotle and Thomas were mistaken to place final felicity in the 'intellect' rather than in free individual expression, that is, in our unique selving in song and action and sensible affects. This is what Hopkins, following Scotus, calls the love of things themselves, *amor obiecti*, the praise of ordinary dappled things – 'all things counter, original, spare, strange'. At which point, the famous Scotist univocity of being (natural, human and divine) may be said to consort with a plurivocity of expression. The haecceity of each creature proclaims itself multiply and uniquely: 'Each mortal thing... / Deals out that being indoors each one dwells; / Crying, What I do is me, for that I came.' ('As Kingfishers Catch Fire').

One last remark on these allusive and elusive matters. The reference to pitch as 'abyss' aptly echoes here the Scotist claim that the ground of individuality is an intrinsic lack of being (*carentia entitatis*) – a void which results in a creature from its being created. Each finite creature is marked by this paradox of a simultaneous possession of positive being and a gap for further possible being, which ensures our constant becoming. Hopkins' notion of singular 'pitch' is an attempt, I submit, to translate Scotus' view that each finite being is individuated by the intrinsic degree (*gradus sibi intrinsecus*) in which it possesses both a positive perfection of its 'nature' and simultaneously a still further possible perfection of its 'being' (still to come in nature). As such pitch can be compared to a hole, or series of holes, in a violin for example, 'into which a peg can be fitted so as to tighten the string; the holes would be the *carentia*, the peg would be an ideal self, the string would be human nature'.[36]

Hopkins usually equates pitch and personality; but once, speaking of pitch as pre-existent, he introduces the key notion of temporal delay or process. Pitch, he concedes, 'is not truly self: self or personality truly comes into being when the self, the person, comes into being (existence) with the accession of nature'.[37] The human self, on this account, is a doubled self, stretched like a violin string between the actual possession of its 'nature' and the desire for ever further perfection of 'being' – a perfection perhaps never fully achievable or understandable, as Scotus held, until we partake of the 'Beatific vision'. For us mortal 'potsherds', immortal wonders are still mediated through mortal wounds. Hence the deep inclination (*pondus*) of each broken finite creature to seek ultimate fulfilment in God as final cause. And if, Hopkins implies, we may glimpse moments of beatific vision in this life – in certain states of epiphany – the human self may even be said to express itself as a triple self, echoing the *vera imago* of the Trinity in one's own ideal soul. The person of Christ being the incarnate self of divinity which invites each mortal being to participate – 'since he was what I am'. In sum, the Father generates the Son through the Spirit not only in the Epiphany witnessed by the Magi two thousand years ago but each and every time infinite being crosses finite being, here and now, and wounded wonder illuminates everyday lives: 'I am all at once what Christ is, since he was what I am, and / This Jack, joke, poor potsherd, patch, matchwood, immortal diamond / Is immortal diamond.' ('That Nature is a Heraclitean Fire')[38]

But epiphanies – whether they be then or now, upper case or lower case – express the fact that individual haecceity is intrinsic to 'being' (divine) prior to 'existence' (actual), and so require a delay to become manifest – an 'overing', a following-through, a re-doing, a witnessing. Existence expresses itself ultimately as epi-phany in that it does not confer individuality on something as matter on form (as Aquinas held) but rather brings out what is already there as 'being', after the event of first creation. Poetic invention, in sum, is discovery! Or as Hopkins portentously put it in his undergraduate essay on Parmenides: 'Nothing is so pregnant and straightforward to the truth as simple yes and is.'[39] Hopkins' poetics, in two words, signals a 'yes' to the 'is' of haecceity. A consent – in and through darkness – to the everyday wonder of being. Epi-phany is ana-theism.

> Each mortal thing does one thing and the same:
> Deals out that being indoors each one dwells;
> Selves – goes itself; myself it speaks and spells,
> Crying Whát I dó is me: for that I came.

ENDNOTES

1   Gerard Manley Hopkins, *The Sermons and Devotional Writings of Gerard Manley Hopkins*, ed. Christopher Devlin SJ (Oxford: Oxford University Press, 1959), p. 263.
2   Ibid, pp. 263–4.

3   Forty days before his death, on 29 April 1889, Hopkins wrote to his friend Robert
     Bridges: 'I am ill today but no matter for that as my spirits are good.' *The Letters of
     Gerard Manley Hopkins to Robert Bridges* (London: Oxford University Press, 1970),
     p. 303. He died on 9 June 1889 at the age of 44 and was buried in a collective Jesuit
     grave in Glasnevin Cemetery, Dublin.

4   Cited Paul Mariani, 'The Mystery and the Majesty of It: Jesuit Spirituality in the
     Poetry of Gerard Manley Hopkins', *The Journal of Jesuit Studies* 47/2 (2015), p. 32.

5   The phrase 'detective ingenuity' is from Christopher Devlin SJ, *Sermons*, p. 221.

6   *Sermons*, p. 265.

7   On Hopkins' notion of poetic 'aftering' see Richard Kearney, *Anatheism and God after
     God: An Anatheist Attempt to Reimagine God* (New York: Columbia University Press,
     2011), pp. 6–7.

8   *Sermons*, p. 264.

9   Ibid.

10   Ibid.

11   *Sermons*, pp. 264–5.

12   Mariani, 'The Mystery and the Majesty of It', pp. 21, 43.

13   *Sermons*, p. 335. Hopkins became fascinated by the visions of Gasgony peasant
     mystic, Marie Lataste, during a retreat in November 1878. He wrote that 'her life was
     all grace and miracle, and her writings full of living sanctity and vigorous perceptions
     of things hidden to the wise'. Hopkins wrote a detailed commentary on her vision,
     entitled 'The Epiphany', which he introduces: 'Marie Lataste one Twelfth Night is
     led by her angel to the stable of Bethlehem'. Devlin provides long extracts of Lataste's
     Epiphany vision and of Hopkins' comments in 'Appendix I' to *The Sermons*, pp.
     325–37. Lataste here takes her place beside the Magi strangers, from afar.

14   Hopkins, *Sermons*, p. 271. Hopkins summarizes the trinity of conversions thus,
     under the overall entry of 'Sunday of Epiphany': 'Christ's three manifestations: at
     Bethlehem, at the baptism, at Cana. (1) Consider *to whom*; (i) to the Magi and by
     them to the Gentiles; in (ii) to St John Baptist, his disciples, and the Jews; in (iii) to
     Christ's disciples... (2) Consider *as what*: in (i) as a child, helpless (*the nativity*); in
     (ii) as in the disguise of a sinner (*the baptism in Jordan*), in (iii), as in the disguise of
     common social life (*marriage feast at Cana*). (3) By what means: in (i) of inanimate
     nature in the star, in (ii) of the divine Persons, in (iii) of his own incarnated power'
     (*Sermons*, p. 259; italics and parenthesis are mine for emphasis).

15   See Emmanuel Levinas, *Totality and Infinity*, (Pittsburgh, PA: Duquesne University
     Press, 1960). On the kairological–eschatological time of epiphany see Richard Kearney,
     Anatheism, (New York: Columbia University Press, 2010) and *Reimagining the Sacred*,
     eds Richard Kearney and Jens Zimmerman, (New York: Columbia University Press,
     2010). The paradoxical structure of time, which Paul called 'eschatological', is
     exemplified in the Palestinian formula for 'remembering the one who is still to come'.
     Or again in John the Baptist's greeting of Christ as the one coming after him who
     came before him. This temporal enigma has been identified with 'messianic' time by
     contemporary thinkers such as Levinas, Benjamin, Derrida, Agamben. They refer, in
     their respective ways, to a special form of 'anticipatory memory' which recalls the past

into the future through the present – what Hopkins, as we saw, called 'aftering' or 'over-and-overing': an ana-aesthetic process which enables us to bear witness to how each simple mortal thing 'deals out that being that in each one dwells; selves'. On the question of epiphanic temporality and remembering-forward see also Julia Kristeva, *Time and Sense. Proust and the Experience of Literature* (New York, NY: Columbia University Press, 1996), pp. 3–22; and Walter Benjamin, 'Theses on the Philosophy of History', *Illuminations. Essays and Reflections*, ed. Hannah Arendt (New York, NY: Harcourt Brace Jovanovich, 1968), p. 230.

16 See Christopher Devlin's scholarly commentary in Hopkins' *The Sermons*, Appendix II entitled 'Scotus and Hopkins', p. 338.

17 *Sermons*, p. 151.

18 Ibid., pp. 339–40.

19 Ibid., p. 340.

20 Ibid., p. 265.

21 Ibid., p. 264–5.

22 Ibid., p. 341.

23 Ibid.

24 Gilles Deleuze & Félix Guattari, *A Thousand Plateaus. Capitalism and Schizophrenia* (Minneapolis, MN: University of Minnesota Press, 1987), pp. 540n33, 262.

25 Gilles Deleuze, *Difference and Repetition* (New York, NY: Columbia University Press, 1995), p. 38.

26 On the relation between Joyce's HCE and Scotus' *Ecce/Ecceitas* see Richard Kearney, 'Epiphanies in Joyce', in Anne Fogarty and Fran O'Rourke (eds), *Voices on Joyce* (Dublin: University College Dublin Press, 2015).

27 *Sermons*, p. 241.

28 Duns Scotus, *Parisiensia* ii, xii, 5, cited Devlin, *The Sermons*, p. 342.

29 See Christopher Devlin, *Sermons*, p. 349. Christopher Devlin offers the following useful gloss on this notoriously difficult question: '[Hopkins] was following Scotus in thinking of self or individuality as the independent possession of one's human nature; but he was also following Scotus in thinking that one's independence as a human nature rests on one's deeper dependence as a human being – and the more perfect the nature the deeper the independence. Further, for both Scotus and Hopkins, the independent possession of one's nature is exercised by the will as *arbitrium*, while the deeper dependence is in the attraction of the *voluntas ut natura* to the infinite, which is its origin.' And Devlin adds, regarding Scotus' use of the word *personalitas*: 'Scotus's thought will be found to conclude at the same point as GMH's – namely, that "we are created in Christ … Personality, for both, is a movement from the ideal to the actual, and back from the actual to the ideal – though it is an ideal which can never be actually reached because it is identical with God himself and the processions of the Trinity. Personality is thus a journey into every increasing never-ending self-realization."' Devlin concludes: 'Pitch, in so far as it is a positive direction from God's will, is *haecceitas* … Each human nature is seen in God's mind as an image of his Essence, but an imperfect image; not merely imperfect because it is finite, but imperfect because it is fragmentary. It is part of a species or pattern

which is incomplete without the other parts; hence it needs a *haecceitas* to complete it for purposes of existence.' (pp. 350–1) Devlin also observes how both Scotus and Hopkins resort to the same musical image to express the multitudinous degrees of perfection in created things, human and non-human – that of a 'choir of voices where each voice retains its individuality but the total effect is a more perfect whole'. (p. 351) This relation between the individual and the whole is central to Scotist ontology. See Etienne Gilson's famous comment on *haecceitas*: 'L'extrême pointe d'actualité qui détermine chaque être réel à la singularité' in *Jean Duns Scot. Introduction à ses positions fondamentales* (Paris: Vrin, 1952), p. 464n2; for a more exhaustive presentation of the Scotist idea of *haecceitas* as a principle of divine individuation see *Jean Duns-Scot ou la revolution subtile*, ed. Christine Goémé (Paris: FAC editions, 1982), pp. 25–9, 32–6.

30 Duns Scotus, *Quodlibet* xii, cited Devlin, *The Sermons*, p. 342.

31 Ibid., p. 153.

32 Ibid., p. 197. See Devlin, p. 342.

33 Ibid., p. 342.

34 Ibid., p. 349.

35 Ibid., p. 345.

36 Ibid., p. 343.

37 Ibid., p. 342.

38 See Paul Mariani's brilliant reading of this poem in 'The Mystery and the Majesty of It' as well as his illuminating comments on the pivotal role of the Trinity in Hopkins' theological poetics and the motif of light-dark mysticism in both his life and work. 'Hopkins – like St John of the Cross before him – had to learn that it was only in darkness that the "infinite God himself becomes the Light of the darkened soul and possesses it entirely with His Truth". Then and only then, "at this inexplicable moment", did the deepest night become day and faith itself turned into understanding.' (Mariani, p. 28). The epiphanic moment, where desolation becomes consolation, in a flash, is poetically captured in the resurrection moment of drowning as rebirth: 'Away grief's gasping, joyless days, dejection / Across my foundering deck shone/ A beacon, an eternal beam.' ('That Nature is a Heraclitean Fire')

39 *Sermons*, p. 293. For further useful commentaries on Scotist 'haecceity', see Gerard Casey, 'Hopkins: Poetry and Philosophy', *Studies* 84 (1995), pp. 160–7; Hans Urs Von Balthasar, 'Hopkins: Oxford, Ignatius and Scotus' in *The Glory of the Lord: A Theological Aesthetics* (San Francisco, CA: Ignatius Press, 1986); and Philip Ballinger, *The Poem as Sacrament. The Theological Aesthetic of Gerard Manley Hopkins* (Leuven: Peeters, 2000), Chapter 3, especially pp. 193–8. See also Julia Kristeva's recent critical retrieval of the Scotist notion of haecceity in her essay, 'A Tragedy and a Dream: Disability Revisited', in *Carnal Hermeneutics*, eds Richard Kearney and Jens Zimmerman (New York, NY: Fordham University Press, 2015).

EDITH STEIN'S PHILOSOPHICAL CONVERSIONS: FROM HUSSERL TO AQUINAS AND NEWMAN

DERMOT MORAN

INTRODUCTION

Edith Stein (1891–1942), who later took the appellation of Saint Teresa Benedicta of the Cross when she entered the novitiate of the Carmelite order, was a brilliant, original, philosophical genius and a deeply spiritual religious believer, whose life was brutally ended in the concentration camp of Auschwitz, Poland, on 9 August 1942, at the age of fifty-one.[1] In recognition of her martyrdom, Pope John Paul II beatified Teresa Benedicta of the Cross in 1987; she was canonized by him in 1998. In this essay, I offer a reflection on her philosophical contribution, with special reference to phenomenology and Neo-Thomist ontology.

Despite her short life, Stein was extraordinarily productive; her complete works have been published in twenty-eight volumes.[2] The divisions of the *Gesamtausgabe* give a flavour of the full range of her production: Biographical Writings, Philosophical Writings, Writings on Anthropology and Pedagogy, Writings on Mysticism and Spirituality, and, finally, translations. Stein's writings cover an impressively wide range of topics, from her early writings on phenomenology and the foundations of psychology, to political writings on the nature of the state, to serious ontological studies, primarily offering an alternative to Heidegger's phenomenological ontology, informed by an original reading of early Neo-Thomism. She wrote on empathy, on the nature of the person, on communal life as well as ontological studies on substance, potency and act, essence and existence, and on the principle of individuation, where she challenged the Aristotelian–Thomistic view that matter is the principle of individuation. She left lectures on an introduction to philosophy, as well as many occasional writings on the role and status of women and on education. She wrote deep meditations on spirituality and mysticism, especially on St John of the Cross.

All in all, Edith Stein remains a most engaging, fascinating, challenging, but paradoxical figure. Although she belonged to a closed order of nuns, the Carmelite Order, she was also an engaged social activist especially on women's rights and access to education. For instance, she was commissioned to write a report for the Ministry of Education on women's education and educational reform. She gave public lectures and radio talks on the topic in the early 1930s.[3] She even spoke on a 'Woman's Hour' programme on Bavarian Radio on the subject of rearing children. She gave an address in Paris to the Thomist Society on the relation between St Thomas and phenomenology. Although in an enclosed order, she was hardly shy or retiring about expressing her views! In the early 1930s she was more or less a leader of the Catholic Women's Movement. Interest was particularly stimulated by her lecture 'The Ethos of Women's Professions' given in Salzburg, Austria, on 1 September 1930.

Stein was particularly interested in the education of women (and the importance of women as teachers of women) and in the different psychological make-up of men and women, some of which are natural and some of which are due to social formation.[4] She maintained that a rounded education required exposure to both male and female teachers, something denied to the majority of girls in the education system of that time. In advising on the education of girls she was clear that they should be taught about sex:

> I would not dodge the questions on sex – on the contrary, one ought to be glad when a spontaneous opportunity arises to speak honestly and clearly on the subject, since it simply will no longer do to send the girls out in the world without having taught them about sex. But one must choose [the topics] carefully, avoiding sultry eroticism. However, teaching the elementary facts of life and their meaning, honestly as well as realistically, is far from dangerous.[5]

She also argued that men and women had different but complementary aptitudes and that both needed to be developed.[6] She opposed the view that women should be confined to domestic life. Following Husserl, she thought about 'male' and 'female' as types. Maleness for her had a tendency towards objectification whereas femaleness had an orientation to the development of the whole person. Both tendencies could be over-developed. But she saw in women a higher potentiality for spirituality.

No one essay could do justice to this extraordinary opus. Here I shall concentrate on describing her philosophical formation and conversions, which paralleled her own religious conversion.

Edith Stein can be said to have gone through various conversions or overturnings of previous convictions. Born into a Jewish family, she declared herself an atheist, but later had an intense religious experience that led to her baptism as a Catholic.[7] She then chose to enter the Carmelite order but she never stopped her academic activities, writing penetrating philosophical and theological studies.

Stein went through several philosophical conversions also. She initially trained in phenomenology with Edmund Husserl, the founder of the phenomenological movement, and was an active participant in the Göttingen philosophical circle of eminent phenomenologists. She volunteered as an auxiliary nurse during the First World War, while studying for her doctorate. She published her doctoral dissertation, *On the Problem of Empathy*, written under Husserl's direction, in 1917,[8] and then worked as Husserl's personal assistant for two years (1916–18), during which she contributed greatly to the editorial organization of his work *Ideas* II,[9] and his *Lectures on Internal Time Consciousness* (which were eventually published by Martin Heidegger with only a small allusion to Stein's editorial work).[10] Stein struggled to be an academic philosopher, for which the *Habilitation* degree was required, but, as a woman and a Jew, could not find a professor to sponsor her. Nevertheless, she went on to develop her own original phenomenology of the person, and completed a major research work that she intended as her *Habilitation* thesis. As a committed phenomenologist, Edith Stein corresponded with Husserl and Heidegger, audited Scheler's lectures in Göttingen, and corresponded with Marvin Farber and many others. She was one of the first to discuss Husserl in relation to Dilthey in her PhD thesis on empathy, which also provided an insight into Husserl's thinking on empathy, at a time when *Ideas* II and the *Cartesian Meditations* had not been published.

At the same time, Stein was also interested in social and political philosophy and wrote several treatises on the nature of social relations, including the nature of collective persons (groups), and a unique study on the nature of the state, *An Investigation Concerning the State* (*Eine Untersuchung über den Staat*), published in Husserl's *Jahrbuch für Phänomenologie und phänomenologische Forschung* in 1925.[11]

Perhaps the main event that changed Stein's life was her conversion to Catholicism.[12] After her conversion, Stein concentrated on Thomist metaphysics, particularly encouraged by her religious mentor, the German-Polish Jesuit priest Erich Przywara (1889–1972),[13] who himself had engaged with the phenomenologies of Husserl and Heidegger, but also read Aquinas and Newman, and had debated with Karl Barth. Przywara had even written a study on Newman and Scheler.[14] He was a very open intellectual, intent on modernizing Catholic theology. He recommended Stein read Augustine and Pseudo-Dionysius, for example.

Stein made detailed studies of Thomas Aquinas over decades, and translated several of his works, including *Quaestiones disputatae de veritate*[15] and *De ente et essentia*.[16] She had learned Greek and Latin in the Gymnasium, which allowed her to carry out this translation work at an impressively high level. She also studied and translated John Henry Newman from English into German, including his classic *The Idea of the University*.[17] It was her mentor Fr Przywara SJ who recommended she read Newman, another convert. Stein had a deep historical sensitivity in her writings on ontology and, in this sense, offered an alternative to Heidegger's reading of its history which was receiving attention after the publication of *Being and Time*.[18] In many respects, Stein's attempted synthesis of Husserlian and Thomistic ontology, especially on the nature of essence (*Wesen*) and being (*Sein*), is meant to offer a corrective of the Heideggerian version.[19] Thus, for example, she opposes the sense of security in Being to Heidegger's *Angst*.

EDUCATION

Edith Stein was born on 12 October 1891 into a middle-class, German-speaking, Jewish family in Breslau, then Silesia in Prussia, now Wrocław, in Poland. When she was just two years of age, her father, Siegfried Stein, died at the age of forty-eight. Her mother, Auguste, a strict Orthodox Jew, was left in charge of the family business – a lumberyard – and at the same time had to raise their seven children. Edith attended a local school, before enrolling in the Victoria Gymnasium in Breslau. There she was a precocious student. A voracious reader, she read books from the library of her secular brother-in-law, Max: 'Max and Else were totally without belief; religion had no place whatsoever in their home.' Stein later wrote: 'Deliberately and consciously, I gave up praying here.' At an early age, she declared herself an atheist. She wrote later in her autobiographical *Life in a Jewish Family*:

> I used my free time principally for reading, preferably drama: Grillparzer, Hebbel, Ibsen, and, above all, Shakespeare became my daily bread. I was much more at home in this colourful world of the great passions and deeds than in the everyday life around me. But the day I produced Schopenhauer's *The World as Will and Idea*, my elder sisters protested energetically. They feared for my mental health; and I had to return the two volumes to the library unread. [20]

At the age of thirteen Stein wilfully decided to leave school, but returned after some months, then excelling in her studies. She took first place in her class in the *Abitur*, the German school-leaving and university matriculation examination.

Stein enrolled at the University of Breslau in 1911 to study psychology but was disappointed with the mechanistic scientific approach of her professors. One of these was the famous child psychologist William Stern, who rejected such an approach and developed a more humanistic psychology. She took philosophy classes with the Neo-Kantian Richard Hönigswald (1875–1947). [21] She spent the summer of 1911 in a Bohemian village with other young women from the university. They were all members of the women's suffrage group. Stein was at that time an ardent young feminist and she signed up to the Prussian Society for Women's Right to Vote and threw herself into student debating societies and other activities. [22] Later, she petitioned the Prussian authorities to allow women to proceed to the *Habilitation*. [23]

In 1913, after four semesters of study, Stein broke off her studies at the University of Breslau and, feeling some grief at leaving her mother behind, transferred to Göttingen precisely because of its fame in phenomenology. [24] As she recounts in *Life in a Jewish Family*, one of her professors, Dr Moskiewicz, who knew Edmund Husserl personally, having studied with him for a semester in Göttingen, gave her a copy of the second volume of Husserl's *Logical Investigations*, and remarked to her that in Göttingen the students philosophized day and night and talked only of the phenomenon. [25] Her mother agreed to the move, on condition that her sister went with her.

Moskiewicz had recommended that she study with Adolf Reinach, who was then *Privatdozent*[26] but had earned a reputation as a wonderful teacher and more accessible than the remote Husserl.

Edith and her sister Rosa Stein arrived in Göttingen in April 1913 and took Reinach's course on 'Introduction to Philosophy' and seminar on 'movement' or 'motion'. Shortly before the semester began, Husserl's *Ideas* I appeared in print and caused consternation because of its idealist turn.[27] Stein also attended the lectures Max Scheler gave – outside the university – on the basis of an invitation from the Göttingen Philosophical Society. He struck her as a fascinating character, with the air of genius, scattering brilliant remarks but not at all systematic in the manner of Husserl.[28] She also attended psychology lectures with Georg Elias Müller, who was deeply opposed to phenomenology, and also met David Katz who was *Privatdozent* in psychology and a student of Edmund Husserl.

Stein quickly became an active member of the Göttingen Philosophical Society, which at that time included Adolf Reinach and Roman Ingarden (who had arrived in Göttingen in 1912), and Hedwig Conrad-Martius (who had come from Munich in 1910), who became a life-long friend. Others in the group included Fritz Kaufmann and Alexandre Koyré (who had arrived from Odessa in 1908). Ingarden (born in 1893 in Krakow) was one and a half years younger than Stein; he completed his doctorate in 1918. According to his own account, he met Stein on her arrival in Göttingen in 1913 but only became close friends with her after she had passed her doctoral degree in 1916.[29] Roman Ingarden went back to Poland but returned in September 1917 and stayed until the end of January 1918, during which time they seem to have become intimate. The surviving correspondence between them begins in 1917 with her writing to him about his dissertation on Bergson.[30]

In November 1917 Ingarden and Stein learned of the death of Adolf Reinach from the *Frankfurter Zeitung*. Her letter to him of Christmas Eve 1917 addresses him as 'Mein Liebling' and expresses the desire to be with him on that day. She speaks of 'difficult days' behind and ahead of her, and she writes him a 'goodbye'. Reading between the lines it appears they had an intimate relationship at this time and that she was ending it. Sawicki reports the claim that Stein had fallen in love with Ingarden but when he went back to Poland he married a local girl and broke it off with Stein. Stein was also particularly fond of Hans Lipps who came from Munich; she supported him even after a personal falling out with Husserl, as is evident from her letters to Fritz Kaufmann seeking to intercede on his behalf in 1919–20.[31]

The outbreak of the First World War in 1914 changed everything. Stein interrupted her studies in order to serve as a volunteer nurse in the Red Cross, working in a military typhoid hospital in Austria, but she herself was struck down with bronchitis and returned to her university studies in October 1914. However she returned to nursing in 1915. She attended Husserl's *Nature and Spirit* lectures which covered some of the ground of the *Ideas* II manuscript that Stein would later work on.

Stein had approached Husserl in 1913 to write a doctorate on phenomenology and his reaction was more or less the same as later to another female student Gerda Walther: he recommended she sit the state teaching examination and not attempt to pursue a doctorate in philosophy.[32] Stein reports in her autobiography that she felt very depressed while struggling with her dissertation in the winter semester 1913–14. She later wrote that she could not cross the street without wishing that a street car would knock her down. Her conversations with Reinach, however, helped her through this difficult period, although all through her life she would struggle with self-doubt.

Eventually Husserl accepted Stein for the doctorate, suggesting empathy as a topic; Stein immersed herself in the work of Theodor Lipps, for whom the sentiment was a key concept. Husserl, however, had now been appointed to the chair in Freiburg so Stein had to follow him there, hoping that he would read her thesis and arrange the viva. Husserl finally agreed to read it and asked for it to be formally submitted to Freiburg. Stein defended her dissertation on 3 August 1916 and received the grade of *summa cum laude*.

Being one of the first women to gain a doctorate in philosophy from a German university, Stein campaigned to be allowed to register for the *Habilitation*, hitherto denied to women. She describes visiting Anna Reinach (née Stettenheimer, 1884–1953), widow of Husserl's assistant Adolf Reinach, after his death on 16 November 1917 and coming away impressed by the manner in which Anna's great faith was obviously a comfort to her.[33] Together with other students of Reinach she arranged for his *Gesammelte Schriften* (Collected Writings) to be published as a memorial volume for him. She managed to persuade Reinach's widow to allow some of his texts to be published even though he himself had become convinced during the war (where he was an artillery commander) that he had no ability as a philosopher and had left instructions for all his papers to be burned on his death.

EDITH STEIN'S PERIOD AS HUSSERL'S ASSISTANT (1916–18)

After Husserl accepted her doctorate, he invited Stein to work as his private assistant. According to Stein, Husserl's deteriorating eyesight meant that he could not read the pencil manuscript of *Ideas* II that he had begun in 1912 around the same time as he wrote *Ideas* I, published in 1913. The shock of his son's death and the upheaval of the move to Freiburg had disrupted his research and he needed an assistant.[34] Since he had been reading her thesis and noticed the anticipation of his *Ideas* II manuscript, she was ideal. Stein, who had begun a teaching career, immediately agreed and moved to Freiburg.

Stein worked as Edmund Husserl's paid assistant from October 1916 until February 1918, when she resigned in frustration.[35] She transcribed and edited Husserl's research manuscripts, including the manuscript of *Ideas* II, which shows considerable evidence of her editorial interventions. She also laboured on Husserl's *Lectures on the Consciousness of Internal Time* (1905–17), although these were eventually brought to press by Heidegger in 1928 (with only the slightest reference to Stein's labours on them). She was actually present in Bernau in 1917 as Husserl was composing these manuscripts on time (the C-manuscripts).[36] Ingarden says that probably her last acts as assistant consisted of her 'adjustment' of the lectures on internal time-consciousness.[37] Ingarden, explaining her position, writes that 'she had been appointed to set Husserl's manuscripts in order and to prepare them for publication. She was authorized to elaborate them, to introduce any changes into their content, or their internal structure, which she considered necessary on account of the subject matter, or on purely formal and didactic grounds. Husserl was supposed to read them in due course',[38] but as Ingarden confirms, whether because of his mental preoccupations or physical health (increasing blindness): 'It was simply impossible to persuade Husserl to re-read, study and correct his old manuscripts. He was usually dissatisfied with what he had already accomplished. He always believed that he now knew the truth about things better than before. His old manuscripts bored him, and he usually gave them up after one or two days reading.'[39]

Stein's letters to Ingarden show that she found this work frustrating as she was unable to interest Husserl in her revisions of his manuscripts, including the draft revision of the Sixth Investigation. Husserl would promise to read what she had written, eventually take it up for a day or two but then be distracted onto new problems and projects. According to her letter to Ingarden of 19 February 1918, Husserl was giving her 'impossible' (*unmöglich*) instructions for arranging the manuscripts. She also felt stifled, because she had no time for her own research, so she offered her resignation. She was not someone who could simply 'obey' Husserl: 'And if Husserl will not accustom himself once more to treat me as a collaborator in the work [*als Mitarbeiterin an der Sache*] – as I have always considered my situation to be and he, in theory, did likewise – then we shall have to part company.'[40] By 28 February 1918 she is writing to Ingarden that 'the Master has graciously accepted my resignation. His letter was most friendly – though not without a somewhat reproachful undertone'.[41] Stein wanted above all to become a university professor.

STEIN'S ATTEMPTS TO PURSUE A *HABILITATION*

In Germany, then as now, a *Habilitation* or higher doctorate was necessary in order to be a university professor. Stein was intent on the academic life, despite lack of encouragement from Husserl, who thought women were not well suited to the lonely life of the academic researcher. There was a general reluctance to accept women as *Habilitation* candidates (for which one needed the support of a professor willing to act as mentor). Stein intended her *Habilitation* thesis for Göttingen to be her study of the nature of psychology as a science. In fact, to this end, she completed a major study, entitled 'Contributions towards the Philosophical Foundation of Psychology and Science', which she intended to submit for the *Habilitation*. Thus, she refers to it as a '*Habilitation* Thesis' in her letter to Kaufmann of 31 May 1920.[42] This text, now referred to as '*Psychische Kausalität*' or *Beiträge zur philosophischen Begründung der Psychologie und der Wissenschaft* was published in Husserl's *Jahrbuch*, Volume 5, in 1922.[43]

There seemed to be a general presumption that women were not permitted to enrol in the *Habilitation*, so Stein agitated to have an official circular sent from the Ministry to the universities (presumably to remind them not to discriminate against women).[44] Her *Contributions to the Philosophical Foundation of Psychology* is a remarkably detailed and mature work, strongly influenced by Husserl's *Ideas* II and also by Max Scheler's writings on the person (especially as found in his *Formalism in*

Ethics, which had been published in Husserl's *Jahrbuch* 1913–16).[45] Here Stein speaks of a 'life-power' (*Lebenskraft*) that varies with each person's psycho–physical constitution and underlies their feelings and affective life: 'The changing conditionalities of life signify an increase or decrease of life-power, and different life-feelings correspond to that as "manifestations".'[46] This concept of *Lebenskraft* is developed in her later work including in her *Finite and Infinite Being*.[47]

Unfortunately Stein was unable to convince a professor to take her on as a *Habilitation* student. In her letter to Fritz Kaufmann of 8 November 1919 she complains:

> For all of ten days, the rejection, in black and white, has been in my pocket, or, more exactly, the document is in our files, closing the matter. [The application] was not even taken up by the faculty, but was quietly dispatched.

> I received a letter from Hermann, the department head, that was meant to appear as an official notification, for a *pre-commission* had decided not even to judge my thesis since the *Habilitation* of women continues to create many difficulties. The following day, evidently after the irregularity of this procedure had been explained to him, he told me orally that the danger had existed of having the thesis rejected because Müller had asserted that it 'would unseat psychology, as it is pursued here' (which is a slight error), and they had wished to spare me that [rejection].[48]

She was convinced that it was the philosopher Georg Misch (who later wrote a comparison between Husserl and Heidegger which favoured Heidegger's hermeneutics) who had been behind the refusal. On the other hand, Müller at Göttingen was deeply committed to empirical psychology and had been equally deeply hostile to Husserl's phenomenological approach when they were colleagues at Göttingen.

CONVERSION TO CATHOLICISM AND TURN TOWARDS NEO-THOMISM

While visiting her close friend Hedwig Conrad-Martius and her husband Theodor Conrad, at their home in the small village of Bergzabern, where they had an orchard and ran an informal but highly serious philosophy seminar, in the summer of 1921, Stein came across a copy of St Theresa of Avila's autobiography which she spent the whole night reading. This was her Augustinian *tolle lege* moment. She felt she had found the truth.[49] Very soon afterwards she converted to Catholicism and was baptized on 1 January 1922 with Hedwig Conrad-Martius as her godmother. Her conversion deeply disappointed her mother and many of her Jewish friends.[50] Stein's conversion meant that she turned her attention to works in the Catholic intellectual tradition and particularly the works of Thomas Aquinas. It is clear that she was familiar with Thomas even before her conversion, especially his account of affectivity. Stein was drawn in particular to St Thomas' account of essence and existence.[51] She also emphasized a certain existential turn in Aquinas. Thus she could write:

> Of course there is a world of difference between Thomas' philosophy and what passes for 'philosophy for life' today. In his philosophy we will look in vain for flights of emotion; all we will find is truth, soberly grasped in abstract concepts. On the surface much of it looks like theoretical 'hair-splitting' that we cannot 'do' anything with. And even after serious study it is not easy to put our finger on practical returns. But a person who has lived for some time with the mind of St. Thomas – lucid, keen, calm, cautious – and dwelt in his world, will come to feel more and more that he is making right choices with ease and confidence on difficult theoretical issues or in practical situations where before he would have been helpless... truth bears fruit of itself.[52]

Having been initially denied permission to follow a *Habilitation*, she taught at a Dominican school in Speyer from 1921 until 1932, when she moved to teach at the German Institute for Scientific Pedagogy in Münster. She continued to correspond with Husserl, Ingarden and others, and contributed an article to Husserl's *Festschrift* (1929), 'Husserls Phänomenologie und die Philosophie des hl. Thomas von Aquin' ('An Attempt to Contrast Husserl's Phenomenology and the Philosophy of St Thomas Aquinas'). This had originally been written in the form of a dialogue between these two thinkers: 'What is Philosophy? A Conversation between Edmund Husserl and Thomas Aquinas'.[53] But Heidegger as editor had asked her to write a more 'neutral' article and Stein recast it as an article removing the dialogue. In its original form, it presents an imaginary discussion between Thomas Aquinas and Husserl in the latter's home in Freiburg. Thomas and Husserl agree that they can do philosophy by discussing the matters themselves with figures who range across history – Plato, Aristotle and Augustine, for Aquinas; Descartes, Hume, Brentano, for Husserl. Both agree that philosophy must be rigorously scientific and must be essentially rational. Thomas, however, recognizes that there are revealed truths that are essentially rational and intelligible in themselves which human reason is required to recognize. Stein suggests that Husserl had an interest in reason in general, whereas Aquinas distinguishes between human and supra-human reason. Much of this discussion is repeated in *Finite and Eternal Being*.

Stein was studying Thomas Aquinas closely through the twenties and even translated his *De Veritate* (*Disputed Questions on Truth*) in her spare time. She acknowledges that she is a neophyte in scholasticism (if not in philosophy) and had no access to the relevant scholarly literature when she was doing her translation.[54] It is clear that she kept up with phenomenology and mentions in a letter of 16 February 1930 to Sr Adelgundis Jaegerschmid, a close friend of the Husserl family, that she has read the *Formal and Transcendental Logic* which Husserl had directed the publishers to send her.[55] Stein would go on to write major books on metaphysics including *Potenz und Akt* (*Potency and Act*) and *Finite and Eternal Being*.[56] She also read Heidegger's *Being and Time* (1927) and *Kant and the Problem of Metaphysics* (1929), when they were published and includes extensive critical discussions of Heidegger in her *Finite and Infinite Being*.[57] Stein praises Heidegger's turn towards Being, but denies that the apprehension of Being can be based on human finitude.

In 1930 Stein made another attempt to register for a *Habilitation* with her *Potenz und Akt* (completed around 1930),[58] this time getting in contact with Heidegger who was by then full professor in Freiburg, having replaced Husserl who retired in 1927. He was helpful and offered to inquire about getting her a study grant but pointed out that if she planned to get a job in a Catholic university she might be better not working with him.[59] She also saw Professor Martin Honecker (1888–1941), who held a chair in Freiburg, who agreed to support her application,[60] and it appears Husserl and his wife Malvine (who remained supportive of Stein) were pleased at this. She was planning to begin the *Habilitation* in Autumn 1931. Her appointment to a teaching post at the German Institute for Scientific Pedagogy in Münster may have been the reason she abandoned plans to complete the *Habilitation*. Her new, proposed *Habilitation* thesis, *Potenz und Akt*, was later incorporated with changes into her posthumously published *Endliches und ewiges Sein* (*Finite and Eternal Being*).

Following the rise to power of the National Socialists in Germany in 1933 Stein was not permitted to give further lectures at Münster, as she put it, 'because of my Jewish descent'.[61] Her official letter of dismissal is dated 19 April 1933. In mid-May 1933 she applied to the Catholic Archbishop for admission to the Carmelite Order. In October 1933 she entered the Carmelite convent at Cologne, and in April 1934 entered the novitiate, taking the religious name Teresa Benedicta of the Cross (Teresia Benedicta a Cruce), after the mystic who had inspired her original conversion. Her family were deeply wounded by her decision to become a Catholic nun at a time when Jews were being persecuted. Her mother died in 1938 but seems to have come to some acceptance of her daughter's decision.

ONTOLOGY: FINITE AND ETERNAL BEING

Stein reworked *Act and Potency* into a vast ontological study, *Endliches und ewiges Sein* (*Finite and Eternal Being*), an attempt to synthesize the diverse philosophies of Aquinas and Husserl, building on the dialogue between these two thinkers that she had contributed to Husserl's Festschrift. *Finite and Eternal Being* is subtitled 'An Attempt at an Ascent to the Meaning of Being' (*Versuch eines Aufstiegs zum Sinn des Seins*). It was completed in her monastery in Cologne-Lindenthal in September 1936, and sent for publication in 1937, but it was blocked from publication because of its author's Jewish heritage. It was not published until 1950 as Volume Two in the Herder series. Stein was in correspondence with Marvin Farber and Fritz Kaufmann, both in the USA, to have it published in America; it has been translated into English by Kurt Reinhart. In a letter to Malvine Husserl in 1940 she describes it as a 'work on the basic ontological questions, comparing and contrasting Thomism and phenomenology'.[62]

It is clear that the book is informed both by phenomenological ontology (especially as found in Husserl, Scheler and Heidegger, and perhaps most especially in the ontology of her friend Hedwig Conrad-Martius) and Neo-Thomist metaphysics, especially through her close dialogue with Erich

Pryzwara. This Neo-Thomism, as Stein acknowledges in her Preface, is one open to Augustine and Pseudo-Dionysius as well as Aristotle and St Thomas.[63]

The book begins with a discussion of the problem of being in the history of philosophy beginning with Aristotle and continued in St Thomas. She writes that 'The inquiry into the meaning of being may be regarded as the dominating theme of both Greek and medieval thought.'[64] She claims that ontology was lost in modern philosophy but was revived 'in the phenomenology of Edmund Husserl and Max Scheler'.[65] She also believes (in a way reminiscent of Heidegger) that the Greek and German languages have more flexibility than Latin in discussing the nature of being. She therefore proposes illuminating Latin in terms of the Greek and generally speaking she looks to the historical origins of terms. She proclaims: 'Medieval scholasticism has not invalidated Greek philosophy and neither has Latin made the Greek language obsolete.'[66] Like Heidegger, Stein proposes her own translations. Therefore, she renders *to on* as '*das Seiende*' and *entelecheia* as 'perfection of being' (*Seinsvollendung*).[67] Stein begins her ontology from the 'fact of our own being',[68] the primal certainty of my own existence.[69]

Stein then discusses the extent to which philosophy is a science aiming at 'ultimate clarity'.[70] She agrees with Thomas that the Christian believer must defer to revealed truth, but otherwise the way of reason must be followed; furthermore, the world takes on new meaning when viewed with the eyes of faith.[71] Faith, as an intelligible illumination, gives knowledge about 'the first existent', i.e. God, which could not be gained by natural reason.[72] Furthermore, it is precisely revealed truths such as the doctrine of creation that led Christian philosophers such as Thomas to distinguish between *esse* and *essentia*. For Stein, Christian philosophy uses faith as a source of knowledge, but it does not thereby become theology. Christian philosophy, for Stein, means not just that the philosopher is Christian, but the ideal of a perfect system of reason.[73] The criterion of reason must be applied in full stringency.

Reflecting on self-being, for Stein, reveals being and non-being or act and potency. I am in the now, but there is a non-being of past and future. The ego lives in an actual, streaming, living present.[74] Nevertheless, from this experience, I can grasp the concept of 'pure being', a being that is pure 'fullness' or plenitude (*Fülle*) and is always in the present, ('the *idea* of true and eternally immutable being').[75] The ego experiences itself as 'thrown into existence';[76] it knows its own being as received being. The idea of fullness becomes the measure of its own being. In contrast to Heidegger, Stein does not see *Angst* as the fundamental mood but rather the sense of the security of being.[77] Human beings by realizing their potentialities develop their true being. Stein introduces many new ideas including the idea of different degrees of 'vitality' (*Lebendigkeit*) of the ego[78] – this is a revival of her notion of *Lebenskraft*, a kind of psychic power that uniquely defines every human being.

Influenced by Duns Scotus and by Max Scheler, Edith Stein was particularly interested in the essences of individual persons.[79] The final chapter of *On Finite and Eternal Being* contains her thought analysis of personal unrepeatability. Much of the discussion concerns the nature of individual being. Stein distinguishes between 'general' (*allgemein*) and 'individual essence' (*Einzelwesen*),[80] drawing inspiration from Jean Héring's careful analysis of essences and 'whatnesses'.[81] The idea of essence as universal is usually contrasted with the individual this, *tode ti* in the philosophy of Aristotle, for instance. But Stein is interested in the 'unrepeatability' and 'incommunicability' of individuals. There is an essence of what it is to be an individual as such, the essence of *individuality*, but there are also individual essences of people like Socrates which are unique. Each self is a 'once off' (*Jedes Ich ist ein Einmaliges*).[82] For Stein, as for Scheler, *individuum* is at the heart of the person. Each individual human being is a distinct essence; there is an 'individual essence' (*individuelles Wesen, Einzelwesen*) proper to a specific person, and the individual is not completely absorbed by the species 'human being'. Furthermore, a person's individuality is not simply a matter of a collection of accidents clustered around the essence of being human. Stein writes in *Finite and Eternal Being*: 'It seems to me that the essence of Socrates is found in his being Socrates (which includes his being human) and I hold that this essence differs not only numerically but also by virtue of a special particularity from the essence of any other human being.'[83] As Stein writes, the unique *goodness of Socrates* is different from the goodness of any other human being. Social conventions hide this inner kernel of the individual.

Stein rejects the Aristotelian–Thomistic view that matter is the principle of individuation as sufficient for explaining the individuality of persons. She posits the ontological principle of 'being-a-carrier' (*Trägersein*)[84] as that which grounds individuality. Following Husserl, she distinguishes between different kinds of 'existence' (*Dasein*) and 'subsistence' (*Selbststand*) – material things have existence, ideal entities such as triangles have subsistence. She takes her orientation from St Augustine's *De Trinitate* and St Thomas Aquinas to articulate the person's 'existence in itself' as 'self-standingness' (*Selbstständigkeit*) and as 'the carrier of essence' (*Wesensträger*). God, for Stein, is 'Being-in-Person' (*Sein-in-Person*).[85] Being a carrier is not defined in terms of communicability of being but rather as 'non-communicability' (*Unmitteilbarkeit*). Individuals, moreover, are self-unfolding. Each individual is a member (has 'membership being', *Gliedsein*), of the human species, but is also a part of a totality where individuals realize themselves.[86] Human beings have a spiritual nature, which for Stein means they are meant to be in a spiritual communion with one another.

FINAL YEARS

Other philosophical and spiritual works followed. In 1938, with the Nazi threat growing, she was transferred to the Carmelite convent at Echt in Holland, where it was thought she would be safe from persecution. There she wrote her important treatise *Studie über Joannes a Cruce: Kreuzeswissenschaft* (*The Science of the Cross*, 1950), a phenomenological study of St John of the Cross,[87] which was prepared as part of the planned 400th celebration of the birth of John of the Cross in 1542.

In 1941 she also wrote a study on the *Symbolic Theology* of Pseudo-Dionysius the Areopagite, entitled '*Wege der Gotteserkenntnis*' ('Ways to Know God'),[88] in German, originally submitted to Marvin Farber for *Philosophy and Phenomenological Research*. Farber thought it a fine study of the stages of religious experience, but, having consulted with Alfred Schutz, who thought it entirely theological, recommended it be submitted elsewhere. In 1944, after her death, Farber submitted it to *The Thomist*, where it was refereed by Rudolf Allers who undertook to translate and edit it for publication. This whole episode shows that Stein continued to see herself as engaged professionally in philosophy and indeed in phenomenology.

Leaving Germany, however, did not ensure Stein's safety. Aware of the dangers for her, Herman van Breda, the Belgian priest responsible for saving the Husserl Archives, travelled by train to see her in Holland to persuade her to leave. The German authorities in Holland demanded that all non-Aryans be registered. The condemnation of Nazi anti-Semitism by the Dutch bishops of occupied Holland, issued in a pastoral letter read in all churches on 26 July 1942, provoked the German authorities to order the arrest of all non-Aryan Roman Catholics. With her sister Rosa, also a Catholic convert, Teresa Benedicta was seized by the Gestapo on 2 August 1942 at the convent in Echt and shipped to the concentration camp at Auschwitz where she arrived on August 7. Survivors of the death camp testified that she helped all other sufferers with great compassion. She was sent to the gas chamber, where she died with her sister on 9 August 1942.

At an open-air ceremony in Cologne on 1 May 1987, Pope John Paul II beatified Edith Stein, that is, declared her worthy of public veneration as a genuinely holy, or blessed, person. In Rome on 11 October 1998 he canonized her. Her beatification treated her as a martyr for the faith; and one miracle is attributed to her after a child who had swallowed paracetamol was cured. In 1999 Stein was proclaimed one of the patron saints of Europe. The Pope wrote that the 'proclamation of Edith Stein as a Co-Patroness of Europe is intended to raise on this Continent a banner of respect, tolerance and acceptance which invites all men and women to understand and appreciate each other, transcending their ethnic, cultural and religious differences in order to form a truly fraternal society'.

Edith Stein, inspired by Newman, and by the Christian mystics whom she studied closely, followed her conscience. Regarding her choice of religious name, she wrote in a letter of 9 December 1938 to Mother Petra Brüning, of the Ursuline Order, from Cologne Carmel: 'By the cross I understood the destiny of God's people which, even at that time, began to announce itself. I thought that those who recognized it as the cross of Christ had to take it upon themselves in the name of all. Certainly, today I know more of what it means to be wedded to the Lord in the sign of the Cross. Of course, one can never comprehend it, for it is a mystery.'[89]

ENDNOTES

1 Alasdair MacIntyre, *Edith Stein. A Philosophical Prologue, 1913–1922* (Lanham/ Oxford: Rowman and Littlefield, 2006); Freda Mary Oben, *Edith Stein. Scholar, Feminist, Saint* (New York, NY: Alba House, 1988).

2 Edith Stein, *Gesamtausgabe* (Freiburg: Verlag Herder, 1950–2018). Hereafter *GA*. Twelve volumes of the *Collected Works of Edith Stein* have been published to date (Washington, DC: Institute of Carmelite Studies, 1986–2014), hereafter *CWES*.

3 Her writings on women are collected in *Die Frau. Fragestellungen und Reflexionen*, *GA* 13, trans. *CWES* 2.

4   See Mary Catharine Baseheart, 'Edith Stein's Philosophy of Woman and Women's Education', *Hypatia* 4/1 (1989) pp. 120–31; reprinted in Linda López McAlister (ed.), *Hypatia's Daughters: Fifteen Hundred Years of Women Philosophers* (Bloomington, IN: Indiana University Press, 1996), pp. 267–79.

5   Letter to Mother Callista Brenzing, 18 October 1932, in *Self-Portrait in Letters, 1916–1942*, CWES 5, p. 121.

6   See Jane Kelley Rodeheffer, 'On Spiritual Maternity: Edith Stein, Aristotle, and the Nature of Woman', *Annual ACPA Proceedings*, 72 (1999), pp. 285–303.

7   See Ulrich Dobhan, 'Vom "radikalen Unglauben" zum "wahren Glauben"', in *Edith Stein Jahrbuch* 15 (2009), pp. 53–84.

8   The title of the dissertation was *Das Einfühlungsproblem in seiner historischen Entwicklung und in phänomenologischer Betrachtung* [*The Empathy Problem as it Developed Historically and Considered Phenomenologically*]. It was published as *Zum Problem der Einfühlung* (*On the Problem of Empathy*) in Halle in 1917 with the first historical chapter omitted. This first chapter was lost.

9   E. Husserl, *Ideen zu einer reinen Phänomenologie und phänomenologischen Philosophie. Zweites Buch: Phänomenologische Untersuchungen zur Konstitution*, (The Hague: Nijhoff, 1991); trans. R. Rojcewicz & A. Schuwer, *Ideas Pertaining to a Pure Phenomenology and to a Phenomenological Philosophy, Second Book*. Collected Works III (Dordrecht: Kluwer, 1989). Hereafter '*Ideas* II'.

10   Originally published in 1928 as E. Husserl, *Vorlesungen zur Phänomenologie des inneren Zeitbewußtseins*, ed. M. Heidegger (Halle: Niemeyer, 1928), trans. James Churchill, *Phenomenology of Internal Time Consciousness*, (Bloomington, IN: Indiana U. P., 1964). Expanded Husserliana edition, *Zur Phänomenologie des inneren Zeitbewusstseins (1893–1917)*, (The Hague: Nijhoff, 1969), trans. John Barnett Brough, *On the Phenomenology of the Consciousness of Internal Time (1893–1917)* (Dordrecht: Kluwer, 1991).

11   E. Stein, 'Eine Untersuchung über den Staat', *Jahrbuch für Philosophie und phänomenologische Forschung* 7 (1925), pp. 1–123, reprinted GA 7; trans. *An Investigation Concerning the State*, CWES 10. In this work, Stein develops the social ontology of Adolf Reinach as found in his *The Apriori Foundations of the Civil Law* (*Die apriorischen Grundlagen des burgerlichen Rechts*, 1913), in order to account for the social ontology (*soziale Ontologie*) of the state, of law and of social acts (*soziale Akte*) generally. See Francesca De Vecchi, 'Edith Stein's Social Ontology of the State, the Law and Social Acts. An Eidetic Approach', *Studia Phaenomenologica* 15 (2015), pp. 303–30.

12   Florent Gaboriau, *The Conversion of Edith Stein* (South Bend, IN: St Augustine's Press, 2002).

13   Erich Pryzwara's major work was *Analogia Entis. Metaphysik* (1932), trans. John R. Betz and David Bentley Hart, *Analogia Entis. Metaphysics: Original Structure and Universal Rhythm* (Grand Rapids, MI: Eerdmans, 2014).

14   Erich Pryzwara, *Religionsbegründung. Max Scheler – J.H. Newman* (Freiburg: Herder, 1923). Pryzwara supported Scheler's rejection of Kant and his realism which he thought could be compared with that of Thomas and Newman.

15 Stein's translation of *De Veritate* is contained in *GA* 23 & 24.

16 Thomas Aquinas, *De ente et essentia – Über das Seiende und das Wesen*, übersetzt von Edith Stein, *GA* 26. See Sarah Borden Sharkey, 'Edith Stein and Thomas Aquinas on Being and Essence', *American Catholic Philosophical Association Quarterly*, 82/1 (2008), pp. 87–104.

17 Her translation can be found in *John Henry Newman, Die Idee der Universität*, *GA* 21; and *John Henry Newman, Briefe und Texte zur ersten Lebenshälfte (1801–1846)*, *GA* 22.

18 Sylvie Courtine-Denamy, *Three Women in Dark Times: Edith Stein, Hannah Arendt, Simone Weil* (Ithaca, NY: Cornell U.P., 2001).

19 See 'Anhang: Martin Heideggers Existentialphilosophie', in *GA* 2, trans. Mette Lebech, 'Martin Heidegger's Existential Philosophy', *Maynooth Philosophical Papers* 4 (2007), pp. 55–98.

20 Edith Stein, *Aus dem Leben einer jüdischen Familie. Das Leben Edith Steins: Kindheit und Jugend (Autobiographie)*, *GA* 7, trans., *Life in a Jewish Family: Her Unfinished Autobiographical Account*, *CWES* 1.

21 Hönigswald was Jewish and was eventually dismissed from teaching by the Nazis in 1933. He was the teacher of Norbert Elias. He published primarily in the area of neokantian epistemology. Stein mentions his interest in the psychology of cognition. See R. Hönigswald, 'Prinzipienfragen der Denkpsychologie', *Kant-Studien* 18 (1913), pp. 205–45.

22 E. Stein, *Life in a Jewish Family*, p. 191. Stein wrote a great deal on feminism and especially advocated the participation of women in higher education. See *Essays on Woman* (*CWES* 2), and Michael A. Carey, *A Feminist Anthropology. Women in the Thought of Edith Stein* (Washington, DC: Pontifical John Paul II Institute for Studies on Marriage and Family, 1991).

23 Indeed the eventual decree explicitly mentions Stein's efforts. See 'Erlaß des Preußischen Ministers für Wissenschaft, Kunst und Volksbildung vom 21. Februar 1920', *50 Jahre Habilitation von Frauen in Deutschland. Eine Dokumentation über den Zeitraum von 1920–1970*, ed. Elizabeth Boedeker (Göttingen: Schwartz 1974).

24 Edith Stein, *Life in a Jewish Family 1891–1916*, pp. 239, 247.

25 Ibid., p. 218.

26 In German-speaking countries '*Privatdozent*' is the title of an academic who qualifies as lecturer by completing a second thesis (*Habilitationschrift*), and has permission to teach at a university without a salaried professorial appointment.

27 Ibid., p. 250.

28 Ibid., p. 259.

29 Roman Ingarden, 'Edith Stein on her Activity as an Assistant of Edmund Husserl', *Philosophy and Phenomenological Research* 23/2 (1962), p. 155.

30 Ingarden would later be of the opinion it was this dissertation on Bergson, when Husserl finally got around to reading it, that stimulated his time meditations in 1917 in Bernau.

31 Lipps was involved in a very unpleasant lawsuit and Husserl would not speak to him.

32 *Life in a Jewish Family*, p. 269.

33 Adolf Reinach and his wife had both entered the Protestant church in 1917. Later his widow had to flee Germany in 1942 to Spain to avoid the Nazis and in later life converted to Catholicism.

34 Stein, *Life in a Jewish Family*, p. 409.

35 Husserl paid Stein the same rate he paid his male assistants; see *Life in a Jewish Family*, p. 495.

36 Edmund Husserl, *Die 'Bernauer Manuskripte' über das Zeitbewußtsein (1917/18)* (Dordrecht: Kluwer, 2001).

37 R. Ingarden, 'Edith Stein on Her Activity as an Assistant of Edmund Husserl', p. 161.

38 Ibid., p. 157.

39 Ibid., p. 158.

40 E. Stein, 'Letter to Ingarden, 19 February 1918', in *Self-Portrait*, p. 22.

41 Ibid., p. 23.

42 Ibid., p. 43.

43 Edith Stein, 'Beiträge zur philosophischen Begründung der Psychologie und der Geisteswissenschaften', *Jahrbuch für Philosophie und phänomenologische Forschung*, 5 (1922), pp. 1–116; reprinted as *Beiträge zur philosophischen Begründung der Psychologie und der Geisteswissenschaften: Psychische Kausalität, Individuum und Gemeinschaft*, GA 7, translated as *Philosophy of Psychology and the Humanities* (*CWES* 7).

44 *Self-Portrait*, p. 44.

45 M. Scheler, *Formalism in Ethics and Non-Formal Ethics of Values* (Evanston, IL: Northwestern University Press, 1973).

46 E. Stein, *Philosophy of Psychology and the Humanities*, pp. 24–5.

47 See Christof Betschart, 'Was ist Lebenskraft? Edith Steins erkenntnistheoretische Prämissen in »PsychischeKausalität« (Teil 1)', *Edith Stein Jahrbuch* (2009), pp. 154–83.

48 *Self-Portrait*, p. 35.

49 See Teresia Renata Posselt OCD, *Edith Stein: the Life of a Philosopher and Carmelite* (Washington, DC: ICS, 2005).

50 Her phenomenological colleague Fritz Kaufmann (1891–1958) broke off all relations with her at that time but she managed to convince him to renew their friendship. She wrote to him in July 1925 on the occasion of his mother's illness and their correspondence renewed. In a letter of 13 September 1925 she congratulated him on his *Habilitation*. He even visited her in her convent. He later made efforts, while in the USA, to have her work published.

51 See Jude Dougherty, 'Edith Stein: The Convert in Search of Illumination' in *Western Creed, Western Identity* (Washington DC: Catholic University of America Press, 2000). On Stein's relation to Thomas, see Ralph McInerny, 'Edith Stein and Thomism', *Carmelite Studies* 4 (1987), pp. 74–87.

52 Edith Stein, 'Husserl and Aquinas: A Comparison', *CWES* 8, pp. 27–8.

53 Both versions have now been published as 'Husserl and Aquinas: A Comparison', in *CWES* 8, pp. 1–63.

54 See her letter of 12 June 1932 to Petrus Wintrath, *Self-Portrait*, p. 115.

55   Ibid., p. 60.
56   Edith Stein, *Endliches und ewiges Sein. Versuch eines Aufstiegs zum Sinn des Seins*, GA 2, trans. *Finite and Eternal Being. An Attempt at an Ascent to the Meaning of Being*, CWES 9.
57   See Mette Lebech, *The Philosophy of Edith Stein. From Phenomenology to Metaphysics* (Frankfurt: Peter Lang, 2015), pp. 147–64.
58   Edith Stein, *Potenz und Akt. Studien zu einer Philosophie des Seins*, GA 10, trans. *Potency and Act: Studies Towards a Philosophy of Being*, CWES 11.
59   E. Stein, 'Letter to Sr. Adelgundis Jaegerschmid 26 January 1931', *Self-Portrait*, p. 82.
60   See Hugo Ott, 'Die Randnotizen Martin Honeckers zur Habilitationsschrift *Potenz und Akt*', *Phänomenologische Forschungen* 26/27 (1993), pp. 140–5.
61   E. Stein, 'Letter to Elly Dursy', *Self-Portrait*, p. 141.
62   *Finite and Eternal Being*, p. 529.
63   Ibid., p. xxxi.
64   Ibid., p. 4.
65   Ibid., p. 6.
66   Ibid., p. 10.
67   Ibid., p. 11.
68   Ibid., p. 35.
69   Ibid., p. 36.
70   Ibid., p. 20.
71   Ibid., p. 21.
72   Ibid., p. 22.
73   Ibid., p. 25.
74   Ibid., p. 52.
75   Ibid., p. 56.
76   Ibid., p. 54.
77   Ibid., p. 58.
78   Ibid., p. 49.
79   See Sarah Borden Sharkey, *Thine Own Self: Individuality in Edith Stein's Later Writings* (Washington, DC: Catholic University of America Press, 2010); Christof Betschart, 'The Individuality of the Human Person in the Phenomenological Works of Edith Stein', in A. Calcagno, ed., *Edith Stein: Women, Social-Political Philosophy, Theology, Metaphysics and Public History: New Approaches and Applications* (Dordrecht: Springer, 2016), pp. 73–86.
80   *Finite and Eternal Being*, p. 81.
81   Jean Héring, 'Bemerkungen über das Wesen, die Wesenheit und die Idee', *Jahrbuch für Philosophie und phänomenologische Forschung* 4 (1921), pp. 495–543.
82   *Finite and Eternal Being*, p. 343.
83   Ibid., p. 478.
84   Ibid., p. 492.
85   Ibid., p. 359.
86   Ibid., p. 507.

87   Edith Stein, *Kreuzeswissenschaft. Studie über Johannes vom Kreuz*, *GA* 18, trans. *The Science of the Cross*, *CWES* 6.

88   Edith Stein, 'Ways to Know God: On the Symbolic Theology of Dionysius the Areopagite', trans. Rudolf Allers, *The Thomist* (1946), retranslated by Walter Redmond in Edith Stein, *Faith and Knowledge*, *CWES* 8, pp. 83–118. The German text was published in the *Tijdschrift voor Philosophie* in Leuven in 1946.

89   E. Stein, 'Letter to Mother Petra Brüning, OSU', *Self-Portrait*, pp. 295–6.

RELIGIOUS SYMBOLS IN THE PHILOSOPHICAL ANTHROPOLOGY OF PAUL RICOEUR

EILEEN BRENNAN

'Transcendence' is not a term commonly associated with the work of Paul Ricoeur, and yet at one time Ricoeur had well-developed plans to address that very topic in a proposed third volume of his *Philosophy of the Will*. Those plans were announced in *Freedom and Nature*,[1] the first volume, and revisited in *Finitude and Guilt*, the second volume, which actually comprises two books: *Fallible Man* and *The Symbolism of Evil*.[2] We know that the third volume was to bear the title *Poetics of the Will*, but that work was never written, at least not in the form originally intended. Ricoeur's project came to a halt with the publication of *Finitude and Guilt*. Opinion is divided as to whether Ricoeur permanently abandoned the project at that point. Olivier Abel and Jérôme Porée argue that subsequent works mark 'a poetic turn' in Ricoeur's phenomenology and hermeneutics. These were *The Rule of Metaphor*, the three volumes of *Time and Narrative* and *From Text to Action*.[3] Abel and Porée do not claim, however, that those writings also represent a turn towards transcendence, a move that would have placed all five texts in a direct line of descent from *Freedom and Nature* and *Finitude and Guilt*. Taking a more factual approach in assessing Ricoeur's path to a 'poetics of the will', Jean Grondin observes that, after *The Symbolism of Evil*, Ricoeur would have been expected to write 'the last volume of the trilogy'. But instead of writing that book, notes Grondin, Ricoeur wrote another based on lectures given at Yale and the Sorbonne during the first half of the 1960s: *Freud and Philosophy. An Essay*

on Interpretation (1965).[4] And that, Grondin suggests, was when Ricoeur's work took a wholly new direction.

Without necessarily getting into the debate about whether or not Ricoeur finished his project on the will by other means, I want to gather the type of evidence that will help us (1) to determine what Ricoeur means by 'transcendence'; (2) to recognize at least two of the forms of transcendence found in Ricoeur's work; and (3) to suggest ways in which Ricoeur's reflections on transcendence served his wider objective of developing a philosophical anthropology, the central category of which is the acting and suffering human being. With those goals in mind, the present essay is divided into four parts. The first part assembles a number of statements that Ricoeur makes about transcendence and the related experience of 'the fault' ('*la Faute*'), with a view to clarifying the meaning of our key term. It also identifies a first form of transcendence. The second part switches attention to the indirect or symbolic form in which the meaning of 'the fault' is expressed. It also discusses the 'methodological revolution' that Ricoeur was obliged to effect in order to understand symbolic meaning. The third part uncovers a second form of transcendence in Ricoeur's work. The fourth and final part situates Ricoeur's idea of transcendence in the broader context of his philosophical anthropology.

WHAT RICOEUR MEANS BY 'TRANSCENDENCE'

It is not possible to say what Ricoeur means by 'transcendence' without first explaining what he means by 'the fault'. To make matters even more complicated, there are also subtle but important differences between what he says about 'the fault' in *Freedom and Nature* and in *The Symbolism of Evil*, differences which we need to bear in mind if we are to have a proper sense of the wide range of meanings that fall under the heading of what Ricoeur considers to be the indissociable 'affirmation of "Transcendence"'.[5] In *Freedom and Nature*, he describes 'the fault' as '*the universe of the passions and of the law*, in the sense in which St Paul contrasts the law which kills with the grace which gives life'.[6] Rejecting any suggestion that passions, like ambition and hate, are just emotions that are 'more complex, more enduring, and more systematic' than others, he insists that passions are *distortions* both of the voluntary and the involuntary in human beings. Then, drawing on a Pauline heritage, he claims that passions and the law are mutually dependent:

This mutual dependence of passion and the law is central: in the context of the fault, passions and the law form the vicious circle of actual existence. Passions eject values from man, alienate them in a hostile yet melancholy transcendence which is, strictly speaking, the law in St Paul's sense of the word, the law without grace. In turn the law condemns without helping: it entices the fault by prohibition and precipitates the very internal decadence which it seems to be designed to hinder.[7]

In these lines Ricoeur depicts the law as a form of transcendence, which is clearly not the 'transcendence' he intended to talk about in the third volume of the *Philosophy of the Will*. The law, all further consideration of which he is about to suspend in *Freedom and Nature*, is 'hostile yet melancholy'; it is 'the law without grace'. Not only does it condemn *without helping* – what we suspect has to be the very opposite of a gracious transcendence – but by prohibiting certain behaviours it actually 'entices the fault', motivating the very thing it seems designed to prevent.

In *The Symbolism of Evil*, Ricoeur will return to the subject of the law, but on this occasion he will offer a description of the Pharisees – who 'are first of all and essentially men of the Torah'[8] – which does not suggest that the law they so assiduously observe puts them at risk of becoming internally decadent. Instead Ricoeur will describe the Pharisees as 'the purest representatives of an irreducible *type* of moral experience', in which we can all recognize one of the fundamental possibilities of our own humanity.[9] He will even encourage us to see Pharisaism as a 'joyous abandonment of the will to direction by the Law'.[10] And he will describe Psalms 19 and 119 as 'the most beautiful lyrical witnesses' that we have of this.[11] Nonetheless Ricoeur will still be able to acknowledge that the scrupulousness of the Pharisees has its limitations: 'Ritualization, sedimentation, separation of the scrupulous conscience – [Nevertheless,] these traits do not make the scrupulous man a monster; the limitations of scrupulousness are the counterpart of its depth.'[12] What Ricoeur says about sedimentation in *The Symbolism of Evil* picks up on a point that he makes in *Freedom and Nature* about the vastness of '*the universe of the passions and of the law*'.[13] He notes that the conscience of the Pharisee is 'an increasingly articulated and subtle conscience that forgets nothing and adds incessantly to its obligations'.[14] He then notes: 'This is not a conscience that begins or begins anew, but a conscience that continues and adds to.'[15] One can expect, then, to see that the already vast universe of the law will continue to expand due to the 'work of minute and often minuscule innovation' carried out by the modern-day equivalents of the Pharisees, who, for Ricoeur, would certainly include people of the Jewish faith.[16]

In *Freedom and Nature* Ricoeur admits that 'We cannot help being impressed by the vastness of the domain [of the fault].'[17] He also summarizes four traits of the fault to which, he says, he will 'constantly allude':

[1] The principle of passion lies in a certain *bondage* which the soul imposes on itself. This bondage has nothing to do with determinism which is only a necessary rule binding *objects* together for a *theoretical* consciousness; the bondage of passions is something that happens to a subject, that is, to a freedom;

[2] The bondage of passions is a bondage to *Nothing*. All passion is *vanity*. Reproach, suspicion, concupiscence, envy, hurt, and grief are various names for chasing after the wind;

[3] Passion introduces an infinite, an excess, which is at the same time a painful infinite, perhaps even an obscure religion of suffering. All passion is unhappy;

[4] The fault is not an element of fundamental ontology... It can be conceived only as an accident, an interruption, a fall.[18]

Nevertheless, Ricoeur's statement that he will 'constantly allude' to these four traits of the fault is misleading. As already mentioned, he is about to suspend all consideration of 'the fault' in *Freedom and Nature*. He will do so as soon as he has completed the General Introduction to that work; and he will not lift that suspension until he starts to write *Finitude and Guilt*, more particularly its second part whose title, as we know, is *The Symbolism of Evil*.

The closing section of the General Introduction is especially relevant to the work of clarifying what Ricoeur means by 'Transcendence'. He introduces the topic via a reflection on a particular aspect of the fault. He writes: 'The integral experience of the fault and its mythical counterpart, the vision of innocence, are closely linked with an affirmation of Transcendence – in one aspect, the integral experience of the fault is the fault experienced as before God, that is, as sin. This is why we cannot dissociate the fault and Transcendence.'[19] Not surprisingly, sin is yet another subject to which Ricoeur will return in *The Symbolism of Evil*. There he will devote a whole section of the chapter, which he dedicates to that particular type of fault, to analysing the meaning of the 'category of "before" God'.[20] His central message is that to understand this category we have to set aside '"thought" in the sense of Greek philosophy'[21] and try instead to re-enact 'the prophetic "oracle"'.[22] As he has already noted, 'sin presupposes a "theistic" perspective'.[23] To be conscious of sin, says Ricoeur, you need to think of yourself as someone who 'finds himself implicated in the initiative taken by someone who, on his side, is essentially turned toward man; a god in the image of man, if you wish, but above all a god concerned about man; a god who is anthropotropic – before being anthropomorphic'.[24] To be conscious of sin, he says, you need to think in terms of a 'preliminary dimension of encounter and dialogue' between a god and the human being that he is concerned about.[25] Once you do that, you can certainly be conscious of sin, which is precisely a violation of that bond, 'a violation of the Covenant'.[26]

Ricoeur is not really in a position, in *Freedom and Nature*, to go into this kind of detail regarding the consciousness of sin. However, he is able to say something about what transcendence can do for the sinner. He writes:

> But above all Transcendence is what liberates freedom from the fault. Thus men live Transcendence, as purification and deliverance of their freedom, as salvation. Transcendence bursts forth on us in relation to a spiritual world in which there are real breaks. All other modes of access, which might appear as short cuts, are in fact alien to that concrete experience of Transcendence which is a sign of our rediscovered integrity. Captivity and deliverance of freedom are one and the same drama.[27]

There is so much we could say about those remarkable lines. To begin with, the first and second lines provide an answer, though certainly not the only one, to what Ricoeur means by 'Transcendence'. In this context, where he has just been talking about sin, it is clear that he uses the term to mean a god, 'a god in the image of man, if you wish',[28] who has the power to liberate human beings from their self-imposed '*bondage*'.[29] Even without the additional and very valuable information supplied by the chapter on sin, in *The Symbolism of Evil*, we can tell that the appropriate perspective to take up here is the theistic one. The third line is one that I find truly fascinating. It is an adaptation of a way of describing the intentional structure of consciousness that Ricoeur borrowed from Edmund Husserl and then used in his Translator's Introduction to the French version of Husserl's *Ideen I*. There Ricoeur talks about a form of consciousness *bursting out towards the world*, thus underlining the capacity of consciousness for some form of transcendence. But in the above-quoted passage, the sinner has a very different experience from that of a consciousness that perceives an object, imagines a scenario, or even decides on a project. Here, instead of bursting out toward the world, 'Transcendence bursts forth on us in relation to a spiritual world in which there are real breaks.'[30] I shall return to this idea of transcendence bursting forth on us when I uncover what I believe is a second form of transcendence in Ricoeur's work.

Although Ricoeur does not say so in as many words in *Freedom and Nature*, it should be obvious that he alludes to two different types of fault in that work: (1) sin; and (2) guilt, an experience that the Pharisees would have had whenever they failed to observe the law. In *The Symbolism of Evil*, as I have already shown, he picks up on those two distinct types of fault – sin and guilt – analysing them in much greater detail. But he does more than that. He also introduces and analyses a third type of fault: defilement. In the next section, I shall discuss the symbolic form in which the meaning of 'the fault' is expressed. I shall also comment on the 'methodological revolution' that Ricoeur was obliged to effect in order to solve the problem of interpreting symbolic or indirect meaning.

A HERMENEUTICS OF RELIGIOUS SYMBOLS

There is a passage in the Preface to *Fallible Man* where Ricoeur recalls his own thought processes as he moved from 'the initial idea of a mythics of bad will' to the course he would finally settle on: developing 'a symbolics of evil'. He writes:

> First it became evident that the myths of fall, chaos, exile, and divine blinding, all of which are directly accessible to a comparative history of religions, could not be inserted in their unrefined state into philosophic discourse. First they had to be put back into their own universe of discourse... It then appeared that myths could be understood only as secondary elaborations of a more fundamental language that I call the language of avowal; this language speaks of fault and evil to the philosopher, and what is noteworthy in it is that it is symbolic through and through. It does not speak of stain, sin, or

guilt in direct and proper terms, but in indirect and figurative terms. To understand this language is to bring into play an exegesis of the symbol, which calls for rules of deciphering: a hermeneutics. In this way the initial idea of a mythics of bad will has been expanded to the dimensions of a symbolics of evil.[31]

We have already seen Ricoeur refer to at least one of the myths that are listed in the first line: the myth of the fall. Commenting on the correlative experience of sin, in *Freedom and Nature*, he announced that it 'can be conceived only as an accident, an interruption, a fall'.[32] There was also an allusion to the myth of exile in that earlier text, although that one is much harder to spot. The sinner has not only fallen from grace; in breaking the Covenant, she has brought exile upon herself, that is to say, she has separated herself from God. The question raised in the above-quoted passage, though not explicitly, is whether myths of the fall and exile, etc., can be 'inserted in their unrefined state into philosophic discourse'. It is hard to imagine a philosopher answering that question in the affirmative, and Ricoeur is no exception. So how does he plan to proceed? And what does he mean by getting the myths of fall, chaos, exile and divine blinding into a refined state, ready for insertion into philosophy? As the second line suggests, Ricoeur wants to create the conditions for a *dialogue* between the largely religious myths and an essentially agnostic philosophy. There is surely potential for a dialogue of that type given that, as the third line states, myths are 'secondary elaborations of a more fundamental language', a language that 'is symbolic through and through'; and that language 'speaks of fault and evil to the philosopher'. However, the fourth line signals that there is a problem here: what is said is said 'in indirect and figurative terms'; and anyone familiar with philosophy will know that most philosophers would have difficulty understanding things that are expressed in such unfamiliar terms. But all is not lost. As the fifth line explains, the solution to the problem of correctly interpreting meanings that are given only in indirect and figurative terms is 'to bring into play an exegesis of the symbol, which calls for rules of deciphering: a hermeneutics'.

Jean Grondin picks up on Ricoeur's use of the phrase, 'rules of deciphering', noting that Ricoeur would appear to lay claim here to the traditional idea of hermeneutics, more particularly to a version of hermeneutics close to that of Wilhelm Dilthey.[33] But Grondin cautions that 'the rules that concern Ricoeur are very different, in their form and spirit, from those of Dilthey'.[34] As he explains in reference to another passage in the Preface to *Fallible Man*, Ricoeur is actually interested in 'rules of transposition' that would allow him to take the symbolism of evil into a new type of philosophic discourse. However, Grondin expresses puzzlement about the content of the sought-after rules of transposition: 'What can such rules consist of?'[35] The answer he gives is that it is hard to tell, partly because there is no obvious route from religious to philosophic discourse, and partly because Ricoeur did not present rules of that type in the Conclusion to *The Symbolism of Evil* even though he had apparently promised that he would. Nonetheless, Grondin insists that those rules of transposition are important, because needing to have them was what led Ricoeur to enter into hermeneutics in the first place.[36]

Grondin's reading not only of the Preface to *Fallible Man* but also of *The Symbolism of Evil* itself represents a challenge to the view, shared by John B. Thompson, Domenico Jervolino, and indeed Ricoeur himself, that in the 1960s he limited the definition of 'hermeneutics' to the interpretation of the hidden meaning of symbols.[37] Grondin's central claim is that while Ricoeur described what he was doing in *The Symbolism of Evil* as offering an exegesis of symbols, what he was really doing was something rather different. Far from searching for rules of deciphering that could be applied to a world of symbols he was in fact searching for 'rules for transposing the symbolics of evil into a new type of philosophic discourse'.[38] In short, despite appearances to the contrary, there was nothing traditional about the hermeneutic exercises presented in *The Symbolism of Evil*. I suggest, however, that Grondin is mistaken, and that a clear distinction should be drawn between what Ricoeur terms 'rules of deciphering', and 'rules for transposing'. As I shall now try to show, the first set of rules is required in order to get the myths of fall, chaos, exile and divine blinding into a refined state, ready for insertion into philosophy. The second set of rules would have come into play only at the point where an effort was made to take up into philosophy the then suitably prepared religious myths.

It may come as a surprise to learn that despite the risks Ricoeur took in trying to establish a dialogue between religious myths and philosophy – Grondin maintains that Ricoeur was in danger of transgressing 'the boundaries of the philosophical' in attempting this – he was quite conservative when it came to observing the philosophical conventions of clarifying meanings, having evidence to support your claim, etc. We learn a lot about Ricoeur's views on the importance of philosophers using concepts, whose meaning is clear and capable of being understood, from reading certain passages in *Critique and Conviction*. There Ricoeur refers to his debt to Gabriel Marcel, who mentored him in the 1930s and 1940s and taught him 'how to do' philosophy as opposed to merely repeat the views of people like Aristotle and Kant. However, Ricoeur also talks about the difficulty he had when it came to emulating Marcel's *style* of philosophizing, something he felt under pressure to do as a young man. The problem, for him, was the lack of conceptual clarity in Marcel's way of thinking. As he notes in *Critique and Conviction*, Marcel's thought proceeded by means of the poetic devices of 'assonance and dissonance'.[39] From as far back as the 1930s, then, Ricoeur wanted to work with concepts whose meaning was clear, and the approach he took in the *Philosophy of the Will*, from *Freedom and Nature* to *The Symbolism of Evil*, was no exception.

We need only consult the first chapter of *Freedom and Nature* to see just how focused Ricoeur is on arriving at clear concepts in advance of any philosophical analysis of what we might term, 'the lived experience' of willing something. In the first chapter of that work, he lists some of the words that he will use when analysing the basic structure of the will – 'decision, project, value, motive, and so on' – noting that all of those words 'have a meaning which we need to determine'.[40] He knows how to set about determining those meanings: by using the 'eidetic approach' pioneered by Edmund Husserl. However, he has certain reservations about 'pure description': 'The gushing reality of life can become shrouded in essences.' Nevertheless, he takes the pragmatic decision to 'first draw from [the eidetic approach] all that it can give us, especially delimiting of our basic concepts'.[41] However, Ricoeur is not in a position to use the eidetic approach in *The Symbolism of Evil*. As we have seen, the indirect and figurative terms in which the myths of fall, chaos, exile and divine blinding are expressed oblige him to effect 'a revolution in method', which amounts to his being obliged to have 'recourse to hermeneutics'.[42] Ricoeur's attitude to that revolution in method is not entirely positive. He sees it as 'the price' to be paid for being able to use the symbols of evil to give 'new life and considerable enrichment to the idea of the possibility of evil or fallibility',[43] but also and perhaps more importantly, it is the price to be paid for being able to take up 'into the element of philosophic discourse'[44] the symbolically structured language of avowal or confession.

There is no denying that hermeneutics in the sense of an exegesis of symbols was essential to the effort to facilitate a productive exchange between the religious symbols and philosophy. Without that intermediary the philosopher would not have been able to understand what was being said to her in a language that was by design 'symbolic through and through'. But Ricoeur, who always insisted on using concepts in philosophy, and not any kind of poetic devices, wanted to go a step further. He wanted to find a *concept of fault* that the philosopher could not only understand but also go on to use in philosophical reflection. To that end, his 'survey' of the symbols of defilement, sin and guilt, in *The Symbolism of Evil*, was arranged so as to demonstrate that 'there is a *circular* relation among all the symbols: the last brings out the meaning of the preceding ones, but the first lends to the last all their power of symbolisation'.[45] In this way Ricoeur managed to orient his exegesis of symbols towards the *concept* of the 'servile will'.[46] The following passage will confirm that Ricoeur's hermeneutics of symbols had that particular orientation; it will also point out that the concept of the servile will is no different from the symbols from which it gets all its meaning; that is to say, it is ineluctably 'indirect':

> The concept toward which the whole series of the primary symbols of evil tends may be called the servile will. But that concept is not directly accessible; if one tries to give it an object, the object destroys itself, for it short-circuits the idea of will, which can only signify free choice, and so free will, always intact and young, always available – and the idea of servitude, that is to say, the unavailability of freedom to itself. *The concept of the servile will, then, cannot be represented as the concept of fallibility*, which we considered at the beginning of this work; for we should have to be able to think of free will and servitude as coinciding in the same existent. That is why the concept of the servile will must remain an indirect concept, which gets all its meaning from the symbolism that we have run through ... this concept, which will occupy our attention in the third volume of the present work ... [is] the intentional telos of the whole symbolism of evil.[47]

Ricoeur's use of italics goes some way towards explaining why he would have seen having recourse to hermeneutics as something that came at a price. What he had to forego in moving from using the phenomenological method, the method used both in *Freedom and Nature* and in *Fallible Man*, to using hermeneutics, the method used in *The Symbolism of Evil*, was any chance of *representing* the concept that was now in sight. Nonetheless, it was a price worth paying. An indirect concept was still a concept. It was also the only acceptable form in which to bring what we might term the 'wisdom of symbols' to the philosopher. As we learn from one of the lines quoted above, it is the concept of the 'servile will' that 'will occupy our attention in the third volume of the present work'. However, as already mentioned, Ricoeur never managed to write the third volume of the *Philosophy of the Will*.

It is interesting to look back to the first of the four traits of fault that Ricoeur identified in the General Introduction to *Freedom and Nature* and to see how well he anticipated the meaning of the indirect concept of the 'servile will'. As already noted he describes that first trait of fault as follows: 'The principle of passion lies in a certain *bondage* which the soul imposes on itself... the bondage of passions is something that happens to a subject, that is, to a freedom.'[48] Looking back to *Freedom and Nature* in this way also serves to remind us that not long after he made those comments, Ricoeur went on to say that 'we cannot dissociate the fault and Transcendence'.[49] With that in mind, I shall now turn to consider a form of transcendence which is linked to one particular element of the cycle of symbols that has led us to the concept of fault: defilement.

A SECOND FORM OF TRANSCENDENCE

Strictly speaking, we are not yet in a position to properly understand the transcendence to which the concept of the 'servile will' is linked. That is because, as Ricoeur notes in *Freedom and Nature*, it is the '*integral* experience of the fault and its mythical counterpart', and not the experience of fault considered in isolation, that are 'closely linked with an affirmation of Transcendence'.[50] But everything we have considered so far in terms of Ricoeur's various interpretations of the symbols of fault has been limited by an abstraction from considerations such as (1) universality; (2) accounts of 'the Beginning and the End of fault'; and (3) narratives that chart the movement from fallibility to fault,[51] all the considerations in fact that come into play as soon as we begin to interpret second-order symbols or myths. Ricoeur explained very early on in the inquiry that it was for 'didactic purposes' that he chose to abstract the 'living experience' of defilement, sin and guilt from the myths of the fall, chaos, exile and divine blinding.[52] Of course none of that stopped him from identifying transcendence, in *Freedom and Nature*, as a god who liberates freedom from the fault.[53] Following that precedent, I propose to discuss a second form of transcendence, one that is found in the opening chapter of *The Symbolism of Evil*.

Ricoeur devotes the first chapter of *The Symbolism of Evil* to the theme of fault in the sense of defilement. He notes that the experience of defilement is marked by feelings of fear, dread, and even terror; the thing that is feared, dreaded, the source of terror is 'the impure'.[54] He is quick to acknowledge that there is nothing in any of this that the philosopher can be expected to understand. He explains: 'Defilement itself is scarcely a representation, and what representation there is is immersed in a specific sort of fear that blocks reflection.' Nonetheless, Ricoeur will find something of educational value in those 'negative feelings', and he will sketch out his position on that point at the end of the chapter.[55] However, there will be an uncharacteristic steeliness in what he goes on to say; and what he finally recommends in terms of 'familial and scholastic' education will not be something that parents and teachers would now consent to. And yet, it is among those same rather harsh sentiments that one finds a statement, one that is almost entirely out of step with all the others, which points to the second form of transcendence that I want to talk about. That statement reads as follows: 'Before casting out fear, love transforms and transposes it.'[56] The curious thing is that it is not Ricoeur himself, but rather one of his former graduate students, Marguerite Léna, who fully recognizes the distinctive intentional structure of a love that transforms and transposes fear.

In her book, *L'Esprit de l'éducation*, Marguerite Léna quotes a very long passage from Ricoeur on the educational value of the feelings of fear, dread and terror. Introducing that passage she says that what Ricoeur is doing here is calling to mind 'the educative function of fear' as well as 'the spiritual transfiguration' to which it leads.[57] However, in her commentary on the passage she is also careful to make a distinction between fears with educational value and those without. She describes the latter as fears that suffocate and paralyse. She thinks that educators should only arouse fears with educational value; and they should cure those that have none. As examples of fears that have no educational value, she cites the fears that very young children have when they look upon the faces of strangers or when they find themselves in unfamiliar surroundings. She also speaks quite tenderly about children who are frightened at the prospect of starting school. Those and similar fears can always be allayed, she says, through what she terms, 'the power of love'. According to Léna, 'A child that is truly loved feels and knows herself to be safe enough not only to take a risk, but also to seek it out and develop a taste for it.'[58]

Léna's reference to fears that suffocate and paralyse recalls Ricoeur's account of the person who dreads the impure. As already noted, that sort of fear is so intense as to 'block reflection'. We saw in the case of the sinner that it would take a god to liberate freedom from its self-imposed bondage. But what would it take to help end the suffering of a person who is in the grip of an intense fear, even and especially an irrational one? Léna has surely found the answer in Ricoeur's text: the kind of love that can transform and transpose fear. And the great benefit of Léna's depiction of the caring teacher who sets about allaying the fears of frightened children is that it is so easy to switch perspective and imagine what it must be like for the children to receive that warm reassurance. It must be as though transcendence is bursting forth on them in relation to a public world in which there are real breaks.

A PHILOSOPHICAL ANTHROPOLOGY INFORMED BY RELIGIOUS SYMBOLS

The only direct quotation from *The Symbolism of Evil*, in Léna's *L'Esprit de l'éducation*, is the one just mentioned, yet it is clear that the book follows the route that Ricoeur carved out in 1960. Léna wants to talk about the 'educative act', which she defines as 'the slow, piecemeal conquest of one's humanity'.[59] Humanity, as Léna understands it, is something that even a very young child is required to 'take on and bring into play'.[60] To do this a child will need to have the benefit of 'a thousand years of experience', something that can be acquired only through an 'act of transmission' on the part of her teachers, parents, etc.[61] There is a nod here to all that Ricoeur puts at our disposal in the vast survey of religious and classical texts offered in *The Symbolism of Evil*. But Léna mentions an additional requirement: the child needs to acquire centuries-old skills like reading, writing and arithmetic. Mastering those skills will be an important step, she says, on a child's journey to 'demonstrating' her humanity. However there is, for Léna and indeed for Ricoeur, one additional thing to do in the course of 'the slow, piecemeal conquest of one's humanity', and that is to learn to value and to nourish a relationship with the sacred.

There are two places in *The Symbolism of Evil* where Ricoeur underscores this idea that having a relationship with the sacred is part of what it means to be human: the Introduction and the Conclusion. In the Introduction, he boldly states that, 'the confession [of fault or evil] lies within the sphere of interest of philosophy, for it is an utterance, an utterance of man about himself; and every utterance can and must be taken up into the element of philosophic discourse'.[62] Ricoeur is clearly thinking about philosophy in the sense of philosophical anthropology. The thought seems to be that if you want to arrive at a properly philosophical – and comprehensive – understanding of what it means to be a human being who acts and suffers in the world, then you need to listen to all the evidence, including the testimony of people who see themselves as having a relationship with the sacred. But we later discover that the phrase 'must be taken up' is not in fact a hypothetical imperative. As the Conclusion clearly demonstrates, Ricoeur is highly critical of the modern age for having lost sight of something that he thinks his philosophy of symbols alone can make visible again: that there is an *essential connection* between human beings and the sacred. Here are the rather dramatic terms in which he identifies both the problem with the modern age and the solution to that problem, namely, his new style of philosophy: 'The historical moment of the philosophy of symbols is that of forgetfulness and restoration. Forgetful of hierophanies, forgetful of the signs of the sacred, loss of man himself insofar as he belongs to the sacred.'[63] It is significant that in the Conclusion to *The Symbolism of Evil*, Ricoeur is no longer talking about unhappy passions or the fault in its various forms. He has switched perspective to talk about the indirect ways in which Transcendence communicates with human beings: through 'hierophanies' and 'signs of the sacred'. His plan is to have the 'philosophy of symbols' restore the visibility of those ciphers, thus highlighting an essential aspect of our shared humanity: our connection with the sacred.

ENDNOTES

1   Paul Ricoeur, *Philosophie de la volonté* I: *Le Volontaire et l'Involontaire* (Paris: Aubier Montaigne, 1950). Paul Ricoeur, *Freedom and Nature: The Voluntary and the Involuntary* (Evanston, IL: Northwestern University Press, 1966).

2   Paul Ricoeur, *Philosophie de la volonté* II: *Finitude et Culpabilité* (Paris: Aubier Montaigne, 1960). Paul Ricoeur, *Fallible Man* (New York, NY: Fordham University Press, 1986) and Paul Ricoeur, *The Symbolism of Evil* (Boston: Beacon, 1967).

3   Olivier Abel and Jérôme Porée, *Le Vocabulaire de Paul Ricoeur* (Paris: Ellipses, 2007), p. 67.

4   Jean Grondin, *Paul Ricoeur* (Paris: Presses Universitaires de France, 2013), p. 75.

5   Ricoeur, *Freedom and Nature*, p. 29.

6   Ibid., p. 20. Italics in original.

7   Ibid., pp. 21–2.

8   Ricoeur, *The Symbolism of Evil*, p. 122.

9   Ibid.

10   Ibid., p. 123.

11   Ibid.

12   Ibid., p. 138.

13   Ricoeur, *Freedom and Nature*, p. 20. Italics in original.

14   Ricoeur, *The Symbolism of Evil*, p. 136.

15   Ibid., pp. 136–7.

16   See ibid., p. 137.

17   Ricoeur, *Freedom and Nature*, p. 22.

18   Ibid., pp. 23–4.

19   Ibid., p. 29.

20   Ricoeur, *The Symbolism of Evil*, p. 50.

21   Ibid., p. 53.

22   Ibid., p. 54.

23   Ibid., p. 51.

24   Ibid.

25   Ibid., p. 50.

26   Ibid., p. 51.

27   Ricoeur, *Freedom and Nature*, p. 29.

28   Ricoeur, *The Symbolism of Evil*, p. 51.

29   Ricoeur, *Freedom and Nature*, p. 23.

30   Ibid., p. 29.

31   Ricoeur, *Fallible Man*, p. xlii.

32   Ricoeur, *Freedom and Nature*, p. 24.

33   Grondin, *Paul Ricoeur*, p. 60.

34   Ibid.

35   Ibid.

36   See ibid., p. 61.

37   For confirmation of Ricoeur and Thompson's shared view on the matter, see Paul Ricoeur, *Hermeneutics and the Human Sciences* (Cambridge: Cambridge University Press, 1981), p. 33. Jervolino positions himself close to Thompson and Ricoeur in Domenico Jervolino, *Paul Ricoeur: Une herméneutique de la condition humaine* (Paris: Ellipses, 2002) pp. 23–45.

38   Grondin, *Paul Ricoeur*, p. 60.

39   Paul Ricoeur, *Critique and Conviction* (Cambridge: Polity, 1998), p. 23.

40   Ricoeur, *Freedom and Nature*, p. 37.

41   Ibid.

42   Ricoeur, *Fallible Man*, p. xliv.

43   Ibid.

44   Ricoeur, *The Symbolism of Evil*, p. 4.

45 Ibid., p. 152.
46 Ibid., p. 151.
47 Ibid., pp. 151–2.
48 Ricoeur, *Freedom and Nature*, p. 23.
49 Ibid., p. 29.
50 Ibid. Emphasis added.
51 Ricoeur, *The Symbolism of Evil*, pp. 162–3.
52 Ibid., p. 10.
53 See Ricoeur, *Freedom and Nature*, p. 29.
54 Ricoeur, *The Symbolism of Evil*, p. 25.
55 See ibid., pp. 44–5.
56 Ibid., p. 45.
57 Marguerite Léna, *L'Esprit de l'éducation* (Paris: Desclée de Brouwer, 1991), p. 110.
58 Ibid.
59 Ibid.
60 Ibid., p. 83.
61 Ibid.
62 Ricoeur, *The Symbolism of Evil*, p. 4.
63 Ibid., p. 349.

ICONS OF INFINITY: ROTHKO, LEVINAS AND JEAN-LUC MARION

MARK PATRICK HEDERMAN

It is the poet and philosopher who provide the community of objectives in which the artist participates. Their chief preoccupation, like the artist, is the expression in concrete form of their notions of reality. Like him, they deal with the verities of time and space, life and death, and the heights of exaltation as well as the depths of despair. The preoccupation with these eternal problems creates a common ground which transcends the disparity in the means used to achieve them. And it is in the language of the philosopher and poet or, for that matter, of other arts which share the same objective that we must speak if we are to establish some verbal equivalent of the significance of art.[1]

Christopher Rothko

What language must we speak if we are to evaluate the contribution of Mark Rothko?[2] His one-time friend, and fellow artist, Barnett Newman tried to articulate the essential project of American artists of the mid-twentieth century as 'an attempt to achieve feeling through intellectual content'. Feeling is the essential barometer but it need not be fuzzy or uncontrolled; it should be rigorously presented and intellectually cohesive. Although feeling, for the artist, is paramount and primordial, its inspiration and its final shape are intellectual: 'heart work', in Rilke's term, filtered through 'head work'. Newman defends 'abstractionism': '[I]n handling philosophic concepts which *per se* are of an abstract nature, it was inevitable that the painter's form should be abstract.'[3]

In early 1950, around the time of his own final transformation as an artist, Rothko travelled to Europe, with his second wife, Mell. It was his first visit since his emigration from Russia to America at the age of ten. He was an admirer of European art but insisted upon the autonomy of new American painting.[4] Early in his artistic career he teamed up with leading American Abstract artists, such as Clyfford Still, Jackson Pollock and Barnett Newman, who were among those known as 'The New York School'. These were some of the first American abstract artists to achieve international recognition. Later, as his own personal style developed more idiosyncratically, he distanced himself from these, and from any such label. He had the greatest disdain for art critics and objected to being identified as an 'Abstract Artist'. He also repudiated the description of himself as 'a great colourist': 'I'm not an abstractionist. I'm not interested in the relationship of colour or form or anything else. I'm interested only in expressing basic human emotions: tragedy, ecstasy, doom, and so on.' The book on Rothko in the Taschen series, by Jacob Baal-Teshuva, from which many of these quotations are culled, is subtitled *Pictures as Drama*.

In this sense, Rothko saw himself as a dramatist developing a theatre of basic human emotions. His first artistic impulses were theatrical. He studied drama in Portland in 1924 and applied for a scholarship to the American Laboratory Theatre in New York in 1925. The following passage describes how he saw the relationship between drama, as he understood it, and his artwork:

> I think of my pictures as dramas; the shapes in the pictures are the performers. They have been created from the need for a group of actors who are able to move dramatically without embarrassment and execute gestures without shame. Neither the action nor the actors can be anticipated, or described in advance. They begin as an unknown adventure in an unknown space. It is at the moment of completion that in a flash of recognition, they are seen to have the quantity and function which was intended. Ideas and plans that existed in the mind at the start were simply the doorway through which one left the world in which they occur.[5]

Rothko saw art as this doorway leading beyond 'ideas' and the contemporary cultural world. He was wary and contemptuous of art critics who explained and interpreted his work according to canons and criteria of a culture already rendered obsolete by his artistic exploration. John Fischer, his friend and the publisher of *Harper's Magazine*, reports him as saying: 'I hate and distrust all art historians, experts and critics. They are a bunch of parasites, feeding on the body of art. Their work not only is useless, it is misleading. They can say nothing worth listening to about art or artists.'[6]

In their manifesto on aesthetic beliefs, written in the early 1940s, Rothko and Adolph Gottlieb presented five basic premises that defined their work. Among these is the idea that 'art is an adventure into an unknown world, which can be explored only by those willing to take the risk … This unknown world belongs to the imagination' and 'is violently opposed to common sense'.[7]

On his way towards total abstraction, Rothko explained his own evolution. It is not so much that 'the figures had been *removed* from the canvas, but that they had been replaced, first by 'the symbols for the figures' and then by forms that evolved into 'new *substitutes* for the figures'.[8] His later abstract style uses very large formats comprising two or three rectangular and symmetrically overlaid colour blocks, separated from the edges of the canvases to give an impression of coloured fields floating in front of undefined backgrounds. 'If previous abstractions paralleled the scientific and objective preoccupations of our times, ours are finding a pictorial equivalent for man's new knowledge and consciousness of his more complex inner self.'[9]

In the early 1950s Rothko was creating wall-scale abstracts that filled the viewer's field of vision until they became something of an environment. He seemed to be exploring the compositional potential of colour and form to play upon the human psyche. 'Any picture which does not provide the environment in which the breath of life can be drawn does not interest me.'[10] Standing in front of such Rothko creations, 'pulsating vibrancy' emanates from the canvases. The ideal distance is 45 centimetres away from them, according to the artist himself. In this intimacy, the viewer is drawn into the fields of colour, with their inner movement and absence of clear borders. 'The people who weep before my pictures are having the same religious experience I had when I painted them, and if you say, you are moved only by their colour relationships, then you miss the point.' 'A painting is not a picture of an experience; it is an experience.'[11] Such a 'religious experience' is to feel, if only momentarily, something of whatever 'sublime' Rothko relentlessly sought to evoke. This has been described as 'an awe for that which could not be understood, together with the freedom to overstep the very limits of human existence'.[12]

The way Rothko eventually approached his task also shows us that with our normal vision we are living an illusion. He does this by entering the illusion and, within it, creating a remedial facsimile which allows us to unmask the illusory structure in which we are embedded. Phenomenologists have described the contours of this illusion but Rothko was able to create the visual equivalent providing an antidote to our otherwise restricted horizon. If we follow him, we will gradually find ourselves inside the structures he has built and eventually be able to look out at the world we used to live in from within the perspective of these structures. Such an artistic re-education process changes our outlook on reality but also our approach to Rothko's work itself. Rather than looking outward at what he has created and trying to understand his artwork from our old, familiar point of view, we embed ourselves in his creation until it becomes the filter of our point of view.

Our visual system is a sensor with 180 degrees of horizontal impact; it scans the horizon superficially. We don't need precision as we scour the landscape. Except for things on which we decide to focus and concentrate, a more vague peripheral vision will do. We are fashioned to see close-up, and our visual apparatus is designed to focus in detail, only on what is directly in front of us. Our eyes see colour and fine detail only where these are directly in the forefront. Our peripheral vision detects movement but has little colour determination. It need only be vague, and in black and white, because its primary use to us for millennia was as an early warning system for detecting aggressors or spotting potential game. Rothko spoke of wanting the spectator to feel inside the pictorial space, the apparitional surfaces and luminosity of his canvases. 'I paint big to be intimate,' Rothko said. 'The surfaces of colour recalled architectural elements, such as columns, walls, doors, windows, giving the viewer a feeling of confinement, yet presenting an unreachable world beyond.'[13] Providing a surrounding circumambience forces us as viewers to become aware of the perspectival framework of our own visionary make-up. Limited frontal vision prevents us from seeing the bigger picture, at least in as chromatic and detailed a way.

Jean-Luc Marion has examined philosophically this aspect of our vision as a working reality. He has applied to it what we normally regard as a theory of painting, especially with reference to the Renaissance painters. 'Perspective should therefore be first understood not as a historically situated pictorial theory (although it is that also) but as a fundamental role of the gaze, without which we would never see a world.' It is the task of phenomenology to describe to us in detail the very basic and ordinary realities about ourselves that we take for granted. Marion observes: 'In whatever place I actually find myself located, a thing among things, I organize – indeed, I open – the space between right and left.' And again, with descriptive accuracy he shows us, what we might have passed by without noticing, namely the reality of 'depth': 'Whatever my travels might be, depth will always remain in front of me as that which I will never be able to traverse, since if I advance myself towards it, it will deepen itself that much more, so that I am never really able to cover it. The opening of depth always precedes me.'[14]

The three dimensions of right, left, and depth are realities which we take for granted. We ignore them to the extent that they themselves are not measured by us even if they make possible every measurement we make of real space. They are the already existing categories which make the visible visible, whereas they themselves remain hidden and never appear as essential scaffolding. Perspective is therefore an a priori condition of all our experience. Perspectivalism, according to Marion, is what produces the 'phenomenality' of phenomena.

To counteract this undeclared scaffolding which supports all our visual experience, Rothko emphasized the flat surface in this later work. In contrast with the so-called 'action painters', another branch of Twentieth Century American Abstractionism, he refused to impose emotional energy by the way he handled paint, or ruffle our sensibilities by putting gestural traces on the canvas. All his surfaces remained cool and austere, effacing any individual marks in favour of a large, flat, stained or soaked area of colour, which he saw as the essential nature of visual abstraction married to the actual shape of the chosen canvas itself. When asked to describe the formula which produced the magic of his art, he replied: 'It's just the paint. These surfaces are expansive and push outward in all directions or their surfaces contract and rush inward in all directions. Between these two poles you can find everything I want to say.'

Marion also provides a useful philosophical tool with which to approach these canvases in what he describes as the 'saturated phenomenon'. This term is probably theological in its origins. Patrick Masterson suggests, in his own translation of a 1949 text,[15] that a similar term is used by the Jesuit philosopher, Joseph Maréchal (1878–1944). John D. Caputo holds that the term derives from Marion's study of Christian Neoplatonic mystical theologians.[16] Whatever the derivation of the term, these 'saturated phenomena' are 'of such overwhelming givenness or overflowing fulfilment' that our standard organs of perception, our natural receivers, whenever faced by them, 'are overrun, flooded – or saturated'. Saturated phenomena have something of the effect on us, to whom they appear, that 'the other person' has in the philosophy of Levinas. They present themselves to those who come across them, undermining the epistemological structures which service our day-to-day commerce with the world around us. Their saturation causes bedazzlement in us and overwhelms our normal receptors. So much do they throw us adrift by their superabundant presence that they alter our identity as subjects who normally stage manage our own surroundings. They corrode the filtering system whereby we process the world as it seeks to enter our interiority. Encounter with them is so bizarre that it flattens us and all our usual responses into a passive receivership, awaiting the saturated phenomenon's unfolding of itself.

What used to be an 'I', as self-confident plenipotentiary, becomes a disoriented inarticulate 'me' awaiting instructions. I am reduced to the status of a secondary or derived subject, one who is constituted rather than one who constitutes the surrounding panorama. I become a 'me' rather than an 'I', in the accusative rather than the nominative case, 'bereft of any limiting role of signification or containment and thereby denied any claim to be the ultimate foundation of the experience of phenomena ... I do not lay hold of the transcendent. It lays hold of me.'[17]

Through this unforeseen impact and my inevitable resistance to it, the 'visibility' of both what presents itself, and of myself as receiver, makes each other recognizable. Marion describes the operation as though the unseen given projects itself onto the given-to, or consciousness, as onto a screen – its impact upon the screen provoking this double visibility, as developing chemicals on photographic paper make an image visible. He takes, as another example, a prism capturing invisible white light and turning it, by refraction through itself, into the spectrum of primary colours, making otherwise invisible light finally visible. And again, he suggests as helpful, the image of electrical resistance where the restriction of the otherwise completely free movement of electrons in a cable transforms this invisible movement into observable light and heat.

Rothko could be said to be creating such saturated phenomena in the colour blocks which he hangs on undefined backgrounds. His images are similar in structure and yet they differ in tonal and emotional effect, 'where a rendering of colours into adjacent but also intersaturating bands maximizes their luminosity'. Such visual imagery constitutes a 'middle term' between the objects of perception and our conscious ideas of these, which means that such works of art create new levels of being. 'The ecstasis effected in Rothko's Red on Red is ... beyond language altogether, a non-linguistic form of knowing, a contact with vision in a purity never possible in everyday looking.' The waves or veils of colour are 'divested of tactile significance because the limits of individual colour-configurations are not experienced as though they were the edge of some kind of tangible thing but as a compelling unbroken continuity'. The painting is silent in a way that is foreign to articulation. 'Here the visual approaches total figurelessness; its maximum significance resides in its opticality alone.' [18] Barnett Newman described such art as 'a time of looking occasioned by colour'.

'In order to understand this very thing that Marcus Rothkowitz understood so intensely that he consented to reform entirely his whole enterprise of painting, we must bring him together with another émigré, his contemporary, coming not like him from Russia to Portland, Oregon, but from Lithuania to Strasbourg, France, Emmanuel Levinas.' So says Jean-Luc Marion.[19] If we follow this train of thought we may ask further: what was 'this very thing' that Rothko understood; what 'reform' did he achieve in 'his whole enterprise of painting', and, finally, what debt did he owe to Emmanuel Levinas? The answer to the last question, again according to Marion, is that: 'Pictorially, he confirms what Levinas establishes in phenomenology, or rather, he puts to work phenomenologically what the phenomenologist shows in concepts.'[20] What does phenomenology show us in concepts in this regard? Phenomenology, from the outset, has had an ambiguous, uneasy relationship with transcendence, with the wholly other, with the numinous.[21] Phenomenology, as Marion emphasizes, is the philosophy of the 'givenness' of the given. It restricts itself to describing carefully and without prejudice whatever is *given* to experience in the manner in which it is so given. Only things of this world are accessible to our 'knowing'. There may, of course, be other realities beyond our ken but we cannot know them, they are beyond us.

Philosophically speaking, the Western world has been epistemologically confined to this hermetically sealed time-space capsule for over two centuries. Pointless to try to escape from the world we live in because our minds have been designed to cope only with this reality. Within the framework of phenomenology, only the subject, as limited receiver of whatever presents itself, can act as presenter of any such reality. In the words of Marion, 'only the given-to in its role of resistance to the impact of the given can bring that which gives itself to manifestation or to show itself as a phenomenon'.[22] So the question remains, can God, or whatever we choose to call the radically Other, the transcendent, that which is beyond the range of normal human perception, show up or appear within the limitations of our horizons and capacities, while at the same time maintaining inescapable otherness or alterity?

What both Rothko and Levinas became aware of, at more or less the same time, was the possibility of transcendence lurking within the bounds of immanence. Jacob Baal-Teshuva suggests that 'the formal tools of his trade served Rothko merely as instruments to relate an experience of transcendental reality',[23] pointing towards the 'spiritual' intentionality of his overall project. For Levinas, there was one reality in the world around us which immediately introduced us to a world beyond our time-space capsule and this was the face of another person. To meet the other person is to have the idea of Infinity.[24] Levinas was dedicated to the phenomenological search for the concrete significance of such alterity. As a phenomenologist he used all the subtlety and sophistication of this philosophical method to describe what happens when we encounter the reality of another person. The human face is present as one object among so many others in our workaday world but genuine encounter with this phenomenon puts us in immediate contact with infinity.

The way in which Marion tries to explain this possibility is by using the example of my gazing into the pupil of another person's eye. The black vanishing point in the pupil of the other person's eye prevents me from reducing this other to total comprehensibility in terms of shape and form and availability to me as a viewer. 'Here in the very midst of the visible, there is nothing to see, except an invisible and untargetable void ... my gaze, for the first time, sees an invisible gaze that sees it.'[25]

This means that the face, as well as being a potential port-hole to the infinite is also a 'façade' in as much as it represents the outer wall of that shell comprising the mug shot of all seven billion people alive today on the planet. There is no automatic access to its infinite potential. We can bounce off it as an object or we can be submerged into it as a subject. The face as object is the outer skin of an irreducible, unrepeatable, unique existence which is the human person. Encounter with this reality is the primary experience that teaches us the truth about who we are. But such an encounter depends upon our good will. If we allow it to happen, our life as truly human begins. We accede to the domain of Ethics, which then becomes 'first philosophy', our introduction to how and what we know, since it concerns our encounter with one another. Responsibility to and for 'the other' precedes any objective search for so-called abstract truth.

This revelation of infinity in the face of the other is not automatic. It is a phenomenon, which means that it is a reality which happens within the epistemological framework; it is something that I can recognize but not necessarily so. It depends upon my free will as to whether the other person appears to me as an object among others or as an inlet to infinity. Marion suggests: 'It is up to me to set the stage for the other, not as an object that I hold under contract and whose play I thus direct, but as the uncontrollable, the unforeseeable, and the foreign stranger who will affect me, provoke me, and – possibly – love me. Love of the other repeats creation through the same withdrawal wherein God opens, to what is not, the right to be, and even the right to refuse Him.'[26]

If we translate this into painterly terms it suggests that as Levinas had established the impossibility of representing the face by a façade, the artist should follow suit. For a painter, 'façade' would mean the canvas or the surface on which the painter applies the paint, a flat surface which is visible to us but without any depth or further dimension. Such a surface façade cannot reveal the secret of interiority, the mystery of the infinity enclosed within.[27] 'The façade confronts (*fait face*), but it closes itself all the more, for if everything is visible there, the seen must necessarily be seen on the plane, reduced to flatness (*platitude*), and therefore the façade closes off access to the intimate.'[28]

One half of the impossibility of representing the human face pictorially comes from our way of seeing. Things only show a façade, even and especially in art (painting), they never show a face as such: 'The façade of a house, isn't it a house that is looking at us?'[29] The façade does not look at us: only a face can do so; only the face comes to reveal itself in the idiom of 'face to face' encounter. Such an encounter cannot be reproduced on a flat surface as a portrait.

Rothko's conversion from figurative work to a more formless pictorial communication anticipated what Levinas articulated philosophically: the façade forbids us to paint the face, which can only be murdered if squashed into the flatness (*platitude*) of the canvas. Levinas published these views in 1951 almost contemporaneously with the maturation of Rothko's later painterly style.

In 1945 Rothko had written:

> I insist upon the equal existence of the world engendered in the mind and the world engendered by God outside of it. If I have faltered in the use of familiar objects, it is because I refuse to mutilate their appearance for the sake of an action which they are too old to serve; or for which perhaps they had never been intended.[30]

Rothko applies to his paintings the same enigmatic phenomenology which Marion describes with regard to the possibility (or not) of seeing infinity or drawing a blank. 'A picture lives by companionship, expanding and quickening in the eyes of the sensitive observer. It dies by the same token.'[31] He even uses the analogy of human intercourse to describe the paradoxical interconnection which has to happen: 'No possible set of notes can explain our paintings. Their explanation must come out of a consummated experience between picture and onlooker. The appreciation of art is a true marriage of minds. And in art as in marriage, lack of consummation is grounds for annulment.'[32]

Jonathan Jones in a review of the newly reopened Rothko Room at the Tate Modern, where some of the murals originally intended for the Seagram restaurant in York are now housed, in a dimly lit and somewhat restricted space, says: 'These are paintings that seem to exist on the skin inside an eyelid.'[33] If we follow this image biologically we can observe that the outer part of the human eye is part of the material reality of the world we live in. However, this outer orifice is the delicate and complicated medium whereby sensual reality is communicated to the brain. It is the brain which elaborates on the visual stimuli we receive, and transforms these into 'artworks'. The brain crafts the optimal scenario from the raw image presented by the eye. Mark Rothko's art tries to subvert this mechanism and provide our senses with primordial and immediate data. The first thing light touches when entering the eye is a thin veil of tears that coats the front of the eye. Behind this lubricating moisture is the front window of the eye, which we call the cornea, from the Latin word for 'horn', the outer shell of the eye. On the other side of this cornea is more moisture, the aqueous humour, a clear watery fluid which circulates throughout the front part of the eye and is the material source of our tears.

If Rothko's paintings could succeed in reaching our tears, before the intervention of our more sophisticated delivery mechanisms, he would have crossed the first essential threshold. To effect such an ambush his paintings had to be massive and sophisticated surfaces that impregnated the eye before it had time or tactics to hold them at bay. The meeting between the viewer and the Rothko canvas had to be somehow subcutaneous. Achieving this effect required knowledge of the eye and the way we see, on the one hand, and a revolution in the way art comes into being. Rothko's revolution could be described as the end of painting as such. Even the way Rothko applied the colour to the canvas is post-painterly. Acrylic allows itself to flow onto the canvas in an osmosis which oil paint cannot achieve. Oils of their nature cover the surface with a layer of paint. By the time of the Houston Chapel experiment 'he had practically eliminated colour as a major player'.

During the last decade of his life, Rothko's ambition was to display his art in an environment where he was in complete control of both the room space and the observer so that anyone entering would experience the paintings immediately as the artist had intended. The very architecture of the room conspired to focus attention on the paintings in the precise way he had intended, and this allowed for the removal from the paintings themselves the architectural features, such as columns, walls, doors, windows, which he had used in the past to give the viewer a feeling of confinement, while at the same time presenting an unreachable world around and beyond them. Now the building could do the architectural work of confinement and the canvases themselves would provide the awnings to an infinity beyond all spatial ingenuity.

Initially, the Chapel at Houston, which is now non-denominational, was to be specifically Roman Catholic, and during the first three years of the project in its planning stages (1964–7) Rothko believed it would remain so. Thus, it appears that both Rothko's design of the building, and the implications of the paintings, were inspired by Roman Catholic art and architecture. The octagonal shape is influenced by the Byzantine church of Santa Maria Assunta, in Venice, which Rothko had visited on his last visit to Europe in 1966, and the format of the triptychs derives from paintings of the Crucifixion. However, even if the architecture of the building is Catholic, the canvases blow the walls into infinity, thereby expressing the intended meaning of the word 'Catholic' as truly 'universal'.

The de Menils, who commissioned the chapel, believed the universal 'spiritual' aspect of Rothko's work would complement the elements of Roman Catholicism. In her dedication speech, Dominique de Menil said:

> The paintings themselves will tell us what to think of them – if we
> give them a chance. They will educate us to judge them. Every work

of art creates the climate in which it can be understood ... Everywhere where creative people are trying to open a new door, there is always more than meets the eye in an authentic work of art ... The more I live with them, the more impressed I am. Rothko wanted to bring his paintings to the greatest poignancy they were capable of. He wanted them to be intimate and timeless. They embrace us without enclosing us. Their dark surfaces do not stop the gaze. A light surface is active – it stops the eye but we can gaze right through these purplish browns, gaze into the infinite. We are cluttered with images and only abstract art can bring us on the threshold of the divine.[34]

As early as 1943, Rothko had written: 'Art to me is an anecdote of the spirit, and the only means of making concrete the purpose of its varied quickness and stillness.'[35] In the Chapel at Houston it is as if Rothko was providing us with the experience of being within that blackness which is the pupil of another person's eye as it silently swallows us up. As Marion puts it: 'For such is the final paradox: the gaze of the other is not seen, at least as an object; strictly speaking, it remains invisible – we do not look anyone in the whites of the eyes, but rather in the blackness and the emptiness of the pupil, in the only "spot" on their body where there is simply a void to see; we face up to the other in his gaze insofar as he remains invisible; but this invisibility, as such, reaches us more than everything of the other's that is visible; it is the other's invisibility that weighs on us, gazes upon us.'[36]

ENDNOTES

1 Christopher Rothko, *The Artist's Reality: Philosophies of Art by Mark Rothko* (New Haven, CT: Yale University Press, 2004), p. 21.

2 Mark Rothko (25 September 1903–25 February 1970), born Markus Yakovlevich Rotkovich, was an American painter of Russian Jewish descent. His father emigrated from Russia to America; Markus and his mother joined him in the winter of 1913. He won a scholarship to Yale at the age of eighteen. He dropped out of university after a year and did not return until he was awarded an honorary degree there forty-six years later. He married twice and had two children, Kate and Christopher, by his second wife, Mell; he died by suicide in his own studio at the age of sixty-six.

3 Barnett Newman, 'The Plasmic Image', in John P. O'Neill (ed.), *Selected Writings and Interviews* (Berkeley, CA: University of California Press, 1992), pp. 154–5.

4 Jacob Baal-Teshuva, *Rothko* (Köln: Taschen, 2003), pp. 45–9.

5 Rothko wrote this text for a journal called *Possibilities*, which was produced in 1947–48 as a magazine devoted exclusively to American art. This essay, 'The romantics were

prompted' (1947), is reproduced in Mark Rothko, *Writings on Art* (New Haven, CT: Yale University Press, 2006), pp. 58–61.

6   Quoted from an article by John Hurt Fischer, 'The Easy Chair: Mark Rothko, Portrait of the Artist as an Angry Man', (*Harper's Magazine*, July 1970), pp. 16–23. The writer, also publisher of *Harper's*, had met Rothko during a trip to Europe in the spring of 1959 when he had apparently taken notes of their conversations. The article was not published until ten years later and some months after Rothko's death in February 1970. This article is reproduced in full in Rothko, *Writings on Art*, pp. 130–8.

7   Mark Rothko and Adolph Gottlieb, letter of 7 June 1943, to the *New York Times* (published 13 June 1943), in Rothko, *Writings on Art*, p. 36.

8   Annie Cohen-Solal, *Mark Rothko, Toward the Light in the Chapel* (New Haven: Yale University Press, 2015), p. 111.

9   Letter to the editor of *The New York Times*, 8 July 1945, in M. Rothko, *Writings on Art*, p. 46.

10   Baal-Teshuva, *Rothko*, p. 45.

11   Ibid. p. 57.

12   Ibid. p. 46.

13   Ibid. p. 61.

14   Jean-Luc Marion, *The Crossing of the Visible* (California, CA: Stanford University Press, 2004), pp. 4–5.

15   Patrick Masterson, *Approaching God* (London: Bloomsbury, 2013), p 40. The text he refers to is Joseph Maréchal, *Le point de départ de la métaphysique* (Bruxelles: Lessianum, 1949), pp. 378–80, where the author describes 'infinite being' as an 'ultimate and saturating goal'.

16   Review by John D. Caputo of Jean-Luc Marion, *The Erotic Phenomenon* in *Ethics*, 118/1, (October 2007), pp. 164–8

17   Masterson, *Approaching God*, p. 16.

18   All quotations on this page come from Jennifer Anna Gosetti-Ferencei, *The Ecstatic Quotidien, Phenomenological Sightings in Modern Art and Literature* (University Park: Pennsylvania State University, 2007), pp. 215–16.

19   Jean-Luc Marion, *In Excess, Studies of Saturated Phenomena* (New York, NY: Fordham University Press, 2001), p. 77; from the French, *De surcroît: Etudes sur les phénomènes saturés* (Paris: Presses Universitaires de France, 2001).

20   Ibid., pp. 77–9.

21   See Dermot Moran, 'Immanence, Self-Experience, and Transcendence in Edmund Husserl, Edith Stein, and Karl Jaspers', *American Catholic Philosophical Quarterly* 82/2 (2008), p. 265.

22   Marion, *The Crossing of the Visible*, p. 26.

23   Baal-Teshuva, *Rothko*, p. 57.

24   Emmanuel Levinas: 'Aborder Autrui dans le discours, c'est accueillir son expression où il déborde à tout instant l'idée qu'en emporterait une pensée. C'est donc *recevoir* d'Autrui au delà de la capacité du Moi; ce qui signifie exactement: avoir l'idée de l'infini.', *Totalité et infini* (The Hague: Nijhoff, 1971), p. 22.

25   Jean-Luc Marion, *Prolegomena to Charity* (New York, NY: Fordham University Press, 2002), p. 82.

26   Ibid., pp. 166–7.

27   Emmanuel Levinas, *Totalité et infini*, p. 167: 'Par la façade, la chose qui garde son secret – s'expose enfermée dans son essence monumentale et dans son mythe où elle luit comme une splendeur, mais ne se livre pas. Elle subjugue par sa grace comme une magie, mais ne se révèle pas. Si le transcendant tranche sur la sensibilité, s'il est ouverture par excellence, si sa vision est la vision de l'ouverture elle-même de l'être – elle tranche sur la vision des formes et ne peut se dire ni en termes de contemplation, ni en termes de pratique. Elle est visage; sa révélation est parole. La relation avec autrui introduit seule une dimension de la transcendence et nous conduit vers un rapport totalement different de l'expérience au sens sensible du terme, rélative et egoïste.'

28   Marion, *In Excess*, p. 77.

29   Emmanuel Levinas, 'L'ontologie est-elle fondamentale?' a text which Marion points out was published in the *Revue de métaphysique et de morale* in 1951, almost at the same time as Rothko's transformation.

30   Mark Rothko, 'I adhere to the reality of things', in Rothko, *Writings on Art*, p. 44.

31   Mark Rothko, 'The Ides of Art: The Attitudes of Ten Artists on their Art and Contemporaneousness' in *Writings on Art*, p. 57. Originally in *The Tiger's Eye* 2 (December 1947), p. 44. Quoted in Marion, *In Excess*, p. 72, footnote 19.

32   From 'Rothko and Gottlieb's letter to the editor, 1943', in Rothko, *Writings on Art*, p 36.

33   Jonathan Jones, 'Tate Modern's rehang cannot diminish the majesty of Mark Rothko', *The Guardian* (22 August 2012).

34   Baal-Teshuva, *Rothko*, p. 74–5.

35   Rothko, 'Personal Statement', in *Writings on Art*, p. 45.

36   Marion, *Prolegomena to Charity*, p. 167.

WISDOM AFTER METAPHYSICS?

MARKUS H. WÖRNER

Wisdom is scarcely a central topic in contemporary philosophy, an occupation originally called the 'love of wisdom'.[1] Today's philosophers may seem to confirm Nietzsche's observation: 'When philosophers meet among themselves they start casting off all sorts of wonderful rubbish; above all ... they hang up the "love of wisdom" like stuffy robes of office.'[2]

WISDOM AS A MODE OF BEING IN THE WORLD AND REPUTABLE OPINIONS

However, wisdom can be found, even though perhaps rarely. It is also undeniably the case that the search for wisdom plays a fundamental personal, political and economic role in making sense of living, in dealing with crises or with decision-making in general. Both individuals and societies tend to strive to live better lives rather than remaining content with mere survival or with continual crisis management based on doubtful decisions. For the most part, they are unwilling to deceive themselves in such matters or to be taken in by what Francis Bacon calls the 'idols of the human understanding'.[3] Wisdom is needed to generate good, better, best answers. If these cannot be found, people commonly say that they are 'at the end of their wisdom'. Even though we may admit that we are not wise absolutely, nonetheless we wish to be wiser than we are. Similarly, we may not wish to live the perfected good life, we may simply want to live better than we have lived until now. Since we wish to live and die well, we require a modicum of wisdom to live better or even to live as we do and to be able to cope positively with our own process of ageing.

Wisdom mostly seems to be required in discernment and judgment when we anticipate that the outcome of events will be uncertain, where there is no expertise or scientific knowledge that is capable of providing the right answer, or even when too much expertise is available that is contradictory. Consequently, especially in dealing with the area of the contingent, of human action in particular, wisdom is of crucial importance. Wisdom is less needed in areas of the necessary or the impossible (such as mathematics or logic), where it almost takes a fool to ignore what cannot be changed.

However, wisdom may not presuppose for its existence a life well lived or the prospect of a happy death, as is frequently assumed. Some heroes of historical master-narratives of wisdom (Jesus, for instance) were prosecuted or died the lives of criminals on the cross, were executed or underwent extreme suffering in their lives. Some survivors of the holocaust, such as Viktor Frankl, are held in high esteem for their wisdom but cannot be said to have lived a good life, at least not while living in concentration camps.

Yet the contrary view is upheld by those who support the assumption that a wise person can be defined as someone who possesses not only extensive factual and theoretical knowledge, and very few unjustified beliefs, but also knows how to live well and is actually successful at living well.[4] This claim is far less clear than it sounds. It is far from obvious how much knowledge a wise person must possess on this account, how many unjustified beliefs are allowed her before she ceases to be wise, or for how long she must live a good life in order to count as wise. Nor is it clear that, supposing someone is prevented by life's circumstances from living a good life, at least in the sense of being able to do what she reasonably wants to do, it is reasonable to think that this excludes her from wisdom. It is thus questionable if these are really necessary and sufficient conditions for wisdom, and in what sense they might be so.

What is meant by 'wisdom'? I should like to suggest an answer by starting from what may be called a common-sense approach and some preliminary pragma-linguistic observations.

Obviously, wisdom has an objective, third-person-perspective aspect as well as a subjective, first-person-perspective aspect, and they are not symmetrical. We can say 'X is wise' but we cannot say – without potentially making fools of ourselves: 'I am wise.' The same asymmetry applies to groups who may create wise deliberations, actions or emotional responses. They cannot unreservedly say 'We are wise but others are not', without being suspected of being foolish in the eyes of the world. It appears that other people, not we ourselves, need to carry out this particular attribution.[5]

This asymmetry between self-ascription and other-ascription also underscores the fact that something which is intended by someone to be wise is not necessarily the same as what counts as wise in a group, society or culture, or what is taken as wise by a particular group of people. We may intend to be wise, for instance, without counting as wise in society, although we may be taken to be wise by our best friends. These differing aspects give rise to the problem of the extent to which wisdom is primarily a characteristic feature of a real or a fictitious individual's character or rather an evaluative criteriological ascription by a public which judges the utterances, emotions or actions of individuals, groups or even whole cultures. In all likelihood, both are involved, though clearly this question demands considerable further exploration.

Moreover, wisdom is taken by some commentators to resemble health. On the whole, a person who is healthy – or wise – is not aware of it, at least most of the time. Health is hidden from the person who is healthy unless she notices that something is wrong with her. 'Health,' H.G. Gadamer claims, 'is not a condition which one feels within oneself, detected by introspection. It is a condition of being-there (*Dasein*), of being in the world (*in-der-Welt-Sein*), of being involved in an active and rewarding engagement with the things that matter in life.'[6]

This parallel between health and wisdom implies that wisdom itself, just like health, is not simply a characteristic feature of an individual's character or an evaluative ascription, but a way of seeing, feeling and acting in the world. This amounts to a mode of being-in-the-world.[7] Folly is its opposite. Most of us embody both ways of being in the world to greater or lesser extents.

Commonly shared intuitions of what wisdom is are noted, for instance, in the Oxford English Dictionary or in empirical (sociological or psychological) studies which collect them. The OED mentions two common types of understanding, according to which wisdom is:

'1a) [A] capacity of judging rightly in matters relating to life and conduct; soundness of judgment in the choice of means and ends; sometimes, less strictly, sound sense, esp. in practical affairs: opp. to folly [...]

2a) Knowledge (esp. of a high or abstruse kind); enlightenment, learning, erudition; in early uses often = philosophy, science.'[8]

Wisdom in the first sense is connected with right judgment concerning human activities. It is not elitist in the sense of requiring a particular education, erudition or highly privileged insight or intuition. Nobody is excluded *per se* from this kind of wisdom. Wisdom in the second sense, however, is elitist, at least tendentially. It divides societies into those who are wise (enlightened, erudite, philosophers, psychiatrists, scientific experts) and those who are not.

The OED definitions may or may not accurately represent 'common-sense' understandings of wisdom, and what counts as common sense in a particular place or time may or may not have claims to be authoritative. Nonetheless we may, as did Aristotle, begin from what seems to be widely believed, and sift such beliefs for what recommends or fails to recommend them. Starting from this twofold OED definition, therefore, I should like to suggest three interpretive assumptions – which I also take to be common-sense assumptions, or at least widely shared, and on convincing grounds:

1. Most people are inclined to say that wisdom may come in degrees and in certain respects. Not everyone is as wise as Socrates, Jesus, Confucius or the Buddha, nor is everyone wise in every respect at all times and under all circumstances.

2. I postulate too[9] that everyone – and not only some of us – has the capacity for wisdom in so far as we belong to the species *Homo sapiens*. Human beings have sapiential competence. To assume that only some human beings have this competence, and that having it is better than not having it, would mean to divide mankind into beings who are better and worse. Hence, wisdom in the first sense may seem more egalitarian than the wisdom of the enlightened elite; admittedly, this is predominantly an ethical and political reason for preferring it.

3. The type of wisdom indicated by the OED is a human good achievable between birth and death, and hence a good achievable by human individuals or groups during their life-courses. As a rule, it is not a gift of Nature or of Grace. Exceptions to the rule may exist, but they are of no direct concern here.

These assumptions, if we accept them, put considerable restrictions on notions of wisdom which have become part of our mainstream Western philosophical and theological traditions. They do not exclude them *per se* but they do make them appear unlikely candidates for expectations that both accord with everyday experience and avoid the division of human beings into 'more' or 'less' human.

Excluded, for instance, are notions of wisdom which either strictly deny that wisdom can be achieved by human beings at all or place its achievement into a Beyond, either into an afterworld (like the wisdom reached through grace in a postmortem beatific vision) or into a pre- or post-history (like the prelapsarian wisdom of Adam or the post-historical wisdom of Nietzsche's *Übermensch*).

They also exclude the view that the completed, overall perfection of an individual, group, society or culture is the *conditio sine qua non* for wisdom. Instead, wisdom itself is understood, here, not as a perfectionist, but as an a-perfectionist, processual phenomenon manifesting itself in human communication and interaction, hardly ever perfected in its entirety and mostly detected in others or by others rather than in oneself. However, the more aspects are realized convincingly, the more apparent it becomes.

Also excluded is an understanding of wisdom as knowledge of first causes and principles of reality as a whole,[10] in so far as only a select few living contemplative lives can truly achieve it. Furthermore, on these criteria wisdom is unlikely to be perfected encyclopedic knowledge of human and divine things[11] or knowledge of divine things only, essentially depending on God's grace.[12]

Following suggestions like the ones represented in the OED, an a-perfectionist notion of wisdom which is neither perfectionist nor anti-perfectionist, flexible enough to be applicable in principle to as many people as possible, appears reasonable as a starting point for discussing the relation between wisdom and master narratives guiding it. Hence, the broad division between wisdom as a perfection attributable to perfect or divine beings, and wisdom as something attainable in degrees and in certain respects by human persons, groups, societies or cultures as a human good, is of crucial importance for an a-perfectionist approach. However, in both cases, sound judgment is one of its necessary components.

WISDOM AS VIRTUE

Judging rightly and sound judgment, particularly in practical affairs, are generally understood as being rooted in a capacity. We judge rightly because we have the capacity to do so more or less well. If we judge rightly regularly, our judging is rooted in a capacity informed by a habit. According to the majority of psychologist researchers on wisdom connected with the Berlin Paradigm Group of the late twentieth century,[13] what appears most characteristic of wisdom is that it is a capacity and expert knowledge (in two senses: knowing that ... and knowing how...) in dealing with fundamental, existential problems related to the meaning and conduct of life.[14] These writers also identify specific features of knowledge (possibly characteristically Western, possibly not universalizable in respect of all possible human societies) presupposed by this capacity: lifespan contextualism, value relativism and tolerance, knowledge about handling uncertainty, including knowledge about emotions connected with it; and knowledge of the limits of one's own knowledge.

The model of wisdom identified by these features involves a coalition of 'cognitive (outstanding knowledge about the self and the world), social (empathetic concern, the ability to give good advice), emotional (the ability to regulate one's own feelings), and motivational (orientation toward personal growth) capacities'.[15] Hence, it involves consideration of intra-, inter- and extra-personal relations, of self- and other-related interests and values. It involves moral reasoning and practice. It also appears to be linked with a specific moral stance, in which other-oriented values and a general interest in the common good, as well as a self-oriented interest in personal growth and insight, are balanced.[16] It tends to be even more other- and environment-oriented than self-oriented. In the context of values, people with this capacity appear to be less oriented to hedonistic well-being than those with a lower level of wisdom-related knowledge. They are more oriented towards 'eudaimonic' well-being connected with personal growth.[17]

Openness to others and to new experiences, on this account, marks wise people's thinking style. Rather than judging whether or not other people's actions or thoughts are right or wrong, persons with wisdom-related knowledge prefer to ask why and how something happened.[18] They keep an open mind instead of adhering to existing rules and judgments, or minimizing change and avoiding ambiguous situations. Hence, they are not conservative or reactionary.

The Berlin Paradigm group assigns a generally normative social role to wisdom and the wise person. However, their claim can hardly avoid the problem of circularity: 'Wisdom as an expert system in the fundamental pragmatics of life can define the most general range of what goals and what means are socially acceptable and desirable in human development.'[19]

In other words: Whatever wisdom declares to be truly desirable, is desirable; whatever is truly desirable is that which wise people would declare as such. The wise see what is wise. Wisdom is what wise persons see. Hence, wisdom and wise persons should be the guides for individual and societal development. But is it only the wise who should decide who is to guide? Who guards the guardians?

Wise persons, it is said, master 'an expert system in the fundamental pragmatics of life'.[20] It is 'a system in human thought and behaviour that coordinates knowledge and virtue, mind and character'[21] or 'a meta-heuristic (pragmatic) to orchestrate mind and virtue toward excellence'. Compared with other definitions of wisdom suggested in recent literature, these definitions proposed by the group appear to be most comprehensive, although they do not speak explicitly about wise groups, societies or cultures.[22]

They appear to reflect prominent features of an Aristotelian account of ethical and intellectual virtues and practical wisdom (φρόνησις) in particular – to the neglect of theoretical, speculative wisdom (σοφία), traditionally concerned with the eternal and the necessary rather than the variable and the contingent. This neglect seems to be motivated by the attempt to understand wisdom strictly *sub specie humanitatis* rather than *sub specie aeternitatis*. However, neglect does not necessarily mean denial.

The generic terms used for wisdom, here, are 'system', 'expert system' or 'meta-heuristic'. These are terms adopted from the recent world of machines, very likely from information technology, insinuating, perhaps not intending, a basically mechanistic point of view of wisdom. However, even if the constituent structure of this 'system' were inborn as sapiential competence, a competence we may all share to a greater or lesser extent as *Homines sapientes*, it still has to be acquired as a relatively permanent disposition before it can constitute sapiential performance in the long run, be it for individuals or groups. It needs to be developed to a sufficient degree to make the resulting coordination or orchestration reliable, right, swift and easy.

We may develop wisdom by engaging or being engaged in situations of thought, action, emotion and will which may change our life course, when we have to activate the sapiential competence of coordinating our thoughts, actions and emotions to find new, previously unimagined yet meaningful ways of being in the world. This development is desirable if the orchestration which it yields involves an adequate integrative process of cognitive, emotional, motivational, communicative and interactional capacities. Each of these capacities can be developed to create relatively permanent dispositions of their own. Traditionally speaking, such acquired and relatively permanent optimal dispositions to think, feel, act and interact are forms of human excellence; they are virtues. However, it is a truism that none of us is perfectly virtuous. We may develop virtues and wisdom to a certain degree or in certain respects only.

It is generally assumed among Aristotelians that bravery, for instance, the standard example of virtue in virtue ethics, is a relatively permanent optimal disposition as regards the emotions of hope and fear in dangerous situations. Wisdom coordinates virtues such as bravery, justice, temperance, liberality or magnanimity, in a holistic way. Virtues coordinated by wisdom are first-order virtues.[23] Since wisdom orchestrates these dispositions to act, to feel or to think, and no other virtue seems to do the same, it is a virtue coordinating virtues. It is a second-order virtue.

Of course, recent years of research have shown that most working definitions pointing to wisdom as a second-order virtue are still agonizingly vague or general, in need of further clarification and empirical study. However, in spite of their vagueness they signify that whatever this system or meta-heuristic is *for* concerns what is right, valuable or true in respect of practical human life. Moreover, wisdom, in my view – and this view is even more agonizingly vague – concerns what is right, valuable or true as regards our way of being in the world (*Dasein*). It involves how we understand, appreciate and interact with things in the world, with others and with ourselves. In this case, wisdom is neither purely theoretical nor purely practical; it embraces both. It is *sapida scientia*.[24] Moreover we possess it in degrees.

In spite of this very general scope of wisdom, momentous implications arise from the fact that problems demanding it are, for the most part, those which expert knowledge alone cannot solve and which crucially involve uncertainty. Responding to them adequately as well as creatively challenges human freedom and responsibility. Uncertainty in human affairs offers the opportunity for reasonable choice, self-determination and self-transformation. In taking the risks frequently connected with wise responses to uncertainty, we form (*gestalten*) ourselves as individuals, small and large groups, and indeed as a human species. We develop our own 'second nature' as a capacity which provides a potentially optimal form of practical, emotional and theoretical rationality in the area of contingent freedom – since wisdom, rather than concealing life, as Wittgenstein may have thought, reveals life.[25] However, this may be true provided that we are prepared to accept that wisdom is a virtue determining not only our way of seeing the world as truly as is possible for us, but also of being and living in it as truly as possible.[26]

WISDOM AS OPENNESS TO TRUTH

When distinguishing between intellectual virtues, Aristotle identified them as modes of revealing truth, of hitting on what is right (ἀληθεύειν);[27] he mentions art (τέχνη), science (ἐπιστήμη), practical wisdom (φρόνησις), theoretical wisdom (σοφία) and intellect (νοῦς). Whatever is true or whatever is right may be there beforehand, as if it were a Platonic idea or a pre-existing reality open only to contemplation. It is brought into being by being realized in action, in utterances or products (ἀλήθεια πρακτική). Nonetheless, it is true; it is 'just right', although it may be surprising, frequently unexpected; it may not have been even imagined as possible. Excellent architects may design truly beautiful houses; but an excellent architect who is also wise will design houses which are not only beautiful but also excellent to live in.

No neat distinction between practical and theoretical wisdom may be adequate to explain the phenomenon of wisdom sufficiently, and this is partly because wisdom is one of the specific modes of revealing what is just right – a kind of truth which may be found, created and revealed by an optimal orchestration of human thought, emotion, desire, will and action in our lives between birth and death, in the lives of communities, states or cultures and between them. Moreover, for any other virtues revealing truth or 'what is just right', wisdom is the virtue orchestrating them optimally with the rest of our capacities. Hence, wisdom is the virtue of virtues, revealing truth that is significant for our being in the world.

Being in the world crucially involves being in time. Wisdom seems to enter a specific relation with this, for instance in that there are right and wrong times for wisdom to come to the fore. It is also a sign of wisdom to find or determine right times consistently. Hence, it is commonly regarded as a sign of a wise person to know the time to speak and when to remain silent, when to act or when to refrain from acting. The kind of time involved here is predominantly a qualitative, fluent, 'token-reflexive' or *kairotic* time, allowing for ascriptions of 'past', 'present' and 'future', guiding emotions or actions, distinct from a static, enduring time which can be dated (McTaggart's B-series of time). The latter only allows for a 'prior', 'simultaneous', and 'posterior' time. Kairotic time, however, can be right or wrong, dragging along, appearing to stand still, or speeding up (McTaggart's A-series).[28] A wise person knows how to deal with time, how to adjust to it adequately and how to determine it. He or she knows how to deal well with life-time. Yet wisdom as a mode of being in the kairotic world only comes in degrees and reveals life in degrees. It is contingent in itself, not perfect, always on the way. It gains strength in going.

WISDOM AND THE BOUNDS OF HUMAN CONVERSATION

For its existence, wisdom as the virtue of virtues, revealing theoretical as well as practical truth, obviously relies on experience and learning from it. Yet, experience without understanding what is experienced remains blind and, therefore, closed to wisdom. Experience must be thematized and reflected upon, whether by conversing with others or with oneself as an Other.[29] Without such a dialogue, or at least meaningful interaction, attempting to verbalize or make sense of whatever was experienced, wisdom cannot come into existence or fulfil its proper function. People would not know what kind of experience was involved, how to respond to it reasonably and how to orchestrate dispositions to feel, to think and to act accordingly. Hence, wisdom needs communication with oneself and with others (based on a language) in order to exist. The same applies to the other virtues as long as they too are based on justified reasons.

This kind of reflective conversation presupposes a phenomenon highlighted in Wilhelm von Humboldt's philosophy of language: 'There is an unchangeable dualism in the basic nature of language, and the possibility of speaking itself is conditioned by address and reply.'[30] Speaking, and language itself, are intrinsically designed for a reply; both are dialogical *per se*. This dualism does not only apply to speaking with others but also to conversing with oneself. Following a hint given by Plato, conversing with ourselves as 'the dialogue with oneself taking place in the soul',[31] means to think.

Moreover, address and reply presuppose that there is common ground between them, a resonance between speaker and addressee and between what they have to say to each other. This makes possible a mutual exchange of thoughts which deal with a joint theme. Such an exchange of thematically focused thoughts in cooperatively alternating conversation, frequently related associatively yet cohesively, and more or less coherently rather than necessarily forming a strictly logical chain, is their rational core. It is conversational thinking.

Obviously, conversation means communication with others. It involves transcending and continuing the ongoing dialogue of the soul with itself – without which, in turn, any inner dialogue would be impossible. Progressing in such an exchange broadens and deepens not only theoretical or practical knowledge, but also sociable interaction (or the unsocial sociability characteristic of human beings – if Immanuel Kant is to be believed).[32] This many-faceted expansion is frequently triggered by the resistance we experience when others may not share our thoughts or feelings or we cannot share theirs. In addition, we may not fully be aware of the kinds of prejudices guiding our own thoughts, emotions or actions or know which of them are justified. We may become aware of them, however, when we encounter dissent from interlocutors. In dealing with fundamental, existential problems related to the meaning and conduct of life it is of particular importance for gaining and sustaining wisdom to be open to these differing thoughts, emotions and actions, while possibly transforming our own ways of thinking, feeling and acting. Hence, these conversations with others or with ourselves, crucial for wisdom, may not deal with specific topics of everyday conversation but frequently involve considerations about who we are and how we live. Here too, conversation may reveal who we are and how we can and should exist with others in this world. The German poet Friedrich Hölderlin emphasized the anthropological importance of conversation in the words '[...] since we are a conversation and capable of hearing from each other'.[33] He does not wish to say that we may lead conversations *ad libitum*, drop them and then turn our attention to other issues. He makes the strong claim that conversation itself defines what we are as human beings. Humans are living beings who understand and determine their mode of being in the world by conversing. We are *Gesprächswesen*. Consequently, wisdom and virtues in general intrinsically involve communication, conversation and interaction.

In spite of its conversational, inherently dialogical and interactive character, wisdom and its inherent structure may still appear to be self-centred. It seems that human beings are unavoidably concerned with their own modes of being in the world, be these of individuals, groups, societies or global communities. Whatever counts as the 'reality' with which wisdom is concerned appears to exist within this 'wordly', self-related conversational horizon. Whatever truth may *transcend* human experience, remains within this horizon. Following Leonid Batkin's remark (ascribed to Ugo Foscolo), wisdom thus circumscribed involves a specific kind of transcendence, potentially beyond human past and present experience and conceptualization, based on the structure of the human pursuit of perfection: 'Probably the most sublime ability of human beings is to aim at a kind of perfection which transcends everything that their own experience is capable of promising.'[34] Hence, wisdom may reach its final horizon with this kind of 'humanist' transcendence, openness to experience of the unexpected as a potential manifestation of human perfection *qua* perfected practical truth in historical time. Wisdom itself may not guarantee or provide this on the basis of past or present experience alone. However, truth of this unforeseeable and hitherto unconceived kind cannot be negated a priori without epistemic dogmatism, since it cannot be proved never to exist. It cannot be proved to exist either, but this does not render its possibility nonsensical. In this situation of undecidability, it is reasonable to assume that wisdom involves an open-minded, if sceptical, optimism, rather than a closed mind. Of course, this does not rule out that this kind of truth may reveal itself as unexpected, utterly unwanted and annihilating, leaving no room for optimism. Either way, transcendence allegedly presupposed in wisdom so understood remains 'wordly' transcendence.

However, there appears to be an even wider horizon for wisdom to expect, to reach out for, to hope for or even to rely on. Religious prayer as a form of conversation appears to presuppose the widest possible horizon for revealing truth. Prayer addresses an Other of a unique kind, different from anything which might be an object of possible experience within any wordly horizon. Despite the fact that this conversation is (mostly) also concerned with the human being and its mode of existence, self-concern is not intended directly for the most part. It may be intended concomitantly. The direct concern of prayer consists in almost the opposite, namely to turn attention away from the Self and focus on the Other in the attempt to contemplate or to communicate, possibly in the most intimate way. This kind of turning from the Self to the Other (which already enriches understanding in everyday conversation or dialogue), seemingly enriches and deepens, for those who are engaged in it, an understanding of who they are, of what there is or what should be. For them, it would amount to a contradiction in terms if they were also to believe that this Other and their own mode of conversing were ultimately based on fiction, even though they may be fully aware that they do not experience what the Other is. It is in this conversation, in 'learned ignorance' (Nicolaus Cusanus), and in simultaneous openness to a transcendent but potentially revelatory truth, that wisdom may find its ultimate source and aim. However, we are free to accept, to reject or to be agnostic about this source and aim. Which kind of horizon of wisdom we choose depends on what kind of persons we are.

ENDNOTES

1 Plato, *Symposium* 203b1–204b7.

2 Cited in W. Welsch, 'Wisdom: Philosophical Aspects', in N.J. Smelser and P.B. Baltes (eds), *International Encyclopedia of the Social and Behavioral Sciences*, vol. 24 (Amsterdam/New York: Elsevier, 2001), col. 16504.

3 Francis Bacon, *Novum Organum*, Aphorism XXXVIII in *The Philosophical Works of Francis Bacon*, ed. J.M. Robertson, (London: Routledge, 1905), p. 263.

4 Sharon Ryan, 'Wisdom', in *Stanford Encyclopedia of Philosophy* (https://plato.stanford. edu/entries/wisdom/), accessed 27 June 2019.

5 'Wisdom, considered not from the outside but from the point of view of someone seeking it,' says Gabriel Marcel, 'can never be looked upon as acquired. If a man were to say of himself "I am a sage", he would at once make himself ridiculous. Is this because a sage is expected to be falsely, hypocritically, modest? I do not think so, I think it is because we know that if wisdom became complacent, it would immediately get stiff in the joints and in the end fall into decay. It does seem in the last analysis that, for the seeker, wisdom is in a sense indistinguishable from the pursuit of it.' Gabriel Marcel, *The Decline of Wisdom* (London: Harvill, 1954), p. 40.

6 H.-G. Gadamer, 'Über die Verborgenheit der Gesundheit', cited in F. Svenaeus, *The Hermeneutics of Medicine and the Phenomenology of Health: Steps towards a Philosophy of Medical Practice* (Dordrecht: Kluwer, 2001), pp. 143–4.

7 Of course, the parallel between health and wisdom does not mean that we may not sensibly say that we are healthy because we should not sensibly say that we are wise! The asymmetry condition for the ascription of wisdom does not apply to health. I thank Ricca Edmondson for this remark.

8 *The Oxford English Dictionary*, vol. 20 (Oxford: Oxford University Press, 1989), pp. 421–2.

9 By 'postulate' I mean a theoretical hypothesis which is nonetheless necessary from the point of view of practical reasoning.

10 Aristotle, *Metaphysics* 1, 2, 982a5–6.

11 Cicero, *Disp. Tusc.* 4, 26, 57.

12 Augustine, *Contra Academicos* 1, 6, 16; *De Trinitate* 13, 19; 14, 1, 3; *Martin Luthers Werke*, vol. 22, (Weimar: Böhlau, 1929), pp. 325, 381.

13 For a concise description of the Berlin Wisdom Paradigm and the kind of research undertaken in its context see Ute Kunzmann and Paul B. Baltes, 'The Psychology of Wisdom: Theoretical and Empirical Challenges', in R.J. Sternberg and J. Jordan (eds), *A Handbook of Wisdom – Psychological Perspectives* (Cambridge: Cambridge University Press, 2005), pp. 110–35; see also Markus H. Woerner and Ricca Edmondson, 'Towards a Taxonomy of Types of Wisdom', *Yearbook of the Irish Philosophical Society* (2008), pp. 148–63; Ricca Edmondson, *Ageing, Insight and Wisdom: Meaning and Practice Across the Life Course* (Bristol: Policy Press, 2015), pp. 155–96; Ricca Edmondson and Markus Woerner, 'Sociocultural Foundations of Wisdom', in Robert J. Sternberg and Judith Glück (eds), *The Cambridge Handbook of Wisdom* (Cambridge: Cambridge University Press, 2019), pp. 40–68.

14 See, for instance, Paul B. Baltes and Ursula M. Staudinger, 'Wisdom: A Metaheuristic (pragmatic) to Orchestrate Mind and Virtue Toward Excellence', *American Psychologist* 55 (2000), pp. 122–36.

15 U. Kunzmann and P. Baltes, 'The Psychology of Wisdom: Theoretical and Empirical Challenges', in R.J. Sternberg and J. Jordan (eds), *A Handbook of Wisdom – Psychological Perspectives* (Cambridge: Cambridge University Press, 2005), p. 113.

16 Ursula Staudinger now argues that we should distinguish between 'general wisdom' such as that discussed in this paper, and 'personal wisdom'. See U. Staudinger, 'The Need to Distinguish Personal from General Wisdom: A Short History and Empirical Evidence', in M. Ferrari and N. Weststrate (eds), *The Scientific Study of Personal Wisdom: From Contemplative Traditions to Neuroscience* (Dordrecht: Springer, 2013), pp. 3–20.

17 Pamela S. Schmutte and Carol D. Ryff, 'Personality and well-being: Re-examining methods and meanings', *Journal of Personality and Social Psychology* 73 (1997), pp. 549–59.

18 U. Staudinger et al., 'The Psychometric Location of Wisdom-related Performance: Intelligence, Personality, and More?' *Personality and Social Psychology Bulletin* 23 (1997), pp. 1200–14.

19 U. Kunzmann and P. Baltes (2005), p. 127.

20 Ibid.

21 Ibid., p. 128.

22 For an overview of definitions of 'wisdom' see J.E. Birren and Ch.M. Svensson, 'Wisdom in History', in R.J. Sternberg and J. Jordan (2005), pp. 14–17.

23 *Pace* John Kekes, *Moral Wisdom and Good Lives* (Ithaca, NY: Cornell University Press, 1995), pp. 9–10.

24 '*Sapida scientia*' ('savoury knowledge') was commonly taken as the 'etymology' of *sapientia* throughout the Middle Ages. According to Thomas Aquinas (*ST* I, 43, 5 ad 2), it is closely related to 'the sort of formation of the intellect by which one breaks forth into the affection of love'. For examples of the common usage of the term see Klaus Kirchert, 'Text und Textgewebe', in: Kurt Ruh (ed.), *Überlieferungsgeschichtliche Prosaforschung* (Tübingen: Niemeyer, 1985), pp. 233–4.

25 See Anthony Kenny (ed.), *The Wittgenstein Reader* (Oxford: Blackwell, 2006), p. 301: Here Wittgenstein remarks: 'It might also be said: Wisdom merely *conceals* life from you.'

26 In this respect wisdom resembles humour, of which Wittgenstein once said when he was staying in Rosroe, Connemara: 'Humour is not a mood, it is a way of seeing the world.' This way of seeing reveals something that is true which goes beyond mere constatives, at least it is revealing for everyone who has a sense of humour and is prepared to listen. Again, it is mostly the listener and not the speaker who decides whether or not the latter is humorous.

27 See Aristotle, *Nicomachean Ethics* 6, 3, 1139b 15–17.

28 J.M.E. McTaggart, 'The Unreality of Time', *Mind* 17 (1908), pp. 457–74. See also F. Ó Murchadha, *Zeit des Handelns und Möglichkeit der Verwandlung: Kairologie und Chronologie bei Heidegger im Jahrzehnt nach Sein und Zeit*, (Würzburg: Königshausen und Neumann, 1999).

29 Probably the most profound discussion of the concept of the 'Other' in twentieth-century philosophy of dialogue can be found in Michael Theunissen, *The Other – Studies in the Social Ontology of Husserl, Heidegger, Sartre, and Buber* (Cambridge, MA.: MIT Press, 1984).

30 Wilhelm von Humboldt (1827), 'Über den Dualismus', in Andreas Flitner et al. (eds), *Wilhelm von Humboldt, Werke 3: Schriften zur Sprachphilosophie* (Tübingen: Narr, 1963), p. 138.

31 Plato, *Sophist* 263e3–5; *Theaetetus* 189e4–190a6.

32 See Immanuel Kant, 'Idee zu einer allgemeinen Geschichte in weltbürgerlicher Absicht', *Berlinische Monatsschrift* (November 1784), pp. 385–411, 'vierter Satz'.

33 Friedrich Hölderlin (1800?), 'Versöhnender, der du nimmergeglaubt' (Dritte Fassung), in Friedrich Beißner and Adolf Beck (eds), *Friedrich Hölderlin: Sämtliche Werke*, Bd. 2.1 (Stuttgart: Kohlhammer, 1946), pp. 136–7.

34 Leonid M. Batkin, *Die Italienische Renaissance: Versuch einer Charakterisierung eines Kulturtyps* (Stroemfeld: Roter Stern, 1981), p. 5. My translation.

EXPERIENCE AND
TRANSCENDENCE

JOHN HALDANE

I

In his book *Approaching God: Between Phenomenology and Theology*, Patrick Masterson presents and discusses at some length Jean-Luc Marion's radical phenomenological approach to issues of experience and transcendence. Marion is well known as an advocate of 'post-onto-theology' which seeks to set aside or reject traditional metaphysical approaches to the question of divine existence and revelation. Instead, he focuses on the idea of the phenomenal *givenness* of the transcendent in 'saturated' experiences, in which the given surpasses the conceptual capacity of thought, and which do not require metaphysical validation or explanation.[1] In some respects, Marion is invoking and interpreting an ancient strand in Christian mystical theology as represented primarily by Pseudo-Dionysius; but his critical aim is to free notions of transcendent experience from requirements of philosophical justification characteristic of later medieval and modern philosophy.[2]

Marion's notion of givenness as a mode of phenomenality, and the displacement of any idea of anterior subjectivity in favour of the notion of 'receptivity' is connected to his deprecation of metaphysical objects (of which the *self* is an instance). But in so far as the transcendent is identified as a dimension or mode of experience, rather than being inferred or postulated as the cause and external object of such, it may seem to be subjective in a non-cognitive sense – a *feature* of experience itself rather than an independent reality encountered in or implied by it. Masterson formulates his own reservations as follows:

In [Marion's] account, all givenness and transcendence, indeed all religious phenomena, are contained within the sphere of immanence, to the exclusion of any ontological realism and metaphysical causality.

But can this immanent bedazzling or bemusing experience of divine transcendence as that which is utterly distant and withdrawn from the range of conceptual comprehension be taken as a dependable revelation, even if only 'through a glass darkly', of God? Or instead of peering more closely at this allegedly unconditioned experience of an immanent transcendence, of a visible invisible, might it not be more appropriate to recognize this experience as a dependent cipher of an ontologically independent transcendent God, to whom one must argue metaphysically from the experienced cipher?[3]

I am in sympathy with these concerns and with the way in which Masterson puts Marion in dialogue with Aquinas in an effort to show the complementarity of a modified phenomenological approach and that of metaphysical natural theology. I want to begin at an earlier stage, however, by placing the notion of transcendence in the context of a series of contrasts with the 'factual', then to subvert a reading of those distinctions that would consign the transcendent to the domain of imagination or non-cognitive subjectivity. This will then lead to some consideration of how experience might signify an ontologically independent transcendent ground.

II

Notions of a *fact*, of *factuality* and of *facticity*, have featured prominently in recent philosophy in the formulation of certain supposedly significant distinctions.[4] Thus, we have 'facts' and 'values', 'facts' and 'interpretations', 'facts' and 'theories'[5], 'factuality' and 'counter-factuality' (by which I mean metaphysically, naturally or conceptually constrained possibility), to which we may now add 'facticity' and 'transcendence'.

If there is any common core to these contrasts it is the idea that the second term in each pair involves 'going beyond' (the) facts. Judgments of value may refer to the factual but they *add* to it; interpretations (and theories) are *additional* to what they interpret; counter-factuality *ranges beyond* the actual into the possible; and transcendence *surpasses* facticity (where the latter is usually specified in terms of the contingent, the empirical, the physical, or the natural). Generally the pairings mean to involve the idea that the factual is what is true, with the implication that the contrast is with something either universally false or *not* properly evaluable as true or false. The actual terms of the contrasts, however, need not carry that assumption, and some have wanted to allow distinctions made in these terms, while also maintaining that statements of evaluation, and of interpretation, as well as contrary-to-fact-conditionals, and statements about transcendents may themselves be true. This raises the question of what is then being contrasted. Here is where the idea of 'going beyond' can do some work, though if it is to apply across the range of classes then its meaning is analogical rather than univocal: for interpretations do not contrast with data in the same way that counter-factuals contrast with factuals. Philosophers who take the contrasts in the earlier sense, as being between what is true and what is otherwise (either universally false, or not false but non-truth-apt), tend then either to affirm the distinction, intending thereby to demote whatever falls under the second term, or to deny it with a view to elevating the latter to the status of truth. A less prejudicial response, however, is the second one: allowing that the contrasts have application but then considering case by case where that leaves the truth status of claims in the second categories.

In the next three sections I aim to show three things using the example of architectural practice: first, that we cannot do without what the second terms represent: *evaluation*, *interpretation*, *counter-factual supposition*, and *transcendence*; second, that these operations and dependencies are related; third, that they may involve objective, correct or truth-apt judgments.

III

Suppose I am an architect and have been commissioned to design a tomb to house the remains of an 'unknown soldier', a memorial that will serve to represent the indefinitely-many who have died in battle and whose bodies were never found, or were buried without identification, or whose place of interment was unrecorded. Some aspects of the brief will be practical relating to size, materials, methods of construction and expected lifetime; others, however, will engage historical, political, aesthetic and ethical considerations, as well perhaps as religious ones.

The practical aspects can be relatively easily stated. The structure should have a base within a given area; it should be recognizable from a range of perspectives and visible from up to a certain distance; it should be in stone or concrete; it should have an interior space of certain dimensions, and so on. These requirements are not self-interpreting but broadly speaking they are specifiable and resolvable at the level of the factual. When, however, one turns from the dimensive and constructive to the other aspects of *design per se* then evaluation, interpretation, counter-factuality and transcendence are certainly inescapable.

How is the theme of the unknown soldier to be treated? Should I emphasize the anonymity and perhaps fragmentary character of the remains, particularly if they may in fact be of several bodies? On reflection I may judge that in order for people to respond to the memorial as something personal *and* national, the individuality should be that of a concrete universal: not *an* unknown soldier but *the* unknown soldier. Some tombs are horizontal, implying a resting figure, others are vertical suggesting a standing one. Which is it to be? We know that on the battlefield, bodies – if buried at all – will have lain in shallow graves, but I might consider the literal counter-factual that the soldier stands upright, uncowering, as will living ceremonial personnel who stand to attention before his tomb: soldier 'facing' soldier. Thus is created in a normative ideational order something acknowledged by fitting responses.

What of the material? Concrete has utilitarian and mundane associations; but if stone is to be used should it be granite, marble or Portland limestone? Or perhaps a variety of stone types drawn from different parts of the country like the soldiers whom the tomb honours? While being from a place, the former transcends the diversity of locations and types; but the latter reflects the realities of those differences. There is also the more obvious aspect of the 'look' whether a unity of uniformity or a unity of integrated variety. Furthermore, a tomb has at once to acknowledge the fact of death but also to counter thoughts of decay. Perhaps then it should represent a timeless life maintained at the age of loss, an embodiment of the ideas expressed in Robert Laurence Binyon's poem 'For the Fallen':

They shall grow not old, as we that are left grow old:
Age shall not weary them, nor the years condemn.
At the going down of the sun and in the morning
We will remember them.

What this intimates, and what the tomb should also aspire to achieve, is for *the* unknown soldier, and for the many other absent and unknown ones, a kind of transcendent presence, a virtual immortal mortality. [6]

These are not factors I *might* wish to consider in conceiving and composing a design; rather they are of sorts that *must* shape both my thinking and making if the task is to be achieved. Just as there are practical necessities to be met so there are these others, evidently more important, to be satisfied. Think also of cultivating a garden, or planning a core curriculum, or counselling someone through the ending of a relationship, or coping with illness, or loss, or deciding whether to enter into a lifelong relationship, or raising a family, and so on.

Each involves practices of *evaluation*, *interpretation*, *counter-factual thinking*, and imagining forms of *transcendence*. As well as being related these are also connected to something which may seem to belong to the 'fact' side of the associated contrasts, namely *description*. One cannot pursue one of these activities save in connection with others. To conceive the transcendent involves drawing contrasts between what is or what may be. This is not because the transcendent is necessarily to be contrasted with the actual but because the conceiving of it involves considering different possibilities and evaluating them as more or less warranted, and thinking how things would be different with regard to the ordinary or immanent on the basis of alternative transcendent possibilities. Besides, interpretations and evaluations are themselves descriptions, and even the prior descriptions upon which they are focused carry evaluative, interpretative, counter-factual and transcendent aspects. If I judge that something is a piece of gold, then that grounds judgments about its properties and effects. It also allows me to make sense of its presence in a given context or its suitability for another, and to make certain counter-factual inferences. Moreover, the use of the kind term 'gold' goes beyond the instance, subsuming it under an elemental classification and committing me to judgments about unencountered earlier, elsewhere, and as yet unactualized instances.

IV

Returning to the pairings 'facts' and 'values', 'facts' and 'interpretations', 'factuality' and 'counter-factuality', and 'facticity' and 'transcendence', someone may complain that I have overlooked the arguments for treating only the former in each case as truth-related. The very point of the distinctions in familiar uses is to mark a contrast between what may be true or false and what may be neither because the 'going beyond' involves adding some subjective aspect: an attitude, a construal, an *ens rationis*, or a wholly imaginary construction. What are these arguments? There are three that should concern us here (I set aside those specifically concerning the status of counter-factuals which involve additional issues): 1) from disagreement, 2) from the nature of experience, and 3) from the nature of reality. All three feature in the writings of David Hume, and since the days of the logical positivists have been recurrently invoked by those who favour reductive naturalisms.

First, then, that from disagreement. Even where people agree about the facts they may disagree in how they evaluate and interpret them, and in what they take to be their implications, if indeed they do take them to signify anything further at all. Obviously, we sometimes disagree in our value judgments and interpretations, but note three points. First, this is rarely a dispute about the cognitivity of evaluation, and generally presupposes belief in it. Typically, it concerns what things are valuable and in what ways they are good, bad or indifferent. Second, in a reflective context we may think of questions of interpretation as having the form 'What does this mean or signify?' But the question 'What is this?' also seeks an interpretation, and this is given by a description that purports to subsume the instance under some relevant kind. Third, and most obviously, disagreement does not imply that there is no fact of the matter, any more than agreement in judgment entails facticity. What needs to be attended to before hypothesizing subjectivism is the *character* of the disagreements, and relevant differences will be found to apply *within* the categories of evaluation and interpretation and not between those and the domain of facts.

Again, not all apparent disagreements are real ones. How beliefs are manifested in actions depends on other beliefs and circumstances. As Adam Smith observes, in a mode more characteristic of his time than of ours, which itself is testament to the point: 'The style of manners that obtains in any nation is often, on the whole, the one that is most suitable to its situation. Hardiness is the character most suitable to the circumstances of a savage; sensitivity to the circumstances of life in a very civilized society.'[7] Similarly, it does not follow from one group valuing something and another not that there is any dispute between them; and again the existence of disagreement does not imply that there is no fact of the matter and that members of different cultures are simply expressing alternative cultural preferences. These several considerations cast doubt on the force of the subjectivist challenge by showing that even if there are intra-cultural and inter-cultural disagreements they do not imply that objectivism is false.

The two other kinds of arguments are linked in that they generally draw on a unified 'naturalistic' view of reality and of experience and I will deal with them conjointly. Advocates of a scientific perspective within particular fields of enquiry and with respect to thought more broadly often express, or presuppose, the idea that credibility in the light of science is a preeminent or even an exclusive guide to truth. The stronger the version of the claim the more likely they are to attempt to explain away putative non-scientific ways of knowing, among which they often include both common sense or 'folk-theorizing', and moral, aesthetic and religious understanding. This way of thinking has also been extended to the assessment of philosophy itself and it has even been adopted *within* philosophy as for example by W.V.O. Quine who described his own 'naturalistic' world view as 'the recognition that it is within science itself, and not in some prior philosophy, that reality is to be identified and described'.[8]

This speaks to the prestige and growing influence of scientific thinking but there is something else at work. One could give full credit to the sciences for revealing and explaining much of the structure and behaviour of nature while yet holding that there are many things which it cannot explain, not because of any deficiency but because they are of a different kind to its proper concerns. We might well look to the materials scientists to explain why certain combinations of pigment and medium are more transparent, or retain an appearance of liquidity, or can be built up by impasto, but it would absurd to think that because they can explain those things they can also speak with authority on which of several works employing such paints is the best *painting*. The physics and chemistry of materials are one thing, the aesthetics of their use are another. Similarly, we may look to the forensic scientist to analyse materials and to testify before a court regarding them, but not to evaluate the morality or the legality of the issue. Or again, returning to the earlier example, a building engineer may advise on the physical integrity of a structure but not by that knowledge judge its aesthetic and ethical merits as a tomb and monument to the fallen.

My present interest in the potential of architecture to embody meaning, including transcendent meaning, is philosophical, not art-critical-cum-historical. Evidently people have built and experienced buildings in other than engineering and utilitarian terms, deploying the language of aesthetic value and transcendent significance, often to contrast the latter pair with the former. Consider, for example, Ruskin on principles of architecture:

There is dreaming enough, and earthiness enough, and sensuality enough in human existence without our turning the few glowing moments of it into mechanism; and since our life must at the best be but a vapour that appears for a little time and then vanishes away, let it at least appear as a cloud in the height of Heaven ... The ambition of the old Babel builders was well directed for this world: there are but two strong conquerors of the forgetfulness of men, Poetry and Architecture; and the latter in some sort includes the former, and is mightier in its reality; it is well to have, not only what men have thought and felt, but what their hands have handled, and their strength wrought, and their eyes beheld, all the days of their life ... It is in becoming memorial or monumental that a true perfection is attained by civil and domestic buildings; and this partly as they are, with such a view, built in a more stable manner, and partly as their decorations are consequently animated by a metaphorical or historical meaning. [9]

What philosophical sense can be made of architecture being animated by transcendent meanings and how far can such significance range? The idea of building in accord with socially, or metaphysically, transcendent values and meanings faces two sorts of challenges. First, which I have discussed, is that values as a category are themselves problematic, and second, that the notion of embodying meaning in physical form is somehow incoherent.

Suppose we think that all knowledge derives from experience and that this is essentially a matter of the impact of the physical environment upon the sense organs. According to Quine this is where traditional empiricism and science coincide: '[T]he watchword of empiricism: *nihil in mente quod non prius in sensu* is a prime specimen of naturalized epistemology, for it is a finding of natural science itself, however fallible, that our information about the world comes only through impacts on our sensory receptors.'[10] One consequence of this view is that so far as knowledge goes, reality involves collections of matter located in time and space, plus an uncertain number of conscious individuals – 'uncertain' because on this view it may be a theoretical question as to whether there is any consciousness other than one's own, for what one *sees* when looking around in a crowd are *bodies*, or the sensory effects of these, and it can only be a conjecture, therefore, that they are also *subjects* of experience. I will return to this point later but here I want to suggest that there is no good reason to accept Quine's account of experience, and there is also reason to resist his interpretation of the principle more familiarly expressed as *nihil in intellectu nisi prius in sensu*. Apart from the matter of whether there are sources of knowledge other than experience, there is the issue of the nature of experience itself. It might be that while what is in the intellect was *somehow* first in experience, the *way* in which it is in the former is different to how it was in sense-experience. Here we may invoke another scholastic principle, consistent with the first, namely *quidquid recipitur ad modum recipientis recipitur*:[11] whatever is received is received according to the manner of the recipient, of which the relevant epistemological application is *cognitum est in cognoscente secundum modum cognoscentis*:[12] the thing known is in the knower according to the mode of the knower. So when we say that knowledge comes through experience, we should distinguish the objects of cognition from the way in which they are known, and within the latter the ways they are known *in sensu*, and *in intellectu*.

V

Traditional and Quinean empiricism seek to describe and explain experience in terms of interactions with the environment, and that can make it difficult to conceive of how anything other than sensible properties could be objects of knowledge. When discussing the design of a public tomb and monument I mentioned the need to imbue it with certain perceptible qualities including a kind of transcendent presence of a concrete universal: *the* unknown soldier, which is neither a singular individual nor an abstract type. In one obvious sense this is not an empirical object but it is the sort of thing that a sensitive and thoughtful person might see and feel. Such is the accommodating character of experience in a larger understanding of it that there is no reason to deny that architecture can embody transcendent social and aesthetic meanings and values.

To see how that might be done we need to start with a correct account of perception. There is a widespread tendency to confuse two different sorts of states and operations. On the one hand, there is the subject matter of neuroscience. This begins with changes in sense organs effected by the surrounding environment and then traces further effects within the brain and central nervous system. On the other, there is the concern of epistemology which starts with the effect of the environment on the sense faculties and looks to the incorporation of these in thoughts about the world. Both processes are real and both deserve study; the mistake, however, is to conflate them, for what is input to the sense-organs may not be what is known to the subject. A better account is one that treats 'impacts on our sensory receptors' as the necessary causal basis for perception but views perception itself as a discriminating activity on the part of intelligent, questioning and interpretative animals. To perceive an apple is not to infer its existence from optical and tactile sensations, but to encounter directly an object of a certain sort whose nature is understood by the observer on the basis of past experience and an implicit theory acquired through language. Anyone in a position to discriminate something as an apple already possesses a good deal of interconnected knowledge about reality. Equally, the belief that there is an apple on the table is not one whose verification could consist in first- or third-person reports of certain sensory activities. One cannot infer from these to the existence of anything beyond them. In short although perception may depend upon sensation as its material basis it clearly transcends this level.

Can this transcendence take us to the level of meanings? Evidently it does, for when we hear someone speaking a language we understand, we grasp his or her meaning directly. Semantic understanding is not inferred from syntactical structure, far less from the physical structure of sound. To be able to make sense of what someone is saying we need to have broadly similar conceptual and linguistic resources to those that she deploys in her speech. In other words there needs to be common knowledge and understanding. The fundamental question of symbolic meaning is not whether we can interpret it but whether it makes any sense as a representation of reality or as an expression of certain values; and the only test of that is whether it helps us to make sense of the world as we already understand and transform it.

There is no saying in advance whether some species of meanings is intelligible or viable. Meanings, signs and symbols must somehow conform to real or possible objects, attributes and structures, be they physical, psychological, cultural or transcendent. The question to ask of a symbolic account is whether it illuminates aspects of the world of which we already have some understanding, doing so either through evaluation, interpretation or some other kind of explanation. There is nothing inherently incoherent about the idea of a symbolic order; nor is there anything in the nature of making and understanding that precludes the possibility of such meaning being embodied in architecture or another medium including that of lived experience and activity. Whether any particular narrative or set of meanings is credible is not something that can be excluded on account of the nature of thought and experience themselves; we need to look hard, read what we find there and think about how it relates to what we already believe and what it may contribute to our own efforts to understand and embody that understanding in buildings, rituals, practices and institutions.

It is a fact of human experience that interior spaces can induce feelings of quietness, reflective calm and natural piety. Equally the massing of volumes upwards may create a sense of transcendence, as if suggesting the possibility (without inducing the belief) that, like the stones themselves, the viewer can rise above the earth on which she stands. These responses are often difficult to characterize and usually they cannot be made precise, nonetheless they are undeniable. If the experience of space and solid forms did not prompt them, then architecture, as contrasted with mere building, would not exist and, a fortiori, religious architecture would be impossible.

Part of what such architecture depends on is the fact that human beings respond in certain ways to shapes, volumes and spaces. What more can be said about this? There is increasing interest in the possibility of explaining aesthetic preferences and affinities in terms of our natural history and one might try to connect the experience of architectural forms to some more primitive and ancient association with places of significance to our primordial ancestors, such as caves and crevices. Without denying the possibility that present experiences have some relation to practical necessities of the long-distant past, such accounts cannot be complete since all they explain are very general features, and do not account for the specificity and particularity of experiences and associated interpretative and evaluative judgments directed towards particular spaces and forms. A natural disposition to enclosures and high structures may derive from ancestral associations but this is an unverifiable speculation and at most establishes a very broad area within which the aesthetics of architecture operates.[13]

What needs adding is the fact that wood, stone and glass, like paper, canvas and paint, may be used as media for the communication of experiences and ideas. Architecture is a form of embodied meaning. To speak of the 'language of architecture' may be misleading if it suggests that buildings are linguistically structured, made up of the equivalent of sentences, themselves composed out of elements corresponding to words. Nonetheless, it is appropriate to think of buildings as vessels of meaning, or as bearing a significance, and in this way it is proper to speak of 'reading' or interpreting a building: working out the meaning of the parts and of the whole.

VI

This discussion began with mention of Marion's radical phenomenological treatment of issues of experience and transcendence, particularly as the latter might relate to religious experience, and with the question raised by Patrick Masterson: '[whether it might not] be more appropriate to recognize this experience as a dependent cipher of an ontologically independent transcendent God, to whom one must argue metaphysically from the experienced cipher'.

In approaching this suggestion I have given attention to analysing various contrasts with the idea of the factual, and shown that what is placed in juxtaposition with this needs to be acknowledged, but not as other-than-possibly-true. Valuation, interpretation, counter-factuality and transcendence are all necessary to making sense of 'facts' and are themselves candidates for the factual in a full(er) sense. The case for this also involved showing the inadequacy and fallacious foundation of the empiricist notion of experience. Value and meaning are part of what we perceive through informed experience and there is no reason to treat them subjectively 'to the exclusion of any ontological realism'. What then of transcendence? As I indicated, like the other categories contrasted with the 'factual', it is a generic classification subsuming diverse species, and I have dealt with some forms of transcendent content in discussing the case of architectural thought, design and experience; but at this point the issue turns to the religiously transcendent and the ultimate case of this: the divine. Could experience signify an ontologically independent transcendent source: God; and is there any reason to believe that it does?

One general form of argument to be further specified by reference to particular kinds of experience, including purportedly mystical ones, might invoke *object-involving* or *object-dependent* thought and perception. Although these expressions are associated with recent neo-Russellian theories of reference,[14] the ideas are much older and are to be found in Meister Eckhart's *Parisian Questions*[15] which may be related to his own emphasis on the mystical encounter with God. Object-involving (OI) and object-dependent (OD) theories maintain that certain kinds of thoughts are only possible given the existence of what their contents 'present'. If it could then be shown that some sorts of experience that seem to present an ontological transcendent as object are indeed of OI or OD types, then the existence of the transcendent follows directly. There are many challenges to such a style of argument but it is not in the ordinary understanding a causal proof. Instances of the latter argue:

A1) E cannot be (or be thus and so) unless caused to be (or be thus and so) by C;
A2) E exists (or is thus and so); hence
A3) C exists.

The present argument, by contrast, is of the form:

B1) E cannot be (or be thus and so) unless C exists;
B2) E exists; hence
B3) C exists.

The ground for asserting B1) is either that E has C as a metaphysical constituent, or that E depends non-causally on C. It may be that in either case how such thoughts come to exist also involves causal activity on the part of C, but that is not the relation that warrants the conclusion.

Such an argument is problematic for several reasons. Some concern externalist accounts of intentional states in general, but others relate to the correct characterization of a thought or experience. The expression 'God-oriented-experience', like 'unicorn-oriented-experience' is ambiguous between referential and non-referential readings. Doubtless there are experiences sincerely reported as being 'of God' as perhaps there are as being 'of a unicorn', but apart from asking what aspect of them suggests the divine there is the obvious rejoinder that, as the unicorn example shows, in one sense of thought or experience one can intend or be aware of what does not exist.

A second kind of argument which is not conceived with mystical experience in mind but can be adapted to it is proposed by Thomas Reid; though more strictly I think that what he writes suggests *two* distinct arguments. In the sixth of his *Essays on the Intellectual Powers of Man* ('On Judgement') Reid asks how a one-year old child comes by the belief that one who nurses him is a thinking being. Reid answers:

Not by reasoning surely, for children do not reason at that age. Nor is it by the external senses, for life and intelligence are not objects of the external senses ... This belief stands on another foundation than that of reasoning; and therefore, whether a man [in whom this belief remains] can give good reason for it or not, it is not in his power to shake it off.

Setting aside this natural conviction, I believe the best reason we can give, to prove that other men are living and intelligent, is, that *their words and actions indicate like powers of understanding as we are conscious of in ourselves.* The very same argument applied to the works of nature, leads us to conclude that there is an intelligent Author of nature, and appears equally strong and obvious in the last case as in the first.[16]

Reid's suggestion can be understood in two ways. First, as an instance of a causal-inductive argument to the existence of other minds based on the recognition of causal relations between one's own thought and behaviour, together with observation of the behaviour of others suggesting the hypothesis that what causes their behaviour is of the same sort as causes it in oneself, namely various kinds of mental states. Likewise, features of the world more generally *indicate*, by bearing the marks of being effects of, minded agency; hence we may conclude that there is an Author of nature. This then looks to an instance of an A-type argument. As such it is triply problematic. First, it involves a generalization made on the basis of a single case, acquaintance with one's own experience, and that experience is itself ambiguous since how does one know that the relation between one's mental states and one's behaviour is causal rather than merely correlative? Second, it would be question-begging to say that the basis on which mindedness is applied to other human beings is the observation of their words and actions if these features are understood intentionalistically, for this already assumes that their authors are minded. Third, the extension of the argument to the works of nature requires that the latter be seen as analogous to or instances of action and utterance (whether conceived intentionalistically or otherwise) but they seem categorically different sorts of things.

Aspects of Reid's broader views are relevant to how one might respond to these objections; but there is a second line of argument suggested (though probably not intended) by what Reid says. On this account when he writes that 'their words and actions *indicate* like powers of understanding', this may be read as saying that they are not *effects* of such powers but *manifestations* of them, as a gesture may manifest and thereby signify anger. Here we would view the relation between utterance and action, and more generally between behaviour and mindedness, as not always one between distinct existences, for the former may be expressive instances of the latter. What on this second account the child is able to do is recognize what is naturally signified, in the sense of being manifested, namely mind. Continuing this line of thought into the supplementary claim of an analogy with nature and God we get the idea that aspects of the world as these are experienced by us may be natural signs, i.e. *manifestations* of divine-mind. Here what does the work in bridging the two kinds of cases is not the analogy of works of nature to words and actions but the idea that both are instances of manifest signification, be it of quite different kinds.

Reid writes of the 'appearance' or 'marks of wisdom and design' in 'the works of nature'[17] and gives as examples 'the fixed stars which afford us light to travel both by sea and land', the mathematical regulation of the solar system, the shape and atmosphere of the earth and the forms and functions of living things – the sorts of things familiarly cited in eighteenth-century design arguments. If we follow the second line of argument the idea would be that these are manifestations of divine activity, direct signifiers rather than effects of it. It does not follow from this, however, that an argument from the significance of these to the existence of God would not be a causal argument, for there remains the question of whether there is an agent whose intelligence is being manifest. One could think that nous is not something apart from its manifestations but a principle of mindedness immanent in nature itself. Here is where further metaphysical argument comes in on the side of making sense of divine personhood and agency.

In conclusion, however, I want to propose as candidates for signs or manifestations of divine activity aspects of our very thoughts, experiences and activities themselves. I am not thinking now of mystical experiences, though not excluding them, but of diverse cases of phenomena charged with valuation and value, interpretation and meaning, including various kinds of transcendent, though not necessarily religious meaning. Another way of conceiving of facts and factuality as these were set against the several contrasting features is in terms of a world devoid of the latter: an austere, qualityless world such as might be represented by physics. But that is not the world in which we live and have our being. Our world is one animated by value, meaning and transcendence, as are we; and the existence of such an axiologically configured reality is inexplicable naturalistically. Just as the existence of composed aesthetic objects points to the existence of an artist as cause, so that of a contingent noetic, axiological, personal structure calls for a transcendent cause. Here, one might accept the inference but see it as compatible with a deistic account; however, it is part of the position advanced by Aquinas that God is a sustaining cause of contingent being; as he writes: 'The preservation of things by God is a continuation of that action by which he gives existence, which action is without either motion or time, so also the light in the air is by the continual influence of the sun', [18] and it is part of the picture I am proposing that God manifests something of his nature in sustaining a meaning-world for and of human subjects: 'for in him we live and move and have our being. As some of your prophets have said we are his offspring.'[19]

This is neither to say that we are part of God in either a pantheistic or panentheistic sense, nor that God is the complete deterministic cause of our intentional, axiological activity; but it would imply that features corresponding to his being and nature radiate into us, while he gratuitously permits us to cooperate creatively in responding to and incorporating meaning and value as aspects of our living.

In these concluding observations, I have made a point of not focusing on mystical experience per se, but it is relevant to end by saying that such might be an additional gift: a more direct and intense form of divine radiation. Meanwhile our inhabiting and having the power to contribute (positively and negatively) to a world of value and meaning including aspects of transcendent meaning are paired gifts. Such a world and such subjects cannot have a scientific explanation but they can have a personal one, and part of the story may include the idea that all of this is a partial revelation, again to quote Patrick Masterson, 'a dependent cipher of an ontologically transcendent God, to whom one must argue metaphysically from the experienced cipher'.

ENDNOTES

1   See Jean-Luc Marion, *Being Given: Towards a Phenomenology of Givenness* (Stanford, CA: Stanford University Press, 2002), and 'Sketch of the Saturated Phenomenon' in Dermot Moran (ed.), *Phenomenology: Critical Concepts*, (London: Routledge, 2004).

2   See Jean-Luc Marion, *Cartesian Questions: Methods and Metaphysics* (Chicago, IL: Chicago University Press, 1999).

3   Patrick Masterson, *Approaching God: Between Phenomenology and Theology* (London: Bloomsbury, 2013), p. 122.

4   See Bede Rundle, *Facts* (London: Duckworth, 1993).

5   Hereafter I will just speak of 'facts' and 'interpretations' subsuming theories within the latter. The notion of theories is itself a broad one encompassing different conceptions, but one non-theoretical use of 'theory' which is more or less synonymous with an everyday use of 'interpretation' is that which features recurrently in Arthur Conan Doyle's Sherlock Holmes stories, as illustrated in the following exchange. Holmes: 'What is your own theory as to what took place?' Lord St Simon: 'I came to seek a theory, not to propound one. I have given you all the facts.' *The Adventures of Sherlock Holmes* (London: George Newnes, 1892) p. 240. Here theory means interpretation-cum-explanation. This is to be distinguished from the logical empiricist notion in which theories deal in unobservables linking them by bridge laws to observable phenomena. The latter also involves 'going beyond the given facts' but in a further sense.

6   Significantly, this stanza appears inscribed in many war memorials and is recited during the Last Post ceremony at the Menin Gate Memorial in Ypres.

7   Adam Smith, *The Theory of Moral Sentiments* (Cambridge: Cambridge University Press, 2002), p. 245.

8   W.V.O. Quine, *Theories and Things* (Cambridge, MA: Harvard University Press, 1981) p. 21.

9   John Ruskin, *The Seven Lamps of Architecture* (London: Smith, Elder & Co., 1849), Chs 5 and 6.

10   W.V.O. Quine, *Pursuit of Truth* (Cambridge, MA: Harvard University Press, 1990), p. 19.

11   Thomas Aquinas, *ST* I 75, 5; I, 3, 5.

12   Thomas Aquinas, *ST* I 12, 4.

13   For a more extensive discussion of the limits of evolutionary and other reductive explanations of experiences of beauty in nature see John Haldane, 'Finding God in Nature: Beauty, Revulsion and Art' in Craig Titus (ed.), *Christianity and the West* (Washington, DC: Catholic University of America Press, 2009) reprinted in Haldane, *Reasonable Faith* (London: Routledge, 2010).

14   See, for example, Gareth Evans, *The Varieties of Reference*, ed. John McDowell (Oxford: Clarendon Press, 1982) and essays in John McDowell and Philip Pettit (eds), *Subject, Thought, and Context* (Oxford: Clarendon Press, 1986).

15   See Meister Eckhart, *Parisian Questions and Prologues*, trans. Armand Maurer (Toronto: PIMS, 1974).

16   Thomas Reid, *Essays on the Intellectual Powers of Man*, ed. Derek R. Brookes (Edinburgh: Edinburgh University Press, 2002), p. 483, my emphasis.

17   See his 'Lectures on Natural Theology' in *Thomas Reid on Religion*, ed. J.S. Foster (Exeter: Imprint Academic, 2017), pp. 74–5.

18   *ST* I 104, 1 ad 4.

19   *Acts* 17: 24.

ETHICS IN THE FOREST: OTHERWISE APPROACHING GOD

JOSEPH DUNNE

I

I still vividly remember the horizon-stretching impact of Patrick Masterson's First Arts course on contemporary atheism in the old UCD at Earlsfort Terrace in 1966. Paddy's lectures opened a terrain that has drawn him, and me, to continued exploration over the intervening decades – the terrain in which we find, or do not find, bearings in relation to God. In his most recent book Paddy gives a magisterial account of three different approaches to finding such bearings: what he calls the 'phenomenological', the 'metaphysical', and the 'theological'.[1] In this essay I want to sketch an approach that is different from all three – though closest to the phenomenological – in focusing on our experiences of *ethical* concern. Three suggestive images, offered by Charles Taylor in a tribute to what he sees as his teacher Iris Murdoch's distinctive contribution to moral philosophy, will give a preliminary intimation of this approach.[2]

The great bulk of ethical theorizing in the Anglophone world since the mid-twentieth century has been preoccupied with what it is right to do, as governed by rules, principles and decision-procedures regarding our obligations to others. The past few decades, however, have brought also a more expansive interest in how it is best to live, in the light of some more or less explicit conception of what it is for a human life to flourish or go well (which, without annulling our obligations to others, provides the wider context within which these obligations have meaning and force). The '*corral*' symbolizes confinement to the first of these, regarding rule-bound duties, whereas the '*field*' symbolizes the second, wider concern about human flourishing and elements that may be essential to it, such as, for example, a happy family life, purposeful and reasonably well remunerated work, solid friendships, a range of interests and pastimes, or devotion to some worthy cause; all of these are characteristically modern concerns that seem to entail personal qualities traditionally recognized as virtues, such as justice, courage, truthfulness, temperance and generosity. Taylor welcomes the shift of attention from corral to field, but suggests the possibility of a further move: not only out of the corral, but beyond the field too – and yonder into the '*forest*'.[3] This term symbolizes an opening in ethical life to the possibility of radical self-transformation through responsiveness to what can most fully inspire one's love, when this is a supremely high good that is irreducible to, and might indeed call for a renunciation of, a rich or flourishing life as identified in the field. Such an opening is revealed for example in the kind of deep reorientation of a person's identity manifested in a religious conversion, as in a Buddhist's shift from self to 'no-self', or a Christian's submission to God expressed in the words, 'Thy will be done.'[4]

My purpose in this essay is to examine how human life is to be understood if our moral topography is expanded so that, beyond constraints of the corral or fulfilments of the field, the forest is acknowledged as defining the ethical horizon of people who find their way into it – if it does not indeed form a more or less unexplored hinterland of all ethical experience. More particularly, I want to examine how a forest perspective might lead us to re-conceive 'virtue' and show human life as related-to-God. In doing so, I shall focus especially on Christianity as the forest pathway with which I am most familiar and which has been most deeply interfused with western philosophical reflection. I shall try to clarify what is most distinctive about a Christian way of life by relating it to the Socratic tradition – which includes Stoicism and, preeminently, the ethics of Aristotle – and to the repudiation of that tradition in contemporary forms of Neo-Nietzcheanism. While I am well aware of how strongly contestable is the ground to be covered here, my intention is not apological. More than three centuries ago Pascal wrote: 'People have contempt for religion; they hate it and fear it may be true. To cure this it is necessary to … show that it is attractive, lovable (*aimable*), so as to make the good wish that it were true; and then to show that it is true.'[5] To support 'a wish that it were true', rather than 'to show that it is true', defines the limit of my ambition in these pages.

II

The forest is the place where one is drawn to a highest good beyond life – in the Christian case, a God who loves the world and in whose love we can aspire to share. But the very height of aspiration here unavoidably confronts us with the lowness of our achievement, with the distance separating us from this supreme good. In the light of this good, suffering in the world is made peculiarly manifest. The depredations of war and famine, apparently random natural disasters, human potential wasted or great need unmet, cruelty inflicted on the innocent, oppressions and injustices unrectified and often even unrecognized: to be drawn to a good God is at the same time to be exposed in one's conscience to all this blighting of human life. But such exposure also confronts one with everything in oneself that obstructs or greatly limits one's capacity to meet the demand that it presents or indeed to discern what, in one's own circumstances, this demand may be.

Adherence to any demanding ethical ideal is likely to be disturbing in this way. Perhaps in moments of special lucidity or experienced wholeness, one is more aligned with the ideal and more freely and fully disposed to respond to it. But such moments may be relatively fleeting and rare. For the rest, one is occupied with daily cares, finding challenge and satisfaction in ordinary responsibilities and tasks, especially in family and work – enough to distract from, though not entirely to extinguish, one's awareness of the more exacting call, which remains as a background source of admonishment and unease. Embarking on a spiritual path brings this background more to the fore and thus entails encounter with the dark or shadow side of oneself; in the Christian tradition, the 'desert' rather than the 'forest' symbolizes the place of this encounter. That this shadow exists is not just due to an egregious failure in moral formation or an arrested state of psychological development. It is seen rather as the default or 'normal' condition of human beings, a normality that leaves us hampered in our ability to meet ethical–spiritual demands that we still find inescapably compelling. Only at the summit of spiritual advance, in the lives of those who are truly holy, is this state of disability overcome so that, in the Christian case, they submit unconditionally to the promptings of an *agapê* that has taken possession of their whole being.

It is the distance between such a saintly state and our ordinary condition that one sets out to traverse when one embarks on a spiritual path; and given the scale and nature of this distance, the path is one of transformation. It will consist centrally of practices and disciplines that aim at an unmaking and remaking of one's character. 'Spiritual exercises' is the common expression here, used for centuries in religious communities (associated most easily but by no means exclusively with Ignatius Loyola), but with wider currency in philosophy now partly because of its centrality in Pierre Hadot's *Philosophy as a Way of Life*. This book demonstrates the extent to which ancient philosophy, especially as practised in the Hellenistic schools, did not consist in 'teaching an abstract theory, much less in the exegesis of texts, but rather in the art of living' – which, from Plato's *Phaedo* onwards, included most testingly the art of dying. Such practice of philosophy was primarily a therapeutics of the passions, especially of 'unregulated desires and exaggerated fears', which aimed at 'a profound transformation of the individual's mode of seeing and being'.[6] Of the two major Hellenistic schools, Stoicism has a spiritual tenor characteristically different from that of Epicureanism: whereas the former emphasizes rational sovereignty through the cultivated ability to limit one's care to matters one can affect and to regard those outside one's control from the perspective of an impassive cosmos, the latter encourages a more insouciant and joyful appreciation of the gifts of existence in each moment. But both schools initiated students into practical disciplines designed to increase vigilance and lucid self-presence in the conduct of life.

These disciplines, if only because of their sanction in the Western philosophical tradition, are helpful reference points here. But there are at least three noteworthy differences between them and their Christian counterparts. First, the idea of renunciation has a force in Christianity that it does not have in Stoicism. The Stoic ethical ideal, although in some respects deeply ascetical, does not entail abandonment of anything that can really be regarded as good: what one has to leave behind is properly to be deemed base, trivial or unworthy of a being endowed with autonomous Reason (*to hêgemonikon*).[7] Christian non-attachment, by contrast, requires the surrender of genuine goods – so that there is real conflict between the full-hearted love of God and what we naturally incline to regard as human flourishing; were it otherwise, conversion could not count as *renunciation*, since nothing valuable would have been given up. But precisely because human flourishing is good and willed by God, it is reaffirmed, on the other side of conversion, which is the fundamental act of consent expressed as 'Thy will be done.' This consent is lived out in a commitment to the flourishing of others and ultimately, in partnership with God, to 'repairing the world' (or '*tikkun olam*', the Hebrew expression that Taylor invokes in making this same point).[8] The commitment is variously manifest in the lives of saintly persons throughout the history of all the great world faiths. In the case of Christianity, it is related to the central mystery of the Incarnation – God entering history in fully human form – and to the fact that hope is not for the immortality of the soul so much as for the resurrection of the body. And the contrast here reflects a deep divergence between Christianity and the whole Socratic tradition in Greek philosophy, a divergence dramatically illustrated in the deaths of the two foundational figures: Socrates facing this final ordeal with supreme composure, his rational sovereignty intact – to the point where it was scarcely an ordeal at all – and Jesus enduring and protesting a brutal, agonizing death, for the most part deserted rather than surrounded by his friends.

The second respect in which the practical disciplines of Hellenistic schools differ from those embodied in Christian spirituality relates to their primary role as edification: they involve remaking, but hardly *un*making, the self. Rigorous discipline and ever-renewed attention are indeed necessary, and building positive habits involves dealing with recalcitrant passions – but with no great emphasis on a central feature of Christian asceticism: the sense of one's own personal crookedness, that is to say one's seemingly boundless capacity for evasion, rationalization and self-deception when faced with the demands of the higher good to which one has, or supposes that one has, committed oneself. A closer parallel here lies in contemporary depth psychology and especially in psychoanalysis, which requires the patient not just to confront instinctual material but also to acknowledge and work through his or her own deeply entrenched resistances to, and defences against, doing so truthfully and with integrity (so that it requires, correspondingly, a great deal of strategic intelligence and hermeneutic sensitivity in the analyst's work of 'outwitting'). This is perhaps not very different, at least in some respects, from the 'purgative' element or the '*via negativa*' – often involving a 'dark night of soul' – that is inseparable from religious practice, especially the practice of prayer. Alasdair MacIntyre, in whose work St Augustine and Freud have long been central figures – especially because of their respective concerns with 'the transformation of desire' and 'the complex connections between desire and knowledge'[9] – offers a striking formulation of analogy here. In a discussion of Augustine, he introduces Freud as a figure 'whose account of sexuality and religion in some respects is an inversion of Augustine's'. But the inversion is so close that it allows this intriguing parallel:

> For both Augustine and Freud there is someone before whom and to whom one talks, so that in the end one's prevarications and concealments and self-justifications are heard as what they are and the truth about oneself, including the truth about one's resistance to acknowledging that truth, is acknowledged. In both cases the talking involves a discipline, in the one case that of prayer, in the other that of psychoanalysis. And both insist that there is no way of evaluating that particular discipline from a purely external point of view, for such evaluation will be frustrated by those same fantasies from which the discipline is designed to free us.[10]

MacInytre's point serves also to bring out another, third, aspect of Christian practice that distinguishes it significantly from a Stoic (and perhaps from a Buddhist) counterpart: its intrinsically relational character, its directedness to an Other in whose presence it is always conducted. If 'talking' is an element here – as manifestly it is in, for example, the Lord's Prayer and the Psalms – it is not, however, the main element. At least for the contemplative tradition within Christianity, the emphasis is more on listening in silence and, more generally, on openness and receptivity. To be sure, there must be an active intention to pray; but the most fundamental act in prayer is one of consent to the presence and action of God in one's life, a 'letting go' in which one is radically vulnerable and dependent – and thereby also open to a grace that can never be received on one's own terms. (If there are things to be done in prayer, the greater need is to allow oneself to be undone.) Carried through, such consent has both a purgative and a unitive aspect. Everything that divides one – ambivalent motivation, unresolved conflict, concealed desire – also diminishes one's capacity for presence. And to invite God's presence is to risk having all this – traditionally covered by the term 'sin' – exposed in a process of purification and healing that is likely to be painful, lengthy and hazardous. Healing is possible because not only may the exposure be fierce and relentless but the Other to whom one is exposed offers a love that is tender and merciful. Progress on this path – and 'progress' is hardly the right word, unless in the Beckettian sense of 'fail again, fail better' – is toward unity with this Other, a unity which, through a conversion of one's willing and desiring, allows one to participate in or become a channel of the divine *agapê*.

Two points may be noted here about the complicated nature of the relationship between 'ordinary' flourishing and the 'fullness of life' that opens on the spiritual path. First, it is only with caution that one should refer, as I have just done, to 'healing'. For if healing is identified with a sin-blind psychotherapy aiming at a conflict-free normalcy, then it has no application here. What one needs to be freed from is not a pathology that distinguishes one from healthy people by disabling one as its helpless victim. Rather, it is a form of affliction to which all human beings are prone and in which they are always to some extent complicit. Moreover, healing can be understood only in the context of an acknowledgement that 'God has given a new transformative meaning to suffering' and that 'following him will dislocate and transform beyond recognition the forms which have made life tolerable for us'.[11]

Second, while it is important not to collapse 'fulness of life' into ordinary flourishing, and therefore to reject any understanding of religion as a recipe for 'happiness' or 'success', one may use these valorized terms to characterize the post-conversion state if proper acknowledgement is made of just how deeply revised or 'transvalued' their meaning has then become. Indeed it is just such use that one finds in the Beatitudes, the quintessentially Christian teaching of the Sermon on the Mount.[12] The venerable formula, 'Blessed are those who...' might equally be rendered as 'Happy are those who ...' (in translation of the Greek, '*makarioi*'). If one has become the kind of person characterized by the qualities recommended in each of the Beatitudes then one truly is happy or flourishing – a fact which may be related to the frequently recurring references to joy, peace and the absence of fear throughout the New Testament. (At the very least, one has unburdened oneself of many of the ways of manufacturing *un*happiness for which we humans have an immense talent.) Here one has to recognize the gulf between renunciation and the *rejection* of happiness, found in extreme form in Schopenhauer, who deeply admired the ascetical element in Christianity and indeed Buddhism.[13] It is here too, and precisely in opposition to such misanthropy, that one can make sense of the following: 'The saints are those who are supremely successful at the exacting task of being human, the George Bests and Jacqueline du Prés of the moral sphere. Morality is not primarily a question of duty and obligation but of happiness or well-being. Why we should want to be happy is ... the very prototype of a silly question.'[14]

This kind of affirmativeness, like much of what I have written above, is inseparable from a claim that, for all the awesomeness of divine transcendence and the abyss separating God's being from ours, there is still some basis here for relationship. Moreover, this basis lies not only in God's gratuitous act of entering redemptively into human history but also in the fact that, on their side, human beings are already imbued with a directedness towards God. However protean and vortex-like it may be, human will is not just an engine of futile, self-frustrating desire, as in Schopenhauer's disparagement of it – or indeed a vehicle of untrammelled power, as in Nietzsche's exaltation of it. Christian understanding here is classically expressed by St Augustine who, as MacIntyre points out, 'like every other ancient author, whether pagan or Christian, takes the intensity of human desire for granted'. 'What we discover in our progress towards self-knowledge,' MacIntyre writes, 'is that our desires are inordinate in respect of their finite objects', and he goes on:

> [T]hey are inordinate because they are at once expressions of and disguises for our love of God. We repress in ourselves the knowledge that we are by nature directed towards God and the symptoms of that repression are the excessive and disproportionate regard that we have for objects that substitute themselves for God, objects, which, when we achieve them, leave us disappointed and dissatisfied. It is only insofar as we make God the object of our desire, acknowledging that to desire otherwise is to desire against our nature, that our desires in general become rightly ordered and that we are rescued from the self-protection of a will informed by pride.[15]

III

Aristotle's conception of virtue (*aretê*) must seem in some respects congenial to the 'forest' perspective, which, with special attention to a Christian variant, I have just outlined. It is a strength of Aristotle that – concerned with action, emotion and desire, as well as with insight and judgment – he understands virtue as a disposition of one's whole being and, in particular, as expressive of what one delights in. It is a further strength that he acknowledges a certain 'primacy of practice',[16] especially with regard to the process through which virtue is acquired and developed: apart from sustained engagement in conducive *activities* – without which one lacks material for the only kind of reflection that is apposite – one has no chance of becoming virtuous. The corollary of this primacy is that there can be no informed understanding or sensible discussion of virtue by someone who lacks the relevant experience. This does not mean, as MacIntyre has tartly observed, that 'in order to become an Aristotelian one first has to become virtuous – even a slender acquaintance with Aristotelians would be enough to dispose of that claim'.[17] But it does mean that some experience of the need for virtue, of its indispensability for the achievement of centrally important individual and common goods, *is* required; no standing start or vantage-point from a neutral ground can compensate for the lack of this 'engaged' or 'insider' perspective. All this, which I take to be standard in any satisfactory account of Aristotelian ethics, is structurally akin to what holds also with regard to the world of spiritually and religiously inflected experience sketched in the previous section.

Still, is there not a great gulf in sensibility, with respect both to what is to be lived and to the kind of reflection that will adequately articulate this living, between this latter world and the world of Aristotelian virtue? This question can be sharpened by briefly tracing a genealogy of the concept of virtue before its appearance in Aristotle's texts. As found in Homer, *aretê* refers to any excellence through which a person shows that he is equal to the demands of a well-defined role, paradigmatically that of the warrior on the battle-field. Physical prowess, courage, and wily intelligence are the eminent *aretai*. To excel, and thereby to deserve and preserve honour, is to be on one's mettle and, if fortunate, to prevail in face-to-face combat with an opponent; one must contend with unpredicatable forces (erupting sometimes within oneself), the imperative not to become a supplicant, and the ever-present spectre of death. This arduous, unsentimental and deeply agonal ethos, in which mastery mattered above all, was partially sublimated through its deflection into the athletic arena and later the law-court and the assembly. And perhaps we can see it interiorized and further sublimated in the philosophical ethics of Plato and Aristotle, which depict the individual soul as composite, as the scene of conflict – between reason (*logos*) and the unruly elements comprising the other parts of the soul – and as virtuous to the extent that in this conflict it is reason that prevails.

Prima facie, then, to juxtapose our two worlds – of field (in broadly Aristotelian terms) and forest (in broadly Christian terms) – seems to confront us with two very different and apparently opposing rhetorics: one of strength, mastery, prevailing, excelling; and the other of vulnerability, yieldingness, dependence, receptivity, surrender, supplication. One question about virtue then will concern the range of qualities that are to count as virtuous – and which qualities, therefore, are to be added to or subtracted from the proposed catalogue of virtues in the *Nicomachean Ethics*. In *After Virtue*, MacIntyre was already dealing with this question in pointing out that, in the genealogy of Aquinas' list of virtues, historical elements (especially the entrance of Christianity, with its emphasis on its own peculiarly historical character) have intervened to make him consider as virtues qualities such as humility and patience which, if they were to be included at all in Aristotle's tabulation, would more likely appear as *vices*.[18] And in *Dependent Rational Animals*, he goes further by both excising Aristotle's great-souledness (*megalopsychia*) as a virtue – precisely because its comfort in masterful giving is only the obverse of its aversion to receptivity or dependence – and adding 'just-generosity', a quality that he associates with 'acknowledged dependence' and finds prefigured in Aquinas' virtue of mercy (*misericordia*).[19] This MacIntyrean revision of Aristotle is consonant with what, in terms of the present discussion, might be characterized as movement toward the forest. And there are still other, related qualities that a forest perspective would also include, notably a capacity for forgiveness (already implicit in charity and mercy), and purity of heart, poverty of spirit, gentleness, forbearance, a capacity for mourning, as urged in the Beatitudes, as well as reverence and 'fear of the Lord' (this Lord being not only Abba, loving Father, but also creator and sustainer of a universe of incalculable scale and complexity).

If great-souledness, at least, is to be deleted from Aristotle's catalogue, the question arises as to how the remaining virtues, and especially the 'cardinal' ones (justice, courage, temperance and practical wisdom) relate to the forest virtues just mentioned above. Obvious issues will arise here such as whether, when, or to what extent in any given case, justice is to to be tempered by mercy. Such dilemmas may seem no different from those that can arise anyhow within Aristotle's own plural scheme when the claims of one virtue pull against those of another, and to call therefore for no more than a routine exercise of the master-virtue of practical wisdom (*phronêsis*). But things may not be so simple if charity (*caritas*, *agapê*) is now the master virtue, not, to be sure, usurping the role of practical wisdom but informing and animating it and, through it, all the other virtues. And a further question is whether 'forest' virtues, even if they can alter or redirect the exercise of 'field' virtues, may not themselves depend on some of the latter. For example, it seems unlikely that, in the account of prayer given above, a person could undergo such a chastening encounter with

God without mustering courage to face and truthfulness to acknowledge what may emerge in and from this encounter. If the relationship between these two sets of virtues seems reciprocal, since each may influence the other in perhaps complicated ways, how can we enquire further about this relationship? Perhaps one fruitful way of doing so is by turning to the developmental or learning process, through which virtues are acquired and perfected as a person advances in ethical or spiritual maturity.

Aristotle thinks that one's early years are the crucial period for the formation of good habits, entailing the repeated performance of good actions and the gradual acquisition of appropriate sentiments and perceptions. A virtuous person desires and is disposed to do good actions, while recognizing and esteeming them *as* good; his practical intelligence has been gradually refined so that he understands better *why* they are good and is more discriminating and sure-footed in doing them. Aristotle is right, I believe, to emphasize the importance of this kind of formation in childhood if a person is to have a fair chance of becoming virtuous. What happens, however, if the conditions are not met – by the adult world of parents, carers and teachers – and this kind of formation does *not* happen? Let us suppose this to be the case in the following passage:

> It is irrational to suppose that a man who acts unjustly does not wish to be unjust or a man who acts self-indulgently to be self-indulgent ... Yet it does not follow that if he wishes he will cease to be unjust and will be just. For neither does the man who is ill become well on those terms. We may suppose a case in which he is ill voluntarily, through living without self-control and disobeying his doctors. In that case it was then open to him not to be ill, but not now, when he has thrown away his chance, just as when you have let a stone go it is too late to recover it; but yet it was in your power to throw it, since the moving principle was in you. So, too, to the unjust and to the self-indulgent man it was open at the beginning not to become men of this kind, and so they are unjust and self-indulgent voluntarily; but now that they have become so it is not possible for them not to be so.[20]

One may regard what Aristotle says here as simply true, practically realistic, or deeply pessimistic (even deterministic) – or indeed as all of the above. Two things in any case stand out: first, that a person who routinely acts badly is not to be let off the hook – there is no hint of exculpation or extenuation on grounds of earlier inadequate nurture or instruction: somehow, even 'at the beginning', it 'was in your power'. And, second, once the routine is established, there is no going back – the gravitational pull of established bad habit is irresistible.

Even if one were to accept the first thesis here – which surely goes against the grain of a great deal of modern psychology and sociology and may seem at odds even with Aristotle's own insistence on the indispensability of a person's having received a sound early formation – the second, practically more significant, thesis surely deserves challenge. A person of poor character, we are being told, is irreformable. But how are we to regard this claim? Can we in good conscience write off perhaps a large proportion of our fellow humans? Indeed can we be sure that we are not ourselves being written off? For, how many of us can claim truly that our own formation was directed towards 'the noble-and-good' (*ta kalokagatha*) – as distinct from many other lesser things – or that our characters are not in serious need of remaking? And even if we were to be placed on the right side of the stark separation proposed here between those who are virtuous and those who are irretrievably beyond the moral pale, should we accept the existence of any such pale? Surely we should reject it, not because of commitment to the risible claim that everyone actually is good but rather because of repugnance at the thought that many of those who are not good – and in the above passage Aristotle does not seem to be referring to deep *evil* – are condemned to remain in that state so that they, and we as their friends or fellow-citizens, are helpless to do anything about it.

What I am pointing to here may be taken as a lacuna in Aristotle's account of ethical development: actually, despite frequent claims to the contrary, he has little enough to offer about development in childhood and even less about it in adulthood. To be sure, we might take it as significant that in the *Nicomachean Ethics*, having given his account of flourishing, voluntareity and the virtues (in Books 1 to 6), and having then offered his account of moral weakness (in Book 7), he immediately follows this with his account of friendship (Books 8 and 9). A good friend, it is clear, is one's greatest asset or ally in one's attempt to integrate contrary inclinations and to remain on the path of virtue. 'Remain' is the important word, however; for, on Aristotle's view, friendship itself is possible only between those who are *already* committed to virtue (so that mutual help in sustaining this commitment is at the heart of their friendship). This is surely a lofty view of friendship – but one that does nothing to address the issue just raised: the fate of those who are *off* this virtuous pathway.

Here is a big breach between core insights of Aristotelianism and those of Christianity. If Jesus was, as Hannah Arendt suggests, '[t]he discoverer of the role of forgiveness in the realm of human affairs',[21] this is related to another central concept in the gospel, that of repentance or change of mind/heart (*metanoia*) – which is itself of course related to the idea of sin. It is perhaps ironic that while Christians differ from Aristotle in seeing human beings both as more deeply embroiled in evil and as called to a more demandingly high level of virtue, they nonetheless see the distance between these two poles as more traversable than Aristotle sees the comparable, and arguably lesser, distance that opens up in his moral ontology. Whereas the very idea of sin is often rejected because it supposedly consigns people to damnation or permanent exclusion (something very like what I am finding in Aristotle), it is in fact both bracingly inclusive and, as Taylor points out, dignifying: rather than damning or pathologizing, it accords all of us the dignity of somehow choosing what will not in fact fulfil us but the 'glamour' of which lures us into supposing that it will.[22] Instead of a defined line separating two irreducibly different moral types, perhaps we might entertain the more richly complex ethical picture suggested by Charles Péguy: 'What is formidable in the reality of life is not the juxtaposition of good and evil; rather it is their interpenetration, their mutual incorporation, their mutual sustenance, and sometimes their strange and mysterious kinship.' Such a depiction allows Péguy also to write:

> No one is as knowledgable as the sinner in matters of Christianity. No one if not the saint. And in principle, it's the same person ... The sinner extends his hand to the saint, since the saint reaches out to help him. And all together, the one through the other, the one pulling the other, they form a chain ... of fingers that can't be disconnected ... The one who is not Christian is the one who does not offer his hand.[23]

One way of expressing the difference between the accounts offered by Aristotelianism and by a spirituality of the forest is that, whereas in the former a failure of formation seems to lead into a moral cul-de-sac, in the latter it can open a path beyond itself toward *trans*formation.[24] While this difference lends attractiveness to the forest, we should have no illusions about any easy passage to the envisaged transformation. And here Aristotle's work is in fact helpful. In marked contrast to much contemporary moralizing, which is as voluble in canvassing very high standards as it is silent about what might help us to meet them, Aristotle allows little scope for illusion, stressing that virtuous character is formed in and not above the 'middle soul', that is to say, the whole seat of appetite, emotion, desire and proneness to pleasure and pain. And he depicts convincingly the outcome of ethical formation when it *is* successfully carried through: the virtuous person attunes all this psychic material, 'resisting' and 'opposing' though it may have been in the pre-virtue state, with a reason capable of truthfully disclosing the noble-and-good.[25]

IV

In referring earlier to Aristotle's ethics as a 'sublimation' of the *aretê* of Homeric figures, I intended no disparagement. For although in modern Western culture we have come a long way from that 'pre-Axial' ethos, we have no good reason to suppose that the humans depicted in its 'heroic' literature are essentially different from ourselves.[26] Otherwise we should be even more surprised than we perhaps are at how vigorously the ethos of that earlier society has been reimagined and reaffirmed in the philosophy of the nineteenth century by Nietzsche and his followers. Nietzscheanism too has its catalogue of favoured virtues and they are of an aristocratic and assertive bent, aspiring to great achievement, without scruple about risk or cost. There is here an easy contempt for the supposed pusillanimity of standard modern morality – including benevolence, respect for equality, democratic participation, and human rights (not to speak of the petty comforts they may assure) – now exposed as little more than a thin disguise for the resentment of the weak against the superiority of the strong. Impatience with restraint (or the 'ascetical spirit' of which Socrates himself is seen as the *ur*-exponent) is linked to a fierce assertion – of life, it may be, but a life willing to expend everything, including itself, in pursuit of 'self-overcoming'. How ever one views this philosophy, what is to be learned from its existence and obvious appeal is a keener sense of the tenacity of the most assertive instincts (especially, in Taylor's view, regarding violence and sexuality), the psychic costs incurred in their curbing, and the relative precariousness, therefore, of a moral order such as our own that is based on such curbing. Going further, Taylor suggests that the appeal of Nietzscheanism can be seen as evidence of an 'ineradicable bent' in human beings towards some good 'beyond life' and of where this bent can take us when it does *not* take us to the forest.[27]

Short of such a provocative claim, bringing the Nietzschean perspective on stage can serve to put pressure on its main contemporary alternative, one or other version of the standard morality mentioned above. In this, or any other, morality, 'curbing' can succeed only if it is real sublimation, that is to say, a non-repressive turning around of these instincts so that their energies are deployed to 'higher' ends – without the inevitable 'return' or 'revenge' inexorably entailed by their repression. But sublimation is a big ask, and Taylor sees no grounds for complacency about our capacity to pull it off in contemporary liberal–democratic societies (a scepticism surely amply confirmed by very recent developments in the moral and political climate of these societies). To be sure, we have learned to internalize many kinds of restraint through disciplinary regimes, the workings of which over several centuries have been powerfully exposed in the writings of Norbert Elias and Michel Foucault.[28] But what moral vision do we have that might make such mechanisms of restraint any more than forms of psychic manipulation and/or coercion (however 'soft' their mode of operation), and how deeply does this vision penetrate to the instinctual level itself? Taylor has no quarrel with the substance of this morality; rather, he laments the widespread failure, as he sees it, to articulate a vision that might support it. We are earnest in the codification and juridification of standards and norms of behaviour – to an extremity of 'corral' consciousness that leads him to speak in *A Secular Age* of 'code fetishism' and 'nomolatry' – but strikingly reticent about what truly ennobles or dignifies, thus providing *sources* that could inspire or enable us to live up to them. This failure matters especially when these standards are so demandingly, indeed unprecedentedly, *high*. 'High standards,' as Taylor remarks, 'need strong sources.'[29]

My purpose in this essay was to articulate a perspective within which a search for strong sources might be less stifled than it often is in contemporary academic philosophy – albeit that the spiritual, and frankly theological, connotations of this perspective are often deemed suspect in the philosophical arena. I have been emboldened to take such liberty here because in Paddy Masterson I was blessed to have a teacher whose deep sympathy with the Christian gospel coexisted with a philosophical disposition that was rigorous and adventurous – and more passionate about wisdom than punctilious about disciplinary boundaries. It is a great pleasure, after more than half a century, to present these thoughts to Paddy, in gratitude for the enduring inspiration of his teaching and with the hope that their errancy will be met by that combination of critically raised eyebrow and benign smile that so endeared him to his students.

ENDNOTES

1 See Patrick Masterson, *Approaching God: Between Phenomenology and Theology* (London: Bloomsbury, 2013). I retain the intentional ambiguity of this title in the sub-title of the present chapter.

2 See Charles Taylor, 'Iris Murdoch and Moral Philosophy', in Maria Antonaccio and William Schweiker (eds), *Iris Murdoch and the Search for Human Goodness* (Chicago, IL: University of Chicago Press, 1996). As will be apparent, Taylor's work, with that of his close contemporary Alasdair MacIntyre, has been an important influence on my thinking about issues covered in this essay.

3 Taylor credits Murdoch with pushing beyond the confines of utilitarian and deontological perspectives on the *right* (the corral), and beyond the eudaimonist perspective on the *good*, linked to the more recent emergence of Aristotle-inspired virtue ethics (the field), to a kind of ultimate concern with the *Good*, shaped by her engagement with Buddhism and by a reading of Plato strongly influenced by the French philosopher and Christian mystic Simone Weil (the forest).

4 Two clarifications are in order here. First, the required reorientation is not toward a form of altruism that would lead one to privilege others' flourishing over one's own; for even heroic feats of altruism could still cleave to the primacy of a flourishing human life. It is when this primacy is denied – or, more precisely, when such denial takes the form of an acknowledgement, indeed a full-hearted love, of some supreme good other than human life – that one is in the forest. Second, to speak of the required reorientation as involving 'renunciation' is not to suggest that concern with flourishing and all the recognizable challenges of ordinary ethical life are suspended. For, as we shall see later, at least in the cases of the two historical 'religions' just mentioned, they reappear in transfigured form. As Taylor puts it, 'In Christian terms, if renunciation decenters you in relation to God, God's will is that humans flourish, and so you are taken back to an affirmation of this flourishing, which is biblically called agape. In Buddhist terms, Enlightenment does not just turn you from the world; it also opens the flood-gates of *metta* (loving kindness) and *karuna* (compassion).' Taylor, 'Iris Murdoch', p. 21.

5 Quoted in Lucy Beckett, *Reading in the Light of Christ: Writings in the Western Tradition* (San Francisco: Ignatius Press, 2006), p. 13.

6 Pierre Hadot, *Philosophy as a Way of Life* (Oxford: Blackwell, 1995), p. 83. Hadot points to the affinities, despite marked differences, between his work and Michel Foucault's later writings on ethics. Other comparable work, in Anglophone philosophy,

is Martha Nussbaum, *The Therapy of Desire: Theory and Practice in Hellenistic Ethics* (Princeton, NJ: Princeton University Press, 1994).

7   This is a key term in, for example, *The Meditations* of Marcus Aurelius.

8   Charles Taylor, *A Secular Age* (Cambridge, MA: Harvard University Press, 2006), p. 17.

9   Alasdair MacIntyre, preface to revised edition of *The Unconscious: A Conceptual Analysis* (New York and London: Routledge, 2004), pp. 7, 3.

10 Alasdair MacIntyre, *God, Philosophy, Universities: A Selective History of the Catholic Philosophical Tradition* (London: Continuum, 2009), p. 29. Characteristically, MacIntyre does not regard prayer as only a matter of interior dialogue with God. As he observes elsewhere, 'productive work' can be 'thought of as a kind of prayer and performed as an act of prayer' – though this is a truth all too likely to be obscured in a fragmented culture that consigns prayer to '"religion", religion conceived of as no more than one more compartmentalised area of activity'. Alasdair MacIntyre, 'Where we were, where we are, where we need to be', in Paul Blackledge and Kelvin Knight (eds) *Virtue and Politics: Alasdair MacIntyre's Revolutionary Aristotelianism* (Notre Dame, IN: University of Notre Dame Press, 2011), p. 323. My use of 'practice' throughout the chapter is intended to counter subjectivist misconstruals of 'interiority' that occlude the indispensable background of socially shared activity and meaning. Taylor is no less aware than MacIntyre that in our 'fragmented culture' this background is pluralized and 'fragilized', a process that leads to 'massive unlearning' with respect to 'some of the great languages of transcendence' and loss of '[s]ome great realizations of collective life'. But he also nicely brings out the fact that in this culture 'other facets of our predicament in relation to God come to the fore' – so that, for instance, whereas to appreciate in the seventeenth century what Isaiah meant by a 'hidden God' 'you had to be a Pascal ... [n]ow we live it daily'. This kind of historical lens allows him to view the Church, at least in its contemporary incarnation, not as 'a grouping of people together on the grounds of their sharing some important property' but rather as 'a skein of relations ... [of] particular, unique, enfleshed people to each other', 'a network of agape' that 'creates links across boundaries', and the institutionalization of which may easily make us 'living caricatures of the network life' and of the 'communion' proper to it. This view (much influenced by Ivan Illich) leads him to urge the need for hospitality on the part of contemporary Christians to 'new unprecedented itineraries ... new paths, opened by pioneers who have discovered a way through the particular labyrinthine landscape we live in, its thickets and trackless wastes, to God'. (Taylor, *A Secular Age*, pp. 532, 739, 755).

11 Taylor, Ibid., p. 655.

12 Matthew, 5, 3–10.

13 See especially Arthur Schopenhauer *The World as Will and Representation*, trans. E.F.J. Payne (London: Constable, 1966), pp. 573–88, 603–33.

14 Terry Eagleton, apropos a Thomist ethical vision, in 'Disappearing Acts' (Review of Denys Turner, *Thomas Aquinas: A Portrait*), *London Review of Books*, 35/23 (5 December 2013), pp. 39–40.

15   MacIntyre, *God, Philosophy, Universities*, p. 28.

16   'The primacy of practice' does not imply any rejection of theory; rather, Aristotle's ethical theory is one that acknowledges and accounts for this primacy.

17   'On Having Survived the Academic Moral Philosophy of the Twentieth Century', in Fran O'Rourke (ed.), *What Happened in and to Moral Philosophy in the Twentieth Century?* (Notre Dame, IN: University of Notre Dame Press, 2013), p. 29.

18   See Alasdair MacIntyre, *After Virtue* (Notre Dame, IN: University of Notre Dame Press, 1984), p. 177.

19   See Alasdair MacIntyre, *Dependent Rational Animals* (London: Duckworth, 1999), pp. 119–28.

20   *Nicomachean Ethics* 3, 5, 1104a, 7–22.

21   Hannah Arendt, *The Human Condition* (Chicago, IL: University of Chicago Press, 1958), p. 238.

22   See Taylor, *A Secular Age*, p. 619.

23   Both passages from Péguy here are quoted in Taylor, Ibid., pp. 750–1.

24   Reference might be made here – and not only because it echoes Aristotle's reference to the drinking bouts of the self-indulgent in the passage above – to the work of Alcoholics Anonymous, work that is transformative on the ethical plane by adhering to forest spirituality. For elaboration of this link, see Ernest Kurtz and Katherine Ketcham, *The Spirituality of Imperfection: Storytelling and the Journey to Wholeness* (New York, NY: Bantam Books, 1994) and, closer to my own elaboration of the forest in this paper, Thomas Keating (with Tom S.), *The Divine Therapy and Addiction: Centering Prayer and the Twelve Steps* (New York, NY: Lantern Books, 2009).

25   See *Nicomachean Ethics* 1, 13, 1102b13–28.

26   The 'axial age' characterizes a period, usually placed between the eighth and third centuries BCE, during which a significant transformation of ethical thinking is claimed to have occurred across several different cultures, associated with pioneering figures such as the Buddha, Confucius, Lao-Tzu, Isaiah, and Socrates. The phrase was first given currency by Karl Jaspers in his *The Origin and Goal of History* (London: Routledge Revivals, 2011).

27   The phrase 'ineradicable bent' occurs in the essay on Murdoch and later in *A Secular Age*.

28   See Norbert Elias, *The Civilizing Process*, vol. 1, *The History of Manners*, and vol. 2, *Power and Civility* (New York, NY: Pantheon, 1982); and Michel Foucault, *Power/ Knowledge: Selected Interviews and Other Writings, 1972–1977* (New York, NY: Pantheon Books, 1980) and *Discipline and Punish: The Birth of the Prison* (New York, NY: Vintage Books, 1977).

29   Charles Taylor, *Sources of the Self: The Making of the Modern Identity* (Harvard, MA: Harvard University Press, 1992), p. 516. In this book Taylor attempts to elucidate the notion of a 'moral source' and to provide his own narrative retrieval of significant sources of modern moral consciousness.

THE CONCEPT OF 'PERSON' IN HEALTHCARE ETHICS

NOREEN O'CARROLL

The Hippocratic Oath represents the ethical ideal of the 'good doctor' even though it is uncertain if Hippocrates wrote it or any of the writings attributed to him. Contemporary medicine is very different to that practised in the fifth century BC; nevertheless the symbolic power of the ancient oath resonates across the centuries. It is grounded for the most part in its identification of two related obligations: that of using medical knowledge and skills to prevent illness and promote health, and taking due care to avoid harming patients: 'I will use my power to help the sick to the best of my ability and judgment; I will abstain from harming or wronging any man by it.'[1] Taking its cue from this ancient tradition of swearing an oath to uphold the ideals of the medical profession, the World Medical Association formulated a modern version at its General Assembly in 1948 known as the 'WMA Declaration of Geneva'. It has been amended regularly, most recently in 2017, and renamed 'The Physician's Pledge'. The WMA hopes this will become a global ethical code for physicians everywhere.

PATIENTS AND PERSONS

The role and obligations of physicians nowadays are more complex than in previous centuries; advances in biomedical technologies have brought with them a range of ethical dilemmas at both the beginning and the end of life. Terms such as 'person', 'personhood' and 'person-centred care' frequently feature in discussions of ethically problematic cases. For example: Is an embryo a person? Does someone in the advanced stages of dementia still manifest the characteristics of personhood? Is someone who has suffered irreversible brain-damage still the person she or he formerly was? These are not simply academic questions. They are fundamental and existential: how we answer them has a direct bearing on how we behave and act towards embryos, foetuses, patients suffering from dementia and those with brain injuries from which they will not recover.

The meaning and use of the term 'person' points to the boundary of ethical practice in healthcare in two ways. Firstly, anyone who merits care does so because they have what is called 'moral status', also referred to as moral standing or moral considerability. To have moral status is to deserve the protection afforded by moral norms and rights.[2] This point, and its implications, was clearly noted by Mary Warnock: 'A person is generally supposed to be a bearer of rights. It is thus often suggested that if we could decide whether an embryo, for example, or a foetus, or a girl in a permanently vegetative state were a person, this would allow us to decide, by rational deduction, whether they had a right to life, or whether we might legitimately cause them to die.'[3] This is the crux of the matter as far as the use of the word 'person' and the related terms 'personhood' and 'person-centred care' in healthcare is concerned. For if it can be established that the designation 'person' may legitimately be applied to embryos and patients with severe neurological disabilities as much as to able-bodied individuals who merit the protection of moral norms and rights, the implications for healthcare provision are considerable. It raises questions about the ethics of research on embryos, abortion, euthanasia and physician-assisted suicide as well a range of other issues.

Secondly, there is the moral principle that it is wrong to deliberately cause harm to others. This is rooted in the common morality or set of norms that are shared by all people committed to morality.[4] It is also the foundation upon which the idea that individual freedom is circumscribed by the state only when harm to others is threatened.[5] Since the primary goal of healthcare is care, it is essential that healthcare professionals have a clear sense of the scope of that care to ensure that harm is not caused to others. Thus the main reason for using the designation 'person' in healthcare is that a person has moral status, and consequently rights that merit respect and protection. The term 'person' originally referred to the dramatic mask worn by actors in Greek and Roman theatre (prosôpon/persona). The notion of persona as indicating a role is found in Roman law and the writings of Cicero. It is interesting that this sense of 'role' is still one of the meanings attached to the term 'person' in healthcare when the question of the ability of a brain-damaged patient or someone suffering from dementia to fulfil their role as a parent, partner, friend or colleague, is called into question.[6]

There is no universally accepted definition of the term 'person', either within or outside of the healthcare context. But when one surveys some of the types of ethical dilemmas encountered by healthcare professionals, one is struck by the diametrically opposed definitions of 'person' that underlie discussions.

ETHICAL DILEMMAS

In discussions on abortion, there are those who state that abortion is not morally wrong because the foetus is not a person, a position expressed bluntly by Peter Singer: 'Since no foetus is a person, no foetus has the same claim to life as a person.'[7] This perspective is shared by John Harris and Michael Tooley and others who, like Singer, advert to the characteristics of rationality and self-consciousness as the criteria for personhood.[8] On the other hand, there are those who state that the embryo or foetus is a person from the moment of conception and that, therefore, abortion is morally wrong in all circumstances. This is the position of the Roman Catholic Church which maintains that there is an intrinsic connection between the ontological dimension and the specific value of every human life: 'The human being is to be respected and treated as a person from the moment of conception; and therefore from that same moment his rights as a person must be recognized, among which in the first place is the inviolable right of every innocent human being to life.' And within that perspective, it proffers further clarification on the moral status of the embryo with the statement: 'The human embryo has, therefore, from the very beginning, the dignity proper to a person.'[9] However, the real issue that needs to be addressed lies underneath both of these positions, that is, how to explain the changes that occur so that individual identity, and hence moral status, are acquired?

In discussions about patients with dementia, there are also different views about what it means to be a 'person'. The idea of 'person-centred care' was developed in response to what was seen as the over-medicalization of dementia. This condition very often leads to such profound changes within the individual that some would argue that they have in effect become a different person, and that relationships with that person will change as a result.[10] One implication is that the person's previous values and any advance decisions they have made are less relevant, or even irrelevant, because the person who held those values no longer exists. A second implication is that close family members might feel they do not have any special duties or commitments to the person with dementia since that person is, in effect, a stranger. However, others have argued that this view bears no relation to how we operate in real life; for example, a granddaughter would continue to recognize her grandfather as her grandfather, even if he no longer recognizes her and his behaviour appears to have changed significantly.[11] There are also other implications to be considered. If being a 'person' confers moral status and if one takes the view that a human being is a person from conception to death, irrespective of his or her state of capacity or incapacity, then the question becomes one of *how* they are to be cared for. But if one defines a 'person' in terms of the characteristics of rationality and consciousness, then such patients would be considered 'non-persons'. That raises the question *whether* they are to be cared for at all. Or it asks, as the Ethox Centre did in its response to the Nuffield Council consultation paper on dementia: 'What is *non*-person-centred care?'[12]

On the care of severely brain-injured and comatose patients, there are those who hold that a patient in a persistent vegetative state is no longer a 'person' because he or she does not exhibit any of the features of personhood, i.e. self-consciousness, rationality or autonomy; therefore, involuntary euthanasia is permissible.[13] This view of personhood is shared by Jeff McMahan, for whom ending the life of such a patient is no more morally objectionable than killing a plant; harvesting the patient's organs for transplantation is therefore permissible. In differentiating 'person' from 'organism' he argues that someone in a persistent vegetative state has ceased to exist as a person and is now simply a living organism. From that he deduces that 'a living organism in which all possibility of consciousness has been lost has much the same moral status as a human corpse ... [and] it can be permissible to use a corpse's organs for transplantation'.[14] On the other hand there are those for whom euthanasia is ethically impermissible on the grounds that there is no real distinction between the organism and the person. Thus the locus of dignity and worth is not a characteristic such as rationality or consciousness that may or may not be present, but is rather an ineliminable feature of the patient's humanity.[15]

TWO DEFINITIONS OF 'PERSON'

Two opposing definitions of 'person' underlie discussion in the three types of situations presented above. One derives from the philosophy of John Locke, the other from the philosophical anthropology of classical thinkers in the tradition of Thomas Aquinas. However, as Wittgenstein noted, 'one is often bewitched by a word',[16] so that one's thinking goes astray philosophically. What is common to many people who base their arguments on the word 'person' derived from the thinking of Locke and Aquinas is its 'bewitching' effect, an enchantment with a particular meaning that distracts from the real problem underneath the word. Wittgenstein referred to this power of language to cloud one's cognitive processes as 'the bewitchment of our intelligence by means of language'.[17]

For Locke, 'person' is a designation for 'a thinking intelligent being, that has reason and reflection, and can consider itself as itself, the same thinking thing, in different times and places; which it does only by that consciousness which is inseparable from thinking, and as it seems to me, essential to it; it being impossible for any one to perceive without perceiving that he does perceive'.[18] Thus Locke grounds personal identity in consciousness: 'For since consciousness always accompanies thinking, and it is that which makes everyone to be what he calls *self*, and thereby distinguishes himself from all other thinking things, in this alone consists *personal identity*, i.e. the sameness of a rational being.'[19] The logical implications of this definition of 'person' are that (i) being a human being is no longer a necessary condition for being a 'person'; and (ii) having the ability to reflect on oneself, to be conscious of oneself as a self and to show some outward signs of rationality, constitute the sufficient condition for being a 'person'. It has even been suggested that it may become possible for creatures who were not formerly considered as 'persons', such as animals that display signs of 'rational behaviour' and a 'sense of self', to be designated 'persons'.[20] It also means that anyone who does not manifest conscious self-reflection is relegated to the status of non-person.

On the other side of the divide are those for whom the meaning of the word 'person', deriving from the Thomistic tradition, is an individual substance of a rational nature, composed of body and soul, which retains its psycho–physical unity from conception to death.[21] St Thomas Aquinas built on the first philosophical definition of 'person', which was formulated by the Roman philosopher Boethius in the early sixth century AD, using

Aristotelian philosophical concepts in his attempt to explain the Christian Trinitarian God as being of one nature, with three distinct persons. Within that theological context, Boethius defined a person as *naturae rationabilis individua substantia*, i.e. 'an individual substance of a rational nature'.[22] Aquinas extended Boethius' definition of 'person' from the theological context to the anthropological. Observing that human beings are the only entities among all the different kinds of things that exist which are capable of reflective choice and control over their own actions, Aquinas concludes that these individuals of a rational nature have a special name, that is, 'person': 'Therefore also the individuals of the rational nature have a special name even among other substances, and this name is *person*.'[23] Aquinas was also deeply influenced by Aristotle's explanation of the world as manifesting an order and teleology that are accessible to human reason. He appropriated Aristotle's hylomorphism or form–matter theory to explain how human beings, as persons, are a unity of body and soul; the rational soul is the 'form' of the body, with which it constitutes a single substance.[24] In that way he avoided, as did Aristotle, a dualist conception of human beings. This enabled Aquinas to ground one's identity as an individual person in one's organic existence, one's bodyliness.[25]

Ethical debates within healthcare are frequently bewitched by the word 'person', which conceals the real problem that needs clarification and resolution; that is, the problem of retaining identity through change. Revealing the cause of the bewitchment is one way to finding one's bearings again, so that one can resolve the problem. But it is doubtful whether anyone would acknowledge being bewitched by the power of a word. People are far more likely to say that they were convinced of the validity of an argument on purely rational grounds, rather than admit that the meaning assigned to the word 'person' has a power of its own. However when one party in a discussion bases their arguments about the provision of care on a specific meaning attached to the word 'person' that conflicts with the meaning upon which the other party in the discussion has based their arguments, then the discussions become arguments about the criteria for personhood; debate becomes deadlocked; people talk past each other and the discourse has no foundation upon which any agreement can be reached because there is no consensus about the meaning of the key term 'person'. While all of this is going on, the real issue that merits exploring is unnoticed: that is, the problem of change and identity. This is the problem that lies at the heart of the ethical dilemmas that present in pregnancy, in dementia, and at the end of life. Thus a coherent explanation for how something or someone can change is a necessary element in resolving ethical dilemmas that arise in cases where the identity of the individual, as well as her moral status, is questioned. Of particular assistance in this task are Aristotle's metaphysical insights, which provide valuable intellectual instruments for explaining the phenomenon of change which impacts on patient care.

THE PROBLEM OF CHANGE

All areas of life are concerned with change. A seed grows into a flower; a baby opens its eyes and becomes aware of the objects around it; a student becomes a doctor; a sedentary individual becomes an athlete. Doctors deal with profound change: the coming into existence of a new human life; the change from health to sickness and sickness to health, and the change from life to death. Patients are at the heart of those changes. It is patients who are considered to merit, or not, the designation 'person' that indicates their moral status and how they are to be treated. So unless a coherent explanation for change is given, i.e. for how someone can become what they were not, the word 'person' cannot be evaluated either as a designation for human beings or as a designation for moral status. However it is one thing to describe instances of change in the world; it is quite another to give a philosophical explanation for change. How does something change and yet remain the same thing? Does something that undergoes radical change still exist?

Aristotle's solution to the problem of change is the pair of concepts 'act' and 'potency',[26] also referred to as actuality and potentiality. These are not separate from each other but depend on one another for coherence. They serve to mark the difference between, for example, a builder who is slapping mortar on bricks, and one who is not doing so but retains the skills required to do so; that is, between something which is actually so-and-so and something which is potentially so-and-so. It is one thing to have a capacity, another to exercise it. Or to put it another way, it is one thing to possess potential; it is another thing to actualize it.

Through this distinction between actuality and potentiality, Aristotle found a way to explain change as the actualization of potential, in so far as it is potential.[27] In other words, change is the passing of something from potentiality to actuality, in so far as the potentiality inheres in the thing in the first place. Using these Aristotelian concepts, one can explain how change occurs: A becomes B, not insofar as it is A, nor in so far as it is not B, but in so far as it has a potentiality for B.

In light of Aristotle's doctrine (substance/accidents, act/potency), we can make sense of the twofold types of change. The first type of change is such that something changes, yet retains its identity. For example, cold water becomes hot; a green tomato ripens and turns red; a woman puts on ten kilos in weight; an acorn becomes an oak tree. The beginning- and end-points of the change are delineated by act and potency. Thus water is actually cold, but potentially hot; the tomato is actually green, but potentially red; the woman is actually light, but potentially heavy; an actual acorn is potentially an oak-tree. The second type of change involves generation and destruction, for example when a new life is generated or when something or someone dies. For example, an actual sperm and ovum together are potentially a zygote; an actual living human being is potentially ashes and dust.

Actuality precedes potentiality in all instances of change, according to Aristotle. When something comes-to-be, i.e. changes, we do not mean that an actual entity becomes an actual entity: an oak tree does not become an oak tree. Nor do we mean that a non-entity becomes an entity, since something cannot come forth from nothing. This is of immense significance in explaining the changes confronted in healthcare, where both types of change are present.

The arguments that occur in healthcare regarding the moral status of patients, whether they are persons or fulfil the conditions for personhood, seem to be ethical disagreements about the type of care that is appropriate in specific situations. But in many instances they are grounded on a lack of conceptual clarity regarding the kind of change that affects human beings. The problem of identity concerns what someone is, and whether someone remains 'the same', *idem*, throughout the changes he or she undergoes. The ethical dilemmas outlined earlier are examples of both types of change identified by Aristotle.

In the question of abortion, the moral status of the embryo must be considered in the context of accidental change, i.e. a change of attributes occurring at the early developmental stages of human life. Applying the concepts of act and potency one can say that an actual embryo with the potential for further development exists, manifesting the nature of the species to which it belongs, which in this case is the species *Homo*. Thus the embryo is fully human though not fully developed. The various stages of development are reflected in the terms we use to describe them: embryo, foetus, baby, child, adolescent, young woman, middle-aged woman, old woman. It is sometimes argued that an embryo lacks moral status because it is not a person, and therefore not entitled to the kind of rights an adult human being is entitled to. However if the term 'person' is a designation for human beings who are individual substances of a rational nature, then an embryo merits the moral status and protections that are guaranteed by personhood at every stage of development. When we examine change using Aristotle's concepts of act and potency, we can say that no-one is fully developed; neither an embryo, child, adolescent nor adult. In each case, there is potentiality for further development, whether of a physical, intellectual, emotional, moral, aesthetic or spiritual kind. They differ in the kind and degree of their development, while having in common the potentiality to develop.

Discussions on dementia suggest that the changes in the patient are sometimes so profound that the question of the moral status of that individual is raised, on the grounds that he or she has suffered a loss of identity and is no longer the same person as before. Aristotle's analysis of change is helpful here too. While the individual has certainly undergone profound changes, with the loss of certain capacities, such as motor ability or cognitive and communication skills, nevertheless the same individual subsists throughout the changes. Individual identity will be relinquished only at death, when no further actualization of potentiality is possible in a material body. The fact that the identity persists, albeit in an individual who is profoundly changed because of a diminution of specific capacities, the individual's moral status requires that his or her rights be respected and protected.

Ethical dilemmas concerning severely brain-injured and comatose patients can also be resolved using the Aristotelian concepts of act and potency. However every healthcare situation is unique; there is no 'one size fits all' solution. In certain cases, *some* capacities of the patient have been destroyed through illness, but the individual retains his or her identity since there is the potentiality for further change, even if that is simply the change from life to death. In other cases, the changes wrought by illness are substantial, and specifically involve the destruction of an actual dynamic unity. In the latter case, any treatment decision would necessarily be one that prolonged life artificially with the aid of bio-technology.

Aristotle's explanation of change using the concepts of act and potency allows us to explain how identity is retained such that we may act appropriately towards someone who has undergone profound change. This raises the question of the adequacy of Locke's and Aquinas' definitions of 'person' in light of the reality of change, and whether one is more fitting than the other as a criterion of moral status in healthcare.

'PERSON' AS A DESIGNATION FOR MORAL STATUS

There are many perspectives on the usefulness of the designation of 'person' as the locus of moral status. Mary Warnock, for example, maintains that the term 'person' is a red herring in healthcare discussions since there are difficulties surrounding its precise meaning; using it has led people astray into a kind of discourse that was either incoherent or circular. She suggests that 'person' is a forensic term: it is essentially a matter for society to decide who is a bearer of rights. She concludes that 'deciding who has rights is the very same decision as deciding who is to count as a person. It is a matter for lawyers.'[28] This perspective is shared by groups in the United States who also advocate that the term 'person' be fixed by legislation, though probably not for the same reasons as Mary Warnock. For example, a proposed law in Colorado that would grant the status of 'persons' to fertilized ova is hugely contentious, given its implications for the claim that a woman has the right to terminate her pregnancy.[29]

The Nuffield Council on Bioethics, in its consultation paper *Dementia: Ethical Issues*, opted for 'person-centred care' as the principle for moral status and, in so doing, appeared to challenge the notion of personhood as used by John Locke, John Harris and Peter Singer.[30] In its response to the consultation paper, the Ethox Centre agreed with that designation though argued that there should be no high bar for personhood.[31]

Beauchamp and Childress avoided the language of 'person', 'personhood' and 'respect for persons' in their *Principles of Biomedical Ethics*, on the grounds that the terminology was of little use in resolving ethical dilemmas in healthcare. Instead they examined other possible bases as a locus for moral status: human properties, cognitive properties, moral agency, sentience and relationships.[32] But although they tried to avoid a controversial criterion, i.e. person, by which ethical decisions and actions might be weighed and measured, they have re-introduced it through theories of moral status built on characteristics and properties that are recognisably human properties, and arguably personal properties.

However, both Locke and Aquinas considered the designation 'person' to be necessary in order to denote something distinctive about human beings. Any account of changes that impacted on the identity of human beings would necessarily be regarded by them as impacting on 'personal identity', which was consciousness for Locke, and integrity of body and soul for Aquinas.

The concept of person deriving from Aquinas confers equal moral status on each and every human being, at whatever stage of development. Practically it means that someone who is pregnant through rape is prohibited from seeking an abortion even at the earliest stages of pregnancy because the embryo has the same moral status, and hence the moral rights, of an adult human being. Even a zygote has moral status. In this regard, Mary Warnock commented that it was doubtful whether many people, despite the instructions from the Vatican, really believed that the death of a two- or four-cell zygote was comparable to the death of a child who has been born.[33] When the concept of person deriving from Aquinas is applied to situations such as this, and subjected to scrutiny as Mary Warnock has done, it appears to be both unreasonable and unworkable. However, one could also argue that the consistent application of the designation 'person' to human life at every stage was a paradigm for equality unrivalled anywhere.

A criticism levelled at those who base their understanding of 'person' on the Thomistic approach is that it is based upon an outdated biology. Aquinas' knowledge of biology and embryology was indeed largely based on Aristotle's empirical studies, so he was unaware of the role of the male and female gametes in human generation. He believed that it resulted from the active, formative influence of male semen on essentially passive and inanimate female menstrual blood; he therefore supposed that it must naturally take some time (about forty to sixty days from conception) for the process of generation to yield a body sufficiently organized to receive and be organized anew by a rational soul. However, John Finnis argues that, had Aquinas known of the extremely elaborate and specifically organized structure of the sperm and the ovum, their chromosomal complementarity, and the self-directed growth and development of the embryo or embryos from the moment of insemination of the ovum, he would have concluded that the specifically human, rational soul, and therefore personhood, was present from that moment. Thus his definition of person as an individual substance of a rational nature would apply from the completion of fertilization until natural death.[34] This perspective is shared by the Roman Catholic Church, which is hugely influenced by Aquinas' concept of 'person' and 'personhood'. Within this perspective, human beings are regarded as persons from conception to death. Therefore abortion is regarded as morally impermissible in all circumstances. Moreover the ethical permissibility of many bio-technologies operating at the origin of life is also questioned.

Locke's understanding of 'person' is likewise contentious as a criterion for moral status. Since a 'person' has the ability to consciously reflect on himself, it would follow that whole categories of human beings must be regarded as non-persons – embryos, infants, comatose patients – and their moral status denied. For those who adhere to Locke's meaning of 'person', many healthcare decisions are unproblematic, e.g. abortion, since the foetus does not qualify as 'person'; or euthanasia in the case of a neurologically disabled patient, since he/she does not qualify as a 'person'.

Wittgenstein noted that the term 'language-*game*' brought into prominence the fact that the speaking of language is part of an activity, or of a form of life.[35] Does this mean that the use of 'person' in discussions is just a red herring, as Mary Warnock argued, or utterly useless, as Beauchamp and Childress suggested? Does it mean that all we can expect in ethical debates in healthcare is an endless cycle of disagreement? Or is there a way forward, towards recognition of the concept 'person' as a legitimate designation for the moral status of human beings? If so, what is it?

At this point, a question raised by Wittgenstein is worth considering: 'Do I want to say, then, that certainty resides in the nature of the language-game?'[36] Certainty is a form of judgment, grounded in an affirmation of what is, or is not, the case in reality. The word 'person' is an attempt to designate something that is judged to be the case about real human beings, about real human life. A judgment on the validity of the Lockean or Thomistic understanding of person requires that each be evaluated on whether it takes account of the reality of lived human experience, with its range of changes from beginning to end of the life cycle, since judgment is grounded in reality. That entails a willingness to engage in metaphysical enquiry, something that sits uneasily with doctors, whose *modus operandi* is that of the scientific world.

CONCLUSION

Healthcare is concerned with human beings, whose bodily constitution can be explained biologically and chemically. However, that does not explain the special kind of vitality that distinguishes human beings from other creatures. In the words of Jerome Lejeune:

This idea that spirit animates matter is, in a way, inscribed in our very language. We use the same word for an idea that comes to mind and for a new being coming into existence. In both cases, we speak of conception. This is not a poverty of our vocabulary but implicit recognition, if I may put it so, that at the very beginning, soul and body, spirit and matter, are so interlocked that it is impossible to speak of one without the other. And language never has. This leads us to consider the biologist's first responsibility: to explain to his contemporaries that molecular biology wholly excludes Cartesian Dualism according to which there is spirit on one side and body on the other. Living matter does not exist; there is only animated body, but animated by the nature of man.[37]

The concept of 'person', in the sense of an individual substance of a rational nature composed of body and soul which retains its psycho–physical unity from conception to death, is an attempt to formulate the unique vitality of members of the human species. 'Personhood' is made manifest in the immense range of symbolic forms created throughout the course of history which reveal a tendency in human beings to transcend themselves and reach towards the very ground of existence itself. This is expressed in various ways: ritually in sites like Newgrange; artistically in paintings like Michelangelo's *Last Judgment*; musically in Palestrina's *Sicut Cervus*; poetically in Milton's *Paradise Lost*; philosophically in Edith Stein's *Finite and Eternal Being*; in literature in Evelyn Waugh's *Brideshead Revisited*; and cinematically in Tarkovsky's *Andrei Rublev*. The kind of vitality that is personal is incarnate in human beings. It is the source of the dignity and value of each member of the human species. All human beings are persons from the moment they come into existence, whether they are able-bodied or physically, intellectually or neurologically impaired. The 'good doctor' is one who recognizes and respects the unique person she or he encounters in health care.

ENDNOTES

1 G.E.R. Lloyd (ed.), *Hippocratic Writings* (Harmondsworth: Penguin Books, 1978). The Greek text: διαιτήμασί τε χρήσομαι ἐπ' ὠφελείῃ καμνόντων κατὰ δύναμιν καὶ κρίσιν ἐμήν, ἐπὶ δηλήσει δὲ καὶ ἀδικίῃ εἴρξειν. W.H.S. Jones translates: 'I will use treatment to help the sick according to my ability and judgment, but never with a view to injury and wrong-doing.' *The Doctor's Oath* (Cambridge: Cambridge University Press, 1924).

2   Tom L. Beauchamp and James F. Childress, *Principles of Biomedical Ethics* (New York and Oxford: Oxford University Press, 2013), p. 64.

3   Mary Warnock, *An Intelligent Person's Guide to Ethics* (London: Duckworth, 1998), p. 54.

4   Beauchamp and Childress, *Principles of Biomedical Ethics*, pp. 2–5.

5   John Stuart Mill, *Utilitarianism* and *On Liberty* (Oxford: Blackwell, 2003), pp. 94–5.

6   For further information see Hans Urs von Balthasar, 'On the Concept of Person', *Communio* 13 (1986); H.D. Amos and A.G.P. Lang, *The Greeks* (London: Duckworth, 2003), p. 133; Cicero, *On Duties* (Cambridge: Cambridge University Press, 2011), pp. 100–21.

7   Peter Singer, *Practical Ethics* (Cambridge: Cambridge University Press, 1993), p. 151.

8   Ibid., p. 87; John Harris, *The Value of Life* (London: Routledge, 1985), p. 15; M. Tooley, 'Personhood', in H Kuhse and P Singer (eds), *A Companion to Bioethics* (Oxford: Wiley-Blackwell, 2012), pp. 137–8.

9   Congregation for the Doctrine of the Faith, *Instruction* Dignitas Personae. *On Certain Bioethical Questions* (Vatican: Libreria Editrice, 2008), pp. 6–7.

10   See Rebecca Dresser, 'Dworkin on Dementia: Elegant Theory, Questionable Policy', *The Hastings Center Report* 22/6 (1995), pp. 32–8.

11   Nuffield Council on Bioethics, *Consultation Paper on Dementia: Ethical Issues* (2008) (http://www.nuffieldbioethics.org) (Downloaded 15 March 2019).

12   The Ethox Centre, 'Response to the consultation by the Nuffield Council on Bioethics on Dementia: Ethical Issues', (2008), p. 22 (http://www.nuffieldbioethics.org) (Downloaded 15 March 2019).

13   Singer, *Practical Ethics*, pp. 191–2.

14   J. McMahan, 'Death, Brain Death and Persistent Vegetative State', in Kuhse and Singer, *A Companion to Bioethics*, pp. 286–98.

15   L. Gormally, 'Euthanasia and Assisted Suicide: Seven Reasons Why They Should Not Be Legalised' (London: Anscombe Bioethics Centre, 1997) (http://www.bioethics.org.uk) (Consulted 15 March 2019).

16   Ludwig Wittgenstein, *On Certainty* (Oxford: Basil Blackwell, 1979), p. 57.

17   Ludwig Wittgenstein, *Philosophical Investigations*, p. 47.

18   John Locke, *An Essay Concerning Human Understanding* (Oxford: Clarendon, 1969), p. 188.

19   Ibid.

20   Alan Kearns, *The Concept of Person in a World Mediated by Meaning and Constituted by Significance* (Dartford: Pneuma Springs, 2007), p. 47.

21   Thomas Aquinas, *ST* I, qq. 29, 75, 76.

22   Boethius, *The Theological Tractates*, trans. H.E. Stewart, E.K. Rand, S.J. Tester (Cambridge, MA: Harvard University Press, 1990), pp. 84–5.

23   Thomas Aquinas, *Summa Theologiae* I, 29, 1.

24   Aquinas, *ST* I, qq. 75–6.

25   John Finnis, '"The Thing I Am": Personal Identity in Aquinas and Shakespeare', *Social Philosophy and Policy*, 22 (2005), pp. 250–82.

26   Aristotle, *Metaphysics* 9, 1, 1049b–1052a.

27 Aristotle, *Physics* 3, 1, 201a10–11.

28 Warnock, *An Intelligent Person's Guide to Ethics*, p. 54

29 Colorado Definition of 'Personhood' Initiative, Amendment 67 (2014) (https://ballotpedia.org) (Accessed 15 March 2019).

30 The Nuffield Council for Bioethics, Consultation paper on *Dementia: Ethical Issues* (2008).

31 The Ethox Centre response to the Nuffield Council consultation paper, *Dementia: Ethical Issues* (2008).

32 Beauchamp and Childress, *Principles of Biomedical Ethics*, pp. 69–70.

33 Warnock, *Dishonest to God* (London: Continuum, 2010) pp. 15, 38.

34 Finnis, 'The Thing I Am', p. 22.

35 Wittgenstein, *Philosophical Investigations*, p. 11.

36 Wittgenstein, *On Certainty*, p. 59.

37 Jerome Lejeune, 'Is There a Natural Morality?', *Anthropotes* 5 (1989) 269–77.

ETHICS WITHOUT TRANSCENDENCE

PHILIP PETTIT

A signature theme in Patrick Masterson's philosophical thinking is that our experience of value, in particular moral value, testifies to the presence of something transcendent to natural evolution in human lives and relationships. I was introduced to that theme nearly fifty years ago when I joined University College Dublin as a young assistant lecturer and was fortunate enough to become a colleague and friend of Paddy's.

The theme still stands near the centre of his vision of humanity and its place in the wider universe, as his recent books testify. His friends know that Paddy views life in full recognition of its tragedies, personal and global, but with a lively, deeply affectionate sense of the comic side to human nature and pretension. Yet for all the sorrows and laughs that contour our human lives, the core message of his writings is that there is a reality beyond those experiences that puts them in illuminating, emancipating perspective. This reality appears in the ciphers, as he calls them, of a God on whom we are radically dependent: in the subjectively registered intimations of an objective, transcendent reality.

The experience of value is prominent among the intimations of divinity that Paddy recognizes. This consists in our ethical sense of what is good and right, decent and just, admirable and noble. It yields ideals that compete with our desires and interests, and that summon us, effectively or ineffectively, to be faithful to their demands. It breaks, as if from without, into our desire-bound, interest-bound existence.

In this essay, I gesture at a rival picture of where our experience of the good and the right originates. I think that Paddy is certainly correct to hold that our experience of value competes with our experience of the attractive, representing a call from beyond the drumbeat of our ordinary desires. But that call, so I hold, is intelligible in wholly naturalistic, humanistic terms; it does not testify in itself to a transcendent reality.

In arguing for this point of view I return to a debate with Paddy, and with our joint friend and erstwhile colleague, Denys Turner, that I recall with keen, nostalgic feeling from Dublin of the late 1960s and early 1970s. As I remember our discussions, I can almost get the whiff of the sawdust and Smithwicks that often provided the ambience for our extended *symposium*: etymologically, and literally, our drinking together.

The essay is in three progressively longer sections. First, I set out some assumptions that are background to the debate, arguing that ethical concepts can be organized around the concepts of the desirable and the responsible and that the experience of value should be equated with the sense of the desirable. Next, I elaborate on an assumption that is common ground between Paddy and myself: that the desirable that we identify in the experience of value really does represent a break with our ordinary desires and our ordinary sense of the attractive. And then in the final section, I sketch a story as to how the notion of the desirable may have come to be available to early humans, and remains available to us, without invoking the impact of a transcendent reality.[1]

I. BACKGROUND: THE RANGE OF ETHICAL CONCEPTS

Before looking at where Paddy Masterson and I agree and disagree, it may be useful to put some basic points in place on the nature of ethics or morality. These will help to identify more precisely the experience of value at issue in our debate. While the points to be made may not secure agreement on all sides, they provide us with common, unambiguous terms of reference and they do not tilt the debate in any particular direction.

There are many ethical concepts that we draw on in everyday usage. These include concepts of the desirable and undesirable, the good and the bad, the right and the wrong; of the permissible, obligatory and forbidden; of responsibility and liability; of rights and deserts; of responses like respect, commendation and reprobation; and of the virtue and the vice that we ascribe to one another, even perhaps to ourselves.

But for all the variety displayed by ethical concepts, they can be organized readily into a workable shape. One way of arranging them is to take the ideas of the desirable and the responsible as basic, together with the notion of 'ought' that they presuppose. Something is desirable if it ought to be desired, and someone is responsible if they ought to be held responsible for living up to the standards of the desirable. Organizing ethical concepts around these core ideals involves some regimentation of ordinary, context-sensitive usage but that is a price worth paying for the clarity it yields.

Taking this approach, the good and related terms are definable in terms of the desirable. The right is definable as that which is more desirable than given alternatives and not so demanding – not so 'supererogatory' – that there is little point in holding someone responsible for failing to choose it. And the permissible, obligatory and forbidden are interpretable in any context by reference to presumptively desirable norms or rules. The forbidden is that which those norms rule out, the obligatory that which they rule in and the merely permissible that which they neither rule out nor rule in.

Rights and deserts are definable also in terms of desirable rules. You have a right to what those rules require others to give you – whether or not the rules are actually established in law or custom – and you deserve any treatment that they support or allow. Respect is appropriate with anyone who is generally cognizant of desirability and fit to be held responsible for pursuing the desirable. Commendation is the response we give to a suitably responsible agent when they act desirably, censure the response we give when they act undesirably. And virtue is the habit of robustly pursuing the desirable, vice the absence of such a habit.[2]

When Paddy Masterson looks on the experience of value as a potential interface with a transcendent reality, I shall take it that his focus is on the notion of the desirable. He assumes that in responding to what we judge to be desirable we often reach beyond the promptings of actual desire – our sense of the attractive – to a sense of what we ought to desire. And he holds that the best explanation of this capacity is that we confront demands that break in on us from without, sourced in a transcendent, divine reality.

II. COMMON GROUND: ETHICS OUTFLANKS DESIRE

There are some who would deny that becoming moral, whether as individuals or as a species, involves breaking free in this way from the grip of the desires that happen to form in us. But I agree with Paddy that becoming moral does involve outflanking the regime of desire, as we might express the idea. This view is supported by three assumptions that we all endorse even in unreflective forms of moral thinking.

THREE ASSUMPTIONS

The first assumption is that whether something is desirable is a function of the other properties or features that it displays and that in the normal run of things, the same is true of the desired or the attractive. Is it desirable for me to speak candidly in a given situation? That depends on the general features of that situation, of the audience present there, and my relation to each; I naturally treat the desirability of any option or prospect as grounded in such independent properties. Do I desire to speak candidly in the situation: do I find that option attractive? If I do, that will also depend on independent features that make the option or prospect appealing; the attraction of the option or prospect, like its desirability, is a function of the properties – the desiderata or attractors – that I identify in the scenario. Thus, whether or not I desire to speak candidly will depend on whether the option or prospect attracts me under this or that aspect: whether the candour envisaged is appealing, for example, or whether it actually makes me flinch and withdraw.

But while the desirable and the attractive are both grounded in independent features of any scenario, the second assumption holds that nevertheless they may come apart from one another. What I judge to be desirable – say, that I speak candidly – may not be what I happen to find attractive: what I turn out to desire. I may flinch at the prospect of embarrassment that candid speech is likely to cause me, for example, and fail to muster a desire that answers to my judgment of desirability. This is the merest common sense, recording an everyday human experience. The spirit of judgment is willing, the flesh of desire is weak.

The third assumption that is built into our common sense of the desirable and the attractive is that when they come apart, as the second assumption holds that they may do, it would be a sort of failure on my part not to do what is desirable. It would represent a form of *akrasia* or weakness of will. The idea is that the desirable makes a higher call on me than the appeal of desire and that a failure to heed that call constitutes a failure, period. In metaphors rehearsed by Paul Ricoeur,[3] it means that I have fallen away from the heights, gone astray on my path through life, lost my innocence or purity of heart.

314 • CIPHERS OF TRANSCENDENCE

If we endorse these three assumptions, then we are more or less bound to think that in becoming moral, whether as individuals or as a species, we break away from the rule of desire. This point is often associated with Kantians, since they depict morality as an enterprise sourced in putting desires at a distance and acting on them only in the event of finding that there are good reasons to do so. But we do not have to adopt the Kantian perspective in order to support the claim. The three assumptions listed, which are embedded in common sense, are already enough to provide it with support.

CHALLENGE FROM SPONTANEOUS ALTRUISM

The claim that ethics or morality outflanks desire may seem to conflict with the thesis that we human agents do not need morality to be prompted to behave in a moral fashion: that in general, we are naturally or spontaneously disposed to do so. In the Western philosophical tradition, amoral subjects were always taken to be not just agents who act spontaneously on their desires, but agents whose desires are in general selfish or self-regarding: they are desires for the person's own welfare or for the welfare of their kith and kin. But what should we say about the claim, **on the one side**, that we are like amoral subjects in acting always and only as our desires prompt us to act but, **on the other**, that we are like moral subjects in being led by our desires to act generally in an altruistic or other-regarding manner?

That we human beings are of this spontaneously altruistic kind receives some support from recent work in evolutionary theory. This theory has begun to support the idea that early humans broke away from other apes in developing more or less altruistic desires and that they did this without yet having developed any ethical concepts and, in particular, without yet having a conception of the desirable. The question is whether, if we admit such a claim, we should take our ancestors at this early stage to have already broken into ethical space.

We have long known from evolutionary theory, and from the natural history of many species, that kin selection can lead siblings to be more protective of one another than of strangers and that tit-for-tat reciprocity can even lead strangers to be reliably cooperative in delivering benefits in return for benefits – and in imposing costs in return for costs.[4] But Michael Tomasello has recently gone well beyond such claims. He maintains that in the period between about 400 thousand and 150 thousand years ago early humans are likely to have developed, not just a feeling for kin and a good eye for tit-for-tat benefits, but also the 'motivation ... to help anyone with certain characteristics or within a certain context'.[5]

Tomasello's claim raises an obvious question. What would have motivated our ancestors to help others in this way? What particular individuals would they have been prompted to aid? His answer is: those individuals they would have needed to collaborate with in foraging, given that the changed ecological conditions in this period left them with no alternative but to forage together. And why would they have become motivated to help those others spontaneously – and to carry over this disposition to a range of independent activities – rather than acting on the perception that helping was to their selfish advantage? The answer is: because their interdependence was such that from the point of view of Mother Nature this was good strategy; it would have been more hazardous to let mutual helpfulness appear only when our ancestors were sharp enough to recognize that this was in their individual interests.

Tomasello's claim that this development took place in the early emergence of *Homo sapiens sapiens* is grounded in child psychology and in the differences it reveals between our species and that of other apes. His theory is built on an accumulating body of data to the effect that, unlike chimpanzees, children between the ages of one and three are 'highly motivated', indeed 'internally motivated', 'to help others, with no need for external incentives' and that this motivation is 'mediated by a sympathetic concern for the plight of others'.[6] The idea is that these dispositions appear too early in children, and are too universally in evidence, to be the result of acculturation; and that the best explanation of their presence is that they were favoured by natural selection in a period when our ancestors had to forage together or die alone.

SPONTANEOUS ALTRUISM IS NOT MORALITY

Let us assume that early humans were as mutually helpful as this line of thought suggests. Should we think that even without access to ethical concepts – even without a sense of the desirable – they were already ethical subjects? Our three assumptions suggest not. Or at least they suggest this, on the assumption that there would have been many situations where altruism would have been outweighed by other desires, so that what our early ancestors were inclined to do did not coincide with the moral option.

There would surely have been many situations like that: situations, for example, where free riding on another would have been so attractive as to silence altruistic desire. And without access to the notion of the morally desirable, our forebears would have been in no position to criticize their own choice or to find ground for indicting or regulating the free-riding temptation.

Spontaneously cooperative agents of the kind envisaged act in pursuit of ends that they find attractive – ends that answer to their desires – but happen to be so constituted that what they find attractive often involves, not just their own welfare, but also the welfare of others. Morally cooperative agents act in pursuit of goals they judge to be desirable, whether or not they find the goals spontaneously attractive. The two psychologies are fundamentally different in character.

While many evolutionary theorists have equated altruism with morality, these sorts of considerations have persuaded others to disagree, including Tomasello himself. [7] But the best case against the equation is probably available from moral phenomenology. The experience of value, the exposure to the claims of the desirable, is phenomenologically very different from the experience of attraction – even altruistic attraction – to this or that course of action.

Agents who act for the satisfaction of their desires, guided by their beliefs about the opportunities and obstacles in their way, answer to a familiar decision–theoretic picture that is widely endorsed in economic and social science. In virtue of their desires, various considerations registered in belief motivate them to action: say, to take examples that early humans might have confronted, that that tree is in fruit, that that hunting group needs more members, that the child of another is in danger of falling in the river. And motivated by such considerations, they act as their beliefs then make it sensible to act: they grab a stick to knock down the fruit, they communicate a willingness to join the hunt, they call out a warning to the child or they make an effort to reach it.

When creatures of this kind act for the welfare of others, as in an attempt to save another's child, there is no reason to think of such action as distinctively moral. If it succeeds we may expect success to be satisfying in the way in which it is satisfying to fulfil any desire. And if it fails, we may expect failure to be frustrating in the same way that the failure to realize any desire is frustrating. As it may be frustrating not to be able to knock down the fruit, so it will be frustrating in the same way if the hunting group is too far off to be able to join it, or the child falls to its death before you can reach it.

But this sort of frustration at not being able to fulfil a desire, even the desire to help others, is very different from the response we associate with a failure to do what seems desirable. Such a failure will elicit a sense of regret, not just frustration, if you were clearly unable to act appropriately. And if you believe you were able to act in that way but failed because of letting your actual desires get in the way of doing what was desirable, the failure will elicit censure of yourself: the feeling, as we describe it, of guilt. Moreover, if others come to believe this of you, then they in turn will be disposed to censure you, regarding you with feelings of resentment or indignation.

Feelings like those of regret and guilt, resentment and indignation, would have had no natural place amongst the sorts of naturally helpful creatures we are imagining. In Amartya Sen's phrasing[8] those creatures must have experienced sympathy for one another's welfare, being disposed to aim at making things better for others in the way in which they were disposed to make things better for themselves. But sympathy is not morality, as Sen himself argues. No matter how much sympathy we ascribe to them, we have no reason to think they would have thought in terms of the desirable, let alone of their responsibility for pursuing the desirable. And equally we have no reason to hold that they would have developed corresponding expectations of themselves and one another and displayed suitable responses to the satisfaction or frustration of those expectations.

III. DIVERGING DIRECTIONS

Paddy Masterson and I agree that acting out of a concern for the desirable does not amount to having suitable desires – in effect, altruistic desires – and then acting in pursuit of what those desires represent as attractive outcomes. We hold that human beings achieve moral status only if they can break free of the control exercised by the desires, egoistic or altruistic, that happen to form within them: only if they cease, in an age-old image, to be slaves of their passions.[9]

The shared claim, in other terms, is that moral agents march to a different tune from agents who have and are moved by spontaneous altruism. But where Paddy thinks that the moral tune can gain a hold on us only because of what it echoes from beyond mundane horizons, I think that its grip on us has roots in the earthy soil of our own social nature.

In this relatively longer section I say a little by way of supporting that point of view. I think that it is our nature as linguistic animals, creatures of the word, that explains how we gain a capacity to identify the desirable; to stand back from what we actually desire; and, where appropriate, to silence our desires in order to serve the cause of the desirable. Returning to early humans, my argument is that as they became capable of using natural language, they would have been inevitably led to make speech acts like avowals and pledges; and that such speech acts would have put them in a position where a sense of the desirable became inescapable.

REPORTING ON OUR WORLD AND ATTITUDES

In exploring this thought let us assume that you and I live in the world of early humans, that we have gained access to natural language, and that we use our words for the most basic purpose of exchanging or trading information – or at least what we take and present as information – about our surroundings. I tell you where the fresh fruit is to be found and you in return tell me where the fish are gathering in the river.

In communicating such would-be information, we provide great benefits for one another if we speak truly and we impose great costs if we fail to do so. But we can each hope to be able to rely on the reports of others only if we ourselves are disposed to prove reliable. Thus, we each have a powerful motive to communicate the truth, or make our best efforts to communicate the truth, especially if we are operating within a small community where the reputation for not being a reliable reporter would put us in danger of being ostracized by others and left to cope on our own.

The desire to prove reliable to one another, and establish a reputation for reliability, is likely to establish a pattern of more or less reliable truth-telling among us. But despite this general pattern you or I may sometimes fail to tell the truth without suffering retaliation or ostracism by others. This will be so when my failure to tell the truth can be explained in a way that shows that nevertheless I was disposed to be reliable: I took care about determining what was the case before I spoke and I reported things to be as they showed up in that exercise. You and others will not want to ostracize me when such an explanation – such an excuse, as we may call it – is available and salient, since that would be to lose out on the benefits you stand to gain from relying on me on future occasions.

There are many excuses of a practical kind that I might offer in the case of not speaking the truth: I may have been under threat of punishment by a third party for telling you the truth, or I may have been subject to some debilitating lapse of memory. But there are two salient excuses of an epistemic kind that I would happily invoke if they were plausible. One is that while I did my best to learn how things were before I made the report, I was misled by the evidence: the fruit looked to be ripe in the dawn sunlight. And another is that while the fruit was there to be picked at the time I saw it, it had been taken by someone else before you acted. Where the world was misleading in the first case, in this second case it changed between the time at which I made the observation and the time at which you acted on it.

In the world of early humans that we are imagining, as well as in our own familiar world, we are going to have motives to communicate with one another, not only about our shared surroundings, but also about our attitudes. I will want to assure you about what I believe or what I desire or intend to do, for example, since this will often be important in getting you to rely on me, in making it possible for me to rely on you, and in coordinating with one another to our mutual benefit. Will I rely just on reporting about my attitudes to you, as I rely on reporting about my environment? I may do so in many cases but it turns out that I am not restricted to that option and that I will have a motive for doing something else instead: for avowing and even pledging my attitudes.

AVOWING BELIEFS

To avow an attitude is to communicate that I have the attitude but to do so in a way that breaks sharply with just reporting its presence.[10] If I report on the presence of a belief or desire or intention, then I leave open the two excuses mentioned earlier. Should I prove not to have the attitude reported, I may in principle try to explain the misreport either by arguing that I was misled about my own mind or that I changed my mind between the time of the observation and the time at which you found that I no longer held the attitude.

Avowing the attitude, to introduce the word in a technical sense, breaks with reporting it by closing down the possibility of invoking one of these excuses: that which invokes a misleading mind to explain the miscommunication.

Avowing a belief or desire or intention means communicating its presence in a way that makes it impossible for me as the speaker to excuse the later absence of the attitude by saying that I got my mind wrong. And it does this manifestly or as a matter of common awareness among ordinary speakers; everyone involved recognizes that the excuse is unavailable, recognizes that everyone recognizes this, and so on.[11]

When I make a report about the presence of such an attitude within me you understand that if I prove not to have that attitude, then I may try to excuse the failure by reference to a misleading mind or a changed mind. When I make an avowal of the attitude, you understand that while I may try to excuse a failure to display the attitude by invoking a change of mind, I cannot try to do so by claiming that I was misled about my mind.

What would have enabled you and me in the world of early humans to avow our attitudes; what would have made that option accessible? And why would we have wanted to take the option; why would it have been attractive?

First the accessibility question. The use of natural language in communicating an external state of affairs – say, in an utterance like 'The fruit on the southern hillside is ripe' – communicates, not just that that state of affairs obtains, but that I believe it to obtain. And it communicates my belief that it obtains in a manner that forecloses a later explanation of error, to the effect that I was confused about my own belief. Suppose it becomes clear that I did not myself act as if that fruit was ripe. I might explain the miscommunication by pointing out that I changed my mind or belief: I learned after making the report that the fruit had been picked. But I could not explain the miscommunication about my belief by saying that I must have got it wrong in the first place: that I must have been misled about the presence of the belief within me.

Why does this mode of communicating my belief foreclose access to the misleading-mind excuse? Because in saying that the fruit is ripe, I indicate that I have made up my mind on that question, so that I do not have to introspect on the state of my mind in order to know what I believe. I may have to observe another in order to know and communicate that they believe that the fruit is ripe. But I do not have to observe myself in order to know that I believe that the fruit is ripe. I can know that I believe this just by virtue of the fact that having looked at the relevant data, I find myself assenting to the proposition that the fruit is ripe. Knowing that I am making up my mind in response to those data, I have a maker's knowledge of holding the relevant belief, not just the knowledge of an observer. And having a maker's knowledge, I cannot invoke an excuse that would only have been available if I had come to know of the presence of the belief on the basis of introspection or observation.[12]

When you ask me whether I believe something – say, to take a plausible example, whether I believe that John is trustworthy – I may choose to report the belief, using words such as 'I think that I believe that', where the expression implies a lack of certainty on my part. But equally, if I am confident enough, I may choose to say simply: 'Yes, he is trustworthy.' And in that case I avow the belief rather than report it. When I report the belief, I may excuse my later proving not to have it – this may appear in a failure to act as if John were trustworthy – by explaining that I must have got my belief wrong. But when I avow the belief I cannot do that. Presenting myself as having made up my mind, not just observed my mind, I cannot invoke the idea that my mind misled me in my observations.

So much for the accessibility of avowing a belief. But why might avowal be attractive? The reason is that words are less credible to the extent that they are cheap, and that the words I utter in avowing a belief are more expensive than the words I utter in reporting it.

In avowing the belief that John is trustworthy, I manifestly deny myself recourse to the misleading-mind excuse in the event of proving not to have the belief. And so, I can give you more assurance than a report would have given that I do indeed hold that belief. Thus, I give you firmer grounds for relying on me and make it more likely that you will indeed put your faith in what I say. This is going to constitute a great benefit for me in a society of mutual reliance. Hence we may expect one another in the society of early humans – indeed expect one another by way of default – to prefer to be taken to avow the beliefs we communicate rather than just to report them.

If we really mean just to report our beliefs, we will have to go out of our way to make that clear by resorting to oblique expressions, as in saying that so far as I can see, I seem to believe that John is reliable. Thus I will be taken to avow the belief – and will recognize that I will be so taken – not just if I say that John is trustworthy but also if I say, without indicating any uncertainty, that I believe that John is trustworthy or that the data support the claim that he is trustworthy or anything of that kind. Under the assumption that avowal has a default attraction for any one of us, I can avow the belief, not just by expressing it in the assertion that John is reliable, but in ascribing it to myself or by indicating why the assertion would is well-supported.

AVOWING DESIRES AND INTENTIONS

Suppose, then, that it is a default assumption in the society of early humans that I should be taken to avow a belief whenever I communicate that I have the belief and do not go out of my way to suggest that I merely have the authority of a reporter. In that case, and for parallel reasons, it will also be a default assumption that when I communicate that I have a desire or intention, and do not go out of my way to indicate that I am speaking just as a self-reporter, I will be taken to avow the desire or intention.

Thus, imagine that I say something like 'I want to establish a relationship of mutual reliance with John' or 'I intend to go to the big game hunt at the weekend.' Assuming that I am in a position to have a maker's knowledge of my desires or intentions – more on this assumption in a moment – I will naturally be taken to avow the desire or intention, not just to report on it with a degree of uncertainty. I will be taken to ascribe the desire or intention to myself in such a way that should I prove not to have that attitude – should I fail to act as if I had it – I cannot claim that I must have misread my own mind. This is because I will naturally be assumed to make my words as credible as possible and to enhance the possibility of getting you to rely on me. The only epistemic excuse I can offer in the case of failure is that I changed my mind since making the report; this will be particularly plausible, if I can point to considerations that might have prompted a shift in my desires or intentions.

In saying that I desire to establish a relationship with John, or intend to go to the hunt, thereby avowing that attitude, I will also give expression to my belief that I have that desire or intention in a way that forecloses the possibility of a misleading-mind excuse. But on the picture adopted here the main goal is to avow the desire or intention, and giving expression to my belief in that desire or intention is instrumental to the primary purpose. It is not something that I choose as such to do, only something I must do as a means of avowing the desire or intention itself.

As already noted, however, I can only avow a desire or intention if it is possible for me to have a maker's knowledge of what I desire or intend. Is that plausible? Yes, it is. Assume, as in the last section, that whenever I desire an option or prospect – or go so far as to intend to realize it among a set of alternatives between which I have to choose – I do so on the basis of the appealing features that I ascribe to it: I desire or intend it on the basis of the desiderata or attractors it promises to realize. Given that assumption, I can form a desire or intention just by attending to those desiderata and deferring to them: by making up my mind about what to desire or intend in light of the features presented.

On this picture, I form the desire or intention in a manner that parallels the way in which I form a belief by attending to relevant data and letting them elicit my assent and belief. And as I can know what I believe by making up my mind about what to believe, so I can know what I desire or intend by making up my mind about what to desire or intend. I can know that I have the desire or intention, not by observing my own mind, but by virtue of having a maker's knowledge that I am deferring appropriately to the relevant desiderata.

Thus I can know that I desire to establish a relationship with John, or that I intend to be at the big game hunt, just by dwelling on the features that make the relationship attractive or that make going to the hunt more attractive than staying at home and by finding that they dispose me appropriately. When the fact that John is an influential member of the community commands my attention and deference, for example, I am in a position to know that I have the corresponding desire. And when the fact that going on the hunt offers a prospect of enjoyment or profit that is lacking in the option of staying at home, my affirmation of those attractive properties puts me in a position to know that I have that intention.

These considerations show that as I may avow beliefs that correspond to my acts of propositional assent in response to relevant data, so I may avow desires and intentions that correspond to my acts of desiderative affirmation in response to suitable desiderata or attractors. I may communicate that I have such desires and intentions, as I may communicate that I hold certain beliefs, in a manner that forecloses the possibility of invoking the misleading-mind excuse for a later failure to display those attitudes.

PLEDGING INTENTIONS

Where avowing an attitude forecloses the misleading-mind excuse, by contrast with reporting the attitude, there is a further speech act that goes one better than avowal by also foreclosing the changed-mind excuse. This is the act of pledging an attitude, which makes sense at least in the case of

324 • Ciphers of Transcendence

an intention. If I pledge an intention to do something, then I will not be able to excuse a failure to act on it either by claiming that I misread my mind or by claiming that I changed my mind since making the pledge.

Thus I may not only avow an intention to be at the big-game hunt but, perhaps in response to your wanting greater assurance about my taking part, I can also pledge it. This is possible because the desideratum of proving to be someone whose word is reliable may be enough to give me a special degree of confidence – the confidence of someone with maker's knowledge – not just that I hold that intention, but having made the pledge that I am unlikely in any foreseeable circumstances to drop it. I can make my words maximally expensive and credible, and it will often be attractive to do so, by putting aside both forms of epistemic excuse. The only excuse I will be able to invoke in the case of not acting on the intention, then – in the case of not turning up at the hunt – will have to be practical rather than epistemic in character: it may consist, for example, in explaining that I broke a leg or that I was physically prevented from getting to the hunt.

Why may I pledge only intentions, not beliefs or desires? I cannot pledge a belief, assuming that belief is responsive to evidence, because I can never be in a position to know that there will not be data available in the future that cause me to change the belief. And I cannot pledge a desire, at least not a desire that presupposes the intrinsic attraction of the option or prospect in question, because I can never be in a position to know that the desiderata that attract me now – say, the excitement that the hunt promises – will not cease to attract me later. I may be able to know that if I make a pledge to be at the hunt, the desideratum of proving to be reliable may reliably get me to attend, even if the hunt ceases to be intrinsically attractive. But if the option ceases to be intrinsically attractive the fact that I still go to the hunt will not mean that I continue in the relevant sense to desire hunting. The desideratum of proving to be reliable may be enough to support an intention, then, but it is not enough to support a desire.

THE SIGNIFICANCE OF AVOWALS AND PLEDGES

Why are these observations about the accessibility and attraction of avowing and pledging attitudes – their accessibility and attraction, not just for us, but for early humans – of particular interest? In a phrase, because they connect up with the idea of what it is to be a person.

The etymology of 'person', as Thomas Hobbes pointed out in the mid-seventeenth century, comes from the Latin word for a mask.[13] It comes in particular from the masks worn by ancient actors to identify the characters for whom they spoke. These were masks through (*per*) which they sounded (*sonare*) their words.

Hobbes endorsed an older, medieval tradition according to which a group assumes a persona – in effect, becomes a person – by licensing or authorizing the voice of a designated spokesperson as their own voice. In this way of thinking, people authorize the voice of a spokesperson in so far as they take the avowals and pledges made in their name as utterances for which they can be held responsible; they can be commended for living up to those claims and censured for failing to do so. Hobbes broke new and important ground in arguing that something similar is also true at the individual level.[14]

We human beings, in his novel view of things, count as persons in so far as we speak for ourselves in avowals and pledges – we represent or 'personate' ourselves in those words – and accept that we can be held responsible for such self-representations. We accept that we can be called upon to live up to our words, thereby exposing ourselves to possibilities of commendation and censure; we assume responsibility for proving to be and to act as our words advertise. This responsibility-centred conception of personhood is endorsed later in the seventeenth century by John Locke, who writes: 'Where-ever a Man finds, what he calls *himself*, there I think that another may say is the same *Person*. It is a Forensick Term appropriating Actions and their Merit.'[15]

The words to which we human beings make ourselves answerable, on this conception, include not just the representations we explicitly avow or pledge but also the representations of ourselves that we endorse by failing to distance ourselves from the manifest expectations of others: for example, the expectation that we will abide by established community standards. We individuals are persons on this view in virtue of assuming responsibility for living up to a pattern of self-representation, explicit and implicit, that we cannot help but support.[16]

Avowals and pledges are important, then, because they reflect our most distinctive feature as human beings – or at least as adult, able-minded human beings: they mark the most striking respect in which we contrast with other animals. Unlike other animals we do not just hold attitudes and manifest them in actions, allowing others to interpret our beliefs, desires and intentions. We interpret ourselves to others and, foreclosing misleading-mind and even changed-mind excuses, do so in a way that claims a special, authoritative status for that self-interpretation.

Thus, when I speak for what I believe or desire or intend in the mode of an avowal, or when I speak for what I intend in the mode of a pledge, I assume a special knowledgeable status in relation to myself. I assume the authority to communicate my attitudes in a way that projects myself in the words I utter, inviting you to rely on them with a confidence that no mere report could support. I give myself a character in those statements, as we might say, and present myself as uniquely licensed to underwrite that character. The message I communicate is: 'This is who I am; this is who you may take me to be in our dealings with one another.'

THE EXPERIENCE OF VALUE

This takes us to the dénouement. Once we recognize what it is to be a person, it becomes intelligible why we should have a use for the concept of the desirable and why we should be able to enjoy the experience of value.

The practice of avowing and pledging attitudes means that there is a sense in which I or you or anyone else has two selves. A first self appears in what I am contingently inclined to believe or desire or intend at any moment, a second self in the beliefs, desires and intentions that I am ready to avow or pledge, explicitly or implicitly, finding them suitably supported by relevant data or desiderata. This division of selves allows for a divergence between the beliefs, desires and intentions I actually hold and the beliefs, desires and intentions I am ready to avow or pledge. And, as we shall now see, it casts that divergence in a way that makes room for the notion of the desirable and the experience of desirability or value.

Suppose you have avowed a certain attitude or pledged a certain intention. And now imagine what you must think of the possibility that at some future time, near or far, you will be subject to an influence that may cause you temporarily not to display that attitude or intention. You have avowed a belief that the gambler's fallacy is a fallacy but you imagine not living up to it in the excitement of the casino. You have avowed a desire for moderate drinking but you imagine an impulse that causes you to binge. You have pledged an intention to keep a secret that a friend told you in confidence but you imagine being moved to reveal it by the desire to impress a third party.

How are you to think in each case of the possibility imagined? You cannot think of it as a scenario in which you change your mind. That would be inappropriate in the pledging case and it would not fit in either case of avowal. You do not envisage that you will be persuaded of the gambler's fallacy in the one situation or convinced of the attraction of binge drinking in the other. In each case you will see the factor that causes you to betray your avowal, as you will see the factor that causes you to renege on your pledge, as a distorter. It will present as a factor that makes you less than fully sensitive to the data and desiderata assumed in the making of avowals and pledges.

We argued earlier that while the desirable and the desired are both grounded in the independent features of any option or prospect, they may come apart and that when they do so, it represents a sort of failure on an agent's part not to go with the judgment of desirability rather than with the desire. What should now be salient is that when I avow a desire or pledge an intention, focusing on relevant desiderata, I see the alternative for which I avow a desire or pledge an intention under an aspect that answers to the concept of the desirable.

That alternative will appeal to me in virtue of its independent features – the desiderata that catch my eye. But it may not be the alternative that I actually happen to desire or intend on a given occasion, due to the influence of a temporary distorter. How am I to think about the divergence in such a case? Should I see it as resulting from a split in my psychology such that it would be OK for me to go with the one or the other? Surely not. I have to identify with the practice of avowal and pledging, since my relationships with others and my standing as a person turn on living up to it. And so I will naturally view the possibility of following the contingently divergent desire as a failure.

This is just to say that having avowed a desire or intention, I am bound to think of the alternative addressed in such a manner that I might use the term 'desirable' to pick it out; I conceive of it, in effect, as the desirable option. Thus I will experience alternatives that answer to my avowals and intentions – and, more broadly, alternatives that are fit to answer in that way, being supported by suitable desiderata – as desirable or valuable possibilities. Specifically, I will experience them as contrasting in that way with alternatives that appeal, not for the presence of such desiderata, but merely because of the influence of temporary distorting influences.

In the days when Paddy Masterson and Denys Turner and I debated the origins of the experience of value, I was particularly keen on the work of Jean-Paul Sartre. One of the more notorious of Sartre's claims in *Being and Nothingness* is that, like any other human being, I am not what I am and I am what I am not. What the rather brief and breezy considerations rehearsed here suggest is that there is a certain truth in that claim and that it explains our experience of value without recourse to a transcendent reality.

When Sartre says that I am not what I am, he may be taken to say that I am not revealed in the contingency of what I happen at any moment to believe or desire or intend. And when he says that I am what I am not, he may be construed as insisting that what I am is the self that I project in my avowals and pledges, whether or not that is a self that I bring to life in my imperfect performance. It is the deliverances of that aspirational self that give us the perspective from which we judge our actual self. And it is those deliverances, I suggest, that break in on the routine of day-to-day desire and give us our intimations of value.

ENDNOTES

1   The present essay draws heavily on the argument in *The Birth of Ethics: Reconstructing the Role and Nature of Morality*, (Oxford: Oxford University Press, 2018).

2   Why not equate vice with the habit of pursuing the undesirable? See Philip Pettit, *The Robust Demands of the Good: Ethics with Attachment, Virtue and Respect* (Oxford: Oxford University Press, 2015).

3   Paul Ricoeur, *Fallible Man* (Chicago, IL: Henry Regnery, 1965).

4   Robert Axelrod, *The Evolution of Cooperation* (New York, NY: Basic Books, 1984).

5   Michael Tomasello, *A Natural History of Human Morality* (Cambridge, MA: Harvard University Press, 2016), p. 47.

6   Tomasello, ibid.

7   See Peter DeScioli and Robert Kurzban, 'Mysteries of Morality', *Cognition* 112 (2009), pp. 281–99; also 'A Solution to the Mysteries of Morality', *Psychological Bulletin* 139 (2013), pp. 477–96. Tomasello agrees that mutual helpfulness does not mean this but argues that the pressures of collaboration would have pushed early humans towards the formation of moral responses proper. For a critique of his argument see Philip Pettit, 'Normative Concepts in Tomasello's History of Morality', *Philosophical Psychology* 31 (2018), pp. 722–35.

8   Amartya Sen, *Rationality and Freedom* (Cambridge, MA: Harvard University Press, 2002).

9   See Susan James, *Passion and Action: The Emotions in Seventeenth-Century Philosophy* (Oxford: Oxford University Press, 1997).

10 See Dorit Bar-on, *Speaking My Mind: Expression and Self-knowledge* (Oxford: Oxford University Press, 2004).

11   See David Lewis, *Convention* (Cambridge, MA: Harvard University Press, 1969).

12   For a fuller defence of this position see Philip Pettit, 'Making Up Your Mind', *European Journal of Philosophy* 24 (2016), pp. 3–26. In taking that position I follow the lines of argument in Victoria McGeer, 'Is "Self-knowledge" an Empirical Problem? Renegotiating the Space of Philosophical Explanation', *Journal of Philosophy* 93 (1996), pp. 483–515; Richard Moran, *Authority and Estrangement: An Essay on Self-knowledge* (Princeton, NJ: Princeton University Press, 2001); Victoria McGeer, 'The Moral Development of First-Person Authority', *European Journal of Philosophy* 16 (2008), pp. 81–108.

13   Thomas Hobbes, *Leviathan* (Indianapolis, IN: Hackett, 1994), ch. 16.

14   See Philip Pettit, *Made with Words. Hobbes on Language, Mind and Politics* (Princeton, NJ: Princeton University Press, 2008).

15   John Locke, *An Essay Concerning Human Understanding* (Oxford: Oxford University Press, 1975), § 26; Carol Rovane usefully emphasizes this Lockean theme; see *The Bounds of Agency: An Essay in Revisionary Metaphysics* (Princeton, NJ: Princeton University Press, 1997).

16   See Christian List and Philip Pettit, *Group Agency: The Possibility, Design and Status of Corporate Agents* (Oxford: Oxford University Press, 2011), ch. 8.

SUFFERING AS A CIPHER OF TRANSCENDENCE

BRENDAN PURCELL

In this essay I wish to suggest that our human sufferings can be a cipher of transcendence. They are, to quote the honorand of the present volume, 'experiential clues that enable us to attain a rational or philosophical affirmation of God... to be "deciphered" by philosophical argument'.[1] My reflections have been provoked, firstly by a dialogue between Peter Singer and myself in St Paul's Anglican Cathedral, Melbourne, in 2012,[2] and secondly by a discussion on Irish radio a week after Stephen Fry's televised denunciation of God as evil on Ireland's RTÉ One television in January 2015.[3] Both Peter Singer and Stephen Fry regard the occurrence of suffering as incompatible with the existence of a good God. It will be appropriate to examine their objections before moving towards a context I think will be in keeping with the approach of Patrick Masterson.

OBJECTION 1. WOULD A GOOD GOD PERMIT THE SUFFERINGS CAUSED BY NATURAL DISASTERS?

Peter Singer certainly doesn't think so. Speaking of the 'vast amount of pain and suffering' in the world, he writes that 'if God is all-knowing' he knows this. And if God 'is all-powerful and all-good he could and would have created a world without so much suffering'. While for Professor Singer, it is 'more plausible to believe that the world was not created by any god', still, 'if ... we insist on believing in divine creation, we are forced to admit that the God who made the world cannot be all-powerful and all good. He must be either evil or a bungler.'[4]

While these remarks refer to any kind of suffering, let us think first of all of the sufferings caused by earthquakes, tsunamis, volcanic eruptions, floods, forest fires and so on. Physicists tell us that gravity is one of the four fundamental interactions keeping our universe together. Should God suspend gravity every time a sentient being is in danger of suffering a fall? But the universe we live in simply could not exist at all if it were not held together by gravity. And neither could we exist. Falling and the risk of it are just part of the human condition. Geologists tell us that forces such as gravity result in the formation and movements of tectonic plates on our planet, earth, with their related earthquakes and volcanoes. The best we can do to alleviate suffering and death from these is with more accurate seismological forecasting and improved architecture for life in areas where such events are most likely.

The more we understand about our many-layered cosmos, the more we grasp the interdependence between the astrophysical, chemical, biological, botanical, zoological and human levels of existence. All of the later levels materially depend for their existence on the lower ones – without the burning out of stars, there would be no carbon or rocky planets; without a billion years of algae making the atmosphere breathable by plants, animals and humans, nothing beyond bacteria and other single-celled organisms could live on earth.[5]

Peter D. Ward and Donald Brownlee have written as follows about plate tectonics (whose shifting movements underlie earthquakes and tsunamis, experienced by us as disastrous events): 'Plate tectonics plays at least three crucial roles in maintaining animal life: It promotes biological productivity; it promotes diversity (the hedge against mass extinction); and it helps maintain equable temperatures, a necessary requirement of animal life. It may be that plate tectonics is the central requirement for life on a planet and that it is necessary for keeping a world supplied with water.'[6] And on earthquakes, Guillermo Gonzalez and Jay W. Richards state: 'Most of us associate earthquakes with death and destruction, but ironically earthquakes are an inevitable outgrowth of geological forces that are highly advantageous to life. Heat flowing outward from Earth's interior is the engine that drives mantle convection and, in turn, crustal motions. A tectonically active crust builds mountains, subducts old sea floor, and recycles the carbon dioxide in the atmosphere, all of which make Earth more habitable.'[7]

Since we cannot imagine a gravity-free universe, maybe some cosmic humility is in order so that we do not expect God to suspend the law of gravity across the 93 billion light years of the observable universe, along with what scientists are now telling us about how important plate tectonics are for keeping our planet habitable. One of the reasons natural disasters wreak such havoc on the less developed parts of the earth is because of their inadequate infrastructure and emergency responses. While major disasters often call forth hugely generous aid from the developed world, more long-term approaches often founder because of political and economic attitudes that resist transformation. At least in our time, it is now possible with early warning systems, if effectively maintained, to greatly lessen the death toll caused by tsunamis.

So the believer or the philosopher can thank God for providing us with an astrophysical universe governed by its basic laws – without which it could not exist. Believers do not say that because we suffer in disasters God does not exist. What we do ask is what our suffering means and how it may be reconciled with God's love.

I completely agree then with Peter Singer's questioning whether natural disasters are compatible with a good God. Nothing can take away the horror of, for example, the over 230,000 people who lost their lives in the Indian Ocean tsunami in December 2004. But I think reflection on the planetary significance of the movement of tectonic plates, along with practical efforts at mitigating their effects, rather than expecting God to miraculously break the laws of nature every time such events occur, is our meaningful response to God's love in gifting us this universe along with our reason, expressed in scientific understanding and technology. It does not seem to make sense to blame God for creating a universe bound together by its four fundamental forces – gravitational, electromagnetic, and the strong and weak nuclear interactions – whose natural operation occasionally cause catastrophic events on our planet.

OBJECTION 2. WHAT ABOUT ANIMAL SUFFERING? WOULD A GOOD GOD NOT HAVE PREVENTED THAT?

As regards animal suffering, you may remember the poignant scene in *The March of the Penguins* when the skua flew in to prey on baby Emperor penguins. The adult penguins do nothing since they cannot fly. Nor should we, since the skua have their own problem of survival. The only way to avoid this kind of suffering is to abolish all carnivorous animals – without seals and salmon on the menu, Alaskan bears could only eat animal conservationists. There just could not be the ranges of land and marine animals we know of, unless they were bound to each other as food resources. So, if you do not want animals suffering, you would have to confine existence to the level of the chemical elements or else find another planet inhabited by some unimaginable pre-bacterial life, since even at that simplest level of life, bacteria survive by feeding on each other.

But if Peter Singer and, I presume, Stephen Fry, accept the theory of evolution and its achievement in giving us a framework within which we can intelligibly link all living things together, then they are surely bound to accept the inevitable suffering that accompanies that enormous biological galaxy of interactions between species at all levels of development.

If then there are laws governing plant and animal growth, occasional breakdowns of these growth processes are statistically always likely to occur in biologically based living beings. Animal pathologies that surely cause pain would seem to be an inevitable consequence of their being endowed with sensation. While anaesthetics prevent a person from feeling pain, and medicine may cure its underlying causes, suffering and pain often warn us about underlying illness and so, in those natural instances at least, are good. What is needed is an examination of the different kinds of suffering.

No more than with the laws of physics (since the universe unfolds not only according to the classical laws of Newtonian physics, but also in accordance with the statistical laws of quantum theory), should we expect God to suspend the laws of growth – including their occasional failure – in plants, animals and humans. And of course, a huge factor in mammals and marsupials happily filling the niches left by the dinosaurs was the K-T (Cretaceous-Tertiary) extinction of three quarters of all animal and plant species 66 million years ago. That catastrophic asteroid strike on the coast of Yucatán, Mexico, blasting out the giant Chicxulub crater, was the condition for the later enormous plant and mammal developments in the story of evolution. So at least some cataclysms involving enormous animal suffering and death can be seen as working towards a huge evolutionary advantage. Meaning that a case can be made for ciphers, if not quite of transcendence, at least for meaningful development, in these apparently unmitigated planetary and zoological disasters.

OBJECTION 3. A GOOD GOD WOULD NEVER HAVE ALLOWED THE SUFFERING OF CHILDREN.

Stephen Fry was asked in the interview referred to above, supposing there was an afterlife, what would he say to God? Fry replied: 'I'll say,

"Bone cancer in children? What's that about?" How dare you? How dare you create a world in which there is such misery that is not our fault? It's not right. It's utterly, utterly evil.' While in no way mounting a complete answer to Stephen Fry's objection about the suffering of children from serious illness, I will muster one example of how a young person could transcend her suffering, while of course not negating it. Chiara Badano, from near Genoa, who died at eighteen from bone cancer in 1988, and was beatified in 2010, certainly would not have agreed that her bone cancer was an unredeemable evil that disproved the existence of a good God.

She was diagnosed at seventeen with osteosarcoma, which turned out to be an untreatable spinal tumour allowing the cancer to spread quickly. When she got home from the conclusive tests confirming its mortal seriousness, her mother, Teresa, who had herself been ill and unable to accompany Chiara to the hospital, wanted to speak to her. But Chiara remarked, 'Don't say anything, Mom.' She went and lay face down on her bed for twenty-five minutes, which her parents think were the most important twenty-five minutes of her life. Teresa had the wisdom not to interfere. When Chiara eventually came in to her, she spoke to Teresa with a radiant smile and said, 'You can speak now, Mom!' Somehow, Chiara, who, like every young person, wanted to live, had said Yes to her new situation. She had made her decision and there would be no going back. Her mother noticed a new glow in her face and words. Whatever struggle had gone on in her heart had been resolved through a deep conversation with God.[8]

Serious illness brings detachments, the gradual loss of our independence and the earlier patterns of our life, while physical suffering wears down our natural capacities. Chiara accepted these detachments, like losing her hair or slowly losing her mobility. For each lock of hair that fell she would say, 'For you, Jesus.' She grew ever more aware that her suffering was a gift. For instance, she was soon telling others: 'Don't ask Jesus to bring me to heaven. Otherwise he might think I don't want to suffer any more. He'll come to take me when the time is right.' To her mother, 'Mom if they asked me if I want to get back walking again I would reply "no" because in this way I'm nearer to Jesus.'[9]

Despite her resolve, she still had her moments of anguish. Would she manage to be faithful to her commitment to love Jesus crucified and forsaken, and live her ultimate encounter with him in death? She remarked: 'I feel so small and the road ahead so hard. Often I feel overwhelmed by suffering. But it's my spouse who's coming to visit me, right?' She found the strength to say often, 'Yes, I'll repeat…: "if you want it, Jesus, I want it too."'[10] One of her doctors, a non-believer strongly critical of the Church, was deeply touched by the way Chiara and her parents had been living: 'Since I met Chiara something changed inside me. There's coherence here, and here I can understand Christianity.' Another doctor, Dr Antonio Delogu, said: 'Through her smile, and through her eyes full of light, she showed us that death doesn't exist; only life exists.'[11]

Chiara Badano would have a right to answer Stephen Fry's 'What about bone cancer in children?', even though when the osteosarcoma struck she was not a child, but a teenager. In Masterson's language, her illness was a cipher of transcendence which her ever deepening contact with 'God as infinite, creative, personal love' enabled her to decipher.

4. THE UNDERLYING OBJECTION: SINGER'S AND FRY'S UNSCIENTIFIC REJECTION OF NATURE

Underlying their rejection of suffering caused by natural catastrophes, by animal predation and human illness, Singer and Fry seem to be in danger of rejecting nature itself, since all of these realities can be understood as an integral aspect of what Bernard Lonergan called emergent probability – that is, a world process unfolding according, not only to the classic laws of Newtonian mechanics, but to the statistical laws of quantum mechanics and to the developmental laws underlying bacterial, botanic and zoological existence.[12] Just because they find suffering meaningless does not mean that the intelligibilities suggested above – at the physical level by plate tectonics, at the zoological level by a non-ideological theory of evolution, and at the human level by a capacity for experiencing suffering as occurring within a transcendent context – are themselves meaningless. Could it be that the denial of nature is profoundly anti-rational and anti-scientific? Of course there is a further consideration, which Masterson summarizes as follows: 'The basic structure of the a posteriori argument [for the existence of God] is a demonstration that various features of the domain of finite beings, whose actual existence we affirm, turn out, on metaphysical analysis, to be incoherent, impossible and contradictory unless they are understood to exist, and in the manner in which they do, because wholly dependent upon a cause beyond the domain of finite being.'[13]

So it is not surprising that atheists like Singer and Fry find what are the effects of the laws of nature working in terms of statistical probabilities and evolutionary developments, unacceptable, since without an ultimate ground, all of finite being is, as Masterson notes, incoherent, impossible and contradictory. A somewhat less consistent but more open atheist like Camus proposes what Aimé Forest spoke of as a consent to being. At the beginning of *The Rebel*, his 1951 study of the ideological thinkers who want to change human nature by force, he writes: 'The analysis of revolt, gives rise at least to the suspicion that there is a human nature, as the Greeks believed, and contrary to the postulates of contemporary thought.' And at the very end of his study he remarks of such ideologists that '[T]hey no longer believe in that which is, in the world and in living man.'[14] Singer's and Fry's rejecting 'that which is', in the case of physical, zoological and human being, makes any further quest for 'a cause beyond the domain of finite being' unnecessary.

5. THE MOST SERIOUS, MORAL, OBJECTION TO THE EXISTENCE OF A GOOD GOD

Does God cause evil? I'd like to reword that question: If God creates us free, and we do wrong and hurt others, isn't it his fault? Surprisingly neither Peter Singer nor Stephen Fry raises what is generally the cause of our greatest suffering, caused by our own evil deeds or those of our fellow human beings. This brings us face to face with a wonder – why did God create us morally free in this way, what was his purpose? Discussing 'Whether God Wills Evils', Aquinas explores this question in his *Summa Theologiae*, concluding that 'God neither wills evil to be done, nor wills it not to be done, but wills to permit evil to be done; and this is a good.'[15]

The basic point is that what God wishes must happen, what he does not wish cannot happen. But he can permit – that is, not cause, but allow happen – the misuse of their freedom by human beings. In Masterson's language, our existence as created free beings entails 'the requirement of love', but if it is to be love, that requirement does not and cannot force our love. Masterson has given a profound interpersonal articulation of this question in his *Sense of Creation*: 'Thus the concrete ethical experience of the transcendence of the other person constitutes a privileged practical foundation for a metaphysical account of creation. Moreover, this experience appears to require such an account as its ultimate truth condition… It is an argument which claims that the asymmetrical transcendence of the other person vis-à-vis oneself affirmed in the fundamental ethical relationship implies, as its metaphysical counterpart, the asymmetrical transcendence of God vis-à-vis creatures asserted in the classical view of creation.'[16]

Why the kind of altruistic action at the core of Levinas' notion of our obligation towards the other is a cipher of transcendence for Masterson is that it cannot be understood except in terms of the intrinsic worth of the other, compelling us to relate to that other as an end in him- or herself. Our readiness to sacrifice ourselves for the sake of another, the existence of moral self-transcendence, can only be rendered intelligible in terms of our common participation in a ground transcending us both. Let me give two contrasting experiences which I think help to clarify Aquinas' paradoxical notion of God's permission of evil, a permission of evildoing for the sake of the good of the creature's free exercise of their autonomy.

First, in the early 1970s I was invited to a meal with a young couple in Brussels. They had decided never to have a child because of the danger of a nuclear war. I remember saying to them that the risk they would be taking if they had a child was not unlike the risk God takes in creating us – the risk that it is better we exist with the enormous gift of our freedom, even though, because we are free, we are also free to refuse to love.

Second, 1968 was not only a year of student revolt in Paris, Berkeley and elsewhere. In Italy, where family bonds were very close, students not only revolted against what they felt was political or cultural oppression, but against their parents. A friend of mine told me how this worked out in her own Milanese family, where her younger sister (I'll call her Rina here) had joined a far-left commune. Complicating the situation were attacks by armed right-wing groups on communes like Rina's. Naturally, Rina's parents were deeply concerned for her, but living out their own commitment to the Gospel, they made sure she was always welcome at home. Among her group, Rina's were almost the only parents still in touch with their young adult children – so she was always able to carry on a dialogue with her parents.

Once she asked her father what he thought of what she was doing. He restrained himself from saying how much he wanted her to leave her group. Instead, he focused on what had been her ideal as a teenager as a committed Catholic in the same Focolare movement as Chiara Badano, saying: 'If you're sure that what you're doing is out of self-sacrificing love for the other, then keep on doing it.' She thought about that, and returned to her group. But a year or so later, realizing the group's leaders were more keen on developing a political profile for themselves, as well as unfairly using the money they had all put in common, Rina, remembering what her father had said, left the group.

I would like to use the experience of Rina's father, and that of any parent, to illustrate God's role in creating us as free persons. Parents face situations like this all the time. They can advise, direct, train, warn, threaten, punish, their children, but each person in the end is free: which means they may know what they should do yet freely choose not to do it, causing suffering for others. Rina's father took the risk of allowing her to use her own freedom, even if that could lead to her moral or physical destruction. The Brussels couple were more like a God who decided endowing human beings with freedom was too risky, that it would be better to keep all animate beings at the level of the inhabitants of Dublin Zoo.

6. ETTY HILLESUM AND THE MYSTERY OF EVIL TRANSCENDED BY THE MYSTERY OF LOVE

Perhaps, as with Chiara Badano, it is better to allow someone who has directly experienced this evil and anticipates her own murder as a direct expression of that evil, to discover in her suffering a cipher of transcendence. Born in the Netherlands in January 1914, Esther (Etty) Hillesum was awarded a Master's degree in Law at the University of Amsterdam in 1939. Her entire family perished in the Holocaust. Through others finding a place for her on the Jewish Council, for some time, Etty escaped the threat of arrest and worse, but chose the task of visiting those Jews already interned at Westerbork camp in northeastern Netherlands.

In her diary she wrote of her mounting dread of the approaching Holocaust she knew would destroy her people: 'I continue to grow from day to day, even with the likelihood of destruction staring me in the face… For us, I think, it is no longer a question of living, but of how one is equipped for one's extinction.'[17] Far from blaming God for the horrific tragedy of the oncoming holocaust, Etty insists that it is human beings who are responsible for the evildoing, not God: 'Neither do I hold You responsible. You may later hold us responsible.'[18] Knowing only too well the motivations of those encompassing her own death and that of her people, along with her growing experience of the God she addressed as 'You', she knows God cannot be held responsible for evil.

Not only does she exonerate God of responsibility for the suffering of the Jewish people, but speaks of helping him, since it seems as if he is unable to change what is happening: 'If God does not help me to go on, then I shall have to help God … I don't fool myself about the real state of affairs, and I've even dropped the pretence that I'm out to help others. I shall merely try to help God as best I can, and if I succeed in doing that, then I shall be of use to others as well.'[19] This is one of her fullest statements of her extraordinary transfiguration of the meaning of her suffering at the hands of her fellow men, through seeking to bring God's love to everyone, friend and foe alike in the place of which she remarked, 'Dante's *Inferno* is a comic opera by comparison.'[20] Yet she fully endorses her friend Liesl's remark, 'It is a great privilege, isn't it, that we have been chosen to bear all this?', and later quotes Matthew 26, 39: 'Not my will, but Thy will be done.'[21]

It is within her lived dialogue with God that Etty develops her insight into what she calls 'the art of suffering',[22] through her having touched the transcendence of the beloved other, whether friend or foe, the transcendence of God, for which she had her own word, mystery – the mystery of 'You' and the mystery of each 'you': 'I love people so terribly, because in every human being I love something of You. And I seek You everywhere in them and often do find something of You… The best and the noblest part of my friend, of the man whose light You kindled in me, is now with You… I stood beside his bed and found myself standing before one of Your last mysteries, my God. Give me a whole life to comprehend it all.'[23]

7. HUMAN SUFFERING AND THE DEATH OF GOD

The question of how a good God can allow suffering is not answered for Christians when we realize that God has suffered with us and for us, but that realization lifts the question into the bigger mystery of God's love for us. If his love is so great that he enters into our suffering, enduring it with us, what does that say about suffering – particularly the suffering resulting from the evil choices of others?

In *The Rebel* Albert Camus glimpsed that mystery of a God who shares our suffering with us, and indeed the harshest of suffering, not only violent physical death occasioned by hatred, but what was somehow experienced by Christ as the death of God: 'The night on Golgotha is so important in the history of man only because, in its shadow, the divinity abandoned its traditional privileges and drank to the last drop, despair included, the agony of death. This is the explanation of the *Lama sabachthani* and the heartrending doubt of Christ in agony. The agony would have been mild if it had been alleviated by hopes of eternity. For God to be a man, he must despair.' And four years later, in his 1955 Athens 'Lecture on the Future of Tragedy', Camus returns to this theme:

> Perhaps there has been only one Christian tragedy in history. It was celebrated on Golgotha during one imperceptible instant, at the moment of the 'My God, my God, why hast thou forsaken me?' This fleeting doubt, and this doubt alone, consecrated the ambiguity of a tragic situation. Afterwards the divinity of Christ was never again called into doubt. The Mass, which gives a daily consecration to this divinity, is the real form which religious theatre takes in the West. It is not invention, but repetition.[24]

Elsewhere I have considered the focus in twentieth-century Catholic, Orthodox and Reformed theology, on this experience of Jesus' forsakenness on the cross,[25] but before many of these theological explorations, Chiara Lubich, founder of the Focolare movement, had made her own spiritual–existential discovery of the centrality of Jesus Forsaken (which also underlay Chiara Badano's approach towards suffering). After she and her followers had consecrated themselves to God-Love in 1943, they discovered that the deepest expression of God-Love was in the very experience Camus mentioned, in Jesus Forsaken and Risen.[26]

Developing theologically Chiara Lubich's experience in his study on the Trinity, philosopher–theologian Piero Coda has an interesting section entitled 'The positive not-being of love'. He explores the contemporary theological understanding of how, in the analogy of love, 'God's being as *Agapê* is penetrated and quickened by mutual not-being, through … the love of each of the divine Persons for the others.'[27] Each of the Persons 'loses himself' for the other, so that the three Persons in the Trinity are One because for each of them, their Love at the same time is and is not. Each Person, in Aquinas' terms, is a subsistent relation,[28] a completely Other-related Person by not being himself. The Father loses himself by complete self-giving to the Son, the Son empties himself by completely accepting to be from-the-Father, the Spirit un-selfs himself, becoming nothing to unite completely Father and Son in Love.

Coda points out how this positive not-being of love, this inner life of the Trinity – of the God St John defines as *Agapê*, 'Love' (1 Jn, 4: 8, 16)

– has been understood in contemporary Christology as most dramatically exploding into our space-time universe at the moment St Paul speaks of when Christ 'emptied himself' (ekenôsen, Phil. 2, 7),[29] whose most dramatic moment of his kenôsis is when both his humanity and divinity are eclipsed in his dual forsakenness. Piero Coda cites Russian Orthodox theologian Sergius Bulgakov who speaks of this moment as 'the most profound kenotic concealment of Divinity'. For Bulgakov, the divine mystery is that 'the Father receives the Son in the devastation of death and watches over him until the Resurrection'.[30] Nor does this self-emptying occur only in the Son: 'This forsakenness of the Son is an act of the Father that signifies the fact that he *assumes* the Son's death and thus participates in it, since for the Father the forsaking of the Son to death on the cross is not death, of course, but a certain image of spiritual co-dying in the sacrifice of love.'[31]

And the Holy Spirit is also deeply involved. Bulgakov remarks: 'The fact that the Son has been emptied of and forsaken by Divinity also signifies that he has been forsaken by the Holy Spirit… The Holy Spirit returned, as it were, to the Father when the death of the God-Man was accomplished in all the intensity of the abandonment by God… Thus, this co-participation of the Holy Spirit in the kenosis of the Son … extends in its own fashion the kenosis of the Son to the third Person. Because this is the kenosis of Love in Person (the Holy Spirit): not to be manifested to the Well-Beloved (the Son).'[32] This means for Bulgakov that 'The sacrifice of the Son presupposes the co-sacrificial love of the entire Holy Trinity.'[33]

'The sacrifice of the Son presupposes the reciprocal sacrifice of the entire Holy Trinity.'[34] In other words, the entire Trinity, through Christ, is profoundly enmeshed in all human suffering which in turn is lifted up into the eternal drama of Trinitarian communion.

ENDNOTES

1   Patrick Masterson, *The Sense of Creation: Experience and the God Beyond* (Aldershot, Hampshire: Ashgate, 2008), p. 2.

2   I wrote a summary as 'Conversation between Peter Singer and Brendan Purcell on "The Role of Reason in Faith and Unbelief"' in *The Melbourne Anglican*, 6 May 2012.

3   See Patsy McGarry, 'Stephen Fry tells Gay Byrne: God is a "maniac, totally selfish".' (*Irish Times*, 2 February 2015). A podcast of my interview with Marian Finucane (31 January 2015) is available on RTÉ Radio 1 website.

4   Peter Singer, 'Good God? Religious people are still unable to provide a satisfying answer to the age-old question of why God allows suffering', *The Guardian*, Saturday 17 May 2008.

5   Recent research on this topic by University of Washington scientists is discussed by Hannah Hickey, 'Early Earth's air weighed less than half of today's atmosphere', *UW Today*, 9 May 2016.

6   P.D. Ward and D. Brownlee, *Rare Earth* (New York, NY: Copernicus, 2000), p. 220.

7   Guillermo Gonzalez and Jay W. Richards, *The Privileged Planet*, (Washington DC: Regnery, 2004) p. 55.

8   M. Baroni and J. Lubich, *Chiara Luce: Life Love Light* (Supplement to *Città Nuova*, 3, 2011), p. 19.

9   F. Coriasco, *Dai tetti in giù: Chiara Luce Badano raccontata dal basso* (Rome: Città Nuova, 2011), p. 88.

10 M. Zanzucchi, *Chiara Badano: A Life Lived to the Full* (London: New City, 2010), p. 49.

11 Ibid., p. 39.

12 Bernard Lonergan, *Insight. A Study in Human Understanding* (London: Longmans, 1961), pp. 121–8. On Lonergan's notion of emergent probability see Brendan Purcell, *From Big Bang to Big Mystery. Human Origins in the light of Creation and Evolution* (Dublin: Veritas, 2011), pp. 93–8.

13 Patrick Masterson, *Approaching God. Between Phenomenology and Theology* (London: Bloomsbury, 2013), p. 52.

14 Albert Camus, *The Rebel*, (New York, NY: Vintage, 1956), p. 305.

15 *Summa Theologiae* I 19, 9 ad 3. See Bernard Lonergan, *Grace and Freedom. Operative Grace in the Thought of St Thomas Aquinas* (Toronto: University of Toronto Press, 2000), pp. 328–48.

16 Masterson, *The Sense of Creation*, pp. 83–4.

17 K.A.D. Smelik (ed.), *Etty: The Letters and Diaries of Etty Hillesum 1941–1943* (Grand Rapids, MI: Eerdmans, 2002), pp. 463, 631.

18 Ibid., p. 489.

19 Ibid., pp. 484–5.

20 Ibid., p. 490.

21 Ibid., p. 542.

22 Ibid.

23 Ibid., p. 514.

24 A. Camus, *The Rebel* (New York: Vintage, 1992), p. 32; 'Lecture Given in Athens on the Future of Tragedy', in P. Thody (ed.), *Albert Camus, Selected Essays and Notebooks* (London: Penguin, 1963), pp. 197–8.

25 Brendan Purcell, 'Towards a Trinitarian Humanism: Piero Coda's Development of a Heuristic of Radical Fraternity as a Lived Theology of History', *Sophia: Ricerche su i fondamenti e la correlazione dei saperi* 4/2 (2012), pp. 247–71.

26 Focolare, the Italian for 'fireside', was the name given to a group which began in Trent, Northern Italy in 1943, whose ideal was to bring about the fulfilment of Jesus' prayer 'That all may be one.' After the war it spread throughout Europe and the

rest of the world, with members from Catholic, Anglican, Reformed, and Orthodox Churches. From the 1970s it has attracted Jewish, Muslim, Hindu and Buddhist members, along with those of non-religious convictions. See A. Torno, *Chiara Lubich: A Biography* (Hyde Park, NY: New City Press, 2012).

27 Piero Coda, *Dalla Trinità: l'avvento di Dio tra storia e profezia* (Rome: Città Nuova, 2011), pp. 567, 570.

28 For example, *Summa Theologiae* I 40, 2 ad 1.

29 Coda, *Dalla Trinità*, p. 569.

30 Sergius Bulgakov, *The Lamb of God* (Grand Rapids, MI: Eerdmans, 2008), p. 314. See Piero Coda, *L'altro di Dio: rivelazione e kenosi in Sergei Bulgakov* (Rome: Città Nuova, 1998), p. 140.

31 Ibid., p. 313.

32 Ibid., p. 314, modified in light of the Italian translation, *L'agnello di Dio. Il mistero del verbo incarnato* (Roma: Città Nuova, 1990), p. 383.

33 Ibid., p. 354.

34 Ibid., p. 314.

IS DESIRE DESIRABLE?
THE QUESTION THAT
DISCLOSES THE PERSON

DAVID WALSH

When we reflect on the theme of desire, we leave desire behind to ask about its desirability. The part is contained by the whole that as such can never arise as a part. We are drawn into the horizon of the person who is capable of asking about desire. Is desire desirable? It cannot be asked without entering the perspective of the person who has thereby gone beyond desire. It is to the reality of the person, disclosed in such self-disclosure, that I would like to devote my reflections. We begin with the admission that the notion of the person is sufficiently underdetermined to require such a re-examination. Despite our familiarity with the term person and its continuous usage from its Greek and Roman beginnings in *prosôpon* and *persona*, we have still to come to grips philosophically with the notion. In many respects, the horizon of the person is what is missing within the classical discovery of mind. The later definition of the person as 'an individual substance of a rational nature', derived from Boethius, is precisely what must be challenged if we are to reach the dynamic of self-transcendence that we know as the defining reality of the person.[1]

Our first step will be to show that this conception of the person is not entirely absent in Plato. His treatment of the parts of the soul continually points toward a whole that cannot be included within them. Instead he invokes particular persons, Socrates and the philosopher king, as the means of expressing what cannot be conveyed in terms of their respective parts. Next we follow the similar strategy that Aristotle employs in his account of the formation of character, where continuous reference to types of persons enables him to sidestep a consideration of the person who can ask about the question of his or her character. Our third step will be to ask about the opening of interiority as an event that goes beyond its mere presupposition in the Greek thinkers.[2] Only then will we arrive at the person who, in taking responsibility for a whole life, is present in the mode of self-transcendence. To reach that realization, however, we must be prepared to go beyond the limits bequeathed by the classical thinkers, to acknowledge revelation as the constitutive horizon of the person. Once that suggestion has been broached we may find we are not too far from the region of modern philosophy in which it is precisely presence in the mode of absence that marks its account of metaphysics.[3]

At the outset we sense that 'desire' cannot be presented as a topic of discourse, apart from the setting within which it finds its place. We must not overlook the person who takes responsibility for desire within a whole life. Yet initially our attention is directed to a part in just the way that Plato divides the soul into its parts in the *Republic*. There we find desire most closely associated with appetites, the part of the soul driven by the material needs that specify them but which, in themselves, lack the transparence of rationality. Like the craftsmen and producers of the polis, appetites pursue fulfilment that falls short of full human fulfilment. In order to reach their proper human good, appetites must be subsumed within the directing guidance of reason, assisted by the auxiliary force of the spirited part. Justice as the ordering virtue is invoked as the source of the harmony that allows all of the parts of the soul to perform their proper function and, thus, the good of the whole to be attained. It is notable that neither in the city nor in the soul is justice fully exemplified. No part possesses it as its distinctive virtue, for all must participate in it in their respective degrees, if justice is to be achieved. So ends the founding play of *Republic*, Book 4, that is ostensibly intended to let us behold the emergence of justice in both the city and the soul. It would seem that the Socratic project of defining justice has missed its mark even if, ironically, many readers still take the definition of the ordering harmony of the whole as his definition.

Anticipation of that failure is surely the most profound insight of the text, for Plato goes on, through the waves of objections, to sketch the only perspective in which the ordering harmony of the whole can be comprehended. That is, within the soul of a person who so orders him- or herself. Socrates surmounts objections to the equality of men and women, the community of property, wives and children among the guardians, to reach the only viewpoint within which they can be comprehended. Significantly, that is the interior perspective of a person, the philosopher king. The anthropological principle, the search for justice on the larger scale of the polis, is discarded by the admission that it really only exists within the inwardness of the philosopher. Even when Socrates returns to the declining political forms of timocracy, oligarchy, democracy, and tyranny, the path of explanation follows the interior changes within individuals that work their way out in the political realm. The accent has shifted so decisively to the interior that one is left to wonder whether the external city could ever understand the condition of its possibility, one beheld nowhere but within the innermost vision of the philosopher. Even the philosopher him- or herself may not be able to articulate what it is, since it ultimately derives from the good that is beyond being. Concerning the transcendent ground of order nothing can be said. That is surely the summit of Platonic wisdom and the crown of philosophy. But it is less than satisfactory when something of its truth must be conveyed to the producers and consumers and the mythically educated guardians who are remote from such eschatological glimpses. It is little wonder that Plato seems not to have attempted such a raid on the inarticulate again, given the unpromising limitations of potential listeners or readers. Rather than embracing the philosophical challenge, of intimating what cannot be said, the later dialogues suggest a retreat into the indirection that myth and conceptual elaborations make possible.[4]

Plato's hesitancy to write anything serious, or to even attempt it, may derive not only from the unsatisfactory condition of the life of philosophy, but just as much from an inability to grasp the full measure of his own accomplishment.[5] Having reached the philosopher–king he does not seem to have realized at what he has arrived. Even for Plato, the philosopher remains too much present in the city. The notion that the city may be contained in the philosopher is only haltingly approached in the closing reference, to the city in speech that exists within the dialogue itself.[6] Missing is the realization that the city distended in history, unfolding through its declining and restorative forms, exists nowhere but within the minds of those who are capable of conceiving it. The idea of the city is its truth. Surely that is the burden of the *Republic*. Yet the dialogue stops short of the realization that the idea is the condition of possibility of the polis that is constituted by those who bear the city within.

Tantalizing echoes of the transcendent perspective of the philosopher and, by extension, of all persons who contain the city inwardly are there. The portrait of the statesman who can exist outside of the polis, and Aristotle's astonishing reflection on the man of preeminent virtue who outweighs the whole, are powerfully evocative.[7] They remain, however, only passing glances at the full realization of the person actually on display in Plato's account of the philosopher, as the one who has turned his soul toward the brightest part of being. By becoming a person, he has revealed the constitutive genesis of that reality. The person stands in relation to the Good that is transcendent, and thereby partakes of what surpasses being in dignity and power.[8] The soul that can order its desires and tame its pre-rational spirit gains this rationality through submission to the ordering pull beyond it. Yes, this was a signal breakthrough to the ground of order in mind and cosmos, but not so definitive that it could forestall the multiple misunderstandings that would afflict its interpretation up to the present. Few are the readers who are prepared to admit that reason is neither an instrument nor a faculty, but a theophanic event.

The veil of self-awareness has not yet been parted to disclose the full magnitude of what has been reached. Revelation has occurred without recognizing the mutuality of persons that make it possible. The Platonic theophany is a distinctly impersonal one and the impossibility of such an impersonal encounter has been largely overlooked. Of course it is always possible, as Eric Voegelin has suggested, that Plato deliberately situated his account within a ring of hesitations as to its full ramification.[9] He spoke of opening toward a beyond without conceding that such an event is only possible if the soul is already constituted by such openness, and the Beyond itself bends toward that which is otherwise incapable of receiving it. The mutuality of revelation is a mutuality only available to persons. Only a person can reveal and only a person can receive the revealer. All of this is abundantly evident in the textual account of the ascent toward the Good, for the visible analogy of the sun serves merely to underline the strictly invisible nature of the unfolding. The movement is interior and can only be accessed by those who are open to the same interior prompting. Yet the revelation is not private, as Plato makes clear, for the philosopher has followed the path available to every soul. At its apex it turns, not on the impartment of information, but merely on a participation in that which is. All that is absent is the admission that what is encountered is also soul. Plato's reluctance to identify Nous as God probably derives from his unwillingness to link it to the intra-cosmic gods of the Homeric myth. As a consequence, the breakthrough to transcendence must be recounted without the self-revelation of the transcendent. We know neither how it is possible for the immanent to grasp that which transcends it, nor how the transcendent can reach that which is immanent.

The language of the soul and its parts is not capable of accounting for their order as a whole, nor can it reach the relationship to the whole, the good, from which the order of the soul is derived. The soul is opaque to itself for it cannot account for its capacity to give itself completely to that which is goodness itself. Equally elusive is the self-abasement of the good as it descends from its dwelling in inaccessible remoteness. How do we know about what lies beyond knowledge, unless we are somehow capable of knowing more than we can know? The more one dwells with the constraints of the Platonic movement toward the Beyond, the more it becomes clear that they can only be resolved within the horizon of the person. Only a person can give more than has been given and only a person can receive more than has been received. The relationship to that which is transcendent calls forth a complete self-giving, just as it is the reception of the One who has already exceeded the limits of self-giving. It is a relationship of mutual self-opening, whether from the human or divine side. And it takes place nowhere but within the mutuality by which alone the inwardness of the other can be glimpsed. Only a person is capable of stepping aside to yield to the other. The one who carries the mask is always more than the mask and always says more than what is said. In every instant the instant is transcended. Some sense of this is intuitively present in the *Republic*, for the whole dialogue is framed by the imperative of souls, whether in the Piraeus or Hades, of choosing the character to which the respective destiny is attached.[10] The question of how we can be forever bound by the decision of a moment is not broached. Yet it is taken on board as the unspoken foundation of the whole work. Each person holds their destiny, in all the decisive aspects, in their own hands. That is what it means to be a person, always more than one is and therefore always capable of hearkening to the One who is more than what is, the One who is also a person.

Without a notion of the person, the formation of character, the main topic of Aristotle's *Ethics*, similarly remains a mystery. To his credit Aristotle admits his puzzlement as to how those who lack a sense of the noble and good might be led to acquire it, since it is precisely that disposition that is needed. To refer to it as a gift of nature is no more satisfactory than to explain the weak-willed man as one whose desires overcome his rationality.[11] Admission of the question-begging nature of the analysis is a strong indication of his awareness of the situation, even if Aristotle did not possess the theoretical means of addressing it. But being Aristotle he did not lack resources and, often, highly suggestive ones that point in the direction of the person. In a manner that parallels the central role that one particular person, Socrates, plays in Plato's dialogues, Aristotle has recourse to types of persons throughout the *Ethics*. There are of course the types that exemplify particular virtues, the courageous man, the magnanimous man, or the incontinent man. But these are by way of illustration. They do not reach the man who makes the ethical life his overarching concern. These are the individuals who exemplify the unnamed excellence of the text, what might be called the existential virtues that make possible the ordering of a life as a whole. It is the life of virtue as a whole that is aimed at in the notion of character, but it can only be specified by particular persons or types. The mature man, *spoudaios*, and the man of practical wisdom, *phronimos*, are the most well-known instances. In each case Aristotle invokes them as a way of naming what cannot be named. That is, the capacity for ordering one's existence as a whole that remains a possibility for persons who, in every instance, are not simply present in their existence. They can hold themselves at a distance and ask if desire is desirable. In other cases, Aristotle introduces such types only to pass over them or leave them unabsorbed in his overall account. One thinks of the man who follows justice in the comprehensive sense who is shunted aside, while Aristotle explores justice in its partial or legal sense without reference to the former.[12] But the outstanding case is surely the friend or friends who frame the horizon of Aristotelian ethics without being fully integrated into it. The uncertainty is announced in the opening discussion of Book 8 where *philia* is said to be a virtue, or involves virtue, or is indispensable to life.[13] No need to decide. Except that by not deciding, Aristotle has lost the one opportunity to anchor philosophy within the relational setting from which its genesis can be understood.

The account of friendship that follows is one that preserves the intellectual distance we have come to associate with the Aristotelian approach. A classification of the types of friendship, as the useful, the pleasant, and the good, remains aloof to the differences between them. Initially, one would be inclined to overlook the author's special affinity with the life of friendship, or the extent to which the analysis offered to his readers constitutes a singular act of friendship. The thinker remains outside of his thought. Mastery of the subject conceals the extent to which the subject masters him. Yet the latter is precisely the case, as Aristotle's own deepening exploration reveals. Eventually it becomes apparent that friendship is not a virtue or a part of the good life but its whole. Even the good man, it turns out, has need of friends. He does not need them for utility or for pleasure (although they provide both), but for the sake of friendship itself. A life without friends, Aristotle finally concedes, is hardly a life. The good life is inconceivable without friends for it is friends who enable us to think. The most characteristic activity, the highest of which human beings are capable, the life of contemplation, is impossible alone. Thinking together, *sunaisthêsis*, intensifies what we do separately, but in such a way that it makes it more real and more self-sustaining. We are not meant to be alone, not even in our minds. But this is not a mere lapsing into fellow-feeling, for we can only be united if we are united in truth, not merely in aspiration or appearance. It is only in truth that we can share the same consciousness, including our own existence and the existence of the friend, in the same intention.[14]

Friendship, it turns out, is not only the whole of virtue but the whole of philosophy as well. Philosophy is impossible without friendship, without the friendship of philosophers. Even the analysis of friendship that encompasses the continuum of individual and social and political relations, is embedded within the commitment to truth and goodness (and beauty, by implication) within which the possibility of friendship is grounded. We cannot even think about friendship without offering it as an act of friendship. The analysis of friendship, as the overarching model of relationships in Books 8 and 9 of the *Nicomachean Ethics*, is so stunning in its range and depth, overflowing the boundaries of associational structures into the reality of consciousness itself, that one is inclined to regard it as the summative text of the Aristotelian corpus. Yet the failure to grasp the account of friendship as the key to his thought seems almost to have begun with Aristotle himself, for he rarely seems to exploit the full potential of the astonishing reflections he has laid before us. Only occasionally are there tantalizing suggestions as to where the attenuations may lead. Surely one of the most fascinating is his reflection in Book 10 when, after dealing again with pleasure and its dynamic within desire, he transitions to the concluding discussion of the life of contemplation as the highest, and therefore that which provides the highest pleasure. In describing contemplation as the life that is most continuously active he exhorts us to follow the life that is beyond the human, even if it launches us on a process of immortalization.[15] Not only is this suggestion evocative of the idea of the person as always more than he or she is, but his visualization extends into the only instances of persons that exemplify that dynamic. That is, the life of the gods that now includes the philosophers who, through their own divine activity, reach up to that level. Confirmation that this extension is not a mere overreaching can only be received in the affirmation that it is offered to us from the divine side. The highest contemplation, reached through the co-contemplation with others, is a participation in the friendship of the gods.

But no sooner is that limiting encounter approached than its evocative potential slips away. In the absence of the self-understanding of the person it is impossible to account for how the elusive glimpse was reached. The interior experience of straining beyond a boundary cannot be retained because there is scarcely an interior without the person. Only the one who can step aside from his or her own experience, who can behold the interior movement of the soul, can grasp the condition of possibility for that experience. The term 'prosôpon' ('mask') was available to the classic philosophers but they did not employ it, for they scarcely apprehended the need to hold onto the experience of their own philosophic illumination. It was enough that they had broken with the externality of the Homeric myths and retained the dramatic enactment of truth in tragedy. As a consequence, they launched philosophy as a symbolic form that remained incapable of explicating the source of its own inspiration. Truth could be exemplified but it could not be grasped, for it was not yet the truth of a person. The priority of the person to truth had scarcely been intimated and thus truth could not yet be seen as a mode of existence. Inwardness was certainly there in the classical founding, but it had not yet acquired the language by which it might be retained inwardly. The focus on concepts and results, and the death struggle the polis itself was undergoing, meant that it was enough to preserve what had been gained. The self-deepening of inwardness would have to await a new impetus, one that would impinge on philosophy from beyond it and yet transform it forever. For now, the topics and categories into which Aristotle was already pouring the liquid of philosophy was the best that could be expected. That would still be a considerable achievement. It might not make it possible to raise the question as to whether desire is desirable and thereby open the perspective of the person who is beyond all desire. But within the philosophical subtlety of an Aristotle it would always be possible to follow his suggestion that desire unfolds as intelligent desire or as a desiring intelligence that already transcends the finitude of desire.[16] To ask how such transcendence is possible would require a fuller opening of the horizon of the person. It would have to await the One who poured himself out on behalf of all. Only the event of unconditional love reveals the amplitude of the person. The actor has not only put himself aside to bear the mask, but has so completely surrendered himself that he now bears the 'impress' of all others.[17]

It is the One who gives himself completely who calls forth the response of complete self-giving. The words of the Gospel capture the astonishing simplicity of the event. They left their nets and followed him. Hardly knowing what it entails they relinquish everything to follow the One who calls them. Explanation is neither needed nor given, for the response is everything. The person who calls outweighs all that might be said. In that moment of self-abandonment the meaning of what it is to be a person is discovered. No longer is the person the bearer of a mask, the enactor of a role, but one who offers himself. Holding nothing back, the person is present in his or her nakedness as the one whose whole life has become visible and who yet remains, as the invisible beholder. The episode of the woman at the well (John 4:1–43) is just such a turning point. It is because he calls for a complete change of heart that Christ can open the perspective on the entire life of the woman. The metanoia he offers is parallel to the *periagogê* of the *Republic* (518c), but it arises more directly and immediately in life. Intellectual distance has been removed as the interlocutors enter into a strictly second person perspective. Who do you say that I am? The call for a complete surrender of self has abolished the leisure for reflection, for there must be nothing held back. Having turned our hands to the plough we dare not look behind, if we are to be worthy of the Kingdom of God. The transcendence of all that one has been, brings into view the self-transcendence of the person as such. Yet within that glimpse of total loss there arises the astonishing realization of the fullness thereby attained. By giving we do not lose but gain, immeasurably. He who loses his life will save it, not in the future but in the now from which the self-giving of the person is always possible. Contrary to the idea of substance so often applied to the idea of the person, it becomes apparent that the person exists only through the outpouring of substance.[18] By giving we receive, not just in the sense of reciprocation, but in the deepest interior of the person. Rather than discoursing about the flash of transcendence, we are living it out. It is a long way from the Greek understanding of the mask, yet it is its ultimate fulfilment. The possibility of the mask derives from the one who places himself behind it. Now it has become possible to see the one who cannot be seen and yet is always seen as the bearer of the mask. Only a person can give or receive a person.

What is remarkable about the New Testament is how far this understanding of the person as transcendence is developed without naming it. The notion of the person is operationally pervasive even if its metaphysics is never made explicit. Yet there is a distinct advance on the Greek intuition. Where the man of practical wisdom is the one who can weigh action in light of the good life as a whole, the follower of Christ has already offered his life without reservations or conditions. It is the encompassing character of the Christian vocation that brings to light the condition of its own possibility. That is, that each is a person and therefore capable of giving him- or herself as a whole. It is a depth of self-giving that surpasses the material limits of what is given. The widow's mite is greater than all that had been dropped into the temple treasury. Even a cup of water given in Jesus' name is a gift that overflows the boundaries of the finite. This is the meaning of the Incarnation, that flesh and blood have become the disclosure of what they cannot, and yet do, contain. The mode of containment, however, is no longer material, for the latter has been subsumed within the transparence of the person. 'Spirit' is too gross a metaphor for what continually denies itself. Breath intimates the lightness and the movement, but not the evanescence that is the heart of what it means to be a person. We are open to one another only because we continually yield place to one another. From the weakest to the strongest, the richest to the poorest, self-giving remains the deepest possibility. The ladder of transcendence is available to all, slave or free. A spiritual hierarchy is a contradiction in terms, for it operates in a realm where the last shall be first.

Even in the New Testament, however, there are degrees of self-perception. All may possess the self that can be freely offered, but not all penetrate its interior dynamics to the same degree. This is what makes the self-reflection of Paul of such signal importance. He is capable of putting into words what all believers intuit, without fully explicating. That is, that there is scarcely a self until it has learned to deny itself in obedience to the good. In the famous wrestling of Romans 7, St Paul acknowledges that the good he *wants* to do is not what he does, while the evil he does *not* want to do is what he does. A self, divided against itself, resonates with universal human experience and yet it had not been so piercingly grasped before this text. The abyss that opens within the human heart is achingly on display. The impossibility of reaching resolution, a resolution that can be counted upon, looms as the fate of free being. It is a harrowing penetration of the emptiness of the heart that far exceeds the Aristotelian grappling with the weak-willed individual. Problems of the latter seem comparatively slight in contrast with the drama that overwhelms us in the self-consciousness of sin. Rather than failure, or the loss of self-approval, we seem to face annihilation as the mounting threat. Only the self-distance that remains within the Pauline reflection provides a slender thread of redemption. How was it possible for Paul to glimpse the innermost dynamic of his soul if he was completely engulfed by it? Even in the descent, the person remains as one who is capable of recognizing and therefore of reversing it. At the extreme, this would mean that the person could even be brought to confess the incapacity to bring about the change of heart so direly needed. The person who can grasp the irresolvable conflicts of the soul, it turns out, depends on a viewpoint that cannot be summoned at will. Self-distance, the mark of the person, is itself a graced moment.

It is the viewpoint of God on each of us. Augustine would go on to make this the basis of the *Confessions*, the accusation of oneself before God. But as such, it is a perspective that goes beyond what we can attain. Yet miraculously there it is, an opening that oversteps all limits, especially the limit of the self-contained self. To see ourselves, as we really are, is to go beyond who we are. Without fully formulating it, this is perhaps the great Christian contribution to the differentiation of the person, a differentiation still unfolding within the arc that stretches from Augustine to Kierkegaard. The possibility of asking if desire is desirable, the question that opens the perspective of the person who stands outside of desire, is made possible by the grace embedded in the question itself. It could not be raised if it did not contain the possibility of going beyond desire. We are not prisoners of desire precisely because we can ask the question of its desirability. Desire is itself overturned, as we know when reflection deflects and deflates the urge of the moment. But this is more than a psychological tripwire that snaps the motive force. The grace of self-distance is the crucial opening that is both the transcendence and the fulfilment of desire. To the extent that desire aims at what it cannot attain it is doomed to unfold in a progression without terminus, the satisfaction of one desire becoming only the beginning of the pursuit of the next. Without a *summum bonum*, as Hobbes diagnosed, we are locked into a joyless pursuit of joy. By contrast, the grace of self-beholding is already a glimpse of the fulfilment that is the opening of unending joy. It could scarcely even be glimpsed if we did not already touch it, however tenuously, and from there intuit the possibility of submitting ever more completely to its ever more powerful attraction. The grace that is the apex of the person is, thus, not an external imposition but the indelible mark of love that lingers at the edges of our consciousness. The person, who exceeds all that has been said and done, is already in the heart of a Love exceeding all limits.

It is the vantage point of overflowing love that is the summit of the self-transparence of the person. The person who stands under judgment, who is called to attain the distance of truth on him- or herself, is at the same time sustained by the intimation of love emanating from the call itself. Ultimately the perspective of truth surpasses our capacity and can therefore only be attained when we have been able to see beyond what we are. Self-transcendence is a gift. What had seemed to be an innate capacity of the person turns out to be a gifted possibility, for it is a sharing in the transcendence of Being itself. How else could we even know about such a reality, a reality that surpasses all else that is, if we were not privileged with access to its inner consciousness? To be a person is thus to be constituted by the consciousness of God. This philosophical–theological high point has been scaled numerous times within the tradition, but it has just as often remained an intimation of the ineffable lost in incommunicability. It is only within the perspective of the person that its structure can be opened up, because it is only the dynamic of mutuality that yields the secret of interiority. The self, that can scarcely know itself through its own resources, can attain self-transparence only when it has reached the horizon of transparence as such. We love because He first loved us.

ENDNOTES

1   For a sketch of what that wider revision would entail see my *Politics of the Person as the Politics of Being* (Notre Dame, IN: University of Notre Dame Press, 2016).

2   The idea that classical philosophy articulated the results of an experiential inquiry it was never able to articulate was a seminal discovery of Eric Voegelin, although he was far from alone in this intuition. See 'Reason: The Classic Experience', *The Collected Works of Eric Voegelin*, vol. 12: *Published Essays*, ed. Ellis Sandoz (Baton Rouge, LA: Louisiana State University Press, 1990), pp. 265–91.

3   For the modern philosophical developments that move in this direction see my *The Modern Philosophical Revolution: The Luminosity of Existence* (Cambridge: Cambridge University Press, 2008).

4   One thinks of the *Statesman* and the *Laws* as such a turn away from the explicitly philosophical mode of reflection. See John von Heyking, *The Form of Politics: Aristotle and Plato on Friendship* (Montreal: McGill-Queen's University Press, 2016), chs. 4 and 5.

5   Plato, *Seventh Letter*, 341c–d: 'There is no writing of mine about these matters, nor will there ever be one. For this knowledge is not something that can be put into words like other sciences; but after long-continued intercourse between teacher and pupil, in joint pursuit of the subject, suddenly like a light flashing forth when fire is kindled, it is born in the soul and straightway nourishes itself.' Trans. Glenn Morrow, *Complete Works*, ed. John Cooper (Indianapolis, IN: Hackett, 1997).

6   *Republic* 592b: 'Indeed he will, said Glaucon: you mean this commonwealth we have been founding in the realm of discourse; for I think it nowhere exists on earth.' Trans. Francis Cornford (Oxford: Oxford University Press, 1941).

7   Aristotle, *Politics* 3, 13, 1284a13: 'For a person of this order may very well be like a god among men.' Trans. Ernest Barker (Oxford: Oxford University Press, 1946).

8   *Republic* 509b: 'And so with the objects of knowledge: these derive from the Good not only their power of being known, but their very being and reality; and Goodness is not the same as being, but even beyond being, surpassing it in dignity and power.'

9   Eric Voegelin, *The Ecumenic Age*, Collected Works, vol. 17, ed. Michael Franz (Columbia, MO: University of Missouri Press, 2000), ch. 4, 'Conquest and Exodus', especially the section on 'The Balance of Consciousness'.

10   The lost souls in the Piraeus of Book 1 are echoed by the souls of the underworld in Book 10 who are called back for a new round of existence. 'Souls of a day, here shall begin a new round of earthly life, to end in death. No guardian spirit will cast lots for you, but you shall choose your own destiny.' *Republic* 617d.

11   Aristotle, *Nicomachean Ethics* (=*NE*) 3, 5, 1114b5–12.

12   *NE* 5, 1, 1130a9–11.

13   *NE* 8, 1, 1155a3–5.

14   *NE* 9, 9, 1170b1–14: 'Now, to perceive that we are living is something pleasant in itself, for existence is by nature good, and to perceive that that good thing is inherent in us is pleasant. Further, life is desirable especially for good men, because existence is good and pleasant to them: they are pleased when they are conscious of the presence in them of what is in itself good. From this it follows that just as one's own existence is desirable for each man, so, or nearly so, is his friend's existence also desirable for him. Now as we saw, his existence is desirable because he perceives his own goodness, and this kind of perception is in itself pleasant. Consequently, he must also include his friend's existence in his consciousness (*sunaisthanesthai hoti estin*), and that may be accomplished by living together with him and by sharing each other's words and thoughts.' Trans. Martin Ostwald (Englewood Cliffs, NJ: Prentice Hall, 1962).

15   *NE* 10, 7, 1177b32–1178a3: 'We must not follow those who advise us to have human thoughts, since we are (only) men, and mortal thoughts, as mortals should: on the

contrary we should try to become immortal (*athanatizein*) as far as that is possible and do our utmost to live in accordance with what is highest in us. For though this is a small portion (of our nature), it far surpasses everything else in power and value. One might even regard it as each man's true self, since it is the controlling and better part.' Trans. Ostwald.

16 *NE* 6, 2, 1139b3–5: 'Only the goal of action is an end in the unqualified sense: for the good life is an end, and desire is directed toward this. Therefore, choice is either intelligence motivated by desire or desire operating through thought, and it is as combination of these two that man is a starting point of action.' Trans. Ostwald.

17 For this aspect of friendship see von Heyking, *The Form of Politics*, p. 15.

18 Jean-Luc Marion points out that the only instance of the use of the term *ousia* in the New Testament, most often translated as 'substance', is in the parable of the Prodigal Son where it is precisely the impossibility of holding onto what substance means for a person that is at issue. 'In other words, the gift is not at all laid out according to Being/being, but Being/being is given according to the gift. *The gift delivers Being/being.*' *God Without Being* (Chicago, IL: University of Chicago Press, 1991), p. 101, italics in original.

About What do Contemporary Atheists and Theists Disagree?

ALASDAIR MACINTYRE

The answer to this question must seem obvious. Just like their predecessors, they disagree about God, about whether or not he exists. But, less obviously, they disagree about explanation and understanding, about what needs to be explained and about what it is to understand. My central claim in this essay is that, if we are to understand why they disagree about God, we need to understand their disagreements about explanation and understanding. I am not claiming that they disagree about God *because* they disagree about explanation and understanding. That question I leave open. So let me begin by saying what I mean when I speak of someone as a theist or an atheist.

Atheists define themselves by denying that the God of theism exists. By the God of theism I mean of course the God of Israel, the God of Abraham and Moses, the same God acknowledged in the New Testament and in the Qu'ran. God, so understood, is taken to deserve and require our worship, obedience and love, because he is not only omnipotent and omniscient, creator of the universe and therefore of us, but also all good. Atheists deny that there is any such being and hold that belief in such a being is a dangerous illusion. There must of course be a measure of agreement between theists and atheists about what they mean by the word 'God', if they are to disagree about him. But we should note that such agreement is compatible with significant disagreement about how far the use of the word 'God' by theists is coherent.

Theists on the one hand speak of God in terms that distinguish him from any finite being whatsoever. He is said to be without limitations on his power, knowledge and goodness. Theists on the other hand describe God's attitudes toward and his transactions with particular human beings in some of the same terms that they use of other human beings. He is said to have spoken to and with Moses, to have acted justly and mercifully, to make and to keep promises. How can these two ways of talking about God be reconciled? The atheist takes their use to be incoherent and therefore as evidence that there is no such being. Theists reply that it is the uniqueness of God, as he manifests himself to such human beings as the Hebrew prophets, which makes it necessary to speak in these two ways, so finding language for what cannot be otherwise expressed. Expressions that have familiar application to finite beings are used when speaking of God by analogy. And this extension of meaning from one sphere to another is after all something that occurs outside theology. Physicists would not be able to speak of space-time as curved or to entertain the possibility of particles with zero mass, but spin, if such transformations of meaning were not allowed.

To this an atheist will retort that this is a question begging reply to the charge of incoherence, since it presupposes that God has in fact on certain occasions manifested himself. But whether this is so, whether indeed it can be said, is what is at issue. Theists will not disagree. Since it was only through those encounters with God in which he revealed himself that first Israel and then the rest of us learned how to speak to and about God, any account of why it is appropriate to speak about God in these two ways will presuppose the reality of those encounters. So the theist's response to the atheist on this point must be question begging. Yet, if this is so, how can atheists and theists agree sufficiently in their use of the word 'God' to be able to disagree as to whether or not God exists? Happily, there are theistic claims that supply an answer. For theists are committed to holding that the universe of finite beings is not all that there is, that the universe of finite beings would not exist or have the characteristics that it does, if there were not a being whose power, knowledge and goodness are not limited as the power, knowledge and goodness of finite beings are limited, and who created and sustains the universe of finite beings. Moreover, if these claims are false, all their other claims are false too. And these claims many atheists have found sufficiently intelligible to be able to deny their truth.

In this essay I will focus on just one of these large claims: that the existence and characteristics of the universe of finite beings, including ourselves, stands in need of explanation.

I

What, from the standpoint of the contemporary theist, stands in need of explanation and what is it to possess an adequate explanation? The answers to these questions have after all a long history. At some early stage in that history our predecessors looked for answers to two sets of questions. One set had the form: 'How am I able to bring about *this* under some conditions by doing *that*?' Or: 'If some agent does *this* and *this* under these conditions, what will happen?' A second set were of the form: 'Given that a good deal of experience has led us to expect such and such, why did so and so happen instead?' Or: 'How should we understand this unfamiliar plant/animal/happening, so that we know what to expect from it?' The first set concern what agents can effect. The second set concern our dealings with the unfamiliar and the unexpected. What emerged from the pursuit of answers to these and related questions was a remarkable grasp of the range of types of explanation and of the different types of causal agent. Consider five different scenarios in which puzzles are resolved and 'Why' questions answered.

'Why do these dolphins hunt for fish as they do?' 'That is the nature of dolphins. As young dolphins develop their powers, they learn how to engage with others in hunting down fish. The taking and eating of fish is an end which dolphins pursue.' Contrast with this: 'How did the fire start?' 'Someone left a cigarette burning in the shack and the material of which it was made is highly combustible.' 'Why was so little damage done?' 'A few minutes later there was torrential rain.' Very different yet again is: 'Why did she recover so quickly?' 'Her heart and other organs were functioning well.' Fourthly: 'Why is this house the way it is?' 'The architect had a number of reasons.' And finally: 'How did she become so frustrated?' 'Her ends and those of the organization in which she worked turned out to be incompatible.' Notice two things about these scenarios.

The first is the variety of the explanations advanced and the range of explanatory concepts deployed. Appeal is made to the specific nature of dolphins, to ends towards which dolphin and human activity are purposefully directed, to the causal chain that runs from a lighted cigarette to a fire, to the matter of which the burning shack was composed, to the difference between a complex system functioning well and functioning badly, to the reasons that someone may have for acting or producing in this way rather than that. All of these concepts, we may note for future reference, find a place in Aristotle's scheme of explanation. A second notable feature of these scenarios is that each explanation invites further questions such as: 'How did dolphins come to behave like this?', 'What are the properties of combustible materials?', 'Under what conditions does the concept of function find application?', 'How do reasons issue in actions?', and 'How do organizations function?' For answers to many of these we have to go to the findings of sciences, including evolutionary biology, chemistry, and psychology. But it is important to note that in drawing on various sciences in this way we are putting their findings to the service of two distinct enterprises, one larger, one smaller, neither of which is the enterprise of science itself.

The smaller enterprise is that of providing an explanation for particular happenings or states of affairs. The larger enterprise is that of answering the question: 'Given our understanding of so many particular and local happenings, what kind of universe do we inhabit and what, if anything, is its underlying order?' To both enterprises a range of sciences now make indispensable contributions, but a good deal more is needed than what they can supply. To understand why this is so we must first identify what it is in nature that physics, chemistry, and biology cannot explain.

II

Begin with a rat, perhaps one of the rats used by Professor Moshe Szyf and his colleagues at McGill in their studies of the relationships between early maternal care and ability to cope with stress in later life. Mother rats which devote themselves to licking and grooming their offspring in the week after they are born trigger epigenetic mechanisms, so that a gene encodes a protein, whose transmission sets up a feedback loop in the hippocampus. The result is a well-adjusted rat. Inject certain chemicals into such a rat however, chemicals whose effect is to suppress the activity of the relevant gene, and the result is a rat liable to fear and anxiety. Why is this rat so liable? No account that is only biological and biochemical is sufficient to explain its fear and anxiety. For what brought it about was the decision by a researcher to inject it with the relevant chemicals. The efficient cause of that fear and anxiety was a human intention, a thought. It is a work of intelligent human design.

My reasons for saying this are no more and no less than the facts of the matter, the causal history that began with the researcher's thoughts and intentions and ended with the rat's fear and anxiety. When I speak of those thoughts and intentions as causes, I do not do so in virtue of there being some set of true law-like generalizations which connect researchers' thoughts and intentions and experimental outcomes. There are no such generalizations. So the causal powers of thoughtful agents are not to be understood in these terms. How then are they to be understood? Consider another example. On 16 October 1843 William Rowan Hamilton was walking with his wife by the Royal Canal in Dublin, when he hit on the idea of quaternions. Hamilton's problem had been that of how to represent complex numbers as points in three-dimensional space. The coordinates of such points are triples of numbers and, while Hamilton knew how to add and subtract triples, he had found no way of multiplying them. But on that walk, as he wrote to John T. Graves, on the very next day, 'there dawned on me the notion that we must admit, in some sense, a fourth dimension of space for the purpose of calculating with triples' and a formula for so multiplying presented itself to him, a formula that he scratched on the stonework of the next bridge over the canal.[1] A quaternion is a quadruple that can be so multiplied.

Karl Popper argued that such major conceptual discoveries cannot be predicted, since, were someone to predict such a discovery, they would have to be able to say what it was that was going to be discovered. But to do that would have been already to have made the discovery. We can and should go one step further than Popper. Not only can we conceive of no generalization formulable before the discovery that would enable us to predict it, there just are no plausible generalizations formulable after such events specifying antecedent conditions such that, were they to be satisfied, that particular discovery would be made. How then are such unpredictable expressions of the power of thought to be understood and explained?

They emerge from a certain kind of history, one in which goals emerge and in which problems are posed about how those goals are to be achieved. In setting and resolving those problems reasoning, both theoretical and deliberative, plays a key part. But it matters that those who set themselves to reason are moved by passions and commitments. They have learned to value reasoning and to distinguish good from bad reasons. So each of them has a history which is fully intelligible in terms of the larger project to which they are contributing and, when we try to understand how they came to think and act as they did, the relevant antecedents of their thoughts and actions are to be found in the preceding events of those histories. So, in so far as we can understand why Hamilton was able to think as he did, it is by placing his thought within the history of mathematics and the history of his own engagement with mathematics. It is by constructing a narrative that we make Hamilton's thoughts and actions intelligible. An account of his neurophysiology would be of interest only in so far as it contributed to the construction of that narrative.

It does of course matter that Hamilton's thought was embodied thought. In his letter to Graves he wrote that 'An electrical circuit seemed to close, and a spark flashed forth', metaphors that suggest a change that we would describe in neurological terms. But what made that change significant was its expression as a thought and, if the embodiment of that thought was some particular neurological happening, then it was what it was because the thought was what it was. The relevant antecedents of that thought were the preceding stages of Hamilton's mathematical enquiry, not the events in his brain. So it is with many examples of embodied thought as an initiator of change in the physical world. Note that it is no part of my case to deny that embodied minds have emerged from a long physical, chemical and biological history or that it might one day be possible to construct a computer with the powers of a thinking agent. What I am now asserting about embodied minds would then be true of that computer.

Consider another example. Someone's knees go through the same sequence of movements several times. What is involved is those knees moving as they do. There is of course a story to be told about those knees as mechanical systems, a story about muscles, tendons and bones. There is a neurological story to be told, a biochemical story, and a story about fundamental particles. But none of these stories explains why those particular knees are repeating this particular sequence at this particular time and place. What does explain this? They are the knees of a ballerina who, in the course of rehearsing her part in *Swan Lake*, is representing the movements of a dying swan, as choreographed by the latest in a long line of choreographers. A conception of her role and how it should be danced that was first elaborated in St Petersburg in 1895 has been translated into bodily movement, and her movements would not have the expressive function that they have, were it not for the movements of the other dancers that enable her movements to be interpreted by an audience, as the choreographers intended. Thought designed her movements and informed the decisions that were their moving or efficient cause. Thought informing her movements was their formal and their final cause.

Compare this with an at first sight very different example. A physicist is conducting an experiment, one in which photons are made to strike calcium atoms in an excited state, so that those atoms emit photons of the same energy. The experimenter intends this effect and she does so because she is, for the purpose of instructing her students, replicating part of the experiment by Freedman and Clauser which first showed decisively that Einstein's appeal to hidden variables in his critique of quantum mechanics was mistaken.[2] This experimenter is staging a piece of theatre, re-enacting a dramatic moment in the history of physics, just as the ballerina was re-enacting the choreographer's conception of the dying swan. It was Martin Eger, that great teacher of physics, who remarked that 'It can almost be said that a new experiment is designed to be performed – again and again – as a dramatic play.'[3] When it is repeated, as our imagined experimenter repeated the experiment of Freedman and Clauser, the physicist contrives that atoms and photons replicate those earlier atoms and photons. That they change as they do cannot be understood and explained except in terms of the experimenter's dramatic intentions. It is those intentions that are at once the efficient, the formal, and the final causes of the changes in those atoms and photons.

We could go on multiplying such examples: construction workers realizing an architect's intention by imposing form on wood and brick, farmers raising cattle intentionally, while unintentionally overgrazing the land, surgeons finding good reasons for remaking parts of human bodies. Every one of these examples would be of a type of project in which things can go wrong and most actual projects of any of these types have a history in which at some point things have gone wrong and this from more than one cause. Sometimes it is some failure in reasoning by the agents involved. Sometimes it is the result of interference by other agents, perhaps benevolently, perhaps maliciously, perhaps accidentally. But sometimes it is quite another type of cause: bad weather, an outbreak of disease, a storm or an earthquake, a drought, happenings not to be explained by reasons, intentions or purposes, but by the law-governed workings of nature. Here the natural sciences and only the natural sciences provide explanations. So we move from an initial recognition of the heterogeneity of types of explanation to the claim that all our explanations in the end fall into one of two classes.

Either they are explanations advanced from within one or more of the natural sciences, explanations appealing exclusively to scientific findings, or they are explanations in terms of the distinctive features of human life and the various social forms that it takes, explanations to which scientific findings may contribute incidentally. Explanations of the former kind, drawn from physics, chemistry or biology identify antecedent conditions and either law-like or probabilistic generalizations such that, given that they are what they are, that particular outcome either had to happen or had a certain probability of happening. To explanations of the latter kind conceptions of intention and purpose, of ends set and achieved or not achieved, of what it is to have good reasons for acting, and of various kinds of cooperative enterprise are central. To provide an explanation is to provide a history informed by such conceptions.

That there are these two distinct and independent types of explanation has however been strenuously denied by those who have insisted that in the end all genuine explanation is scientific explanation. We do indeed advance and make use of explanations of the latter kind – we could not conduct our daily lives without doing so – but we have to understand that everything is as it is because and only because the laws of physics are what they are and the constitution of the physical universe is what it is. This is a thesis that has been advanced in a number of versions since the eighteenth century, a thesis that commits those who assert it to the truth of atheism, as they themselves have happily recognized. God, as Laplace insisted against Newton and rightly, has no part to play in scientific explanations and, if all explanation is in the end scientific explanation, then the theistic account of the nature of things must be false.

We have now taken a first step towards justifying the central claim of this essay, that the disagreement between theists and atheists is in key part a disagreement about explanation. For here we have a case where it is a particular account of explanation that entails atheism and therefore rejection by theists, and by theists who insist that they have no reason to believe and a number of reasons to deny – among them some of the examples that I have just cited – that everything is as it is only because the constitution of the physical universe is what it is. What then are the explanatory commitments of theists?

III

In 1901 the young Raïssa Oumansoff and Jacques Maritain were students of the natural sciences at the Sorbonne. They greatly admired their teachers, most of them atheists like themselves, but were perplexed by the materialism that they professed. For that materialism excluded any conception of truth as a good such that recognition of it and allegiance to it could change the direction of a life. The materialist understanding of the causal order had no place for such goods and their account of truth was a weakened relativist account. Yet on Oumansoff's and Maritain's view a life not defined by its relationship to such a good would be a life without meaning. Moreover the evils of the world are such that, if there is no meaning to life, to go on living would be intolerable. So they decided to commit suicide, if they could not find grounds for rejecting the materialism of their teachers. Happily they did find such grounds. Péguy sent them to hear Bergson's lectures and Bergson provided them with badly needed philosophical resources.[4]

Later, as everyone knows, the Maritains became Catholics and later still Thomists. What connection might there have been between their later theism and their earlier insistence on the place of a regard for truth in human lives? I am not trying to reconstruct the path actually taken by the Maritains, but rather to ask more generally what connections are to be found. So let me begin by returning to Hamilton's discovery of quaternions, a key moment both in the history of mathematics and that of mechanics. Quaternions now enable us to represent rotations in areas as different as that of robotics and that of orbital mechanics, so arriving at truths that are crucial for further enquiry. They find an indispensable place in a history of reasoning about the world, reasoning directed towards the achievement of truths, some of which are inconceivable and therefore unimaginable until they are discovered. And numerous scientific lives only have the directedness that they have because of the part that a regard for the good of truth, expressed in the search for such truths, plays in their lives. So there is a history of how mathematics and the natural sciences came to be, a history of the forms in which a search for the truth about this or that aspect of nature came to be embodied. And that history is itself fully intelligible only as part of a larger cultural history of how human beings have pursued and pursue a range of different goods.

To explain this or that episode in either of these histories is simply to identify its place in the development of the embodied thought that provides that history with its subject matter, thought always partly formed by and reflective of material circumstances, but thought informed by standards of truth and rationality, thought directed towards the achievement of goods. How do such explanations relate to the explanations furnished by the natural sciences, explanations of the formation of glaciers and the eruptions of volcanoes, of the genesis of stars and the evolution of species? The aim is to understand how things came to be as they are and not otherwise by, as we noted earlier, identifying the antecedent conditions and the causal or probabilistic law-like generalizations that determined that they should be as they are. But, as we also noted earlier, every such explanation poses further questions.

If to explain is to provide evidence that under these conditions this kind of effect results from that kind of cause, then the next question is: In virtue of what does this kind of cause produce this kind of effect? The answer to this question will be a story of causal sequences at a more fundamental level and about these causal sequences the same question will arise and the answer to it will be a further such story. Moreover, as we spell these stories out, we turn out to have been contributing to a larger story, that of the cosmos. We can begin anywhere, perhaps with everyday accounts of how the planting of seeds issues in the flowering and fruiting of apple trees, and proceed to stories about the molecular interactions necessary for photosynthesis and from them to causal narratives that substitute for an account of molecules and chemical reactions one of fundamental particles and their interactions. There will be in each case a story that can be completed by calling on the relevant sciences. No kind or degree of complexity defies this kind of explanation. We learn what happened at each stage in the history of change and how it happened as it did, moving from less to more fundamental explanations, until we have a cosmological story that takes us from hadrons, leptons and bosons to apple trees and indeed to those who cultivate them for the sake of their fruit, reaching a point or looking forward to reaching a point when there will be nothing further to be explained by biology, chemistry or physics and, from the standpoint of the contemporary atheist, nothing further to be explained.

Yet what is astonishing is that nature so understood has the structure that it has. A story that begins with hadrons, leptons and bosons ends with horticulturalists and atheists, agents who do this for the sake of achieving that. But a world of hadrons, leptons and bosons is one where there is no application for the concept of acting 'for the sake of'. What is astonishing is not the improbability of the outcome. Given any initial distribution of fundamental particles, the laws of quantum mechanics, and an extended period of time, any particular outcome will be highly improbable. What is astonishing is that this universe, the universe as characterized by quantum mechanical and relativistic theorists, should be hospitable to the agency of embodied mind, and be transformable by that agency. This is what, unless one is an atheist, cries out for explanation.[5]

The universe could after all have been quite other than it is. So why is it as it is? What accounts for the fact that the universe cannot be accounted for by physics? Contemporary physics has a place for hadrons, leptons and bosons, for strong and weak forces, for electromagnetism and gravitational attraction, and perhaps for strings and eleven dimensions. What it has no place for, as we already noted, are intentionality-informed agents, intentionally effective agents – something insisted on by Quine – and therefore for physicists. If we take what contemporary physics asserts to be true, then it is difficult to understand how physicists are possible. It is even more difficult to understand how intentionally effective agents, among them physicists, are able recurrently to restructure this or that part or aspect of the order of nature so that it functions as they intended.

The questions that I am asking cannot be answered by drawing on the findings of physics or any other natural science. When natural scientists have completed their work, when there are no more gaps in their stories, these questions will remain unanswered. What may be said in reply is that there is neither need nor occasion to ask these questions. If anyone insists on posing them, the response should be: That is just how things are. When explanation by physics and the other natural sciences terminates, explanation terminates. And, if anyone answers them by asserting that the only possible explanation is that the universe depends for its existence and determinate character on the act of a being whose powers are not limited as the powers of all finite beings are limited, the response should be that we have no compelling reason for looking for explanations beyond what the sciences can afford.

Yet, as the theist will remark, if at earlier stages requests for explanation had been denied because 'That is just how things are', then enquiry would have been frustrated at a much earlier stage. So why is it reasonable to terminate it at this stage? And the theist may voice a suspicion that the atheist fears that the only way to avoid giving the theist's answer is to avoid asking the theist's question. But to this atheists have an important reply. Let us concede, they may say, the possibility of asking the theist's question. It remains impossible for a rational agent to give the theist's reply. For were the universe to be the work of an omnipotent, omniscient, and all good being, it would be quite otherwise than it is. The account of the heterogeneity of explanation that has been advanced makes it plain that the universe lacks the unity that it would have, if it were the work of a single creator. And the multiplicity of kinds of evil and of evils makes it incredible that the will of a single god creator prevails. So admit the theist's question and you will get the atheist's answer.

To which the prudent theist will respond by revisiting the arguments of Book 3 of Aquinas' *Summa Contra Gentiles*. Evils are intelligible only as deprivations of goods and are frustrations of and afflictions of just those agents actually or potentially directed by reasoning and intention towards the achievement of goods. Just as there is no adequate scientific explanation of the existence of such agents in a universe whose physical constitution is what it is, so there can be no adequate scientific explanation of the part played in their lives by their frustrations and afflictions. The only adequate explanation of why the universe is as it is must allow that God in creating the universe made evil possible.

IV

Not all theists believe that belief in God can be rationally justified. What I have suggested is that commitment to belief in God can be rationally justified only if certain theses about the nature and limits of scientific explanation can be justified. It is possible of course without inconsistency to be convinced of the truth of those theses and to remain unconvinced by theistic arguments. I have gestured towards, but not spelled out the arguments that theists would need to advance, if they were to have sufficient grounds for asserting not only that the universe or certain features of it need to be explained, but also that it or they can only be adequately explained as the work of a creating and sustaining God.

Atheists sometimes speak as if the mistake made by theists is only that they believe in one being too many. If we were to enumerate all the items that compose the universe, there would be nothing about which atheists and theists would need to disagree until the catalogue of finite beings was complete and the theists added an infinite being. On this view disagreement about God is consistent with agreement about the universe. What I have suggested is that, where the most influential types of modern atheism are concerned, disagreement about God entails disagreement about the nature of the universe.

ENDNOTES

1   William Rowan Hamilton, *London, Edinburgh and Dublin Philosophical Magazine and Journal of Science* 25 (1844), pp. 489–95.

2   Stuart J. Freedman and John F. Clauser, 'Experimental Test of Local Hidden-Variable Theories', *Physical Review Letters* 28 (April 3, 1972), pp. 938–41.

3   Martin Eger, *Science, Understanding, and Justice: The Philosophical Essays of Martin Eger* (Chicago, IL: Open Court, 2006), p. 46.

4   Raïssa Maritain, *We Have Been Friends Together* (New York, NY: Longmans, Green, 1942), pp. 68–85.

5   The argument that I have just presented is a revised and expanded version of part of my 'On Being a Theistic Philosopher in a Secularized Culture', *Proceedings of the American Catholic Philosophical Association* 84 (2010), pp. 23–32.

'REMEMBERING BÓTHAR BUÍ'

SEAMUS HEANEY

Remembering Bóthar Buí

Hazel stealth. A trickle in the culvert.
Athletic sealight on the doorstep slate,
On the sea itself, on silent roofs and gables.

Whitewashed suntraps. Hedges hot as chimneys.
Chairs on all fours. A plate-rack braced
and laden.
The fossil poetry of hob and slate.

Desire within its moat, dozing at ease --
Like a gorged cormorant on the rock at noon,
Exiled and in tune with the long glitter.

Re-enter this as the adult of solitude,
The silence-forder and the definite
Presence you sensed withdrawing first time round.

For Frankie, with love,
a year and several
revisions later
Seamus
January 1990

MY LIFE IN PHILOSOPHY*

PATRICK MASTERSON

Thank you for inviting me to speak this evening in this beautiful church and to such a discriminating audience. It is an honour but also a challenge. Instead of a technical philosophical lecture which you can download from the internet, I thought, in view of the special venue and context, I might provide a more autobiographical, even confessional account of my personal itinerary of philosophical reflection on the central questions in philosophy of religion. There are basically three such questions. Firstly, a question of existence – does God exist? Secondly a question of meaning – how should we think philosophically about the divine nature? Thirdly, a question of coexistence – in particular how are we to envisage the coexistence of God and ourselves?

I had a conventional Catholic family upbringing on the Northside of Dublin during and after the Second World War. I left school with my matric at the relatively early age of sixteen and found myself articled to become a chartered accountant instead of pursuing my preferred option of law, which my mother thought would be a dead end as we had no legal connections. By reaction to, or to escape, the mysteries of balance sheets and annual reports I decided I might have a vocation to become a simple missionary priest and entered for a brief period the seminary of the Vincentian priests who had taught me at Castleknock College. Here I experienced my first introduction to philosophy with some elementary study of basic logic. Why is it valid to argue that 'If all cats have two heads and if Tabby is a cat then Tabby has two heads', but invalid to argue that 'If all cats have four legs and if Tabby has four legs then Tabby is a cat?' I became interested in the formal structure of logical or rational argument and this respect for rational argument extended later into my reflections about the existence and nature of God and has remained with me throughout my life. In this regard my thinking would be very different to great Protestant theologians such as Martin Luther and Karl Barth who are suspicious of the claims of natural reason in discussion about God.

I went on to study philosophy in much greater detail for my BA at University College Dublin, reading widely in subjects such as logic, psychology, ethics, political philosophy, metaphysics and Natural Theology. This interest developed into a passion and began to replace my commitment to the life of a simple Vincentian missionary. Eventually when it was noticed that the mortality rate of the day-old chickens consigned to my care in the seminary farm rose to an alarming 23 per cent by comparison with a national average of 5 per cent, it was mutually agreed that if I could not be a minder of chickens I was unlikely to be a successful fisher of men. When my father, who was a busy general practitioner with a large family, collected me from the seminary he asked me kindly what I would now like to do after two false starts. I told him that I was now sure that what I wanted was to be a professional philosopher. When he failed to convince me to do medicine first, and then perhaps to continue my philosophical studies, he agreed doubtfully to my decision but warned me that in his humble opinion philosophy would never butter parsnips!

I returned with great enthusiasm to my studies and in the final year of my BA I became particularly interested in what was then called 'Natural Theology'. This was the area of philosophy concerned with what might be known about the existence and nature of God by means of natural reason alone. The philosophy of Thomas Aquinas, as developed in modern times by scholars such as Jacques Maritain, Etienne Gilson, Frederick Copleston, Peter Geach and the vibrant school of philosophy at Louvain, was the main source of inspiration at this stage of my studies and Aquinas has remained for me a remarkable resource of philosophical insight.

Amongst Aquinas' various reflections on the existence and nature of God I devoted particular attention to his famous Five Ways of proving the existence of God. These begin with some familiar feature of our experience, such as things depending causally upon other things like a picture depending on a hook and the hook depending on a wall and so on, or such as contingent things coming into being and later ceasing to be, or such as the different levels of reality such as mineral, vegetable, animal and human, or such as the way in which things with no intelligence seemed to act in purposeful ways like spiders weaving webs to catch food. Aquinas argued that such ordinary experiences when analysed deeply turned out to be inexplicable and even contradictory unless understood as ultimately caused by an infinite intelligent being, namely, God, who is not included amongst such experiences. He was keen to emphasize that this causality by God is not like the ordinary causality of our experience where something already existing, for example a billiard ball, interacts with something else, such as another billiard ball, and causes it to move. He argued that God's causality was what we call creation, namely a causality which does not presuppose things already existing, as does the causality in a game of billiards, but originates and sustains from absolutely nothing the entire order of finite things. This idea of God as creator was nowhere to be found in the philosophies of Plato and Aristotle whom he greatly respected. For them god or gods were just special parts of the world who attracted or moved other things around. The idea of God as creator was a distinctly Judaeo–Christian idea which Aquinas thought could be confirmed by natural reason. This confidence in the power of natural reason to attain some truth about the existence and nature of God I found very appealing.

After obtaining a good BA degree I proceeded to study for an MA degree by written thesis. I took for my subject Aquinas' fourth way of proving the existence of God. This is the argument which starts from the observation that we are aware of different degrees or levels of perfections such as being, intelligibility, beauty and goodness. We are aware that some things have greater existential perfection than others. Thus we realize that trees have a greater measure of being than stones, animals than trees, and humans than animals. Aquinas argues that this hierarchical scale of being is made ultimate sense of by the affirmation of God as its infinite creative source.

This kind of reasoning was popular in Christian thought but it stretches back to Plato's philosophy. Plato argued that we could compare things as more and less good or beautiful only by reference to a supreme example or idea of goodness and beauty of which we were aware in a previous existence and which we can come to know again by a dialectical process of reflection upon the limited expressions of these perfections of which we have experience. Aquinas was not keen on this Platonic idea that through a process of reflection we could come to a direct knowledge of a supreme goodness, beauty and being. For this would imply that we could come to know God directly in this life, which we cannot. Instead he claimed that we could argue validly that God must exist as the supreme unlimited perfection who causes or creates the existence of the different levels of perfection which we know through experience. It is an indirect argument to an affirmation of God as creator, not one in terms of directly attained knowledge of him. (The similarity yet hierarchical diversity of the various levels of existence requires, he argued, the existence of God as their ultimate cause, a cause who is beyond the scaled order of finite perfection whose existence he creates.)

One challenge to this kind of vertical thinking which explains lower reality in terms of a higher supreme perfection is posed by the development of modern science and especially by Darwinian theory of evolution. This proposes a more horizontal account of levels of perfection and seeks to explain the higher in terms of the lower. Ideally it would explain all difference in materialist terms as simply complicated products of elementary particles governed exclusively by laws of physics, chemistry and biology.

For my MA work I was fortunate to obtain a Travelling Studentship from the National University of Ireland to study for a PhD at the famous ancient University of Louvain. Here I spent two and a half years attending lectures by famous professors and writing my PhD thesis (under the direction of Professor Gerard Verbeke who was also Secretary of the Royal Academy of Belgium.) The subject of my PhD was a development of my interest in Aquinas' Natural Theology or Philosophy of Religion. I was interested in elaborating his account of the ultimate philosophical meaning of finite being and of infinite being. This seemingly rather abstract topic was of considerable philosophical interest particularly from a Christian viewpoint. Aquinas wanted to develop and defend a philosophical idea of God as Infinitely Perfect Being. For the Greek philosopher whom he most admired, namely Aristotle, the idea of an infinitely perfect being made no sense. For the Greeks 'finitude' and 'perfection' were equivalent terms. Clearly delineated finite forms, so evidently etched in Greek sunlight, mathematics and architecture were the symbols of completeness and perfection. The infinite, the 'apeiron', by contrast, signified the indefinite, the formless, the chaotic, the imperfect which needed to be contained by or determined into some definite form. The Greek gods, the most perfect beings, were finite in form and the idea of an infinitely perfect being would have struck the Greeks as nonsensical – the ultimate oxymoron. This was one problem that Aquinas would have to address philosophically.

At the other extreme there was a strong Christian tradition, partly influenced by the Platonic thought that I have mentioned, which claimed that the idea of infinite being was a perfectly coherent idea and that when we affirm something to be a finite being we do so only by reference to this coherent idea of infinite being. St Augustine, the Pseudo-Dionysius and St Bonaventure are in this tradition. However, the most famous, or most notorious, was the eleventh-century monk St Anselm, who formulated his famous Ontological Argument for the existence of God. He argued that from our perfectly coherent idea of God, as a being than which no greater perfection can be conceived, we can argue directly to his real existence as distinct from his existence only in our imagination. For since a being that exists in reality as well as in the mind is obviously greater and more perfect than a being that exists only in our mind; therefore God understood as a being than which nothing greater can be conceived must exist in reality as well as just an idea in our minds. This is an argument, some version of which has continued to convince some philosophers throughout the following centuries even to this day. For example, the founder of modern philosophy in the seventeenth century René Descartes remarked in his *Meditations on First Philosophy*: 'Nor should I imagine that I do not perceive the infinite by a true idea, but only by a negation of the finite ... for on the contrary, I perceive that there is manifestly more reality in infinite substance than in finite, and therefore that in some way I have in me the notion of God before that of myself.'

Aquinas rejected this kind of a priori shortcut response to questions about the existence and nature of God. He argued that until we know through faith or rational argument that God, understood as infinitely perfect being, actually exists we cannot be sure that this idea of him is a coherent one rather than a contradictory one like the idea of a square circle. Remember how for the Greeks it would have been a contradictory, nonsensical idea. Aquinas argued that we do not deduce the existence of God from our coherent idea of him, but rather establish the coherence of our idea of him by proving his existence. This we must do in an a posteriori manner by arguing from familiar finite features of our experience to his existence as their transcendent infinite cause or creator.

Aquinas did not believe that to know that something is a finite being we need to have an idea of infinite being. The fact that this being is not that being, or that it began to be and will cease to be, is clear evidence of its finitude. As he said 'finite is predicated absolutely and not in virtue of any reference to an infinite'. He went on to develop a detailed analysis of what in the deepest sense constitutes the finitude of any being. His conclusion was that something is finite, not simply because it is just one material instance of a particular species such as this cat rather than that cat, but because in it the perfection of existence is limited or confined to a specific form such as human, dog, fish or perhaps even angel. When he has shown that the entire order of such beings depends for its existence upon a creative cause not belonging to this order, he can affirm the reality of God, not as a Platonic form or idea, but as infinite perfection of existence. In this context finite beings can be re-described as limited participants in God's infinite perfection of existence. Mercifully for you I won't go into this in more detail but simply remark that Aquinas achieved a remarkable metaphysical synthesis in the face of objections from both Greek philosophy and some Christian thinkers. It is a synthesis which has provided me with a solid basis for philosophical discussion of the main questions concerning the existence and nature of God and his coexistence with creatures.

As I was completing my research on this metaphysical theme I was becoming increasingly interested in various forms of modern and contemporary philosophy such as existentialism and phenomenology, which instead of abstract impersonal metaphysical reflection about the structure, and dimensions, and ultimate foundation of finite being, concentrated attention on the central philosophical significance of human consciousness and the drama of individual human existence. In particular I became interested in the development of modern atheism.

I explored this topic in a series of lectures during the Sixties in UCD where I was appointed as a very junior lecturer in philosophy over fifty years ago in 1963. The topic could be posed in the form of a question. Why was it that until about the seventeenth century a person was said to be alienated, estranged or out of touch if she didn't believe in God ('The fool says in his heart there is no God'), whereas today it is often claimed that it is the person who believes in God who is alienated, estranged and out of touch with contemporary sensibility? How did the relationship between the ideas of atheism and alienation come thus to be reversed?

Eventually in 1971 my reflections on this theme found a wider audience in my first sole-authored book entitled *Atheism and Alienation. The Philosophical Sources of Contemporary Atheism*. To my surprise and gratification this book was well received and was published not only in Ireland, but also in the United States and then in paperback by Penguin in the UK and even, a year later, in translation in Japan. (I must confess to some amusement pretending, during a meeting of the Academic Council in UCD, to read the Japanese translation from back to front as required.) My argument was basically that the two main philosophical sources of contemporary atheism were the development of modern science inaugurated by such geniuses as Copernicus, Galileo and Newton, and the development of modern philosophy inaugurated by such geniuses as Descartes, Hume and Kant.

With modern science one has a more active interventionist conception of authentic scientific knowledge than the characteristically speculative metaphysical approach employed previously. One began to seek knowledge by interfering in the course of nature through recourse to experiments. Instead of appealing to spirits or even God to account for events in the world, a scientific method was developed which was empirical in a twofold sense. Not only did it start from sense experience, it also accepted only explanations which could be verified through a return to sense experience. It sought to understand the world from within the world accepting only mathematically modelled theoretical explanations which could be verified by a return to experience through experiments which could test the value of the explanations.

When this experimental method is elevated to the status of the only acceptable source of scientific knowledge one adopts a form of philosophy known historically as Positivism and later as Logical Positivism. When this is allied with a Neo-Darwinian materialist view of evolution one has a very influential reductionist source of contemporary atheism according to which all valid theoretical knowledge is confined within the limits of physics, chemistry and biology. In this tradition one finds thinkers such as Richard Dawkins and Daniel Dennett.

The second main historical source of contemporary atheism is the modern philosophical revolution inaugurated by Descartes' redirection of attention away from an intelligible, presumably divinely ordered, external world existing independently of our consciousness. Instead he focused attention inwards upon the resources of human subjectivity and sought to understand all meaning and value as somehow deriving from the resources of our human subjectivity.

Thus Descartes doubted the significance and even existence of everything except the one thing he could not doubt, namely, his own existence as a thinking being. From within his famous '*Cogito ergo sum*' ('I think therefore I am') he sought to re-establish the existence of everything else which he had provisionally and methodologically doubted, such as his own body and the external world. As I mentioned earlier, in this exercise he relied greatly on his own idea of infinite being from which he thought he could deduce the existence of God. He then relied on the trustworthiness of this infinitely perfect God to restore his belief in the existence of the external world because a trustworthy God would not deceive him by giving him false beliefs. So finally in Descartes it is ambiguous whether it is God or man who is the ultimate source of meaning and value. And so the problem of the coexistence of man and God becomes perhaps an even more important philosophical issue than the existence and nature of God.

In the subsequent course of philosophy one witnesses the progressive tilting of the balance away from God in favour of man as the ultimate source of all meaning and value. With the philosopher Kant, space and time, substance, causality, relationship, etc are viewed as forms and categories which we impose on our raw experience. Likewise morality is something we give ourselves – we do not derive it from God. God is neither an object of knowledge nor a basis of morality. He is at best an object of hope that a good life will be rewarded.

In the early nineteenth century the philosopher Hegel tried to resolve this problem of the coexistence of man and God by arguing that they were simply two aspects of the same reality. Mankind is simply the necessary medium through which God comes to know himself. The story of human history and religion is the story of the process through which God comes to full and explicit knowledge of himself. In Hegel's own words: 'Without the world God is not God.'

However this Hegelian defence of the coexistence of man and God, of finite and infinite, a defence weighted in favour of God was soon reversed. Karl Marx turned the issue of the coexistence of finite and infinite over on its side and it became an issue of the coexistence of the finite individual estranged from his infinite species reality in the future communist society. This issue of the Coexistence of finite and infinite was not to be resolved by Hegelian philosophy but by class warfare and the revolution of the proletariat. Religion was not a medium through which, when interpreted philosophically, God comes to know himself. It is a self-administered opium of the people which must be overcome if humanity is to attain its true reality in the Communist society.

Another powerful reaction to Hegelian metaphysical thinking, particularly in the twentieth century, was the style of philosophy broadly described as existentialism and more technically as existential phenomenology. Existentialism highlighted as of fundamental importance the anguished existence of the individual subject who must accept responsibility for choosing the orientation of his own life even though it is ultimately meaningless. There were of course religious versions of existentialism, for example, with Kierkegaard and Gabriel Marcel. However, the most influential proponents such as Sartre, Merleau-Ponty, Camus, and Heidegger, were profoundly atheistic and collapsed the issue of the coexistence of finite and infinite into an expression of bad faith on the part of the individual subject failing to face up to the ultimate absurdity of her existence as the only source of meaning and value in her life.

This history of the sources of contemporary atheism, of which I have given you a very potted outline, had a profound influence on my philosophical outlook. I realized that however much I valued impersonal, objective, metaphysical discussion of questions concerning the existence and nature of God, one could not isolate it from the contemporary focus on human subjectivity and the irreducible role of human consciousness as an essential co-relative in any knowledge claim. One could no longer rely exclusively on an account of how things are objectively in themselves independently of our knowledge of them. One must advert particularly to how things appear to, and exist for, human consciousness and subjectivity. The affirmation of the existence of God is not just the registration of another fact such as that water boils at one hundred degrees centigrade at sea level. It is an intrinsically self-involving affirmation with radical consequences for my evaluation of the meaning and value of my existence. The claim of modernity that talk about how things are objectively in themselves, independently of our knowledge of them, is subordinate to how they appear to human consciousness assumes great significance. One heard less talk of metaphysics and Natural Theology and more of Philosophy of Religion, understood as the philosophical appraisal of the religious experience of human subjects. Since then I have been trying to determine the appropriate balance in discussion about God between objective metaphysical discussion and the consideration of how things appear from the perspective of their givenness to human subjectivity, and have published various articles on this topic.

In the mid-eighties my philosophical quest for God was interrupted for a period of sixteen years. For the first eight of these I had the honour of being President of University College Dublin, and for the second eight I was invited to be President of the European University Institute in Florence. When I retired from Florence my beautiful wife Frankie and I divided our time between Dublin and a remote village in the Languedoc region of France. Here I located my library and had the leisure to renew my philosophy studies.

In 2009 I published a book entitled *The Sense of Creation. Experience and the God Beyond*. In it I renewed my interest in the idea of creation, according to which God is the cause of the world, not as an element within it and interacting with it, but rather as the transcendent cause of its entire existence and activity. As creator he is that which enables it to be and to act as the world which it is. His causality does not interact directly with what happens in the world in the way, for example, that alcohol might interact with my concentration and affect my driving. It is a causality which enables me to exist and to continue in existence and to exercise causality in the way that I do. It is a causality not of the same order or kind as mine where cause and effect imply one another. I depend radically upon God but he does not depend upon me. The relationship between me and God is a one-way asymmetrical one – I am really related to God as totally dependent upon him but he is not really affected or modified by creating me, but only thought of as so affected.

In the book I sought to disclose various ciphers or traces or analogies of this curious asymmetrical relationship. I thought that if similar asymmetrical relationshps were to be found within our experience they would help us to make sense of the idea of creation and it in turn would help to make sense of them. I considered, for example, the relationship between the world and our knowledge of it. I argued that when we come to know something about the world, such as the effect of the moon on the tides, our knowledge is really related to and dependent upon the intrinsic intelligibility of the world. However the intelligibility of the world exists independently of our knowledge of it, and is in no way dependent upon it. Our knowledge of the world is an asymmetrical relationship – a one-way dependency relationship.

Another example, this time in the moral sphere, is the way in which the other person, in her need, can make an absolute ethical demand upon me which is not simply the counterpart of what I can demand of her. The centre of my moral being is outside myself in an asymmetrical relationship of dependence upon an appeal addressed to me by my vulnerable neighbour.

I am ethically invoked absolutely by the other person and not simply in virtue of some corelative obligation.

These are just two of various examples which I adduced as finite examples given within our experience of the sort of asymmetrical relationship which obtains in the relationship of creation between us and God. They help us to think constructively about the idea of creation and it helps to make sense of these paradoxical relationships which we experience.

Last year, to the disgust of my disrespectful children who would have preferred me to write a sexy thriller and make some money, I published another book on philosophy of religion. It was titled *Approaching God. Between Phenomenology and Metaphysics*. In it I tried to explore the relationships, if any, between three basic approaches to God, namely, through metaphysics, through phenomenology, and through theology. Each approach is an attempt to provide an overall view of everything and each is governed by a first principle or animating concept – the concept of 'being' in the case of metaphysics, the concept of 'human consciousness' in the case of phenomenology, and the concept of 'God' in the case of theology. One can try to understand everything as a kind of being, or as an object of human consciousness, or as revealed by God.

In metaphysics we try to understand everything as a particular kind or level of being. In phenomenology, which is the characteristic form of contemporary continental philosophy, following in the tradition inaugurated as we saw by Descartes, we try to understand everything as somehow given to human consciousness. This can include trying to understand our sense of wonder, our sense of the numinous, our sense of the sacred or the holy, various religious feelings of need, exaltation or salvation, mystical experiences of encounter with the divine, and experiences of receiving a response to our deepest yearnings. In theology we try to understand everything from the perspective of what God has allegedly told us about himself and our relationship to him. Each of these approaches is sometimes proposed as the only correct and adequate one. I argue that, on the contrary, they are each incomplete and require each other as complementary to one another.

The metaphysical approach is important because its emphasis is upon how things are independently of our knowledge of them. Its affirmation of God as Infinite Being is an affirmation of what would be the case even if there was no human consciousness to affirm it. However, its findings are rather limited and impersonal. It may attain the affirmation of God as infinite creator but tells us very little of the personal relationship which can exist between us and God.

The phenomenological approach, concentrating upon how things are given and appear to human consciousness, is better equipped to deal with our personal sense of God and his significance for our lives. It considers the existence of God as he is for us – as corresponding to very deep longings and emotions for ultimate meaning in our lives. It resonates to St Augustine's remark 'Thou hast made us for thyself O Lord and our hearts are restless until we rest in thee.' However considered simply in itself it cannot disclose the deeper meaning of our relationship to God disclosed in Revelation and developed by theology. Moreover considered in abstraction from the objective claims of metaphysics about the ultimate nature of realty itself there will always remain the suspicion that perhaps the so-called findings about God disclosed in our religious or mystical experience are only an illusion or, as Marx claimed, 'the opium of the people'.

Theology as our attempt to elaborate in a systematic way God's divine revelation to us culminating in the incarnation, life, death and resurrection of Jesus Christ is certainly a much more comprehensive account of God and our relationship to him than we could have ascertained by our own reason alone. However even Christian theology has to rely upon philosophical concepts to elaborate its two great central truths, namely, that God created us and that he has divinized us beyond our status as mere creatures to participate in his own divine life of love. It seems to me that our objective metaphysics of being is best suited to develop an understanding of the revealed truth that we are created beings. The more personal approach of a phenomenology of human consciousness is best suited to elaborate the revealed truth that we are elevated by divine grace to fellowship in God's own love.

It should be no great surprise that we need a combination of various approaches to speak in what will still be a very faltering and limited way about the God who created us and loves us. We might do well to recall that we still use the complementary terminologies of waves and particles when discussing the behaviour of much more mundane phenomena such as radiation and light.

These philosophical reflections on the existence and nature of God, and our coexistence with him, have for me in recent months, assumed a new, more personal form since the sudden death last year of my beloved wife Frankie after almost fifty years of a very loving marriage. I ask myself how can it be that I still love her as an abiding reality and not just as a beautiful memory. It seems to me that despite her death I love her as emergent into a new level or form of reality. It would be hard to make any sense of this except in terms of a loving God who is the creative source of all emergence, including her emergence from death and my love of her as still alive. However in the final analysis I am truly able to love her and to love God not simply in virtue of my naturally emergent but also fundamentally advenient capacity to love: I am also enabled in virtue of the advenient gift of the Holy Spirit, which is the spirit of divine love, to love her and to love God because I and she have been enabled to participate together in the love which God is.

This has led me to undertake serious reflection on the very interesting concept of emergence. And this reflection has led me to agree with the conclusion in a recent book, *Mind and Cosmos*, by the distinguished atheist American philosopher Thomas Nagel that the Neo-Darwinian materialist conception of nature, which is the prevailing scientific orthodoxy, is almost certainly false. The contention of this prevailing viewpoint is that a properly scientific explanation of any object of enquiry, including the origin of life, of consciousness, and indeed of all mental activity must be provided, or at least sought, exclusively in terms of a reductive account which avails itself only of the laws of physics and chemistry.

The concept of emergence provides a context and perspective for an alternative to this reductive assumption. It is an alternative which is open to the possibility that the ultimate foundation of the entire multi-layered reality which we experience is not just an anonymous material universe operating exclusively in accordance with impersonal physical laws but rather and more basically the result of a benevolent decision by a loving God.

The fundamental characteristic of emergence is that it is a defining property of an entity which is neither deducible from, nor reducible to, the properties of the components from which it has emerged. It is not simply 'a result' of the nature, combination and operation of its components. As examples of such mere 'resultants' one might instance a sandcastle or indeed any mechanical object, such as a motor car, assembled from and intelligible in terms of the co-ordination of its components. To describe an entity as emergent is to signify that it obtains and acts in a novel manner, one quite different from the manner in which entities arise non-controversially as a result of the combination of their various components. Think, for example, of the manner in which the first written version of 'Hamlet' emerged from Shakespeare's bottle of ink. No microscopic analysis or random distribution of the contents of the ink bottle will disclose the text of the play. Yet the play has appeared from a particular distribution of the ink. One can meaningfully affirm that it has emerged from or through or in the medium of ink to which it is irreducible.

That the origin of life is emergent in this innovative way is a plausible if hotly disputed claim. I don't intend to enter into this debate. However, as one moves up the scale of the various levels of being it seems increasingly reasonable to maintain that here we have clear evidence of the phenomenon of emergence. Animal consciousness cannot be adequately explained as a mere extension or complication of physical evolution. There is an even more compelling case to claim that reason, including its claim to access objective truth, moral value, aesthetic judgment, cannot be explained as a mere extension or complication of consciousness. An even more remarkable example of emergent activity is the exercise of unselfish love of another. One has moved from the domain of impersonal third-person objects to increasingly profoundly personal levels of first-person subjectivity. One has the emergence of levels of novelty which exist and exercise causality in a radically novel way, a way quite different from and irreducible to that of the physical components in which they subsist and from which they have emerged. Of course all of this needs to be argued more thoroughly but I believe that it can be and this is what now preoccupies me.

I think that a particularly powerful example of emergence is the emergence of human love. This love is a rational activity extending far beyond instinctual response. It can even extend beyond the erotic love of another person because she fulfils all one's desires. It can extend to the agapeistic non-self-regarding love of and solicitude for the inherent goodness and lovableness of the beloved.

Such love is certainly emergent from and irreducible to the material-embodied medium from which it has emerged. It can even extend to being an unselfish loving solicitude for the inherent goodness of the beloved as spiritually emergent after death from her previously physically embodied context. If the experience of this love as love of an abiding and really existing person, and not just love of a memory of her, is not an illusion, a significant question presents itself about how this is possible. It seems to me that only the affirmation of a loving God who is the foundation and source of all emergence can provide an answer to this question. At least this is the perspective which I am at present trying to explore more effectively and develop as a convincing viewpoint.

It is curious that at this late stage in my life I find myself involved in a kind of reflection which moves in an opposite direction to my previous philosophical approach. Heretofore, I have sought to establish certain objective truths about the existence and nature of God by reason alone. This provided the basis for the reasonableness of the free act of faith which gives rise to hope, a hope which is a theological virtue giving trusting access to the love of God. Now instead I find myself starting with love, love of my beloved Frankie and love of God, and working back to hope and thence to faith and rational conviction. Perhaps both approaches are valid and complementary.

In conclusion I will simply say that philosophical and theological reflection on the existence, nature, and coexistence with us of a loving God seems to me a valid, fruitful and rewarding activity. It is one in which I have blessedly been enabled to engage in for nearly sixty years and I recommend it wholeheartedly as an activity which is not an illusion but one which sheds light on the great question of the ultimate meaning and value of human existence.

ENDNOTE

* Text of a talk given in Haddington Road Church, Dublin, 27 November 2014.

SELECT BIBLIOGRAPHY
OF PATRICK MASTERSON

'Our Image of God', *The Irish Theological Quarterly* 30 (1963), pp. 262–72.

'La définition du fini implique-t-elle l'infini?', *Revue Philosophique de Louvain* 62 (1964), pp. 41–68.

'An Open Church?,' *The Irish Ecclesiastical Record* 102 (1964), pp. 417–32.

'The Laity in the Church', *Doctrine and Life* 15 (1965), pp. 438–51.

'Contemporary Atheism', *Studies* 54 (1965), pp. 131–51.

Foreword, Ignace Lepp, *A Christian Philosophy of Existence* (Dublin: Gill, 1965), pp. 7–13.

'Natural Law Today', *Select Proceedings of Guild of St Luke SS Cosmas and Damian* (Dublin, 1966), pp. 12–18.

'For a Laity Articulate and Informed', *Christus Rex* 20 (1966), pp. 287–96.

'The Laity: Commentary on Chapter 4', *Vatican II: The Church Constitution*, ed. Austin Flannery (Dublin: Scepter, 1966), pp. 109–30.

'Ecumenism Today', *Doctrine and Life* 17 (1967), pp. 137–43.

'Christian Faith in Today's World', *The Capuchin Annual* 35 (1968), pp. 217–26.

'Christian Faith in Today's World', *The Christian in his World*, ed. B. Devlin (Dublin: Gill, 1968), pp. 13–30.

'Hegel's Philosophy of God', *Philosophical Studies* 19 (1970), pp. 126–47.

Atheism and Alienation: A Study of the Philosophical Sources of Contemporary Atheism (Dublin: Gill and Macmillan / South Bend, IN: University of Notre Dame Press; 1971 / London: Penguin, 1973). Japanese Translation: Kyoto, 1980.

'Kierkegaard's View of Time: A Reply to J. Heywood Thomas', *The Journal of the British Society for Phenomenology* 4 (1973), pp. 41–4.

'Does Natural Theology Rest on a Presumption?', *Spode House Review* (1974), pp. 9–22.

'Self-involvement and the Affirmation of God', *Miscellanea Albert Dondeyne: Godsdienstfilosofie / Philosophie de la religion* (Leuven: Leuven University Press, 1974), pp. 263–77.

'The Co-existence of Man and God in the Philosophy of St Thomas Aquinas', *Images of Man in Ancient and Medieval Thought: Studia Gerardo Verbeke ab amicis et collegis dicata*, eds. F. Bossier et al. (Leuven: Leuven University Press, 1975), pp. 335–51.

'Aquinas's Notion of God Today', *The Irish Theological Quarterly* 44 (1977), pp. 79–89.

'Structuralism: The Demise of Man', *New Blackfriars* 58 (1977), pp. 4–20.

'Is Atheism now a Problem?', *Hermathena: A Dublin University Review* 103 (1977), pp. 26–33.

'The Concept of Resentment', *Studies* 68/271 (1979), pp. 157–72.

'The 29th September', *The Phoenix Park Dublin, 29th September 1979: The Pastoral Visit of Pope John Paul II* (Dublin: Academy Press, 1979), pp. 11–18.

'Experience and the Affirmation of God', *Neue Zeitschrift für Systematische Theologie und Religionsphilosophie* 22 (1980), pp. 17–32.

'Religion and Morality', *Ateismo e Dialogo* 17 (1982), pp. 167–74.

'Ethics and Absolutes in the Philosophy of E. Levinas', *Neue Zeitschrift für Systematische Theologie und Religionsphilosophie* 26 (1983), pp. 211–23.

'The Arts Degree in an Age of Science and Technology', *The Crane Bag* 7/2 (1983) pp. 33–40.

'God and Grammar', *Philosophical Studies* 29 (1983), pp. 7–24.

'Arguing from Intelligibility to God', *Essays in Memory of Alexis FitzGerald* (Dublin: Incorporated Law Society of Ireland, 1987), pp. 63–74.

'Does Natural Theology Rest on a Presumption?', *At the Heart of the Real*, ed. Fran O'Rourke, (Dublin: Irish Academic Press, 1992), pp. 177–94.

'A European Dimension to Higher Education and Research', *Unity and Diversity* (Brussels / Montreux: European Quality Publications, 2001), pp. 366–7.

'Feuerbach and the Apotheosis of Man', *Nineteenth Century Literature Criticism*, vol. 139, (New York, NY: Thompson-Gale, 2004), pp. 260–66.

'Remembering Vatican Two', *Remembering Vatican Two Facing the 21st Century: Historical and Theological Perspectives*, eds, Dermot A. Lane and Brendan Leahy (Dublin: Veritas, 2006), pp. 40–54.

'Cultural Diversity and Human Solidarity', *Articulations: Poetry, Philosophy and the Shaping of Culture* (Dublin: Royal Irish Academy, 2008), pp. 27–43.

'Natural Law Today', *An Irish Reader in Moral Theology: The Legacy of the Last Fifty Years*, vol. 1, ed. Enda McDonagh (Dublin: Columba Press, 2009), pp. 251–7.

'Morality and Transcendence', *An Irish Reader in Moral Theology: The Legacy of the Last Fifty Years*, ibid., pp. 324–31.

'Richard Kearney's Hermeneutics of Otherness', *Philosophy and Social Criticism* 34 (2008), pp. 247–65.

The Sense of Creation: Experience and the God Beyond (Aldershot: Ashgate/ Burlington, USA), 2008.

Approaching God: Between Phenomenology and Theology (London/New York, NY: Bloomsbury, 2013).

Quality Time at St Chinian (Dublin: Liberties Press, 2017).

'Philosophical Reasonableness of Theism', *The Furrow* 68 (2017), pp. 28–32.

CONTRIBUTORS

Eileen Brennan has a doctoral degree in philosophy from the Institut Catholique de Paris. She is an Assistant Professor in philosophy and the history of education at the Institute of Education, Dublin City University. A former co-editorial director of *Etudes Ricoeuriennes/Ricoeur Studies*, she has published articles on French philosophy as well as translations of works by Paul Ricoeur, Julia Kristeva, Jean Greisch, and Dominique Janicaud.

Deirdre Carabine studied at the Queen's University of Belfast and University College Dublin, gaining a PhD in philosophy from the former and a PhD in Classics from the latter. She was one of the first post-doctoral Newman Scholars at UCD and taught both there and at Queen's from the mid-1980s to the early 1990s. She relocated to Uganda in 1993 to teach at the newly founded Uganda Martyrs University. She was co-founder and Vice-Chancellor at the Virtual University of Uganda, the first fully online-only university in sub-Saharan Africa. Her scholarly interests include Neoplatonism and medieval philosophy with emphasis on the apophatic tradition and the Fathers of the Church.

Desmond Connell was born in Dublin on 24 March 1926. He was educated at St Peter's National School, Phibsboro, and Belvedere College. He studied at University College Dublin, St Patrick's College, Maynooth, and the Université Catholique de Louvain, where in 1953 he received his PhD *summa cum laude* for a dissertation on the French philosopher Malebranche. He was appointed Professor of General Metaphysics at University College Dublin in 1972. In 1981 he was awarded a DLitt by the National University of Ireland. He was appointed Archbishop of Dublin in 1988, and created Cardinal in 2001. He died on 21 February 2017.

John Dillon graduated in Classics from Oxford in 1961, and gained a PhD from the University of California at Berkeley in 1969, after which he joined the faculty of the Department of Classics at Berkeley. In 1980 he was appointed Regius Professor of Greek at Trinity College Dublin, where he remained until his retirement in 2006. He is the author or editor of many publications in Greek Philosophy, in particular the history of the Platonic tradition, including *The Middle Platonists* (1977), *Alcinous, The Handbook of Platonism* (1993), *Iamblichus, De Anima* (2002), *The Heirs of Plato: A Study of the Old Academy, 347–274 BC* (2003), and four collections of essays, *The Golden Chain: Studies in the Development of Platonism and Christianity* (1991), *The Great Tradition: Further Studies in the Development of Platonism and Christianity* (1997), *The Platonic Heritage* (2012), and *The Roots of Platonism* (2018).

Joseph Dunne is Cregan Professor Emeritus of Philosophy and Education at Dublin City University. He taught for forty years at St Patrick's College Dublin and has also taught at Duke University, the University of Oslo, and the University of British Columbia. He is author of *Back to the Rough Ground: Practical Judgement and the Lure of Technique* (1997), and co-editor of *Questioning Ireland: Debates in Political Philosophy and Public Policy* (2000), *Childhood and its Discontents: The First Seamus Heaney Lectures* (2002), and *Education and Practice: Upholding the Integrity of Teaching and Learning* (2004). He is currently completing a book, *Persons in Practice: Essays between Education and Philosophy.*

John Haldane is the J. Newton Rayzor Sr Distinguished Professor of Philosophy at Baylor University, Texas, and Professor of Philosophy at the University of St Andrews, Scotland. He is a Fellow of the Royal Society of Edinburgh and Chair of the Royal Institute of Philosophy in London. He has published widely in aesthetics, ethics, metaphysics, philosophy of mind, philosophy of religion and history of philosophy.

Mark Patrick Hederman has been a monk at Glenstal Abbey, a Benedictine monastery in Limerick, for the last fifty years. He is former headmaster of Glenstal Abbey secondary school. He studied in Paris with Emmanuel Levinas during the 1968 student revolution when universities were closed, after which he wrote his MA dissertation on Levinas under the direction of Patrick Masterson at UCD. He received a PhD in Education from

University College Cork. He is author of a number of books, the latest of which, *Living the Mystery*, combines his interest in philosophy with his vocation to monastic life. He is co-founder, with Richard Kearney, of the cultural journal *The Crane Bag*.

Richard Kearney is the author of many books on modern European philosophy, literature and politics. He has also published novels and poetry and is international director of the Guestbook Project – Hosting the Stranger: Between Hostility and Hospitality. His most recent books include *Anatheism: Returning to God after God* (2012), *Reimagining the Sacred* (2015), and *Imagination Now* (2019).

Alasdair MacIntyre is Emeritus Research Professor at the University of Notre Dame, having previously taught at a number of universities in the UK and USA. Throughout a career of seven decades his work questioning the meaning and rational justification of moral judgments has made him one of the leading philosophers in the English-speaking world. He is a prolific writer, the author of fourteen monographs and four volumes of collected essays, the co-author of two books, and editor of five other volumes. He has published more than two hundred journal articles and book chapters and more than eighty book reviews. His most important book, *After Virtue* (1981), called for a searching re-evaluation of modern liberal individualist moral and political philosophy and a reappraisal of Aristotelian ethics and politics. This book and its four sequels exerted a major influence on subsequent moral theory in the late twentieth century. MacIntyre's most recent book, *Ethics in the Conflicts of Modernity* (2017), returns to the general question of the meaning of moral judgments and their rational justification, weighing the claims of emotivist and expressivist theorists against the Thomistic Aristotelian accounts of human action and practical reasoning.

Patrick Masterson was born in 1936 and grew up on the North Circular Road near the Phoenix Park in Dublin. He was educated at Belvedere and Castleknock colleges. In 1958 he received his MA degree with First Class Honours at University College Dublin and was awarded a Travelling Student Scholarship to pursue doctoral studies at the Université Catholique de Louvain. He was appointed lecturer in UCD's Department of Metaphysics in 1963, and Professor of Philosophy of Religion in 1972. His early book, *Atheism and Alienation: The Philosophical Sources of Contemporary Atheism*

(1971), was translated into Japanese. In 1983 he became Registrar of UCD, and in 1986 was appointed President. In 1994 he was appointed President of the European University Institute in Florence. Since his retirement in 2002 he spends much of the year in a small village in France near Saint Chinian where he has written two works in Philosophy, *The Sense of Creation* (2008) and *Approaching God: Between Phenomenology and Theology* (2013). He tends a small vineyard and has been appointed 'Chevalier dans la Confrérie des Vignerons de Saint Christophe'. His comic novel *Quality Time at St Chinian* (2017), about an imaginary provincial French university subjected to an external quality appraisal, is his first novel. He is a member of the Royal Irish Academy and the Lisbon Academy of Sciences. He has received honorary doctorates from Trinity College Dublin, Champlain College, and New York University.

Dermot Moran is the inaugural holder of the Joseph Chair in Catholic Philosophy at Boston College. He was previously Professor of Philosophy at University College Dublin. He has held Visiting Professorships at Yale University, Northwestern University, Rice University, Connecticut College, the Chinese University of Hong Kong, and Wuhan University, as well as the Gadamer Chair at Boston College (2015). He is a Member of the Royal Irish Academy and the Institut International de Philosophie. He was awarded the Royal Irish Academy's Gold Medal in the Humanities in 2012. He was President (2013–18) of the International Federation of Philosophical Societies (FISP) and President of the 24th World Congress of Philosophy, Beijing, August 2018. He received an Honorary Doctorate from the University of Athens in 2015. His publications include *The Philosophy of John Scottus Eriugena* (1989), *Introduction to Phenomenology* (2000), *The Phenomenology Reader* (2002), *Edmund Husserl: Founder of Phenomenology* (2005), *Husserl Dictionary* (2012), and *Husserl's Crisis of the European Sciences and Transcendental Phenomenology* (2012).

Noreen O'Carroll lectures in medical ethics at the Royal College of Surgeons in Ireland. She completed her PhD in Philosophy at University College Dublin and carried out further studies in healthcare ethics and philosophy of medicine at the Society of Apothecaries, London. Her research interests include bioethics, methods of ethical reasoning in healthcare, human rights and natural law. She has been a member of the Royal Irish Academy's Ethical, Political, Legal and Philosophical Studies Committee since 2014.

Cyril O'Regan is currently Huisking Professor of Theology at the University of Notre Dame. He received his BA and MA in Philosophy from University College Dublin, and his PhD in Philosophy of Religion from Yale, where he also taught for a decade. He specializes in the genealogy of modernity, the relation between philosophy and theology, especially continental philosophy and Catholic theology, while also attending to the history of mysticism and the interaction between religion and literature. He has written on philosophical figures such as Hegel, Heidegger, Kant, Kierkegaard, Marion, Benjamin, Derrida, and Girard, and theological figures such as Karl Rahner, Hans Urs von Balthasar, Newman, Meister Eckhart, and Augustine. His books include *The Heterodox Hegel* (1994), *Gnostic Return in Modernity* (2001), *Gnostic Apocalypse* (2002), *Theology and the Spaces of Apocalyptic* (2009), and *Anatomy of Misremembering* (2014).

Fran O'Rourke is Emeritus Professor of Philosophy, University College Dublin, where he taught for thirty-six years. A graduate of University College Galway, he studied in Vienna, Cologne, Louvain and Leuven. He has held Fulbright and Onassis fellowships, and in 2003 was Visiting Research Professor at Marquette University. He has published widely on Plato, Aristotle, Neoplatonism, Aquinas, and Heidegger. His most recent book, *Aristotelian Interpretations*, was published in 2016. He recently received a second PhD for a dissertation on James Joyce, Aristotle, and Aquinas. As well as philosophical influences on James Joyce, he has researched Joyce's use of Irish traditional song. He regularly performs recitals of Joyce-related songs with John Feeley, Ireland's leading classical guitarist. Together they have performed in Shanghai, Washington, New York, San Diego and Philadelphia. A CD of their concert in Monaco, on St Patrick's Day 2015, has been published (www.joycesong.info).

Philip Pettit teaches Philosophy at Princeton University and the Australian National University. He has worked in a range of areas, including ethical and political theory, the theory of collective and corporate agency, and the philosophy of mind. Among his recent publications are *Just Freedom* (2014), *The Robust Demands of the Good* (2014), and *The Birth of Ethics* (2018). He gave the Tanner Lectures in Human Values in Berkeley in 2015 and the John Locke Lectures in Philosophy in Oxford in 2019. *Common*

Minds: Themes from the Philosophy of Philip Pettit was published in 2007 by Oxford University Press.

Brendan Purcell studied at University College Dublin, the Lateran University, Rome, and the University of Leuven. He was ordained a priest in 1967. He taught psychology and philosophy at UCD from 1972 to 2008. Since 2010 he has been parochial vicar at St Mary's Cathedral, Sydney, and adjunct professor at University of Notre Dame (Australia). His publications include *From Big Bang to Big Mystery: Human Origins in the light of Creation and Evolution* (2011), and *Where is God in Suffering?* (2016). A Festschrift in his honour, *The Human Voyage of Self-Discovery* was published in 2013.

Andrew Smith is Emeritus Professor of Classics at University College Dublin. His publications include *Porphyry's Place in the Neoplatonic Tradition*, the Teubner Edition of Porphyry's fragments and *Plotinus, Porphyry and Iamblichus: Philosophy and Religion in Neoplatonism*. He is currently coediting with John Dillon the Parmenides Press series of translations and philosophical commentaries on Plotinus, to which he has contributed *Enneads* I.6 and V.8.

Denys Turner: Now half-retired, Denys Turner taught philosophy and theology at University College Dublin, at Bristol, Birmingham and Cambridge universities in the United Kingdom, and at Yale University in the United States; he now teaches part-time at Princeton University. Though he prefers teaching to writing, he is the author of a number of books on Marxism, mysticism, and on reason in theology, including *Darkness of God* (1995), *Faith, Reason, and the Existence of God* (2004), and more recently, intellectual biographies, including *Julian of Norwich, Theologian* (2011) and *Thomas Aquinas, A Portrait* (2013). His most recent publication is *God, Mystery, and Mystification* (2019).

David Walsh is Professor of Politics at the Catholic University of America in Washington, DC. He is the author of a three-volume study of modernity addressing totalitarian catharsis, the resurgence of liberal democracy, and the philosophical revolution of the modern world. Intended as a guide to the multiple facets of the age in which we live, the volumes appeared as *After Ideology: Recovering the Spiritual Foundations of Freedom* (1990), *The Growth of the Liberal Soul* (1997), and *The Modern Philosophical Revolution:*

The Luminosity of Existence (2008). Three other books provide tangential perspectives on this modernity project: *The Mysticism of Innerworldly Fulfillment: A Study of Jacob Boehme* (1983), *Guarded by Mystery: Meaning in a Postmodern Age* (1999) and *The Third Millennium: Reflections on Faith and Reason* (1999). His most recent publication is *Politics of the Person* (2016), which will be followed by *The Priority of the Person*.

Markus H. Wörner is Emeritus Professor of Philosophy and former Head of Department at the National University of Ireland, Galway (1986–2009). After his *Lektorat* in Theology at the Dominican *Studium Generale* in Germany in 1993 he completed his studies in philosophy and theology at the University of Bonn with the degree of Dr. phil. (1975). He taught fundamental theology and medieval philosophy at the Free University of Berlin while finishing his Habilitation in Philosophy (1985). He has taught as Visiting Professor at Boston College (1990) and FU Berlin (2000). His major book publications are *Performative und Sprachliches Handeln* (1978), *Das Ethische in der Rhetorik des Aristoteles* (1990), *Glückendes Leben* (2000), *Verstehen an der Grenze* (2003), and Thomas von Aquin, *Summa Contra Gentiles* IV (1996). He has edited four Latin-German editions of the complete *Summa Contra Gentiles*. He is a Fellow of the Royal Astronomical Society.

INDEX

EDITOR'S ACKNOWLEDGMENTS

I express my sincere gratitude to the following for their invaluable encouragement and support: Maeve Convery, Andrew J. Deeks, Renaud Dehousse, Sinead Dolan, Fiona Dunne, Órfhlaith Ford, Conor Graham, Sinead Kelly, Helga Kerstin, Brigid Laffan, Kelvin Mann, Sinead McGowan, Mihaela Magdic, Eilis O'Brien, Brendan O'Byrne, Brian O'Connor, David O'Donoghue, Sarah Prescott, Patrick Sammon, Colin Scott and Mark Simpson.

I am most grateful to Stoney Road Press for their kind permission to reproduce the artwork of Patrick Scott.

I thank my friend Mihai Cucu for providing photographs of the portrait by Derek Hill and the poem by Seamus Heaney.

I am exceptionally grateful to the Heaney family for their gracious permission to reproduce the autograph of 'Remembering Bóthar Buí' by Seamus Heaney.